Corporations and Partnerships in Japan

Corporations and Partnerships in Japan

Second Edition

Ichiro Kawamoto
Yasuhiro Kawaguchi
&
Takayuki Kihira

This book was originally published as a monograph in the International Encyclopaedia of Laws/Corporations and Partnerships.

General Editors: Roger Blanpain, Frank Hendrickx
Volume Editor: Koen Geens

Wolters Kluwer

Published by:
Kluwer Law International B.V.
PO Box 316
2400 AH Alphen aan den Rijn
The Netherlands
Website: www.wklawbusiness.com

Sold and distributed in North, Central and South America by:
Wolters Kluwer Legal & Regulatory U.S.
7201 McKinney Circle
Frederick, MD 21704
United States of America
Email: customer.service@wolterskluwer.com

Sold and distributed in all other countries by:
Turpin Distribution Services Ltd.
Stratton Business Park
Pegasus Drive, Biggleswade
Bedfordshire SG18 8TQ
United Kingdom
Email: kluwerlaw@turpin-distribution.com

ISBN 978-90-411-6854-2

This title is available on www.kluwerlawonline.com

The Authors

Ichiro Kawamoto was a professor of law at Kobe University and taught Commercial Law, Law of Bills and Notes, Company Law and Securities Regulation. He was a member of the Securities and Exchange Council of the Ministry of Finance and a member of the Department of Commercial Law of the Legislative Council of the Ministry of Justice. He is currently a member of the Japan Academy. He is the author of Modern Company Law (9th edition, 2004), Securities Regulation (2nd edition, 1984), Commentary of Bills and Notes (3rd edition, 1976), etc. He is a graduate of Kyoto University and took the degree of Doctor of Laws at Kobe University. He is the emeritus professor of Kobe University and Kobe Gakuin University.

Yasuhiro Kawaguchi is a professor of law at Doshisha University and teaches Commercial Law, Company Law, Securities Regulation and Banking Regulation. He is the member of Subcommittee of Financial System Council. He was the visiting scholar of standard Law School in California during 1996–1998. He is the author of Financial Instruments Regulation (2012), Modern Financial Institution and the Law (4th Edition, 2012), etc. He earned a master degree (Master of laws) at Kobe University. He took the degree of Doctor of Laws at Kobe University.

The Authors

Takayuki Kihira is a corporate and M&A partner with the Japanese law firm of Mori Hamada & Matsumoto, one of the few full-service Japanese law firms with approximately 380 lawyers. He has been selected by various media as a recommended lawyer in corporate and M&A sector in Japan, including Chambers Global (2015) and Chambers Asia (2015). During 2006–2007, he worked with the international law firm of Shearman & Sterling LLP in New York. In 2015, he was appointed as adjunct professor of law (fall term) at Cornell Law School where he taught 'Global M&A Practice'. He is a graduate of Cornell Law School (LL.M.) in Ithaca, New York and Hitotsubashi University (LL.B.) in Tokyo, Japan.

Table of Contents

Table of Contents

List of Abbreviations

BIS	Bank for International Settlements
CP	Commercial Paper
DPJ	Democratic Party of Japan
FSA	Financial Services Agency
IAA	Independent Administrative Agencies
JNR	Japan National Railways
LDP	Liberal Democratic Party
METI	Ministry of Economy, Trade and Industry
MITI	Ministry of International Trade and Industry
NASD	National Association of Securities Dealers
NTT	Nippon Telegraph and Telephone
SDP	Socialist Democratic Party

List of Abbreviations

Preface

After World War II, Japan's rapid economic growth contributed to the characterization of the nation as a developed country. This economic expansion witnessed the growth and development of Japanese companies – earning global attention to 'Japan Inc' (*nihon kabushiki kaisha*). The first edition of this book was published in 1994 and was written to introduce Japanese corporate law and practice to the world.

By the turn of the twentieth century, however, Japan's economy had slowed and weakened. An important structural factor contributing to Japan's relative slow economic growth is its low birthrate and rapidly aging population. But there have also been a number of economic 'shocks' that have taken a toll, from the bursting of the asset bubble in the early 1990s to the more recent 'Lehman shock' and global economic crisis and dramatic rise in the value of the yen.

In order for Japan to restore its economic growth, Japanese companies need to become more globally competitive through, among other things, the shedding of unprofitable businesses and strategic mergers and restructurings. To accommodate these needs, there have been a series of amendments to the Commercial Code, resulting in the eventual adoption in 2005 of a new 'Companies Act', which created a new and independent code embodying Japanese corporate law. It was the adoption of the new Companies Act that compelled us to undertake a complete rewrite of our book for this new edition.

This book is not only intended to provide a commentary on Japanese corporate law, but also to paint a picture of relevant governmental, social and economic factors. Due to the ever-changing nature of this field, it is our intention to update this book periodically going forward.

We would like to express our gratitude to Ms Mina Shibahara and Ms Helen Veitch for their assistance in the preparation of the English manuscript of this book. Lastly, a special thank you to the editor.

Ichiro Kawamoto
Yasuhiro Kawaguchi
Takayuki Kihira
February 2012

General Introduction

§1. Introduction

I. Economic Development and Background

1. Japan's nominal Gross Domestic Product (GDP) in 2013 was USD 4.921 trillion.[1] Globally, Japan's GDP accounted for 6.5% of the world's total GDP, while the GDP of the United States (US) represented 22.0% of the total. Japan's share has decreased year by year, falling to below the 10% mark in 2006 (14.6% in 2000, 10.0% in 2005, and 8.9% in 2006). In contrast, China's nominal GDP was USD 5.824 trillion in 2010, and China has now surpassed Japan to become the world's second largest economy. Such outcome is attributed to Japan's declining economic growth rate while China has accomplished significant economic growth.

Japan's GDP per capita was the largest in the world in 1993. This gradually decreased during the 1990s, leaving Japan in nineteenth place in 2012.[2] Germany also fell from seventh place in 1993 to fifteenth place in 2012. Germany and Japan had both enjoyed sustained economic growth as global manufacturing powers exporting high-quality goods, predominantly in the heavy and chemical industry. However, countries that had not previously been major manufacturing nations have shown significant growth as a result of the development of a new sector in IT (Information Technology) industry.

2. However, Japan's economy still represents nearly 10% of the world's total GDP, and is the third largest economy behind the United States and China. American economics magazine 'Fortune' also lists fifty-seven Japanese companies in the 2014 Fortune Global 500, putting Japan in second place behind the United States's 133 listed companies. However, Japan's line-up remains largely unchanged.

3. With regard to Japan's public finances, according to the Ministry of Finance the amount of national debt was JPY 1,173 trillion at the end of the 2013 fiscal year. The JPY 96.3 trillion in expenditure under the budget for the 2015 fiscal year stood in stark contrast to the JPY 54.5 trillion in tax revenue. This shortfall was covered primarily by JPY 41.8 trillion in government bonds. At the end of 2014, Japan's

---

1. Institute for International Trade and Investment, International Comparative Statistics. GDP is the total value of goods and services produced in a country in a given year. This is different from real GDP, which has been adjusted for inflation.
2. Institute for International Trade and Investment, *ibid.*

national debt reached 230% against its GDP. This stands out among other debt-to-GDP ratios of 110% in the United States, 96% in the United Kingdom, and 79% in Germany. Yet, unlike Greece, which fell into financial crisis with a debt-to-GDP ratio of 115%, Japan managed to avoid such crisis because over 90% of its government bonds are held domestically.

4. Japan is a small island nation in the far east of the Asian continent. Its land area of 377,780 km^2 makes up only 0.3% of the world total and 73% of the land is mountainous. It is a country scarce in natural resources. For this reason, Japan's energy self-sufficiency rate is extremely low, at only 0.1% for oil and 0.6% for natural gas in 2012. With inclusion of water and nuclear power, the primary-energy self-sufficiency rate is 19.9%. In a country with small land area and few natural resources, corporate business activities have been the mainstay of people's livelihoods.

5. In 1965, Japan was 86% food self-sufficient in terms of production value and 73% on a calorie-basis. By 2013, however, this fell to 65% and 39%, respectively.[3] Other than the special case of the United States, which is the world's biggest grain exporter, an international comparison shows that the United Kingdom is 72% self-sufficient, Germany is at 92%, and that France has an export surplus of 129% (all figures are on a calorie-basis for the 2011 fiscal year). The Japanese government aims to raise its food self-sufficiency to 50% by 2020.

6. In Japan, agricultural land ownership and farm management by stock companies were strictly restricted. This was because since the post-war agrarian reforms, efforts have been poured into transferring land ownership to independent farmers. However, the number of individuals engaged in the agricultural sector have decreased, and the aging of population has been progressing. There is also an increase in untilled farmlands that have been abandoned. Under such circumstances, it was argued that stock companies should be permitted to own and lease farmland, and thus be more involved in the farming industry. The 2000 amendment to the Agricultural Land Act permitted agricultural production corporations (*nougyo seisan houjin*) in the form of stock companies. However, as such deregulation was subject to certain conditions such as the majority of the officers required to be engaged in full-time farming and the company shares required to have restrictions on transfer, it merely resulted in the incorporation of farms by existing farmers. In 2003, stock companies were permitted to lease disused farmland in structural reform special zones (*kouzo kaikaku tokku*) and engage in the agricultural business. In 2005, this policy was expanded nationwide. However, it remains difficult for stock companies to enter into the agricultural industry as the leases are permitted only for disused farmlands.

7. The population of Japan was 127.29 million (the world's eighth largest) in 2013 (National Census figures), which was 253,000 less than that of the previous year. What is important, however, is that the natural increase of population (i.e., the

3. Website of the Ministry of Agriculture, Forestry and Fisheries.

balance of number of births and number of deaths) has continued to be negative since 2007, and a decrease of 232,000 was recorded in 2013. There is a concern that such trend of birth rate and aging society may lead to an era of shrinkage. One of the reasons for the low birth rate is that the double-income couples are having fewer children. To reverse this trend, it is essential that an appropriate support is provided to the female workers to continue working after childbirth and balance both work and parenting. On the other hand, it is also important for companies to maintain access to talented workforce. While Japanese companies are continuing to improve their maternity-leave systems (see paragraph 36), public support, such as services of child-care facilities, has become an urgent issue.

II. Governmental System

8. The Japanese Constitution was established in 1946. It clearly states that sovereignty rests with the people, and that the Emperor is a symbol of the nation.[4] Freedom to choose occupation is acknowledged to the extent that it does not interfere with public welfare, and companies may freely engage in business activities.[5] The Constitution also provides separation of power, dividing the State authority into three separate branches: legislative, executive and judicial (Figure 1).

Figure 1 Government Organization

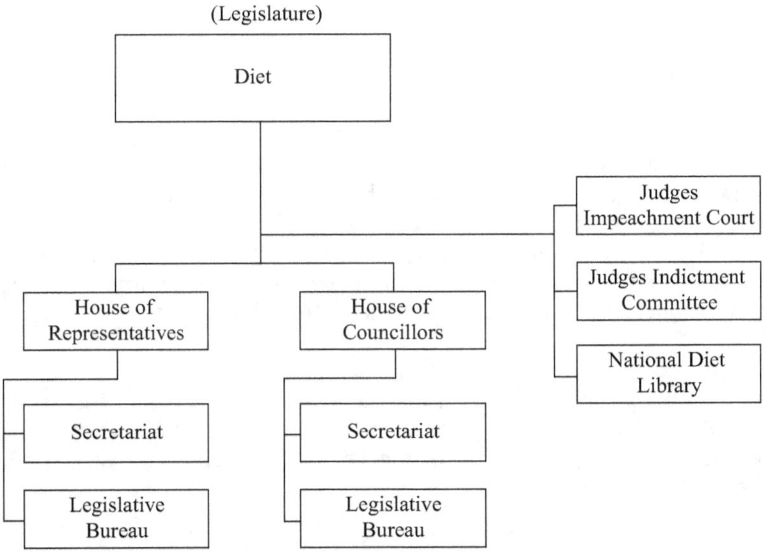

4. Article 1, Constitution.
5. Article 22, para. 1, Constitution.

(Judiciary)

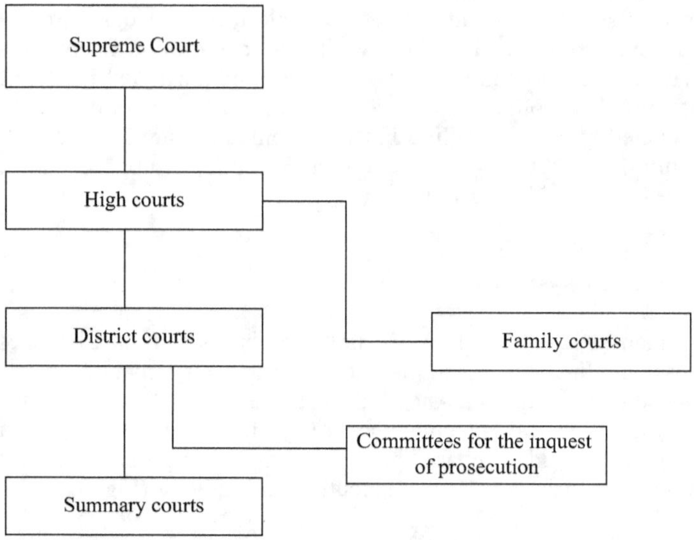

A. Politics

1. Framework of Political System

9. The Diet is the highest organization of State power and the sole legislature of the State.[6] It consists of the House of Representatives (*shugiin*) and the House of Councillors (*sangiin*).[7] The members of the houses (Diet members) are elected as the representatives of the people.[8] The term of office of members of the House of Representatives is four years, subject to earlier termination if the house is dissolved.[9] The term of office of members of the House of Councillors is six years, and half of its members are re-elected or replaced at elections that take place every three years.[10]

10. Executive power is vested in the Cabinet, which consists of the prime minister and other ministers of State.[11] The prime minister is designated from among the Diet members by a resolution of the Diet.[12] The prime minister appoints the

6. Article 41, Constitution.
7. Article 42, Constitution.
8. Article 43, Constitution.
9. Article 45, Constitution.
10. Article 46, Constitution.
11. Article 65; Art. 66, para. 1, Constitution.
12. Article 67, para. 1, Constitution.

ministers of State, the majority of which must be chosen from among the Diet members.[13] Such governmental system, where the majority of members of the administration are elected from the legislature and the executive branch is accountable to the legislature, is called the parliamentary cabinet system (*giin naikakusei*). Japan's first prime minister was Hirobumi Ito, taking office in 1885. Current prime minister Shinzo Abe is the 63rd (and 57th) prime minister.

2. Origins of the Liberal Democratic Party

11. Japan has developed based on the capitalism ideology and conservative politics. The first post-war general election was held in 1946, with the Liberal Party (*Nihon Jiyuto*) emerging as the leading party with 141 seats. The Progressive Party (*Shinpoto*) and the Socialist Party (*Shakaito*) took ninety-four seats each, and the Communist Party (*Kyousanto*) also took five seats for the first time. Following this election, a Liberal-Progressive coalition was established under Liberal Party leader, Shigeru Yoshida (succeeding Ichiro Hatoyama, who was banned from public office), and the first Yoshida Cabinet was formed. This is considered as the roots of the current Liberal Democratic Party (LDP).

12. The 1947 general election was held shortly before the New Constitution was to come into effect and was won by the Japan Socialist Party. However, they only managed to gain 31% of the 466 seats, which was not sufficient to form a single-party government. The Katayama Cabinet was the product of a three-party coalition with the Democratic Party (*Minshuto*) (not the current Democratic Party of Japan (DPJ)) and the People's Cooperative Party (*Kokumin Kyoudoto*). The Liberal Party, led by Shigeru Yoshida, was not taking part of this coalition. Tetsu Katayama declared that his administration will make a transition from capitalism to socialism. However, the House of Representatives consisted of four capitalist parties, including the Liberal Party and the Democratic Party, holding 300 seats, and the Japan Socialist Party and the Communist Party together held only 148 seats. The political situation which was later called the 1955 system – the 'one-and-a-half-party system'– was already established by this time.[14]

13. The Katayama Cabinet collapsed after only nine months, as a result of the Japan Socialist Party's internal discord. In March 1948, the leader of Democratic Party, Hitoshi Ashida, was appointed as prime minister. The Ashida Cabinet was also forced to resign in October of the same year following the Showa Denko scandal. Meanwhile, the Liberal Party merged with Democratic Party defectors to form a 152-seat-strong Democratic Liberal Party (*Minshu Jiyuto*), after which its leader Shigeru Yoshida became prime minister for the second time. In the 1949 general election, the Democratic Liberal Party won a 269 (58%) seat majority and the third Yoshida Cabinet was formed. In this election, Eisaku Sato, Hayato Ikeda (both

13. Article 68, para. 1, Constitution.
14. 'One-and-a-half party system' is a parodic term referencing the more common 'two-party system'. It implies that no change in the ruling party will occur.

future prime ministers) and many other senior government officials won seats. The Democratic Party was dissolved in 1950, with some members joining the Democratic Liberal Party, which then was renamed the Liberal Party (*Nihon Minshuto*). It was during the three-years-and-eight-month term of the third Yoshida Cabinet – in 1951 – that the San Francisco Peace Treaty was concluded. Internal disputes surrounding the ratification of this treaty split the Socialist Party into right and left wings.

3. Establishment of the '1955 System'

14. Yoshida went on to form the fourth and fifth Cabinet. In 1953, Hatoyama supporters from the Liberal Party established the Japan Democratic Party, and waged a campaign to topple the government. This resulted in Yoshida resigning from the Cabinet and party leader. His five Cabinets had governed for a total of seven years and two months. After such a long-standing administration, expectations on Ichiro Hatoyama were high, and the nation experienced an unparalleled 'Hatoyama boom.' The next general election was held under the Hatoyama Cabinet in 1955. Despite the reunification of the Japan Socialist Party, the reformist camp only obtained one-third of the seats. Then, in response particularly to pleas from the business community which was concerned with how the Japan Socialist Party – particularly the leftist wing – was growing in power with each election, the Japan Democratic Party joined forces with the Liberal Party to form the LDP. From the outset, the Japan Socialist Party only obtained less than half of the seats held by the LDP, which meant that it was not realistic for them to become a ruling party. As a result, Japanese politics have seen the two parties continue repeated deals and compromises behind the scenes. This post-war political framework is known as the '1955 system'.

15. Labour unions in Japan do not have strong political influence. Most Japanese companies are Small Enterprises (SMEs) (see paragraph 53) and employees of these companies have no labour union. Although employees of larger companies join labour unions, the leaders of unions are mostly company employees. In other words, most large Japanese labour unions are internal company organizations. This explains why Japanese labour unions did not possess the organizational power – in qualitative or quantitative terms – to oppose the LDP administration (Table 1), and this is one of the reasons why the LDP administration remained in power for so long.

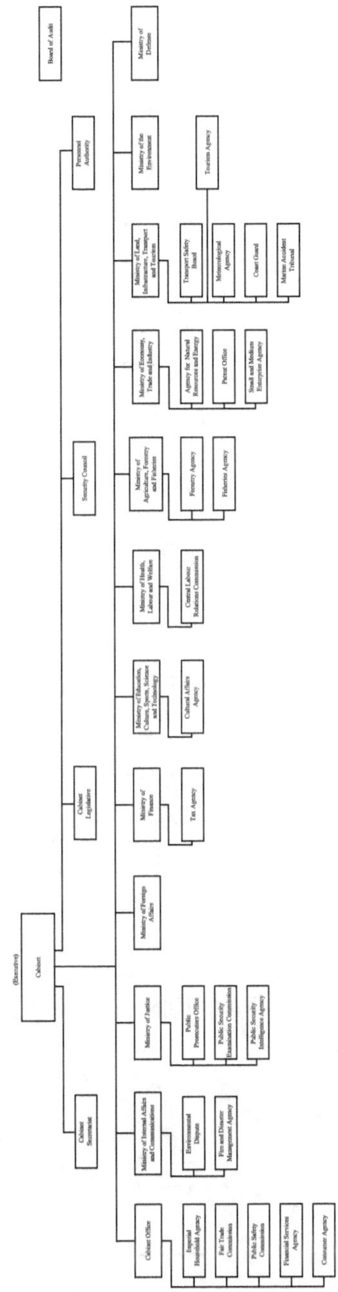
(Executive)
Cabinet
Board of Audit
Personnel Authority
Security Council
Cabinet Legislative
Cabinet Secretariat
Cabinet Office
Imperial Household Agency
Fair Trade Commission
Public Safety Commission
Financial Services Agency
Consumer Agency
Ministry of Internal Affairs and Communications
Environmental Dispute
Fire and Disaster Management Agency
Ministry of Justice
Public Prosecutors Office
Public Security Examination Commission
Public Security Intelligence Agency
Ministry of Foreign Affairs
Ministry of Finance
Tax Agency
Ministry of Education, Culture, Sports, Science and Technology
Cultural Affairs Agency
Ministry of Health, Labour and Welfare
Central Labour Relations Commission
Ministry of Agriculture, Forestry and Fisheries
Forestry Agency
Fisheries Agency
Ministry of Economy, Trade and Industry
Agency for Natural Resources and Energy
Patent Office
Small and Medium Enterprise Agency
Ministry of Land, Infrastructure, Transport and Tourism
Transport Safety Board
Meteorological Agency
Coast Guard
Marine Accident Tribunal
Tourism Agency
Ministry of the Environment
Ministry of Defence

Table 1 Labour Unions and Their Members

Year	*Number of Unions*	*Number of Members (1,000 People)*	*Estimated Membership Rate (%)*
1978	34,163	12,383	32.6
1979	34,112	12,309	31.6
1980	34,232	12,369	30.8
1981	34,200	12,471	30.8
1982	34,477	12,526	30.5
1983	34,539	12,520	29.7
1984	34,579	12,464	29.1
1985	34,539	12,418	28.9
1986	34,216	12,343	28.2
1987	34,033	12,272	27.6
1988	33,750	12,227	26.8
1989	33,683	12,227	25.9
1990	33,270	12,265	25.2
1991	33,008	12,397	24.5
1992	33,047	12,541	24.4
1993	32,552	12,663	24.2
1994	32,581	12,699	24.1
1995	32,065	12,614	23.8
1996	31,601	12,451	23.2
1997	31,336	12,285	22.6
1998	31,062	12,093	22.4
1999	30,610	11,825	22.2
2000	31,185	11,539	21.5
2001	30,773	11,212	20.7
2002	30,177	10,801	20.2
2003	29,745	10,531	19.6
2004	29,320	10,309	19.2
2005	28,279	10,138	18.7
2006	27,507	10,041	18.2
2007	27,226	10,080	18.1
2008	26,965	10,065	18.1

Year	*Number of Unions*	*Number of Members (1,000 People)*	*Estimated Membership Rate (%)*
2009	26,676	10,078	18.5
2010	26,367	10,054	18.5

Source: Ministry of Health, Labour and Welfare, General Survey on Labour Relations, Basic Survey on Labour Unions.

4. Demise of the Japan Socialist Party

16. In 1993, Morihiro Hosokawa formed a seven-party anti-LDP coalition to establish the Cabinet after defeating the LDP administration for the first time. He was succeeded by Tsutomu Hata, another leader of anti-LDP coalition, only for the LDP to subsequently return to power once again. This was in the form of a LDP-Socialist-Sakigake three-party coalition (Sakigake was an LDP breakaway) led surprisingly by Japan Socialist Party chairman, Tomiichi Murayama. Murayama radically transformed Japan Socialist Party policies, supporting the Japan-United States Security Treaty and declaring the Self-Defence Forces constitutional. The background of such transformation was the changing global context defined primarily by the collapse of socialism in 1991 throughout the former Soviet Union and Eastern Europe. Murayama resigned in 1996, after which the Japan Socialist Party renamed itself the Socialist Democratic Party (*Shakai Minshuto*).

17. When Murayama stepped down, LDP leader, Ry tar Hashimoto, was elected as prime minister on a coalition in January 1996. Some members of the Socialist Democratic Party and the New Party Sakigake then merged to form the former Japan Democratic Party, and appointed Naoto Kan and Yukio Hatoyama as their joint leaders. In the same year, the first general election was held under the single-seat-constituency (*shou senkyoku*) and the proportional-representation (*hireid-aihyou*) systems. The LDP earned the most votes but it was not sufficient to hold a majority, leaving Japan once again with a coalition government. The Socialist Democratic Party, having won only fifteen seats, effectively closed its history – in name and reality – and ended the anti-conservative reformist presence in the Japanese politics.

5. Change in Ruling Party

18. The Hashimoto Cabinet resigned in 1998 and was succeeded by Keiz Obuchi, who formed a coalition with the Komeito Party. After prime minister Obuchi's death in 2000, the Yoshir Mori Cabinet was formed. During the 2001 House of Representatives general election, the privatization of the three businesses (national postal mail, savings and insurance services) (see paragraph 202) became a huge point of contention. Junichiro Koizumi received public support for his favour of the privatization of the three postal services, and he was elected as prime minister. The

Koizumi Cabinet implemented a series of structural reform policies and remained in power with high popularity ratings until September 2006. Deregulation of industry was also progressed under the Koizumi administration. However, these policies have since received criticism for bringing about social disparity, polarizing society into rich and poor. Koizumi's successors, Shinzō Abe, Yasuo Fukuda and Tarō Asō, each resigned after one year. These three prime ministers all struggled to control the government, as they failed to achieve a majority in the House of Councillors despite holding a majority in the House of Representatives. This divided State is commonly referred to as the 'twisted Diet' (see paragraph 20).

19. The DPJ then gained a majority in the 2007 House of Councillors election, and went on to win a historic landslide victory in the 2009 House of Representatives election. The DPJ won 193 new seats, taking its total seats to 308, or 64.2%. The LDP, on the other hand, lost 181 seats, leaving it with only 119 seats and losing its position as the leading party for the first time since the 1955 conservative merger. However, the LDP regained its position as the leading party in the 2012 House of Representatives election, leading to the inauguration of the new Abe Administration (see Table 2)

6. Twisted Diet

20. The prime minister will be designated from among Diet members by a resolution of the Diet.[15] If the House of Representatives and the House of Councillors disagree, the designation of the House of Representatives takes precedence.[16] The same applies for decisions on the budget.[17] With respect to the passing of bills, if a House of Representatives resolution is not passed in the House of Councillors, the bill will be subject to a repeat vote in the House of Representatives and will only become valid if it is passed by a majority of at least two-thirds of the members present.[18] If the ruling party holds a majority in both houses, the House of Councillors is effectively rendered useless. On the other hand, not occupying majority of seats in the House of Councillors makes it extremely difficult for the ruling party to implement its policies. This is known as the 'twisted Diet'. This phenomenon has occurred several times in the past.

Table 2 Diet Members by Political Party (House of Representatives (as of 30 April 2015))

Party	*Number of Diet Members*
Liberal Democratic Party	291(25)
Democratic Party of Japan (including Club of Independents)	72(9)

15. Article 67, para. 1, Constitution.
16. Article 67, para. 2, Constitution.
17. Article 60, Constitution.
18. Article 59, Constitution.

Party	*Number of Diet Members*
Japan Innovation Party	40(1)
New Komeito	35(3)
Japanese Communist Party	21(6)
Others	14(1)
Total	475(45)

Figures in brackets are the number of female members.
House of Councillors (as of 6 December 2011).

House of Councillors (as of 29 April 2015)

Party	*Number of Diet members*
Liberal Democratic Party	114(6)
Democratic Party of Japan and Shin-Ryokufukai	58(9)
New Komeito	20(3)
Japan Innovation Party	11(0)
Japanese Communist Party	11(4)
Party for Future Generations	6(1)
Others	10(2)
Total	242(38)

Figures in brackets are the number of female members.

7. Lawmaker-Initiated Bills Relating to the Companies Act

21. The Diet is Japan's sole legislature (see paragraph 9). In Japan, it is usually the Cabinet that presents legislative bills to the Diet (government bills). If a bill is presented by a Diet member, it is referred to as lawmaker-initiated legislation. A Diet member must obtain a certain number of other supporters to legally present a bill.[19] The 1997 Organ Transplant Act, the 1998 Act on Support for Reconstructing Livelihoods of Victims, the Act on Promotion of Specified Non-profit Activities (the so-called NPO act) and the 1999 Act on Special Measures against Dioxins are examples of high-profile lawmaker-initiated bills. There are also lawmaker-initiated bills relating to the Companies Act. In 1997, an amendment introduced stock options. In 1998, a temporary legislation on treasury shares was enacted (see paragraph 152). The restrictions on treasury shares were deregulated in 2001, shifting from general prohibition (with limited exceptions) to general permissibility subject to certain conditions (see paragraph 156), with a 2003 amendment further facilitating companies to purchase their own shares by a resolution of the board of

19. Article 56, para. 1, Diet Act.

directors pursuant to the authorization by the articles of incorporation (see paragraph 162). The Commercial Code was further amended in 2001, reducing directors' liabilities to the company (see paragraph 159). This amendment was legislated, despite opposition from scholars. This was a lawmaker-initiated legislation established in response to lobbying by the business community.

B. *Administration*

1. Formality of Parliamentary Cabinet System and Substance of Bureaucratic Government System

22. Japan has a parliamentary cabinet system. The prime minister, head of the Cabinet, is appointed from among Diet members elected at the general election. The Cabinet, composed of ministers of State appointed by the prime minister, possesses the executive power.[20] The role of governmental officers is to provide support to the Cabinet, under the direction of the ministers of State. However, it has been argued that the governmental officers currently play a more central role and that the government is actually run under a bureaucratic Cabinet system. This trend can be traced back to the beginning of the Meiji era, when Aritomo Yamagata assembled a bureaucrat wing to work for him, consisted solely of officials who had passed the public examination. This was the basis for the examination of career officers (the current Type-I officers examination for the National Public Service, successful candidates of which are known as 'career' officers), which was a prerequisite for recruitment into the elite bureaucracy. The 'career' system is a long-standing tradition rather than a legal framework. All other officers fall into the non-career category. The 'career' officers are guaranteed rapid promotion, whereas the promotion of non-career officers may be limited, creating a sort of class system.

23. This means that the Japanese government is effectively run by the officers assigned to each government ministry. This is particularly true for industrial policy, in which the Ministry of Economy, Trade and Industry (METI) (until January 2001, the Ministry of International Trade and Industry (MITI)) has absolute influential power. The public and private sectors managed to develop unified industrial policies after the end of the Second World War based on the strong connections between MITI and the industrial community. Recently, METI was actively involved in the amendments to the Companies Act.

2. Appointment of Governmental Officers to High Positions in Private Organizations *(Amakudari)*

24. As the elite 'career' organizations of Japanese bureaucracy takes a pyramid shape, there are fewer positions available at higher classes and therefore it has become customary to arrange for the existing officers certain positions at affiliated or related organizations of their ministry. This tradition of setting up parachutes for the existing officers is called *amakudari*. As the personnel departments of each

20. Articles 65–68, Constitution.

ministry have been handling their own recruitment, salary payment and other personnel matters since the beginning of the Meiji era (in essence, the minister's appointive power has no substance), they are also responsible for arranging the re-employment of existing officers. In order to secure *amakudari* positions, each ministry establishes under its control special corporations, independent administrative institutions, authorized corporations and public interest corporations, and provides them with subsidies to ensure their continuity. This results in a waste of taxpayers' money. According to a survey carried out by the research department of the House of Representatives in May 2009, there are 4,504 organizations employing a total of 25,245 *amakudari* re-employees, approximately half of whom – 10,614 – are employees or officers positioned equivalent to directors. Organizations with *amakudari* officers have received a total of over JPY 12.1334 trillion in subsidies through government ministries.[21]

3. Administrative Reform

25. Under the abovementioned bureaucratic system, if the Cabinet – composed of Diet members elected at general elections – attempts to push through policies that are not in line with the interests of the relevant ministry, there will be a strong resistance from such ministry's bureaucrat wing. There have been efforts made since the LDP era to restore the traditional parliamentary cabinet system. The 2007 amendment to the National Public Service Act under the Abe Cabinet clearly set out that a governmental officer's career should not be defined by the class of recruitment examination.[22] However, there has not been much change. In 2008, the Fukuda Cabinet passed a bill for the Basic Act on the Reform of the National Public Service System with a cross-party majority.

The main purpose of this reform was the following:

- Recruitment of 'national strategy staff' (assisting the prime minister) and 'national affairs staff' (assisting individual ministers) widely from both inside and outside the administrative organizations, thereby creating a politician-led government.
- Control by the cabinet on the HR matters concerning executive and administrative staff.
- Greater transparency on the relationship between Diet members and the governmental officers.
- Abolition of 'career' system upon introduction of a new recruitment system.
- Establishment of a new Cabinet Personnel Bureau (*naikaku jinji kyoku*).

This has allowed the prime minister to liaise with the chief cabinet secretary and ministers of state to make decisions on the appointment of administrative vice minister (*jimu jikan*), chief of bureau (*kyokuchou*) and other senior officials based on information provided by the Cabinet Personnel Bureau.

21. See Koichiro Ichimura, *Amakudari no Shinjitsu* 'The Truth about *Amakudari*', 95.
22. Article 27, National Public Service Act.

26. While the Basic Act on the Reform of the National Public Service System set out the principles for reform, individual statutes must be passed to implement such principles. In 2010, the Hatoyama Cabinet presented a public service reform bill to the House of Representatives. The cornerstone of this bill was the establishment of a Cabinet Personnel Bureau to centrally manage the appointment of senior governmental officers (administrative vice ministers, chief of bureau, etc.). The establishment of the Cabinet Personnel Bureau inside the Cabinet Secretariat gave ministers the power to appoint new senior governmental officers from a cross-sectional list of candidates at all government ministries and agencies. A specialized committee would also be established to review and oversee the *amakudari* practices involving ministries, as well as job applications of individual officers. This bill was passed by the House of Representatives, but was scrapped after it was left pending in the House of Councillors.

27. In an effort to establish a simple, efficient and transparent government and thus redress the ballooning fiscal deficit (see paragraph 3), several statutes were enacted in July 1999 relating to the reform of central government. These reforms reorganized the one Cabinet and twenty-two ministries into one Cabinet and twelve ministries (see Figure 1).

C. *Judiciary*

28. Finally, the judicial power belongs to the Supreme Court and lower courts. In general, Japanese people tend to avoid lawsuits, preferring to try to resolve disputes through discussions or negotiations. The number of lawsuits filed in Japan is low compared with other industrialized countries. For many years, Japanese people have maintained cultural and racial homogeneity, sharing one sense of values and preferring to try and understand other people. However, this also leaves Japanese people to some extent defenceless when a lawsuit is filed against them. Since Japanese companies came to actively participate in overseas markets, they have been faced with lawsuits filed by non-Japanese companies. Some of these cases have resulted in Japanese companies paying substantial settlement compensation for patent infringement or sexual harassment. There have even been domestic cases where the courts have passed a series of guilty rulings on large companies for their involvement in company extortionist (*soukaiya*) payoffs, loss compensation and fraudulent accounts. There is an urgent need to establish corporate governance mechanism for companies to comply with laws and corporate ethics.

III. Industrial Framework

29. After Japan recovered from the economic devastation of the Second World War, its heavy chemical and machinery industries started to grow in 1965. It was also around the same time that the full-scale export of Japanese manufactured goods to overseas markets started. In 1968, the trade deficit turned to a trade surplus. The major industries supporting this growth were the iron and steel, shipbuilding and car manufacturing industries. Japan became a major economic power during this period, with its GNP reaching the second largest in the world. This was followed by the worst oil crisis after the Second World War, from which Japanese companies recovered by energy-savings and development of alternative technologies, leaving Japanese industry more competitive in the international market than ever before. In particular, advances in electronic technology improved the performance of machines and manufactured products, making them one of Japan's major export items.

30. Based on such framework, Japan's industry continued to develop, with per capita GDP at times thc largest in the world. More recently, however, the Japanese economy dropped to nineteenth place (see paragraph 1). In 1990, the International Institute for Management Development (IMD) ranked Japan as No.1 in worldwide competitiveness, but in 2010 Japan's ranking dropped to No. 27. METI's 2010 Industrial Structure Vision (announced in June 2010 by the Industrial Competitiveness Committee, a committee established under the Industrial Structure Council of the METI) may help us understand how such drop happened.

31. Since the start of the twenty-first century, Japan's growth has been dependent on its internationally competitive manufacturing industries, especially the car manufacturing industry. Between 2003 and 2007, nominal GDP increased by JPY 13 trillion, approximately half of which – JPY 6 trillion – was attributed to car manufacturing and its related industries. The electronics industry, which until the 1980s had maintained extremely high levels of international competitiveness, declined during the 1990s. Subsequently, it was only the car manufacturing industry that was generating profits in the global market. Then, despite the fact that domestic financial institutions suffered only small direct losses in the recent financial crisis, devastating damages to the real economy were caused by the total collapse of the Japanese economy in the wake of a sudden fall in demand for consumer durables – including cars – during the subsequent global recession.

32. In the upcoming decade, Japan needs to shift from an industrial framework that relies heavily on car manufacturing to a more multipolar structure. The following are some of the areas that have been identified for development:

- Infrastructure related/system exports (railways, water and nuclear power) and cultural industries: Markets which seem ready to expand as a result of the rising income levels in Asian countries.
- Green industry and medical, nursing and health care and child-care services: Industries addressing global issues where Japan is playing a leading role in their resolution.
- Robotics and space: Cutting-edge areas where Japan can use its strength – technology – for further growth.

33. In analyzing the various industries, we find that the Japanese companies were successful in the global market as those companies were the winners of tough competition among many domestic competitors, which had emerged as a result of the dismantling of conglomerates after the Second World War (see paragraph 65).

On the other hand, this has been pointed out as one of the reasons why the profit rates of Japanese manufacturing companies have been extremely low compared with their overseas competitors. For example, in the sectors of information and telecommunications equipment, heavy electrical, semi-conductor, chemical and cement, the average profit rates of Japanese companies are less than half of such profit rates of overseas competitors. This has been attributed to Japanese companies' exhausted conditions as they have been worn out by the fierce domestic competition. Unlike South Korea, where the government promoted large-scale intensification of industries in the wake of the 1997 Asian currency crisis, Japanese companies have not quite focused on the management strategy of concentrating on core competencies. Japanese companies will need to carry out a strategic reorganization of their businesses domestically, expand the scale of investment and make rapid decisions to compete in the global market.

34. Japan is also quickly losing its locational competitiveness. A global company would seek to invest in locations where they expect functions such as regional headquarters, R&D and manufacturing. Recently, Japan has lost its competitiveness as an Asian business hub in all aspects to countries such as China, India and Singapore. In fact, there have been a series of non-Japanese companies choosing to relocate their regional headquarters and R&D centres from Japan to other parts of Asia. The main reason is said to be the insufficiency of Japan's business infrastructure. First, compared with other countries, Japan's effective corporation tax rate is extraordinarily high (41%, compared with an industrial-country average of 26%). Second, the quantity of freight handled by Japanese ports and airports has become less than Incheon in South Korea and Shanghai in China. And third, non-Japanese companies recently tend to consider the listing of their shares in Asia on the stock exchange in Singapore over Tokyo or Osaka. The efforts of individual companies alone will not be sufficient to rebuild the Japanese economy in the face of this challenging situation; government and industry must collaborate as one unit.

IV. Company Management and Labour Force

35. The working population of Japan in 2014 was 63.51 million (see Table 3). In 1980, 10.4% of workers were employed in the primary industries, but this has since dropped to 4.5%. In contrast, the service industry has expanded by approximately 70% since 1980, with 69.6% of the workforce now employed in the tertiary sector (see Table 4).

Table 3 Number of Employees by Industry (Unit: 10,000 People)

Industry	*2002*	*2003*	*2004*	*2005*	*2006*	*2007*	*2008*	*2009*	*2014*
Total	6,330	6,316	6,329	6,356	6,382	6,412	6,385	6,282	6,351
Agriculture/ forestry	268	266	264	259	250	251	245	242	209

Industry	*2002*	*2003*	*2004*	*2005*	*2006*	*2007*	*2008*	*2009*	*2014*
Other (total)	6,063	6,050	6,064	6,097	6,132	6,161	6,140	6,040	6,142
Fisheries	28	27	22	23	22	21	23	20	21
Mining	5	5	4	3	3	4	3	3	3
Construction	618	604	584	568	559	552	537	517	505
Manufacturing	1,202	1,178	1,150	1,142	1,161	1,165	1,144	1,073	1,040
Utilities	34	32	31	35	36	33	32	34	29
ICT	(158)	(163)	(171)	(175)	(180)	192	189	193	203
Transport and postal	(327)	(335)	(326)	(320)	(328)	330	342	348	336
Wholesale and retail	(1,108)	(1,095)	(1,085)	(1,084)	(1,075)	1,077	1,067	1,055	1,059
Finance and insurance	169	161	159	157	155	155	164	165	154
Real estate	(101)	(97)	(98)	(101)	(107)	113	111	110	112
Science and research	(204)	(203)	(205)	(207)	(204)	198	200	195	212
Restaurant and hotel	(396)	(388)	(385)	(381)	(374)	380	373	380	385
Entertainment	(243)	(240)	(239)	(238)	(242)	233	236	241	238
Education	(277)	(275)	(279)	(281)	(282)	279	283	287	301
Health and welfare	474	502	531	553	571	579	598	621	757
Compound services	76	79	81	76	75	71	56	52	57
Service (incl. other unclassified)	(374)	(379)	(413)	(447)	(467)	478	485	463	397
Government (excl. other unclassified)	217	227	233	229	222	227	223	222	234

Source: Ministry of Internal Affairs and Communications Statistics Bureau, Labour Force Survey.

Table 4 Employment Structure

Total Number of Employees (10,000 People)	*Composition (%)*			
Primary	*Secondary*	*Tertiary*		
1950	3,563	48.3	21.9	29.8
1960	4,372	30.2	28.0	41.8

Total Number of Employees (10,000 People)	*Composition (%)*			
Primary	*Secondary*	*Tertiary*		
1970	5,204	17.4	35.1	47.5
1980	5,536	10.4	34.8	54.8
1990	6,249	7.2	33.6	59.2
1995	6,457	5.0	33.0	62.0
2000	6,446	4.9	30.7	67.3
2005	6,329	4.5	27.7	67.8
2008	6,385	1.6	28.8	69.6

36. Japanese women have made rapid strides forward in entering the labour market. In 2013, the working female population was 28.04 million, making up over 40% of the total labour force (see Table 5). Female labour in Japan takes on the pattern of an M-shaped curve, with the participation rate dropping around the age at which most women have children and increasing once again afterwards (see Figure 2). This graph shows that as women recently tend to marry at a higher age, the participation rate for the 25–29 age group has increased, and counter to this, the trough is shifting from the late-20s to the early-30s age group. With women's continuing social advancement, a statutory maternity-leave was established in 1991, enabling women to return to work after taking time off to have children.

Table 5 Women in Employment (Unit: 10,000 People)

Year	*Women*	*Men*	*Percentage of women*
1985	1,548	2,764	35.9%
1986	1,584	2,795	36.2%
1987	1,615	2,813	36.5%
1988	1,670	2,868	36.8%
1989	1,749	2,929	37.4%
1990	1,834	3,001	37.9%
1991	1,918	3,084	38.3%
1992	1,974	3,145	38.6%
1993	2,009	3,193	38.6%
1994	2,034	3,202	38.8%
1995	2,048	3,215	38.9%
1996	2,084	3,238	39.2%
1997	2,127	3,264	39.5%
1998	2,124	3,243	39.6%
1999	2,116	3,215	39.7%

Year	*Women*	*Men*	*Percentage of women*
2000	2,140	3,216	40.0%
2001	2,168	3,201	40.4%
2002	2,161	3,170	40.5%
2003	2,177	3,158	40.8%
2005	2,203	3,152	41.1%
2006	2,229	3,164	41.3%
2007	2,277	3,194	41.6%
2008	2,297	3,226	41.6%
2009	2,311	3,149	42.3%
2010	2,783	3,850	41.2%
2011	2,768	3,822	42.0%
2012	2,766	3,789	42.2%
2013	2,804	3,773	42.6%

Figure 2 Female Labour Participation by Age

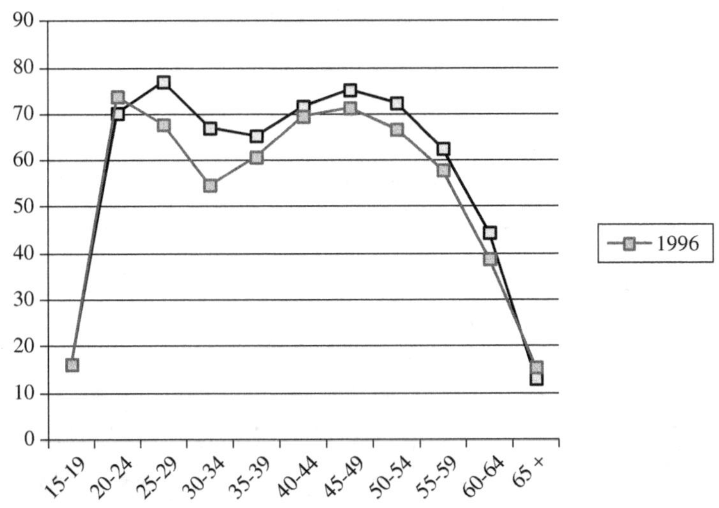

Source: Ministry of Internal Affairs and Communications Statistics Bureau, Labour Force Survey.

37. In June 1997, the Diet passed a resolution to amend the Equal Employment Opportunity Act and to remove provisions for the special treatment of women (under which they had been subject to restrictions on overtime and work on public holidays, and forbidden from night shift work) from the Labour Standards Act. This was one of the priority policy areas in the deregulation of the labour market, and has raised concerns that women will also be involved in burdensome long working hours.

38. The social advancement of women and increase of nuclear families have caused the number of births to drop to a low level. At the same time, the higher average lifetime has caused the number of elderly aged at least sixty-five to increase rapidly. In 1970, only 7.1% of the entire population was aged sixty-five or older, but data for 2014 showed that this had risen to 25.9%.

39. To adapt to such aging population, companies are increasingly setting their mandatory retirement age at 60. There are also an increasing number of companies applying the employment extension system (i.e., allowing employees to continue working past retirement age) as well as the re-employment system (i.e., allowing employees to return to work after retirement). In large companies, secondment has become more common. This usually involves aging employees being seconded to smaller companies. In a sense, SMEs provide working places for the older staff retiring from larger companies.

40. Traditionally, Japanese companies have used the seniority-based wage system, where new graduates are hired on a relatively low starting salary (see Table 6) but are provided regular pay rises in accordance with their length of service. Recently, there has been an increase in companies preferring the annual salary system. Here, annual salary is determined based on performance and results, with gross salary changing in principle each year. In Japan, management staff are promoted from among regular employees under the internal promotion system. This leads to the extremely low salaries of management members in comparison with Europe and the United States (see paragraphs 42 and 43). The seniority-based wage system and lifetime employment system, as well as in company unions, are the three main distinguishing features of companies and labour in Japan.

Table 6 Starting Salaries of New Graduates

Year	*Men*	*Women*						
University Graduates	*High School Graduates*	*University Graduates*	*High School Graduates*					
JPY 1,000	*(%)*	*JPY 1,000*	*(%)*	*JPY 1,000*	*(%)*	*JPY 1,000*	*(%)*	
1976	94.3		76.9		87.6		73.4	
1977	101.0	(7.1)	81.9	(6.5)	95.3	(8.8)	78.4	(6.8)
1978	105.5	(4.5)	85.9	(4.9)	99.9	(4.8)	82.0	(4.6)
1979	109.5	(3.8)	88.6	(3.1)	103.7	(3.8)	84.7	(3.3)
1980	114.5	(4.6)	92.8	(4.7)	108.7	(4.8)	88.3	(4.3)
1981	120.8	(5.5)	98.4	(6.0)	115.0	(5.8)	93.1	(5.4)
1982	127.2	(5.3)	103.4	(5.1)	119.1	(3.6)	97.5	(4.7)
1983	132.2	(3.9)	106.2	(2.7)	124.1	(4.2)	100.0	(2.6)

Year	*Men*	*Women*						
University Graduates	*High School Graduates*	*University Graduates*	*High School Graduates*					
JPY 1,000	*(%)*	*JPY 1,000*	*(%)*	*JPY 1,000*	*(%)*	*JPY 1,000*	*(%)*	
1984	135.8	(2.7)	108.8	(2.4)	128.7	(3.7)	103.0	(3.0)
1985	140.0	(3.1)	112.2	(3.1)	133.5	(3.7)	106.2	(3.1)
1986	144.5	(3.2)	115.4	(2.9)	138.4	(3.7)	108.5	(2.2)
1987	148.2	(2.6)	118.1	(2.3)	142.7	(3.1)	110.1	(1.5)
1988	153.1	(3.3)	120.3	(1.9)	149.0	(4.4)	113.8	(3.4)
1989	160.9	(5.1)	125.6	(4.4)	155.6	(4.4)	118.3	(4.0)
1990	169.9	(5.6)	133.0	(5.9)	162.9	(4.7)	126.0	(6.5)
1991	179.4	(5.6)	140.8	(5.9)	172.3	(5.8)	133.2	(5.7)
1992	186.9	(4.2)	146.6	(4.1)	180.1	(4.5)	139.5	(4.7)
1993	190.3	(1.8)	150.6	(2.7)	181.9	(1.0)	142.4	(2.1)
1994	192.4	(1.1)	153.8	(2.1)	184.5	(1.4)	145.5	(2.2)
1995	194.2	(0.9)	154.0	(0.1)	184.0	(-0.3)	144.7	(-0.5)
1996	193.2	(-0.5)	154.5	(0.3)	183.6	(-0.2)	146.1	(1.0)
1997	193.9	(0.4)	156.0	(1.0)	186.2	(1.4)	147.3	(0.8)
1998	195.5	(0.8)	156.5	(0.3)	186.3	(0.1)	147.9	(0.4)
1999	196.6	(0.6)	157.6	(0.7)	188.7	(1.3)	148.3	(0.3)
2000	196.9	(0.2)	157.1	(-0.3)	187.4	(-0.7)	147.6	(-0.5)
2001	198.3	(0.7)	158.1	(0.6)	188.6	(0.6)	148.7	(0.7)
2002	198.5	(0.1)	157.5	(-0.4)	188.8	(0.1)	148.8	(0.1)
2003	201.3	(1.4)	157.5	(0.0)	192.5	(2.0)	147.0	(-1.2)
2004	198.3	(-1.5)	156.1	(-0.9)	189.5	(-1.6)	147.2	(0.1)
2005	196.7	(-0.8)	155.7	(-0.3)	189.3	(-0.1)	148.0	(0.5)
2006	199.8	(1.6)	157.6	(1.2)	190.8	(0.8)	149.4	(0.9)
2007	198.8	(-0.5)	158.8	(0.8)	191.4	(0.3)	150.8	(0.9)
2008	201.3	(1.3)	160.0	(0.8)	194.6	(1.7)	154.3	(2.3)
2009	201.4	(0.0)	160.8	(0.5)	194.9	(0.2)	153.0	(-0.8)
2010	200.3	(-0.5)	160.7	(0.1)	193.5	(-0.7)	153.2	(0.1)
2011	205.0	(2.3)	159.4	(-0.8)	197.9	(2.3)	170.5	(1.4)
2012	201.8	(-1.4)	160.1	(0.4)	196.5	(-0.7)	153.6	(1.2)
2013	200.2	(-0.8)	158.9	(-0.7)	195.1	(-0.7)	151.3	(-1.5)
2014	202.9	(1.3)	161.3	(1.5)	197.2	(1.1)	154.2	(1.9)

41. This traditional Japanese-style employment may change for the following reasons. The seniority system was a custom that grew out of a society whose workforce comprised fewer older employees than younger employees. This balance will be affected, however, by the falling birth rate and aging population. The fluidity of labour will likely increase due to the young-people-centred job culture with an increase in specialized positions, performance-related pay, as well as their tendency to change jobs. As a streamlined management technique, companies have been employing more female part-time workers and temporary staff rather than permanent employees.

42. The disclosure requirements under the Financial Instruments and Exchange Act have been amended from the fiscal year ending 31 March 2010 to require the disclosure of the names and earnings of board members receiving salaries of at least JPY 100 million in their annual securities reports. In 2014, there were 191 companies which disclosed board member earnings of at least JPY 100 million, with the total number of individuals receiving such salary being 361.[23]

43. The problem lies in the difference between the salary levels of executives and regular employees. As most directors of Japanese companies traditionally started off as regular employees, it has been pointed out that enormously high compensation of directors would not be feasible. In fact, directors typically earn ten times that of new graduate employees. When the average of directors' salary was compared with the average annual salary of regular employees, the directors were found to be earning an average of JPY 34.84 million, which is 4.8 times the average regular employee salary of JPY 7.25 million.[24]

44. The number of young adults in Japan who are not in employment, education or training (so-called NEETs) is increasing. This is attributed to the decrease in new graduate recruitments by companies as well as the companies' demand for work-ready graduates. Other reasons cited are the increase of NEETs due to insufficient communication skills and tendency to depend on the parents financially for longer periods. In Japan, there are also a high number of 'freeters' (i.e., youngsters who engage in part-time low paid works for a living without regular employment). NEETs differ considerably from freeters in that they have no intention to seek employment. There is a concern that such NEETs will have a negative social influence on the community.

45. In the past, labour shortage was a serious problem in Japan. However, the prolonged recession has reversed labour supply and demand. Through a gradual recovery in the economic climate, the unemployment rate in June 2013 fell below 4.0% for the first time in four years and eight months, and the effective opening-to-application ratio passed 1 in November 2013 for the first time in six years and one month. The employment situation in Japan is seeing steady improvement.[25]

23. Tokyo Shoko Research survey.
24. Nikkei newspaper, 22 Sep. 2013.
25. Ministry of Health, Labour and Welfare, 2014 White Paper on the Labour Economy, 9.

§2. PRIVATE BUSINESS ENTITIES: FACTS AND FIGURES

I. Private Business Entities

46. As shown in Table 7, there are 4,128,215 private businesses in Japan (as of 2012). Of these, corporate entities account for 47.3%, while sole proprietorships account for 52.7%. In recent years, the number of sole proprietorships has been on the decline, whereas the number of corporate entities has increased significantly.

Table 7 Number of Enterprises and Amount of Sales

Industrial Major Division	*Enterprises (Total)*	*Percentage by Industries (%)*		*Sales (JPY mn)*	*Percentage by Industries (%)*	
		Corporate Entities	*Sole Proprietorship*		*Corporate Entities*	*Sole Proprietorship*
Total	4,128,215	47.3	52.7	1,335,508,287	97.9	2.1
Agriculture/ forestry / fisheries (excluding individual proprietorships)	24,616	–	–	3,884,692	–	–
Mining and quarrying of stone and gravel	1,766	88.6	11.4	714,500	99.5	0.5
Construction	468,199	65.0	35.0	83,384,100	97.4	2.6
Manufacturing	434,130	64.1	35.9	343,085,349	99.5	0.5
Electricity, gas, heat supply and water	759	100.0	–	21,871,668	100.0	
Information and communications	45,440	94.9	5.1	47,616,605	100.0	0.0
Transport / postal	75,783	73.3	26.7	54,971,022	99.8	0.2
Wholesale/ retail	930,073	47.5	52.5	415,122,173	97.6	2.4
Finance/ insurance	32,419	78.1	21.9	113,927,926	100.0	0.0
Real estate/ goods rental and leasing	329,449	52.5	47.5	35,663,570	97.1	2.9
Scientific research/ professional and technical services	192,062	46.7	53.3	28,905,972	93.5	6.5

Industrial Major Division	*Enterprises (Total)*	*Percentage by Industries (%)*		*Sales (JPY mn)*	*Percentage by Industries (%)*	
		Corporate Entities	*Sole Proprietorship*		*Corporate Entities*	*Sole Proprietorship*
Accomodations/ eating and drinking services	545,801	18.4	81.6	19,980,711	83.7	16.3
Living-related and personal services/ amusement services	385,997	17.2	82.8	37,313,822	95.8	4.2
Education/ Learning support	116,051	23.8	76.2	13,919,827	97.7	2.3
Medical/ healthcare / welfare	276,972	39.7	60.3	74,537,763	93.0	7.0
Compound services	6,469	48.0	52.0	7,474,813	99.7	0.3
Services, n.e.c.	262,229	79.0	21.0	33,133,774	98.3	1.7

Source: Statistics Bureau, Ministry of Internal Affairs and Communications '2012 Economic Census for Business Activity – Tabulations across Industries'.

47. According to Table 8, the number of branches or places of business was 5,768,489, and the number of employees working at these places was 55,837,252.

48. From the composition of different industries, we find that the following industries comprise a high percentage of sole proprietorships: living-related services and amusement services (82.8%), accommodations, eating and drinking services (81.6%), and education and learning support services (76.2%). The following industries are made up of a high percentage of corporate entities: information and telecommunication services (94.9%), mining, etc. (88.6%), and financial services and insurance services (78.1%).

Table 8 Number of Enterprises and Employees by Industrial Major Division

Industrial Major Division	*Number of Enterprises*				*Number of Employees*				*Employees Per Enterprise(Persons)*		
	2009	*2012*	*Rate of Change(%)*	*Percentage of the Total (%)*	*2009 (Persons)*	*2012 (Persons)*	*Rate of Change (%)*	*Percentage of the Total (%)*	*2009*	*2012*	*Rate of Change (%)*
Total	61,999,222	5,768,489	▲ 6.9	–	–	–	–	–	–	–	–
Subtotal	5,886,193	5,453,635	▲ 7.3	100.0	58,442,129	55,837,252	▲ 4.5	100.0	9.9	10.2	0.3
Agriculture/ forestry /fisheries (excluding individual proprietorships)	32,307	30,717	▲ 4.9	0.6	377,595	356,215	▲ 5.7	0.6	11.7	11.6	▲ 0.1
Mining and quarrying of stone and gravel	2,915	2,286	▲ 21.6	0.0	30,684	21,427	▲ 30.2	0.0	10.5	9.4	▲ 1.1
Construction	583,616	525,457	▲ 10.0	9.6	4,320,444	3,876,621	▲ 10.3	6.9	7.4	7.4	▲ 0.0
Manufacturing	536,658	493,380	▲ 8.1	9.0	9,826,839	9,247,717	▲ 5.9	16.6	18.3	18.7	0.4
Electricity, gas, heat supply and water	4,199	3,935	▲ 6.3	0.1	210,533	201,426	▲ 4.3	0.4	50.1	51.2	1.1
Information and communications	71,900	67,204	▲ 13.7	1.2	1,724,414	1,627,310	▲ 5.6	2.9	22.1	24.2	2.1
Transport / postal	147,611	135,468	▲ 8.2	2.5	3,571,963	3,301,682	▲ 7.6	5.9	24.2	24.4	0.2
Wholesale/ retail	1,555,333	1,405,021	▲ 9.7	25.8	12,695,832	11,746,468	▲ 7.5	21.0	8.2	8.4	0.2
Finance/ insurance	91,888	88,831	▲ 3.3	1.6	1,587,909	1,589,449	0.1	2.8	17.3	17.9	0.6
Real estate/ goods rental and leasing	407,793	379,719	▲ 6.9	7.0	1,546,688	1,473,840	▲ 4.7	2.6	3.8	3.9	0.1

Industrial Major Division	*Number of Enterprises*				*Number of Employees*				*Employees Per Enterprise(Persons)*		
	2009	*2012*	*Rate of Change(%)*	*Percentage of the Total (%)*	*2009 (Persons)*	*2012 (Persons)*	*Rate of Change (%)*	*Percentage of the Total (%)*	*2009*	*2012*	*Rate of Change (%)*
Scientific research/ professional and technical services	239,969	219,470	▲ 8.5	4.0	1,781,721	1,663,790	▲ 6.6	3.0	7.4	7.6	0.2
Accomodations/ eating and drinking services	778,048	711,733	▲ 8.5	13.1	5,700,699	5,420,832	▲ 4.9	9.7	7.3	7.6	0.3
Living-related and personal services/ amusement services	509,966	480,617	▲ 5.8	8.8	2,713,386	2,545,797	▲ 6.2	4.6	5.3	5.3	▲ 0.0
Education/ Learning support	168,172	161,287	▲ 4.1	3.0	1,725,610	1,721,559	▲ 0.2	3.1	10.3	10.7	0.4
Medical/healthcare / welfare	344,071	358,997	4.3	6.6	5,629,966	6,178,938	9.8	11.1	16.4	17.2	0.8
Compound services	38,586	33,357	▲ 13.6	0.6	406,920	342,426	▲ 15.8	0.6	10.6	10.3	▲ 0.3
Services, n.e.c.	367,161	356,156	▲ 3.0	6.5	4,590,926	4,521,755	▲ 1.5	8.1	12.5	12.7	0.2

Source: Statistics Bureau, Ministry of Internal Affairs and Communications '2012 Economic Census for Business Activity – Tabulations across Industries'.

II. Companies

49. Table 9 shows that at the end of June 1992 there were 3.024 million companies registered in the Japanese commercial register (see paragraphs 104–111, Types of companies). These companies are broken down as follows:

- Stock companies (*kabushiki kaisha*): 1.295 million.
- Limited companies (*yugen kaisha;* now abolished, see below): 1.633 million.
- General partnership companies (*goumei kaisha*): 19,000.
- Limited partnership companies (*goushi kaisha*): 78,000.

In comparing these figures with those of 2005, we find that the number of stock companies with stated capital of less than JPY 10 million dropped considerably during the thirteen-year period. This is due to the amendment to the Commercial Code in 1990, which introduced a minimum capital requirement for stock companies.

Table 9 Company Numbers by Type and Capital

	November 2005	*June 1992*	
Stock Company	*Capital JPY <10mn*	*11,000*	*739,000*
Capital JPY > 10mn; JPY <100mn	1,103,000	523,000	
Capital JPY > 100mn	38,000	32,000	
Total	1,152,000	1,295,000	
General partnership company	18,000	19,000	
Limited partnership company	87,000	78,000	
Limited company	1,933,000	1,633,000	
Total	3,190,000	3,024,000	

Source: Judicial System and Research Department, Minister's Secretariat, Ministry of Justice.
Note: Figures have been rounded to the nearest 1,000.

50. The commercial register also includes the records of dormant companies. Dormant stock companies will be dissolved upon certain conditions under the Companies Act. That is, a stock company which has not made any registration changes for a certain period of time will be deemed to have been dissolved, upon completion of certain prescribed procedures (see paragraph 860).[26]

51. This means that it is impossible to discern from the commercial register how many of the registered companies are actually active. This can be determined from

26. Article 472, para. 1, Companies Act.

tax figures. According to tax figures, at the end of December 2004, the number of active companies by company type was as follows (Table 10a):

- Stock companies: 1,040,379.
- Limited companies: 1,432,883.
- General partnership companies: 7,775.
- Limited partnership companies: 43,504.

Table 10a Number of Companies: Tax Figures

Capital:	*JPY <10mn*	*JPY > 10mn; JPY <100mn*	*JPY > 100mn; JPY <1bn*	*JPY > 1bn*	*Total*	*%*
Stock company	4,940	998,551	29,866	7,022	1,040,379	40.4%
Limited company	1,346,087	85,852	896	48	1,432,883	55.7%
General partnership company	6,590	1,168	16	1	7,775	0.3%
Limited partnership company	40,678	2,813	12	1	43,504	1.7%
Other	19,862	26,533	969	183	47,547	1.8%
Total	1,418,157	1,114,917	31,759	7,255	2,572,088	100%
(%)	(55.1%)	(43.3%)	(1.2%)	(0.3%)	(100%)	–

Source: National Tax Agency, Planning Division, The actual state of corporate enterprises from the taxation statistics (for 2004).

52. The Companies Act integrated limited companies into stock companies (certain special limited companies (*tokurei yugen kaisha*) – a traditional type of limited company – were allowed to continue their existence) (see paragraph 113). Also, in addition to general partnership company and limited partnership company, the Companies Act created a new type of company: the Limited Liability Company (LLC) (*goudo kaisha*) (see paragraph 1020). As of the end of December 2014, the number of companies in Japan was as follows (Table 10b):

- Stock companies: 2,469,378.
- General partnership companies: 4,092.
- Limited partnership companies: 20,553.
- Limited liability companies: 73,510.

Table 10b Number of Companies: Tax Figures

Capital	*JPY <10mn*	*JPY > 10mn; JPY <100mn*	*JPY > 100mn; JPY <1bn*	*JPY > 1bn*	*Total*	*%*
Stock company	2,110,271	336,571	16,948	5,588	2,469,378	95.1
General partnership company	3,901	180	8	3	4,092	0.2
Limited partnership company	19,824	728	0	1	20,553	0.8
Limited liability company	28,066	256	39	9	28,370	1.1
Other	51,700	20,062	1,229	519	73,510	2.8
Total	2,213,762	357,797	18,224	6,120	2,595,903	100.0
(%)	(85.3%)	(13.8)	(0.7)	(0.2)	(100.0)	

Source: National Tax Agency, Planning Division, The actual state of corporate enterprises from taxation statistics (March 2014).

53. Most stock companies in Japan are small-scale companies. Only 0.9% of all stock companies have stated capital of JPY 100 million or more. Forming a stock company was originally considered more suitable for large-scale companies. The reason for small enterprises preferring to form stock companies will be discussed separately (see paragraph 59).

54. At the end of the 2014 fiscal year, there were 3,541 companies listed on Japan's stock exchanges, with 3,491 of them on the Tokyo Stock Exchange (Table 11) (see paragraph 415, IPO). The Tokyo Stock Exchange has also launched a so-called Mothers market, which is aimed to accommodate venture companies (see paragraph 417). The number of listed non-Japanese companies has been on the decline since 1991, leaving only eleven at the end of the 2014 fiscal year.

Table 11 Listed Companies on the Tokyo Stock Exchange (Unit: Company)

First Section	*Second Section*	*Mothers*	*JASDAQ Standard*	*JASDAQ Growth*	*Tokyo Pro Market*	*Total*
1888 (7)	544 (1)	214 (1)	789 (1)	45 (0)	11 (0)	3,491 (10)

Source: Website of the Tokyo Stock Exchange (as of 1 May 2015) (foreign companies).

55. As of the end of March 2015, there were a total of 45.75 million holders of shares in companies on the Japanese stock exchanges (see Table 12). Some of these shareholders also hold shares in more than one company. Approximately 97% are individuals. However, these individual shareholders altogether hold only 18.7% of the total number of shares. Financial institutions (banks and insurance companies), business corporations, and securities companies (financial instruments and exchange sector) hold 50.3%. This means that almost half of all shares in companies on the Japanese stock exchanges are company-owned. With the exception of the extremely small number of family businesses, names of individuals are no longer found in the list of large shareholders published in companies' annual reports. The number of non-Japanese corporate shareholders is on the increase, having reached 30.8%. It is anticipated that non-Japanese investors will use their voting rights at shareholders' meetings to exert greater pressure on company management.

Table 12 Number of Shareholders and Percentage of Shares Held

	Number of Shareholders (%)	*Percentage of Shares Held*
Total	47,047,951 (100%)	100%
National/ local government	1,332 (0.0%)	0.2%
Financial institutions	94,095 (0.2%)	26.7%
Securities companies	80,959 (0.2%)	2.3%
Business corporations, etc.	766,391 (1.6%)	21.3%
Foreign corporations, etc.	351,085 (0.7%)	30.3%
Individuals, etc.	45,754,089(97.2%)	18.7%

Source: Tokyo Stock Exchange, etc., Outline of Stock Distribution Survey for FY 2013.

56. One reason behind the phenomenon of companies holding the majority of shares in listed companies is the practice of cross-shareholding between companies in the same corporate group (see paragraph 963, Regulations on cross-shareholding). There are several types of corporate groups. There are the 'big six corporate groups'. They consist of the Mitsui, Mitsubishi, and Sumitomo groups, which are the direct descendants of the pre-war *zaibatsu* of the same names, and the Fuji, Sanwa, and Dai-Ichi Kangyo bank groups, which were formed by major 'city' banks during the period of rapid economic growth (starting in 1955) and centred on their corporate clients. The member companies making up these corporate groups exchange shares in each other, a business practice which is referred to as cross-shareholding. It is rare for cross-shareholdings of individual member companies to exceed 10%. However, on a group basis, cross-shareholdings within the big six corporate groups averaged 20.05% (Figure 3).

Figure 3 Cross-Shareholding within Company Groups (Unit: %)

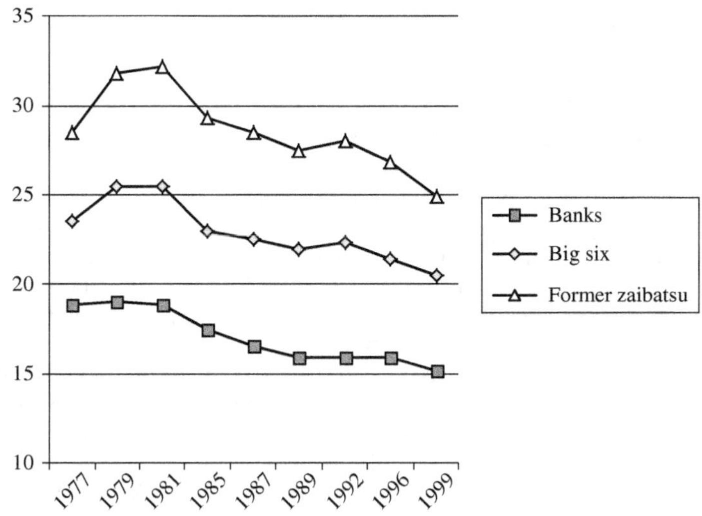

Source: Japan Fair Trade Commission, 7th survey of corporate groups in Japan.
Note: 1. 181 member companies surveyed, excluding life insurance companies.
2. Cross-shareholding rate = sum of the percentages of shareholding ratios held by member companies in each member company / Number of member companies.

57. As the Japanese economy grew, the big six corporate groups came to wield enormous influence; their influence on the competitive order should also not be ignored. However, the strong mutual ties that had developed within these groups – based on capital, exchange of personnel and business relations – are generally weakening.[27] In particular, 37.11% of the companies in the big six corporate groups have taken on an executive officer from another member company. This is 11.43% lower than at the time of the previous survey. There is, however, an increase in the number of directors coming from banks. This is attributed to an increase in numbers of outside directors sent from banks.

58. In most companies, cross-shareholding is on the decline. However, the percentage remains at a high level for companies affiliated with the big six corporate groups: 20.25%, compared with 6.77% for other companies. Although the cross-shareholding is in process of unwinding within the big six corporate groups, this is being replaced by cross-shareholdings with external companies. We are also seeing the ongoing consolidation of financial institutions through, for example, mergers between the core banks of the big six groups. Mega-bank groups have formed out of mergers between Sumitomo and Sakura; Tokyo Mitsubishi, Mitsubishi Trust and

27. Actual Conditions of Corporate Groups (seventh survey), Japan Fair Trade Commission published May 2001.

Banking Corporation and Nippon Trust Bank; Fuji, Dai-Ichi Kangyo and the Industrial Bank of Japan; and Sanwa, Toyo Trust and Banking and Tokai (which later merged with the Mitsubishi group). How each group will restructure following these bank consolidations is being closely watched.

III. Reasons for Forming Different Company Types

59. Owners of sole proprietorship choose to incorporate a company for tax purposes. Companies generally pay less tax than sole proprietorships with the same income (see paragraph 977, Taxation on stock companies). The Commercial Code treated stock companies, limited companies, general partnership companies and limited partnership companies as companies. Accordingly, incorporating any one of these four company types should be effective in reducing business tax. However, since business owners want to benefit from limited liability, they have tended to form either a stock company or limited company. Stock companies were originally more suited to large-scale enterprises, and limited companies were provided for smaller enterprises. Nevertheless, small businesses in Japan have tended to prefer incorporating stock companies. This was due first to inadequacies of the legal framework, but it was also down to a sense of social pride among Japan's business managers, who preferred to run the more highly regarded stock company.

60. Before the 1990 amendment to the Commercial Code, a minimum of JPY 100,000 in capital was necessary to form a limited company. There was no minimum capital requirement to form a stock company; however, forming a stock company required at least seven incorporators, each of whom had to hold at least one share at a minimum issue price of JPY 50,000 (see paragraph 252). This meant that in effect a total of JPY 350,000 was necessary to form a stock company. Until 1 October 1982, such minimum issue price per share requirement was only JPY 500, and therefore it was possible to set up a stock company with just JPY 3,500. But when businesses are faced with the choice of incorporating as stock company or limited company, this difference in amount of required capital is not actually the overriding factor. Since the title 'stock company' sounds more socially credible, this was why even small businesses have tended to opt for stock company, despite such businesses being inherently more suited to limited company.

61. Of course stock companies need to conform to stricter regulations, such as the public notice requirement of financial statements. This was, however, not being carried out by the large majority of small companies, and there have also been no reports of fines for failure to comply with the public notice requirement. This kind of abuse of the stock company system has bred a kind of lawlessness in this area. The 1990 amendment to the Commercial Code introduced a minimal capital requirement of JPY 10 million for incorporating a stock company in an effort to rectify such abuses (see paragraph 255).[28] At the same time, the minimal capital

28. Article 186-4, Commercial Code prior to amendment.

requirement for limited companies was raised from JPY 100,000 to JPY 3 million.[29]

62. However, setting the minimum capital requirement at JPY 10 million was not an appropriate level for separating large-scale companies from smaller ones. The Companies Act has now abolished the minimum capital requirement altogether. A company can be set up with just JPY 1. Further, in order to redress the gap between law and reality, limited companies and stock companies have been integrated into the single category of stock company, establishing a legal framework for small-scale stock companies (see paragraphs 112 and 168).

§3. 'Japanese-Style Capitalism'

I. Changing Perceptions in 'Japanese-Style Capitalism' (*Nihongata Shihonshugi*)

63. There was a time when the 'Japanese-style capitalism' was highly regarded as Japan's economy recovered after the Second World War and further accomplished rapid growth thereafter. It was originally pointed out-in Ezra Vogel's *Japan as Number One: Lessons for America* (1979).[30] Indeed, during the 1980s – and particularly the late 1980s – Japan's manufacturing companies became extremely competitive in the global market. However, in December 1989, the so-called bubble economy topped out, and Japan entered into what was to become a long period of severe economic recession. The recession was difficult to overcome and there were concerns that the economy was falling into a deflationary spiral (where decreases in prices lead to further decreases). This caused Japanese-style capitalism to lose its glorified status and rather a fundamental overhaul was advocated. Japan has since undergone considerable reform in many areas.

II. History of 'Japanese Capitalism' and Its Unique Features

A. Development of Its Framework

64. It was the General Headquarters of the Allied Forces, essentially the United States, which occupied Japan after the end of the Second World War, that developed the framework for Japanese capitalism. The United States carried out a complete reform of agricultural land and the educational system, developed labour unions and dissolved the military and *zaibatsu* conglomerates. Agrarian reform led to the birth of independent farmers and gave rise to an equality in the area of agriculture. Educational reform established a 6-3-3-4 system of education, widening access to higher education and creating an equal-opportunities society where higher education provides equal opportunity for success. The development of labour

29. Article 9, Limited Company Act prior to amendment.
30. Translated into Japanese in 1979 by Wakako Hironaka & Akiko Kimoto.

unions created equality within companies. Japanese labour unions experienced many twists and turns before finally settling as relatively moderate in company unions. Combined with lifetime employment and seniority-based pay, the so-called Japanese employment system was established and hugely contributed to the development of Japan's capitalism economy. There is also an influential view arguing that Japanese capitalism actually existed before the post-war era, and originated in the wartime regime established in around 1940.[31]

65. The *Zaibatsu* headquarters, which controlled large companies before the war through their holding companies, were dissolved and the shares held by the holding companies were disposed of. The Anti-Monopoly Act, which was established at the same time, prohibited the establishment of holding companies (see paragraph 935 for details of the lifting of this prohibition). Large companies were also split and over 3,000 directors of major companies were ousted, to be replaced by a younger generation and leading to the separation of management and ownership. This restructuring exposed Japanese companies to fierce domestic competition. It was not surprising that the nine car manufacturers, five steel manufacturers and seventeen household electrics manufacturers that survived the world's toughest domestic market at the time were so strong in the international markets.

B. Characteristics of 'Japanese Capitalism'

66. In relation to the Companies Act, the following illustrates the relevant features of Japanese capitalism.

1. Increase of Corporate Shareholders: Corporate Capitalism

67. Upon the dissolution of *zaibatsu* which led to disposal of the shares they held, approximately 60% of shares in Japanese companies initially went to individual shareholders. Later, with the liberalization of capital flows in the late 1950s, domestic companies established the so-called cross-shareholding system to stabilize shareholders with the aim of preventing non-Japanese investors from acquiring their shares. As holding companies were prohibited under the Anti-Monopoly Act, there was no other way to stave off such takeovers.

68. By the time the financial bubble peaked in 1989, over 70% of shares in Japan's largest companies were held by financial institutions (46%), business corporations (24.8%) and securities companies (2%). The remaining 30% were held by a large number of individual shareholders. As such individual shareholders have little interest in the management of company, the large number of such shareholders

31. See Tetsuji Okazaki & Masahiro Okuno (eds) *Nihon Keizai Shisutemu no Genry* (The Origin of the Japanese Economic System) (1993) & Yukio Noguchi *1940-nen Taisei – Saraba Senji Keizai* (The 1940s System Japan under the Wartime Economy) (1995).

would exert very little influence on the company's management. In turn, major corporate shareholders had significant influential power, thereby giving strong power to the management members of such corporate shareholders. Yet, the relationship between companies and their corporate shareholders was not tense in most cases, and it was rather mutual dependency. This practice – referred to as corporate capitalism – collapsed with the sharp drop in share prices after the collapse of Japan's bubble economy (see paragraphs 87–89).

2. Shareholders Meetings: A Mere Formality

69. With such structure of share ownership, the shareholders meetings used be a mere formality. Annual shareholders meetings in Japan tended to be concentrated at the end of June every year, on the same day and at the same time, and usually concluded in a very short time (figure 5 and Table 19). This was also because it was companies that hold the majority of issued shares. Except in special circumstances, the representatives of corporate shareholders do not tend to ask questions in the shareholders meetings of other companies. The management would take great care to collect their corporate shareholders' proxies and voting forms, but tended to pay no attention to their individual shareholders. The only individual shareholder that the management would be concerned with were the corporate extortionists (*soukaiya*). However, such practice has undergone major changes (see paragraphs 557–561).

3. Companies as Employee Communities

70. Japanese companies are said to be communities of employees. Management selection in Japanese companies involves a lengthy process, with management members being appointed from among company employees. This is known as an internal promotion system. A typical ambition of new graduate employees is to become a director of the company. And to make this a possibility, the number of directors in a company ends up growing. Labour unions have a very strong interest in keeping employees, and may refrain from demanding pay rises if necessary to maintain employment. Managers are also anxious to keep employees. Compared with other countries, particularly the United States, the difference in compensation between top management and ordinary employees is small. This has in some sense served to establish the trustworthy relationship between management and unions.

In summary, the three main features of the traditional Japanese employment systems are lifetime employment, seniority-based pay and in company unions. However, they have all undergone certain changes (see paragraph 90).

4. Traditional Indirect Financing System

71. Direct financing takes place when investors purchase securities, such as shares and bonds, that a company has issued in the market, with these funds flowing directly to the company. Indirect financing is when a financial intermediary – usually a bank – collects funds from investors and then loans them to companies. The United States is a typical example of a direct financing system; Japan is at the opposite of the spectrum with its traditional indirect financing system. In the post-war era, it was common practice to obtain financing from bank loans for economic recovery and rapid growth. This meant that the scrutiny by the banks – the lenders – functioned as external monitoring systems. However, banks lost this function as the bubble economy grew (see paragraph 78).

72. An important feature of indirect financing in Japan is that the financial assets of individual investors are largely in the form of cash or bank deposits. A comparison with the United States provides further clarity. In the 2007 fiscal year, among Japan's household total assets of JPY 1,520 trillion, cash or bank deposits represented 51.6%, whereas investment trusts or shares represented only 14.3%. In the United States, on the other hand, among the total household assets of USD 49.8 trillion, investment trusts or shares represented 47.9% and cash or bank deposits represented only 12%. With the drop in share prices during the financial crisis that struck in the latter half of 2008, family assets in both the United States and Japan suffered huge losses. However, compared with the United States, Japan's family assets escaped with less damage due to the relatively low rate of high-risk assets.[32] In 2001, the government tried to instigate a shift from savings to investment, but without much success.

III. Growth and Collapse of Bubble Economy

A. Emergence of the Bubble

73. The Japanese economy during the latter half of 1980s – based on the Japanese capitalism characterized by the abovementioned employment system and cross-shareholding – was proclaimed as a global model. The economy flourished due to the extreme rises in real estate and share prices. But upon entering into the 1990s, real estate and share prices started to drop dramatically, and by 1992 deep recession had set in and the boom of the late 1980s was referred to as a bubble.

74. A bubble occurs when the speculative prices of assets, such as shares, land, buildings or art objects, increase excessively, resulting in inflated asset value which creates the illusion of massive price appreciation. Historically, there have been several instances of such bubbles, famously the Dutch tulip bubble during the seventeenth century. People in the Netherlands were creating security interests on their estates to buy just one tulip bulb, and ended up losing their entire fortunes. After a while, this tulipomania subsided and the market price crashed, resulting in a series of bankruptcies among long-established trading companies. It took many years for the Dutch economy to recover. Then how did Japan's bubble era come about?

---

32. 2009 Cabinet Office Annual Report on the Japanese Economy and Public Finance, 130 (English version available in summary only).

75. One of the reasons concerns the relationship with the United States. The trade friction between Japan and the United States was exacerbated in the early 1980s. Anti-Japan hard-liners in the American Congress became more powerful, to a degree where it was feared that economic factors might endanger the Japan-United States Security Treaty. Faced with such crisis, on 22 September 1985 in New York, the Japanese government entered into an agreement – known as the Plaza Accord – with the other G5 finance ministers to induce appreciation of yen against the US dollar (with strong yen and weak US dollar, it is difficult for Japan to export to the United States). The subsequent coordinated interventions and interest rate cuts on the currency markets caused the pre-Accord exchange rate of JPY 240 to the US dollar rise to JPY 152 in 1986. The strength of the yen pushed the Japanese economy into recession. However, Japan's export industries managed to overcome this crisis through major streamlining efforts.

76. This clearly shows that currency exchange adjustments were not enough to reduce Japan's exports, which escalated trade friction between the United States and Japan even further. The United States demanded that Japan implement more effective measures to stimulate domestic demand. Haruo Maekawa, the former head of the Bank of Japan, outlined Japan's response in spring 1986 in his Maekawa Report. In this report, Japan pledged to the world to significantly reduce its huge trade surplus by stimulating domestic demand and opening up Japanese markets to foreign products. In a bid to boost domestic demand, in May 1987, the Nakasone Cabinet announced public spending policies (expansion of public works projects) to the unprecedented level of JPY 5 trillion. In the meantime, since the Plaza Accord, the Japanese government consistently kept interest rates low and implemented official rate cuts. These low interest rate policies and public spending to stimulate domestic demand caused an overflow of money in the domestic market. This money was concentrated in shares and land, and the bubble economy started to develop.

B. Reality Behind the Bubble Economy

77. The land price bubble developed as follows. In the latter half of the 1980s, companies, believing in the 'land myth' that real estate prices would continue to increase, granted their lands to create security interests to obtain bank financing. With this bank financing, they purchased more land. As there was an overflow of money – as mentioned above – the banks also continued to lend money. However, whereas banks would normally offer loan-to-value ratios of 70% of the value of the land; during the 1980s they were offering 100% or even land-secured loans greater than the value of the land. It was similar when shares and other securities were granted to secure bank loans.

78. As such, during the bubble years, in the process of lending in anticipation of rising land-security values, banks lost their function to scrutinize as the external monitors of the borrowers, which is essential in indirect financing. Companies used a large proportion of these borrowings – counting on future rises in land and share prices – to purchase more shares and land, and to invest in corporate investment funds or fund trusts. This had the effect of pushing up the price of land and shares further. Company balance sheets ended up comprising accumulated land and securities on the assets section and accumulated bank loans in the liabilities section.

C. Collapse of the Bubble

79. In the final trading day of 1989, the Nikkei average hit a record high (JPY 38,915). Thereafter, share prices crashed, and although they temporarily recovered to some extent, they basically followed a downward trend (Table 15). The 'land myth' also collapsed: land prices in the commercial areas of Tokyo plummeted by over 80% against their prices during the peak of 1991 (Figure 4). As a result, while the amount of company liabilities in the liabilities section of their balance sheets remained unchanged, the land and securities in the assets section suffered huge unrealized losses, damaging the financials of the companies involved. In a predominantly indirectly financed Japan, the credit risk was borne by the banks. This was the underlying cause of the banks' bad debt problems.

Figure 4 Volatility in Land Value

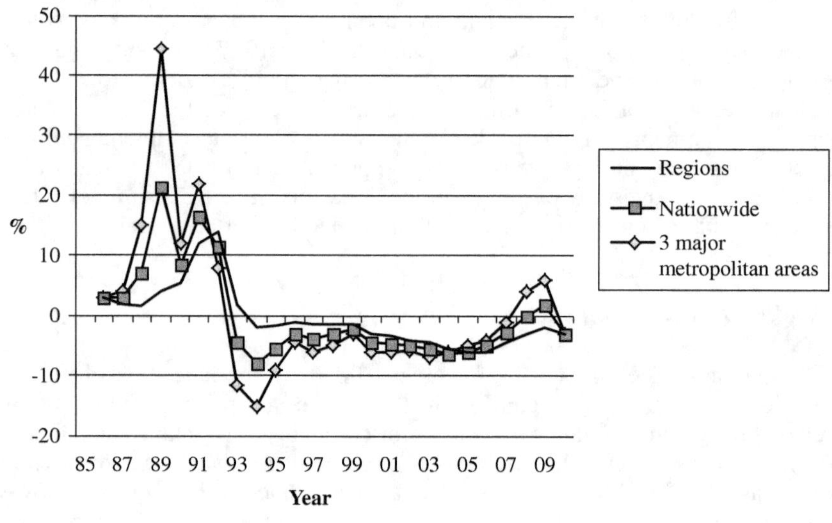

Source: Nikkei forecast for 2010.
Key dates:
1985 = Plaza Accord.
1986 to 1990 = Bubble era.
1989 = Nikkei average hits a record high.
1990 = Limitation on real estate loans.
1998 = Special Purpose Company Act enacted to promote securitization of real estate.
2001 = Initial listing of real estate investment trust on the Tokyo Stock Exchange.
2002 = Restrictions on floor-area ratio for urban areas relaxed.
2002 to 2007 = Period of economic recovery.

IV. The Lost Decade

80. The ten or fifteen years after the collapse of the bubble are referred to as Japan's lost decade. It is illustrated in Japan's economic growth during this period: In 1992, Japan's real GDP growth rate was less than 1%, and except for the temporary recovery between 1995 and 1996, zero growth continued until the 1997 fiscal year, after which the economy entered into a phase of negative growth. Growth picked up again in the 2005 fiscal year, at 2.4%, but fell again to 2.1% in the 2006 fiscal year. The average economic growth rate between 1991 and 2009 was 0.89% (see paragraph 1).

81. Japan's governmental finance is also in trouble by international standards. The national and local government budget deficit continued to grow until it totalled JPY 773 trillion (150% of GDP) at the end of the 2007 fiscal year (see paragraph 3).[33] In the post-bubble economy, corporate bankruptcies increased and corporate downsizing pushed up unemployment, taking the national unemployment rate to a new record high of 5.5% (or 3.5 million people) by November 2001.

82. Commodity prices also fell, and the domestic wholesale price index and the consumer price index also began their steady decline in 1998. This is known as deflation. Low prices may appear to benefit consumers, but in a deflationary economy, companies implement pay cuts to cover the drops in revenue, and unemployment increases as a result of downsizing and bankruptcies, which then further exacerbate the recession. Commodity prices remained in a long-term deflationary trend, but started to improve again in around 2004 (see paragraph 100).

83. Finally, there is the banks' bad debt problems (see paragraph 79). Japanese banks were forced to dispose of JPY 72 trillion in bad debts between 1992 and 2000. Given that the total of their outstanding lending was around JPY 500 trillion, this is a huge number. As their operational results recovered, banks eventually disposed of all remaining bad debts, and the problem has now been solved (see paragraph 93).

V. Structural Reform and Deregulation

A. Background

84. The economic stimulus package worth JPY 10.7 trillion instituted in post-bubble August 1992 was a traditional method of combating recession. The government aimed to prevent a slump in GDP by making up for the low capital investment and private demand with public investment. At the same time, the Bank of Japan cut the long-term and short-term interest rates and implemented monetary easing. But neither budgetary nor monetary measures led to economic recovery.

33. Cabinet Office 2007 Annual Report on the Japanese Economy and Public Finance, 88 (English version available in summary only).

85. Under such circumstances, structural reform through deregulation was advocated. Namely, the supporters argued that: the Japanese economy is struggling to recover at a time when the American economy is enjoying powerful growth; the structural cause of Japan's economic downturn is attributable to the variety of governmental regulations which do not exist in the United States. Such arguments that deregulation is essential for economic recovery swept across Japan during the mid-1990s. While the request for deregulation covered a wide range of areas, the following will focus on Japan's financial 'big bang', as this is most relevant to the Companies Act.

B. The Financial 'Big Bang'

86. The major reform of the financial system began in 1998. The amended Foreign Exchange and Foreign Trade Act came into effect in April, completely liberalizing foreign financing and capital transactions. In June, the Financial System Reforms Act (abbreviation for the Act on Revision of Acts Related to Financial System Reforms) was passed. This act provided a major transformation of financial administration, which was said to be a 'convoy method' (*gosou sendan houshiki*), to revitalize Japan's financial markets through financial liberalization, aiming to develop an international financial market to compete with the markets of New York and London. Specifically, the reform made it easier to enter into the securities sector by dismantling the fences of financial industries and replacing the licensing requirement with a registration requirement which should facilitate the development of new financial products. In addition to the deregulation in the securities sector, which included the liberalization of share trading commissions, the reform also aimed to remove the operational regulations of banks and insurance companies to develop a more efficient financial market.

VI. Reforms Related to the Companies Act

A. Dismantling of Cross-Shareholdings

87. Corporate capitalism – a unique feature of the Japanese economy involving companies' holding of shares in other companies – played a big role in strengthening companies during the period of rapid economic growth, when rises in share prices produced high unrealized profits. However, when share prices crashed with the collapse of the bubble, it reduced unrealized profits, and further incurred high unrealized losses. This became particularly evident at the end of the 2001 fiscal year when it was required to revalue cross-shareholdings at market value, which resulted in surfacing the unrealized losses of the banks that held a large amount of shares in other companies. In a bid to avoid realizing these losses, the banks sold such shares and used the proceeds to write off bad debts. As a result, the cross-shareholdings of banks (long-term credit banks, city banks and regional banks) dropped to 4.6% by the end of 2006. At its height in 1985, bank's cross-shareholdings amounted to 20.9%. Cross-shareholding among business corporations also fell, dropping to 20.7% by the end of 2006.

88. The Act on Limitation of Shareholding by Banks and Other Financial Institutions was established on 21 November 2001 and came into effect on 28 November 2001. This act prohibited banks from owning shares to a total value greater than their own net capital after 30 September 2006. The Banks' Shareholdings Purchase Corporation (*ginkou tou hoyu kabushiki shutoku kikou*) was established to purchase their shares before this cut-off date.

89. As such, Japan's corporate capitalism, which characterized Japanese capitalism, was showing signs of collapse. But this has been having a positive effect on corporate governance as a result of the changes to shareholder composition. Since 2006, cross-shareholding between business corporations expanded again to prevent hostile takeover attempts (see paragraph 98). In an effort to address this issue, the Financial Services Agency (FSA) amended the Cabinet Office Ordinance on the Disclosure of Corporate Information, etc. (effective as of 31 March 2010) to require disclosure of the purpose and certain other matters of share ownership for the top thirty stocks on the company balance sheet on a book value basis (except for shares held for the purposes of net investment) in cases where shares held by the company exceed 1% of its stated capital.

B. Changes in the Japanese Employment System

90. As previously indicated, the three main distinguishing features of the Japanese employment system were lifetime employment, seniority-based pay and in company unions (see paragraphs 66–70). Many Japanese companies, however, shifted from lifetime employment and seniority-based pay to a performance-based pay system after the collapse of the bubble economy to overcome the problems of surplus debts, staff and facilities. However, there have been increasing moves to reinstate these traditional employment practices as economic recovery shifted to economic expansion. In 2007, there was a rapid drop in the number of companies expanding their performance-related pay systems, particularly large companies with 300 or more employees, and the trend to expand such performance-related pay systems that progressed from the mid-1990s has settled down.[34]

91. A notable feature of recent employment is the increasingly high percentage of non-regular workers (part-time staff, temporary staff, agency staff, contract staff, consultants, etc). It has been increasing steadily from 20% in 1990 to 33.9% in 2008. This means that one of three employees is a non-regular worker. Between January and March of 2009, the number of non-regular workers fell by 420,000 people to 33.3%. This was a result of the lay-offs of temporary workers (*haken-giri*) in the wake of the global financial crisis in the latter half of 2008. In 2010, the percentage of non-regular workers climbed back up to 33.6%. The main reason behind this increase in non-regular workers was the companies' policy to cut down personnel costs in the post-bubble economy. Wages of non-regular workers are set

34. 2009 White Paper on the Labour Economy, 189 (English version not available).

considerably lower than those of regular employees, which has widened the income gap among young workers.

C. Introduction of New Business Combination Methods

92. There is a wide range of approaches to restore, maintain and strengthen companies' competitiveness, including spin-off of non-core businesses, mergers and business integration using a holding company scheme. The Commercial Code was amended to meet such needs. For example, merger rules were revised in 1997 (see paragraph 879); share exchange and share transfer procedures were introduced in 1999 to facilitate the formation of 100% ownership relations (see paragraph 940); the company split was added in 2000 (see paragraph 948); and regulations on companies' purchasing their own shares were liberalized in 2001 (deregulation of treasury shares) (see paragraph 388). In 2005, the Companies Act was enacted (see paragraph 167).

VII. Reality Behind Economic Recovery and Growth

93. The Japanese economy started to recover from around summer 2003. It finally emerged from the lost decade (see paragraph 80). Companies' excess investments, debts and employees, as well as structural issues such as the problematic financial system had held back the recovery process for a long-time. Companies restored the profitability of their business activities and shifted to an upward trend by reorganizing their past capital investments and surplus workforce, and on the financial front, by reducing the interest-bearing debts and increasing their net capital. Such recovery efforts supported economic expansion, which – surpassing the fifty-seven-month 'Izanagi economic boom' between 1965 and 1970 – entered its sixth year in February 2007.[35] Employment also continued to rise: the unemployment rate of 5.5% in April 2003 fell to less than 4% by 2007. The performance of companies was said to have hit a new all-time high.

94. But while companies were recovering and developing, per capita income dropped and consumer spending was sluggish. In other words, employees were not sharing the fortunes of the companies' performance. In this respect, the recovery phase was different from the rapid growth years, as the workers' wages did not increase nationwide. Seemingly, the wages have been controlled due to the wave of globalization caused by the enormous supply of low cost and high-quality labour in China and other Asian countries onto the capitalism market.

95. As wages did not increase, consumer spending and other indicators of domestic demand slowed, and wide-spread problems of social and economic

35. 'Izanagi' refers to Japanese mythology, where the creation of the Japanese islands is attributed to God Izanagi and Goddess Izanami.

disparity became noticeable. Disparities emerged between large companies and SMEs, regular employees and non-regular workers, and cities and regions.

96. In the meantime, Japanese companies have been actively engaged in mergers and acquisitions (M&A). According to a survey of 100 presidents published in the Nikkei newspaper at the start of August 2007, 86% of management members in major companies actively encourage M&A transactions. In fact, in September 2007, Daimaru and Matsuzakaya merged to establish a holding company, and in October of the same year Mitsubishi Pharma Corporation and Tanabe Seiyaku Co. Ltd. merged to form Mitsubishi Tanabe Pharma Corporation. According to Recof Corporation, an M&A consulting company, there were 2,725 M&A transactions in 2005, and 2,775 in 2006. The recent trend of a shrinking population has led companies, particularly those dependent on domestic demands, such as department stores and restaurants, to engage in M&A activities as a means to increase their market share.

97. Acquisitions of Japanese companies by non-Japanese companies have also increased. The US Citigroup acquired Nikko Securities in 2007 using the triangular merger (see paragraph 900) that was introduced with the Companies Act (when Citigroup later fell into financial difficulty, the company was transferred to the Mitsui-Sumitomo group). In M&A terminology, M&As between domestic companies are called 'in-in', outbound acquisitions are called 'in-out' M&As, and inbound acquisitions are called 'out-in' M&As. It is important to note the drastic increase in cross-border M&A transactions between Japanese and other Asian companies. This was particularly noticeable in 2010, when M&As between Japanese and Chinese companies increased significantly. By July 2010, the total number of in-out acquisitions had reached twenty-eight for China (twenty-five for mainland China and three for Hong Kong), twelve for Taiwan, nine for Singapore and eight for India. Out-in acquisitions totalled twenty-two for China (sixteen for mainland China and six for Hong Kong), six for Taiwan and five for South Korea. These figures illustrate the sharp increase in both outbound and inbound M&A activities relating to China.[36] With a total of fifty deals, approximately 40% of Japan's overseas M&A activities are related to China. These figures are also evidence of China's high growth potential (see paragraph 1).

98. Recently, one of the highly debated issues involves hostile takeover defence measures. The dispute on anti-takeover measures instituted by Bull-Dog Sauce Co., Ltd. to prevent the hostile takeover attempt by Steel Partners Japan ended up in the Supreme Court.[37] As a precaution against such hostile takeover attempts, there are some companies that introduce so-called anti-takeover measures. In Japan, many such companies adopt advance warning type anti-takeover measures. These entail the triggering of rules to be followed by acquirers seeking to make large-scale share purchases, which rules are formulated and publicly announced by the target company in advance, and in situations such as when the acquirers do not follow such rules, the target company takes defensive measures. A commonly used defensive measure is

36. See MARR 2010, 8 (Recof's M&A trade journal; available in Japanese only).
37. 7 Aug. 2007, Supreme Court Collection of Court Decisions on Civil Actions 61-2215.

share options (*shinkabu yoyakuken*). In Japan, as of March 2014 there were 512 companies that had introduced anti-takeover measures, accounting for around 15% of all listed companies. However, the number has been on a gradual decline.

Table 13 Company Anti-takeover Measures (Advance Warning Type)

			2007	*2010*	*2014*
Procedures	Introduced by	Determination by board of directors	57	18	15
		Approval by shareholders meeting	341	518	476
		(Those requiring amendment of articles of incorporation)	(92)	(223)	(214)
	Triggered by	Determination by board of directors	330	252	186
		(With establishment of a committee)	(298)	(241)	(181)
		Confirmation of shareholder intentions	18	51	49
		(With establishment of a committee)	(3)	(24)	(24)
		Intermediate type	50	233	256
		(With establishment of a committee)	(43)	(227)	(249)
Contents	Acquirer criteria	15% or more	14	10	10
		20% or more	374	516	474
		25% or more	10	10	7
	Evaluation (careful deliberation) period	Up to 90 days in principle	384	527	485
		90 days in principle	14	9	6
	Defensive measures	Share options only	159	189	187
		Others	239	347	304
Effective term (or renewal term)	1 year		94	44	23
	2 years		58	45	30
	3 years		212	436	427
	Other		34	11	10
Number of companies	-		398	536	49

Source: MARR (February 2015).

VIII. Japan's Post 'Lehman Shock' Economy

99. As stated above (see paragraph 93), the Japanese economy emerged from the years of recession following the collapse of the bubble in 1990, and gradually began to pick up. But after the peak in October 2007, the economy entered into a sluggish phase. It was then directly hit by the global financial crisis triggered by the Lehman Brothers bankruptcy in September 2008, otherwise known as the Lehman shock. Fortunately, Japan's banks and securities companies managed to avoid the crisis of financial systems based on their experience from the bubble collapse. However, the United States-originated financial crisis caused the real economies of all industrial nations into major recession, hitting Japan's economy particularly hard. This was because Japan's industrial structure relied heavily on car manufacturing (see paragraph 31), which meant that when car sales in industrial countries slumped, the Japanese economy was hit very hard.

100. The deflation that weighed heavy on the Japanese economy after the collapse of the bubble (see paragraph 82) appeared to have ceased but was once again causing a problem after the Lehman shock. The Japanese government confirmed in November 2009 that the Japanese economy was in a mild deflationary state. Prices continued to fall as a result of demand shortages and supply surpluses. Although lower prices provide temporary relief for household budgets, it also means that company sales slump, profits fall, wages are cut and lay-offs and bankruptcies increase. This then results in lower consumer spending, which exacerbates the recession and causes the economy to shrink. In such situation, tax revenue from corporate tax on company revenue, income tax on individual earnings and consumption tax remain low, which puts a further strain on the nation's fiscal purse. As mentioned above, the only way to break out of the ensuing stalemate is for Japan to venture into new areas of industry (see paragraph 32).

IX. Abenomics and the Japanese Economy

101. When Shinzo Abe took office as prime minister in December 2012, he implemented a policy based on three 'arrows': expansionary fiscal policy, large-scale monetary easing, and a growth strategy. The first arrow sought to stimulate business activities by encouraging aggressive money supply by the Bank of Japan (such as through large volume purchases of government bonds). The second arrow involved aiming for economic recovery through aggressive spending on public works. The third arrow entailed aiming for sustained economic growth by strengthening corporate and industrial competitiveness through regulatory reform and the like.

102. The yen was selling in the JPY 75–JPY 80 range to the US dollar until mid-November 2012. As a result of the first arrow, and because of a stronger dollar due to a buoyant US economy, there was a rapid weakening of the yen, and in March 2015 it had recovered to the JPY 120 range to the dollar. The weak yen saw increased price competitiveness for Japanese exports, while falling crude oil prices brought about reduced energy costs for businesses. Underpinned by factors such as these, Japan saw significant recovery particularly among exporters.

103. Share prices also rose. The closing price of the Nikkei average on 14 November 2012 was JPY 8,665. In April 2015, the Nikkei average hit JPY 20,000 for the first time in fifteen years. Behind this rapid rise in share prices was aggressive buying by overseas investors and an increase in investment by Japan's public pension funds (leading to the current share market sometimes being called a 'ministerially manufactured market' (*kansei soba*)). The sharp depreciation of the yen has weakened the performance of importers. The success of the third arrow will be essential in order for to see true recovery of the Japanese economy through widespread improvement in the performance of Japanese companies.

§4. Japanese Companies

I. Types of Companies

104. The Companies Act provides for stock companies (*kabushiki kaisha*), general partnership companies (*goumei kaisha*), limited partnership companies (*goushi kaisha*) and limited liability companies (*goudou kaisha*). General partnership companies, limited partnership companies and limited liability companies are categorized as membership companies (*mochibun kaisha*). The Companies Act divides companies into two categories: stock companies (Part II, Companies Act) and membership companies (Part III, Companies Act).

105. A stock company is characterized by the limited liability of its shareholders, the ban on return of investment to shareholders who wish to withdraw their investment, the free assignability of its shares, as well as the principle of majority control. In a stock company, liability of shareholders is limited to the value of their subscription (see paragraph 312).[38] And since shareholders are protected from liability to creditors of the company, creditors can only rely on the company's assets for their claims. To prevent company assets being reduced by the company buying back stocks, in principle, shareholders are not permitted to withdraw their investment. On the other hand, shareholders are allowed to assign their shares to recoup their capital investment (see paragraph 371).[39] The limited liability of shareholders enables stock companies to solicit capital investments widely from various investors. The shareholders provide the capital investment and as such are indeed the owners of the company. Stock companies apply the principle of majority control, which means that rather than each individual shareholder being entitled to one vote, shareholders are granted voting rights in proportion to the number of shares that they hold (see paragraph 573).[40]

38. Article 104, Companies Act.
39. Article 127, Companies Act.
40. Article 308, para. 1, Companies Act.

106. Stock companies hold a shareholders' meeting to elect directors. These directors consist of the board of directors. The board of directors then appoints one or more representative director(s). The Companies Act allocates the power to make managerial decisions among the shareholders meeting, board of directors and one or more representative directors. Company auditors (*kansayaku*) are also appointed at the shareholders meeting, tasked with supervising the directors. Another option is to use Companies with Nominating Committee, etc. or Company with Audit and Supervisory Committee (see paragraphs 816–842), which involves a very different corporate governance to ordinary stock companies. Small companies are permitted under the Companies Act to adopt a simpler organizational structure (see paragraphs 545 and 554).

107. In a general partnership company, each member is, in principle, entitled to execute operations on behalf of the company, and shares the liability of the company (see paragraphs 1004–1015, General partnership companies).[41] It is possible to limit the execution of company operations to some of the members by the articles of incorporation.[42] The company operations are determined by a majority vote among all members, or, where applicable, a majority vote among members entitled to execute such operations.[43] Day-to-day company activities may be carried out independently by all members.[44] All members are jointly and severally liable to creditors of the company, and this liability is unlimited.[45] A member may withdraw from the company at will, whereupon the invested equity interest must be bought back.[46] On the other hand, for the assignment of equity interests, the unanimous consent of all members will be required.[47]

108. These characteristics set out by the Companies Act mean that each member of a general partnership company, in their capacity as equity holders, may advocate a different management strategy. This lack of essential unity makes it impossible to run the company smoothly; there is additional risk that the company may be forced to dissolve as a result of members withdrawing their investments. The only way to avoid such risk may be to allow only blood relatives or people known to be trustworthy to invest in the company.

109. A limited partnership company consists of members with limited liability as well as members with unlimited liability (see paragraphs 1016–1019, Limited partnership companies).[48] The members with limited liability are jointly and severally liable to the company creditors but this liability is limited to the value of their investment.[49] A limited partnership company involves limited liability members

41. Article 590, para. 1, Companies Act.
42. Article 590, para. 1, Companies Act.
43. Article 590, para. 2, Companies Act.
44. Article 590, para. 3, Companies Act.
45. Article 580, para. 1, Companies Act.
46. Article 606, para. 3; Art. 611, Companies Act.
47. Article 585, para. 1, Companies Act.
48. Article 576, para. 3, Companies Act.
49. Article 580, para. 2, Companies Act.

investing in a company run by members with unlimited liability and receiving a share of the company's profits. Here, we start to see signs of separation of ownership and management. Since human relationships are critical to connections between members in a limited partnership company, there are restrictions on the assignment of equity interests of members with unlimited liability.[50] As to the assignment of equity interests of limited members, the rules have been relaxed to some extent, but restrictions remain in place.[51]

110. In a LLC, all members are subject to limited liability (see paragraphs 1020–1025, Limited liability companies).[52] Limited liability companies are similar in this regard to stock companies. To enable all members to enjoy limited liability, there are statutory regulations imposed on the payment of dividends as well as mandatory procedures regarding creditor protection. Internal company relations and relations between members are regulated similarly to partnerships under the Civil Code. There are virtually no default rules on the organizational structure or the rights of the members, which may be freely agreed by the members. In this regard, limited liability companies are similar to general partnership companies or limited partnership companies.

111. Before its amendment in 2005, the Commercial Code did not permit general partnership companies, limited partnership companies or stock companies to convert to different types of companies. The Companies Act, however, permits stock companies and membership companies to convert into one another by entity conversion.[53]

II. Special Limited Companies (*Tokurei Yugen Kaisha*)

112. Before the Companies Act was established, four types of companies were legally recognized: general partnership companies, limited partnership companies, stock companies and limited companies. The rules on limited companies (*yugen kaisha*) were provided under the Limited Company Act.[54] Although limited companies were not recognized as companies under the Commercial Code, they did not differ in substance from companies under the Commercial Code and, in the eyes of other laws, they were not actually considered any different to companies recognized by the Commercial Code.[55] Limited companies are similar to stock companies in that their members are subject to limited liability. However, their incorporation procedures and structures were much simpler than those of stock companies, and their

50. Article 585, para. 1, Companies Act.
51. Article 585, para. 2, Companies Act.
52. Article 576, para. 4, Companies Act.
53. Article 743, Companies Act.
54. Act No. 74 of 1938.
55. Article 53 of the Commercial Code prior to amendment; Art. 89 of the Limited Company Act prior to amendment.

closed nature was reinforced in that, for example, there are restrictions on the number of members permitted. It was anticipated that small businesses would use this type of company.

113. Upon the enactment of the Companies Act, the Limited Company Act was abolished. When the Companies Act came into force, limited companies that had been established under the Limited Company Act (former limited companies) automatically continued their operations as stock companies.[56] It was therefore not necessary to implement special procedures to make changes to the articles of incorporation or commercial registration. The Companies Act also provides for small-scale stock companies, and their regulations are very similar to those in the Limited Company Act. However, since these regulations are not identical, special provisions were made for former limited companies so as to maintain the rules applicable under the Limited Company Act.[57] Limited companies which elected to be subject to such rules (so-called special limited liability companies) were required to include the words '*yugen kaisha*' (limited company) in their company trade name to be distinguished from ordinary stock companies.[58] By changing their registered trade name in the articles of incorporation to include the word '*kabushiki kaisha*' (stock company), special limited liability companies may make the transition to ordinary stock company.[59]

III. Characteristics of Companies

114. A company must aim to distribute profits earned though its business activities to its members. Profits may be distributed either in the form of dividends of surplus (see paragraph 635) or by distributing the residual assets (see paragraph 866). A company must engage in business that has the potential to generate profits for the company. Accordingly, it is not permitted to set up a company with the aim of contributing to social welfare, supporting retired long-time employees, or political donations or contributions for the benefit of a company or sector as a whole. It is also not permitted to set up a company for the purpose of carrying out activities that can only be engaged in by persons with certain qualifications, such as lawyers or tax accountants.

115. Article 52 of the Commercial Code prior to its amendment in 2005 defined company as an association formed for profit-seeking purposes.[60] The Companies Act does not have such provision. Since shareholders or members of the company

56. Article 2, para. 1, Act on Arrangement of Relevant Acts Incidental to Enforcement of the Companies Act.
57. Articles 2-44, Act on Arrangement of Relevant Acts Incidental to Enforcement of the Companies Act.
58. Article 3, para. 1, Act on Arrangement of Relevant Acts Incidental to Enforcement of the Companies Act.
59. Articles 45 and 46, Act on Arrangement of Relevant Acts Incidental to Enforcement of the Companies Act.
60. Article 1 of the Limited Company Act prior to amendment.

are granted the right to dividends of surplus and distribution of residual assets, it was considered unnecessary to stipulate a provision on profit-seeking purposes for the distribution of company profits to members.

116. A company is an association. An 'association' (*shadan*) means a group of people. A 'foundation' (*zaidan*), on the other hand, means a group of property. The concept of 'association' can be contrasted with that of a 'partnership' (*kumiai*). In a partnership, the partners – the equity holders- are directly connected to each other by contractual relations. In an association, the members are indirectly connected by means of the relationship between the members and the association. Given that 'association' refers to a group of people, it follows that it must consist of more than one person. Companies with one shareholder or one member are called single-member companies. As an association, it renders the concept of single-member company somewhat problematic.

117. As discussed above, single-member companies will need to be recognized to set up wholly-owned subsidiaries (wholly-owned subsidiaries are single-member companies, with the parent company as the sole shareholder). In a single-member company, the number of members may potentially increase by assignment of shares or equity interests, and therefore it is construed to possess the nature of an association (see paragraph 253, Single-member companies). Under the Commercial Code prior to its amendment in 2005, if the number of members of a general partnership company or limited partnership company was reduced to one, the company was forced to dissolve.[61] These provisions did not apply to stock companies. Today, under the Companies Act, membership companies with only one member are also permitted.

118. The Commercial Code prior to its amendment in 2005 defined company as an association. On the other hand, since the Companies Act contains various provisions that govern the relations of an association, an express provision to this effect was omitted.

119. All companies have legal personality.[62] As a juridical person, a company can execute contracts, obtain rights and owe obligations in its name; and act as a litigant in its own name with respect to such rights and obligations. Incorporating a company makes it simple to deal with the various legal relations that will arise. But the most important reason for incorporating a company is that any property invested in the company will be separated from members' or shareholders' personal assets. This means that any creditor of individual members or shareholders cannot have their rights satisfied from company property. On the other hand, if the legal personality constitutes an abuse of rights or has no substance, the company may be precluded from the limited liability (see paragraphs 291–296, The doctrine of piercing the corporate veil).

61. Article 94, item 4; Art. 162 of the Commercial Code prior to amendment.
62. Article 3, Companies Act.

IV. Large Company (*Dai Kaisha*) and Public Company (*Koukai Kaisha*)

120. 'Large Company' is a stock company whose balance sheet states either stated capital of at least JPY 500 million or total liabilities of at least JPY 20 billion at the end of the previous business year.[63] Before the Commercial Code was amended in 2005, the Act on Special Measures for the Commercial Code concerning Audits of Stock Companies (Commercial Code Special Measures Act) provided special provisions for Large Companies. There are over 1 million stock companies in Japan, and they range from large-scale companies to small, family-run businesses. As it was not feasible to provide for all of these different scales of companies under the Commercial Code, the Commercial Code Special Measures Act was introduced in 1974. It was also necessary to include special provisions for large-scale companies in the Companies Act, and similar criteria were used to define Large Companies (the Act on Special Measures for the Commercial Code defined large companies as companies with stated capital of at least JPY 500 million or total liabilities of at least JPY 20 billion; this definition required complicated interim measures to take into account the capital fluctuations during the business year).

121. The Commercial Code Special Measures Act set out special provisions regarding the authority of company auditors in small stock companies with stated capital of JPY 100 million or less and liabilities of less than JPY 20 billion. In such companies, the authority of the company auditors was restricted to accounting audits only. However, from the point of view of corporate governance, it was generally considered desirable for company auditors to have the authority to audit the company operations, regardless of the scale of the company. It was also considered that there was no benefit in the Companies Act to make further distinctions between companies based on their scale, other than the distinction of Large Companies and non-Large Companies. The Companies Act therefore does not include special provisions for small companies. As a result, the Companies Act grants, in principle, company auditors with the authority to audit not only company accounts but all company operations.[64]

122. 'Public Company' is usually a company that lists its issued shares on a stock exchange (see paragraph 415). However, the Companies Act defines all stock companies – other than those that impose restrictions on transfer of all classes of shares – as Public Companies.[65] This means that stock companies that impose restrictions on transfer of only some classes of shares are also categorized as Public Companies.[66] It is customary for closely held companies to place restrictions on share transfers (see paragraph 374). However, there are also large-scale companies, such as subsidiaries, that exhibit a closed nature.

63. Article 2, item 6, Companies Act.
64. Article 381, Companies Act.
65. Article 2, item 5, Companies Act.
66. Article 2, item 5, Companies Act.

123. As they typically have a large number of shareholders, Public Companies are expected to ensure the separation of ownership and management. For this purpose, it is necessary to establish a management mechanism, and as a result having the board of directors is mandatory. On the other hand, large-scale companies often have many customers and creditors. Large Companies are therefore obliged to have accounting auditors for creditor protection. In the Companies Act, companies are divided into the following categories (see paragraph 548):

(i) Public Company + Large Company.
(ii) Non-public Company (i.e., stock companies with restrictions on share transfer) + Large Company.
(iii) Public Company + non-Large Company (small and medium companies).
(iv) Non-public Company + non-Large Company.

V. Parent Company and Subsidiary

124. Many companies establish subsidiaries to carry out their business operations. This occurs not only under a pure holding company structure: companies often sort out operations that they wish to be carried out by subsidiaries. In the present social climate, appropriate rules are needed for the entire corporate group, rather than simply for individual companies. The Commercial Code prior to its amendment in 2005 defined subsidiary as a stock company or limited company whose majority of voting rights are held by another stock company; and it defined a parent company as a stock company holding the majority of voting rights in such case.[67] Here, the quantity of voting rights was used as a formality criterion. The Companies Act determines whether a parent-subsidiary relationship exists based on whether the parent company is deemed to actually control the management of the subsidiary, in addition to the holding of a majority of voting rights. This criterion is provided in an ordinance of the Ministry of Justice (see paragraph 964).[68]

VI. Companies under General Law versus Companies under Special Laws

125. Companies that fall under the provisions of the Companies Act are deemed to be companies under general law, whereas companies subject to the provisions of special laws are deemed to be companies under special laws. Special laws can be applicable to specific companies, for example, the Kokusai Denshin Denwa Co., Ltd Act, the Electric Power Development Promotion Act, the Japan Tobacco Inc. Act, the Nippon Telegraph and Telephone (NTT) Corporation Act and the Act Concerning the Japan Railway Companies and the Japan Freight Railway Company.[69]

---

67. Article 211-2 of the Commercial Code prior to amendment; Art. 24, item 1 of the Limited Company Act prior to amendment.
68. Article 2, items 3 and 4, Companies Act.
69. Act No. 301 of 1952; Act No. 27 of 1952; Act No. 69 of 1984; Act No. 85 of 1984; Act No. 88 of 1986.

Special laws can also apply to any company whose purpose is to engage in specific types of business activities, for example, the Banking Act, the Trust Business Act, the Insurance Business Act and the Railway Business Act.[70]

§5. History of the Companies Act

I. 1899: Establishment of the Commercial Code

126. Before the Meiji Era (1868–1912), businesses in Japan were operated as sole proprietorships. During the Meiji Era, Japan's economy shifted from feudalism to capitalism. This transition required the introduction of a modern company system. The company system was first approved by the National Bank Act of 1872, which was modelled after the national banking system of the United States.

127. In an effort to develop Japan into a modern nation, the Japanese government supported industrialization, initially focusing on the textiles industry. By 1890s, the Japanese cotton spinning industry had well developed, and the modern steel manufacturing industry was also established by the foundation of the government-run Yahata Steel Mill in 1897. In response to these economic developments, the former Commercial Code was established in 1890 as a generally applicable company law which would apply to all areas of industries. The former Commercial Code, which was drafted by a German citizen named Herman Roesler and contained the companies law in part I, Chapter 6, was not well received in Japan, and its enactment was postponed several times. However, due to the commercial needs of the business community to implement a companies' law, the companies law section was enacted in 1893 by separating other sections of the former Commercial Code, along with the Bills of Exchange and Promissory Notes Act and the Bankruptcy Act.

128. In 1899, a new Commercial Code came into effect in place of the former Commercial Code. Part II of the new Commercial Code covered the companies law in a substantially improved form. While it has thereafter undergone many amendments, the new Commercial Code is still in effect in Japan.

II. 1911 and 1938: Amendments to the Commercial Code

129. Around the time of the Russo-Japanese War from 1904 to 1905, the steel industry expanded dramatically and the chemical industry also emerged. However, once this war ended, many 'bubble' companies disappeared. This was attributed to the dysfunction of the Japanese companies law, particularly the provisions concerning stock companies. To address this, the Commercial Code – particularly the part relating to the companies law – was drastically revised in 1911. This amendment

70. Act No. 59 of 1981; Act No. 65 of 1922; Act No. 105 of 1955; Act No. 92 of 1986.

clarified the civil liability of incorporators, directors and company auditors, and added their criminal liability.

130. The First World War led to the rapid growth of the Japanese economy. However, the financial crash of 1927 caused monopolization and prompted moves for a further amendment of the companies law. This amendment was passed in 1938 and came into effect in 1940. Concurrently, the Limited Company Act – modelled on German law – was also introduced. This amendment limited the authority of directors by giving greater power to the shareholders meeting and also provided a greater civil and criminal liability of directors with an aim to address the trends of emerging gigantic companies, dispersed shareholdings and the separation of company ownership and management. Further, this amendment permitted non-voting shares, convertible shares and convertible bonds to expand company financing. Improvements on accounting, expansion of the court involvement in company matters and the special liquidation procedures were also provided.

131. In summary, Japanese companies law, particularly the rules on stock companies, was originally established in 1899, developed into a modern stock company law – centring on the shareholders meeting – by the 1911 amendment and was finalized by the amendment in 1938.

III. 1950: Amendment to the Commercial Code

132. Japan's economy was in ruins following its defeat in the Second World War. Japanese society and the economy both underwent 'Americanisation' under the occupying US forces. Company law was no exception.

133. As discussed above, Japanese company law was initially based on German law, but was later greatly influenced by the common law during the period of postwar US occupation. When the Commercial Code was amended in 1950, an authorized share system modelled on US law was introduced to facilitate corporate financing. In principle, the authorized shares granted the board of directors the authority to issue new shares within a certain extent. Bonds were also permitted to be issued by a decision of the board of directors. The adoption of no-par value shares also aimed to facilitate financing. As par value shares were not permitted to be issued at a price below par value, the companies were unable to issue new shares if the market value of shares fell below par value. No-par value shares were aimed at solving this issue.

134. In response to the growing separation of company ownership and management, the authority of the shareholders meeting – traditionally the highest and all-powerful company organ – was restricted, and directors were vested with greater powers. On the other hand, the board of directors was introduced as an organ with the authority to determine the company's operations. The board of directors would also elect a representative director to execute its resolutions. As a result, the board of directors must also supervise the representative director's performance of his or her duties. As the board of directors was assigned to supervise the representative director's duties, the company auditors' powers were limited to the auditing of company accounts.

135. As directors were given greater authority, the power of shareholders were also enhanced. Specifically, shareholders were granted the right to file derivative actions to pursue directors' civil liability, as well as other rights, such as the right to seek enjoinment against illegal acts of directors, the right to inspect accounting books, the right to seek dismissal of directors and the right to petition for dissolution of the company. The principle of free assignability of shares was provided to protect the interests of shareholders as investors. The amendment also provided an appraisal right for the dissenting shareholders of merger so that they could demand that the company purchase their shares. It also required the existence or restrictions on the shareholders' subscription rights (*shinkabu hikiukeken*) to be provided in the articles of incorporation. Shareholders' subscription rights were subsequently removed, in principle, by the amendment in 1950.

IV. 1962: Amendment to the Commercial Code

136. This amendment entailed significant changes in provisions relating to company accounts, and by widely incorporating advancements made in the field of accounting, enabled periodic profit and loss accounting. In 1963, the ordinance concerning balance sheets, profit and loss statements, business reports and detailed schedules of stock companies was enacted, prescribing in detail what should be contained in financial statements.

V. 1966: Amendment to the Commercial Code

137. This amendment abolished the principle of free assignability of shares that had been introduced in the 1950 amendment, and allowed stock companies to provide in their articles of incorporation that an approval of the board of directors be required for transfer of shares. This amendment addressed the need to maintain the closed nature of small and medium-sized stock companies which make up a large proportion of Japan's stock companies. Other changes included abolishing endorsements (*uragaki*) upon transfer of registered shares, introduction of non-possession of share certificates and diverse exercise of voting rights.

VI. 1974: Amendment to the Commercial Code

138. The Korean War which broke out in 1950 triggered a 'special procurement' boom, taking Japan's economy into a period of rapid growth. This rapid growth was sustained by aggressive capital expenditures by companies. However, excessive capital expenditures resulted in production surplus, which caused many SMEs, as well as some large companies, to go bankrupt. It was later found that most of these bankrupted companies were involved in accounting fraud. A prime example was the collapse of Sanyo Special Steel Co., Ltd in 1965.

139. The 1974 amendment was intended to prevent such accounting fraud by giving company auditors greater authority: the authority to oversee directors' performance of duties – abolished in the 1950 amendment – was granted to company auditors. In addition, the Act on Special Measures for the Commercial Code concerning Audits of Stock Companies was established separately. This Commercial Code Special Measures Act provided that accounting audits must be carried out by an appointed accounting auditor (*kaikei kansanin*), either a certified public accountant or an auditing firm. Small companies were not required to appoint accounting auditors as the authority of their company auditors remained limited to accounting audits.

VII. 1981: Amendment to the Commercial Code

140. In the process of the abovementioned multiple amendments, it was strongly argued that a more comprehensive revision of stock company law is necessary. The Ministry of Justice started a study on such comprehensive revision immediately after the 1974 amendment was enacted. However, a series of corporate bankruptcies occurred due to the reckless management of their autocratic presidents, highlighting the urgent need to introduce the companies' voluntary oversight mechanism and leading to yet another partial amendment.

141. The 1950 amendment had introduced the board of directors, a corporate governance mechanism tasked with supervising the performance of representative directors. However, as the outcome of such mechanism was not sufficient, the 1981 amendment explicitly set out the supervisory role of the board of directors to caution the directors of their duty. To further strengthen supervisory functions of company auditors, it was provided that large companies must appoint a minimum of two company auditors, at least one of whom must be full-time. Other changes included granting company auditors greater authority and guaranteeing their independence. Accounting auditors, who had been appointed by the board of directors, were required to be appointed at the shareholders meeting. This also aimed to strengthen the independence of accounting auditors.

142. To reinforce the shareholders' supervision on directors, shareholders were granted a right to seek explanations from directors and company auditors at the shareholders meeting, as well as the right to submit proposals at shareholders meetings. A written ballot was also introduced so that the shareholders' views could be directly reflected at the shareholders meetings. Further, to eliminate corporate extortionists – one of the main reasons that Japanese shareholders meetings had become a mere formality – companies were prohibited from providing corporate extortionists any financial benefits on the company accounts.

143. While giving shareholders greater powers as described above, the minimum value of one share in a newly established company was raised to JPY 50,000 to eliminate extremely small shareholders. For existing companies, a temporary round-lot shares (*tanyi kabu*) were introduced.

144. Given the reality of shareholders meetings of large companies, it was not considered appropriate to raise matters requiring specialist knowledge and expertise – such as reviewing the balance sheet or profit and loss statement of the company – on the agenda for discussion. It was therefore permitted that the board of directors approve the company's financial statements without requiring the approval at the shareholders meeting, to the extent that company auditors and accounting auditor provided unqualified opinions on the financial statements.

145. As the Japanese economy developed, the number of individual shareholders also increased. However, the proportion of shares they held actually decreased, while the proportion of shares held by corporate shareholders increased to over 70%. As the cross-shareholding among companies increased, various negative effects emerged. With an aim to regulate cross-shareholdings, the 1981 amendment prohibited subsidiaries from acquiring the shares of their parent company. Also, if company *a* holds more than one quarter of issued shares in company *b*, company *b* was no longer permitted to exercise the voting rights associated with the shares it holds in company *a*.

VIII. 1990: Amendment to the Commercial Code

146. This amendment established the minimum stated capital requirement for stock companies at JPY 10 million. The minimum stated capital requirement for limited companies was raised to JPY 3 million. This change anticipated that relatively large-scale businesses would be incorporated as stock companies and smaller businesses would opt for a limited company. In the meantime, taking into account that most stock companies were actually small companies having a closed nature, the amendment also provided the pre-emptive rights of the shareholders of such companies.

IX. 1993 and 1994: Amendments to the Commercial Code

147. The 1993 amendment was unique as it was an emergency measure in response to the requests from the United States in the United States-Japan working group on the Structural Impediments Initiative. The United States requested the following amendments to Japanese company law:

(i) Improvement on shareholder access to company accounting books: Relaxation of the minimum ownership ratio to inspect records (from 10% to 1% of all issued shares).

(ii) Earlier deadline to dispatch convocation notice of shareholders meeting (from two weeks to one month).
(iii) Establishment of audit committees comprised of outside directors.
(iv) Deregulation of repurchase and holding of treasury shares to eliminate cross-shareholdings.
(v) Establishment of a mechanism to ensure that non-resident shareholders will be able to exercise their voting rights.

While the Japanese declined items (ii) and (v) above, the Commercial Code was amended as follows.

First, the threshold of ownership ratio to inspect and request copies of accounting books was reduced to 3% of all issued shares. In response to the request to establish audit committees comprised of outside directors, the Commercial Code was amended to reinforce the supervisory function of company auditors. This involved extending the company auditor's term of office from two years to three years, and, particularly in large companies, increasing the number of company auditors and establishing outside company auditors and board of company auditors. At the same time, a cap of JPY 8,200 was established on the litigation expenses to be paid by the shareholders for filing a derivative action, regardless of the amount of claim. This had not been requested by the United States, but the Japanese government decided to take this opportunity to realize changes that it had long been discussing independently with a view to vitalizing shareholders' derivative actions.

As to the deregulations on acquisition of the companies' own shares, the Japanese government independently introduced new rules in the 1994 amendment without any reference to elimination of cross-shareholdings.

148. The 1993 amendment also resolved the long-standing issues concerning bonds by an amendment separately from the rest of the Companies Act. Significant changes included abolishing the limitation on the amount of bonds that may be issued, requiring the appointment of a bond management company, as well as clarifying the powers of bond management companies, and adjusting the provisions on bonds in the Commercial Code and the Secured Bonds Trust Act. These amendments were enacted in response to the fundamental reform of Japan's financial and securities system that came into effect on 1 April 1993 (see paragraph 961). The limitation on the amount of bonds that may be issued by a company was abolished as a result of the further development of 'securitization of finances' and the increasing need of the companies to finance by issuing bonds. On the other hand, mandatory appointment of bond management companies was introduced to protect bondholders from the risks associated with the abolition on limitation of bond issuance. While banks (including trust banks) were qualified to act as bond management companies, the activities of bond management companies were expressly limited to the management of bonds after issuance to prevent banks from interfering with the terms of bonds in the process of bond issuance. The terms of bonds should be determined exclusively by the bond issuing company and underwriters. Banks, however, have thereafter become qualified to engage in the underwriting of bonds through subsidiary securities companies.

X. 1997: Amendment to the Commercial Code

149. The 1997 amendment included a revision of merger rules – an issue that had been pending for many years. This amendment lifted the requirement of briefing meetings (*houkoku soukai*) on absorption-type mergers as well as establishment meetings (*souritsu soukai*) in the case of consolidation-type mergers. This had been requested by the business community. Creditor protection procedures were also revised, following strong demands from the business community for the streamlining. Specifically, if public notice was made in the official gazette and daily newspaper, as provided in the articles of incorporation as the method of public notice, individual notices to creditors will no longer be required. In addition, the company will no longer be required to take certain measures, such as repaying debts or providing reasonable security if there is no risk of harm to the creditor stating objections.

Simplified procedures for mergers were also established. If the total number of new shares to be issued by the surviving company was equal to or lower than one-twentieth of the total number of shares issued by the surviving company, and the consideration payment to shareholders was equal to or less than one-fiftieth of the surviving company's net assets, the surviving company was no longer required to obtain a resolution at the shareholders meeting to approve the merger.

In an effort to enhance merger disclosures, the pre-merger disclosure (*jizen kaiji*) requirements of merger documentation were improved and post-merger disclosures (*jigo kaiji*) were also established.

150. In the 1997 amendment, a lawmaker-initiated legislation was also enacted in a rush to revise the stock options. The legislative process was extremely unusual in that the bill was passed without any preparatory discussions at the Commercial Code subcommittee of the Legislative Council of the Ministry of Justice. The Act on Special Provisions of the Commercial Code concerning the Procedure of Cancellation of Shares was also a lawmaker-initiated legislation, which allowed the companies to cancel shares by the profits of the company upon resolution of the board of directors if so permitted in the articles of incorporation.

151. In addition, penalties in the Commercial Code were reinforced after scandals came to light during the year involving large Japanese companies paying off corporate extortionists (*soukaiya*).

XI. 1998: Amendment to the Commercial Code

152. Following the emergency economic policies set out by the LDP in 1998, two temporary statutes (effective until 31 March 2000) were enacted as lawmaker-initiated legislation. First, the Special Measures Act on Cancellation of Shares – which required only a resolution of the board of directors for cancellation of shares – was amended to permit companies to use their capital reserves to cancel shares. Second, the Act Concerning Revaluation of Land was enacted. The discrepancy between the book value and market value of commercial lands owned by companies for a long period of time was often significant. This act aimed to redress the issue by allowing companies to obtain a fair evaluation of their assets. Primarily, it allowed financial institutions to increase their capital adequacy ratio.

XII. 1999: Amendment to the Commercial Code

153. In 1997, the Anti-Monopoly Act was amended to deregulate the prohibition on pure holding companies, except in cases where it would cause an excessive concentration of economic power. Under the Commercial Code, there were no feasible measures to establish a 100% ownership relationship between companies due to the strict regulations on post-formation (*jigo setsuritsu*) and contribution in kind (*genbutsu shusshi*). The 1999 amendment to the Commercial Code introduced share transfer (*kabushiki iten*) and share exchange (*kabushiki koukan*) which would facilitate the creation of such 100% ownership. With an aim to protect the interests of the shareholders of the parent company after share transfer or share exchange, the amendment provided certain obligations on the parent company to disclose the details of the operations of potential wholly-owned subsidiaries. Other changes included the valuation of monetary claims at market value to standardize corporate accounting.

154. The Act Concerning Revaluation of Land was also amended. In connection with the introduction of the tax-effect accounting method (*zeikouka kaikei*), the valuation difference on land revaluation, which was previously booked in the liabilities section of balance sheets, was changed to be booked in the shareholders' equity section after deducting deferred tax liabilities. In addition, for certain large companies, up to two-thirds of the amount of such valuation difference were permitted to be used to cancel treasury shares. This amendment also extended the deadline for revaluation of commercial lands to 31 March 2001.

XIII. 2000: Amendment to the Commercial Code

155. The previous amendments involved the establishment of certain business combination methods, such as streamlining merger rules and introducing share exchange. As part of such amendment, the Commercial Code was again amended in 2000 to provide for company splits (*kaisha bunkatsu*). In this amendment, the stock options were also improved, allowing both the treasury shares method and warrants method. In addition, as to the prohibition on payoff to shareholders, a payoff in the account of the company's subsidiaries was also prohibited to prevent any circumvention of the existing rules on payoffs. In addition, for purposes similar to those of simplified merger and share transfer, simplified procedures on acceptance of entire business was permitted under certain conditions.

XIV. 2001: Amendment to the Commercial Code

156. The Commercial Code was amended three times during 2001. First, as a reform of the share system, the share unit (*tangen kabu*) was established as an alternative to the round-lot shares (*tanyi kabu*) which had been adopted as an interim measure. In addition, par value shares – the significance of which had been questioned – were abolished to unify all shares as no-par value shares. Another important amendment concerned treasury shares. The general prohibition on acquiring own shares was amended to allow companies to purchase own shares at the discretion of the board of directors, to the extent so authorized by a resolution at the shareholders meeting. Once acquired, there was no time limitation on the holding period of treasury shares (*kin-ko kabu*). Treasury shares may be cancelled or used as substitute shares in M&A transactions by the resolution of the board of directors. The amendment concerning treasury shares responded to strong demands from the business community, which were also heavily supported by the LDP.

157. Second, following a study by the Companies Act subcommittee of the Legislative Council of the Ministry of Justice, common shares were permitted to be issued as non-voting shares, which had previously been permitted only for preferred shares. It was also made possible to allow limited voting rights where voting rights could be exercised only on limited matters for resolution. These shares with limited voting rights were treated as class shares. In addition, it was permitted to provide in the articles of incorporation that a resolution at a class shareholders meeting will be necessary on all or part of the matters to be resolved at the shareholders meeting or board meetings. In addition, convertible shares, which allow the shareholders to convert the shares to another class of shares, were conceptually replaced by shares with conversion option, and it was also made clear in the statute that compulsory conversions at the election of the company may be also provided.

158. The amended Commercial Code also introduced share options, pursuant to which companies may grant stock options by issuing share options. Bonds with share options were also established as an equivalent to the traditional bonds with stock acquisition rights and convertible bonds. Another noteworthy amendment came in response to the increasingly wide-spread use of the Internet and allowed certain written documents and notices between the company and shareholders to be in electronic format.

159. Third, a lawmaker-initiated legislation allowed certain limitation of liability of directors to the company. The LDP subcommittee on the Commercial Code had outlined proposed amendments to the Commercial Code on corporate governance in 1997 and again in 1998, and announced guidelines for proposed amendments to the Commercial Code on corporate governance in 1999. These proposals involved limiting the liability of directors in derivative actions. The amendment permitted the companies to limit directors' liability, in general, to their annual remuneration for four years (six years for representative directors). In exchange for such limitation of liability, the powers of company auditors were reinforced to provide further independence by, for example, having their term of office extended from three years to four years.

XV. 2002: Amendment to the Commercial Code

160. The 2002 amendment included important changes in the corporate governance of stock companies. In the amendment, outside directors were expected to play key roles in the new corporate governance model similar to US companies. In addition to the traditional governance model of board of directors and representative director, the new model introduced committees (i.e., nominating committee, compensation committee and audit committee) consisting of a majority of outside directors, and executive officers (*shikkouyaku*) who execute company operations. Companies were able to choose whether to keep the existing governance model or to adopt the new committee model. Separately, a material asset committee (*juyou zaisan iinkai*) was also introduced as an option in an effort to accelerate the decision-making mechanisms of the board of directors. Other amendments on corporate governance included relaxing the quorum for special resolutions at shareholders meeting and simplifying convocation procedures for shareholders meetings.

161. On company accounts, description matters on financial statements were delegated to the ordinance of the Ministry of Justice, and consolidated financial statements were introduced for Large Companies under the Commercial Code Special Measures Act. As to shares, the amendment included new rules on lost share certificates and sale of shares held by shareholders whose residence is unknown. The account transfer system of bonds was also established.

XVI. 2003: Amendment to the Commercial Code

162. The 2003 amendment allowed the companies to acquire own shares as treasury shares by a resolution of the board of directors based on authorization under the articles of incorporation. The Act on Special Measures for the Commercial Code concerning Procedures for Cancellation of Shares, established in 1997, had restricted the company's own shares to be acquired solely with a view to cancel such shares by resolution of the board of directors. However, when the 2001 amendment permitted companies to acquire own shares regardless of the purpose of acquisition, the special measures act was abolished. The 2003 amendment was a response to the demands from the business community to use the treasury shares in a flexible manner, and lawmaker-initiated legislation was adopted that enabled companies to purchase own shares by a resolution at the board of directors based on authorization in the articles of incorporation.

163. The 2003 amendment also revised the calculation method for the upper limit of interim dividends to be paid out. Prior to the amendment, if the stated capital or legal reserve was reduced after the end of the last accounting period, the calculation excluded the total amount of stated capital and legal reserve prior to the reduction, as well as the amount of treasury share purchases authorized at the annual shareholders meeting. This raised concerns that if stated capital is reduced to utilize the reduced amount for the authorized treasury share acquisitions, the above calculation will not take into account the reduction of stated capital and therefore could prevent the payment of interim dividends. Thus, under the amended Commercial Code, if the stated capital or legal reserve was reduced after the end of the last accounting period, an amount equivalent to the reduced stated capital or legal reserve was excluded in the deductions from the net assets for the purpose of calculating the distributable amount.

XVII. 2004: Amendment to the Commercial Code

164. Two amendment bills were passed in the ordinary session of the Diet in 2004: the Act for Partial Revision of the Commercial Code, etc., for Introducing a System of Electronic Public Notice and the Act for Partial Revision of the Act on Transfer of Bonds, etc., for Streamlining and Rationalizing Settlement of Trades of Stock and Other Securities. The former amendment introduced public notices in electromagnetic form, and the latter allowed companies to elect not to issue share certificates.

165. Public notices of stock companies were published pursuant to their articles of incorporation either in the official gazette or daily newspaper which publishes news on current affairs. The 2004 amendment provided an additional option of making public notice via an internet website, allowing companies to make use of this less costly and simpler method, taking advantage of the development of information technology.

166. Previously, all stock companies were required to issue share certificates. However, it was costly for the issuing company and also caused a risk for shareholders, such as losing the certificate. The amendment allowed companies to provide in their articles of incorporation that no share certificates will be issued by the company. Such companies will not need to issue share certificates regardless of the shareholders' request. The abolition of share certificates was accompanied by an amendment concerning share transfer method. In addition, special rules apply to a non-Public Company that even if the company had not provided in the articles of incorporation that share certificates will not be issued, no share certificates are required to be issued until a request to such effect is made by a shareholder. In fact, many companies had not issued share certificates in practice, and the amendment was established to ensure consistency with such practice. Upon the introduction of such non-issuance of share certificates in the Commercial Code, the Act on Book-Entry Transfer of Company Bonds, etc., was also amended accordingly with regard to the procedures for transfer of shares.

XVIII. 2005: Establishment of the Companies Act

167. Since 2002, the Legislative Council of the Ministry of Justice (*housei shingikai*) had intensive discussions on a large-scale revision of 'The Modernization of Japanese Company Law.' The aim was to modernize company law by implementing the following strategies:

(i) Converting the *katakana* (one of two phonetic-based scripts used in Japanese) text used in the provisions of part II of the Commercial Code, the Limited Companies Act and other acts into the more colloquial *hiragana* (the other phonetic-based script used in Japanese).
(ii) Reorganizing the legal terminology, as well as, where necessary, revising the wording to ensure explicit interpretation.
(iii) Compiling part II of the Commercial Code, the Limited Companies Act, the Commercial Code Special Measures Act and other relevant acts into a single body to simplify the rules.

The council also aimed to redress any unbalance among the rules applicable to companies, as well as to carry out substantial amendments to the company law to match the recent social and economic changes. On 29 June 2005, the Companies Act bill passed the Diet together with the bill for the Arrangement of Relevant Acts Incidental to Enforcement of the Companies Act (Arrangement Act) (*seibihou*), and was subsequently enacted containing the following provisions.

168. Limited company (*yugen kaisha*) was integrated into stock company, thereby explicitly allowing small-scale stock companies. The concept of limited company was abolished, and existing limited companies were in general converted to stock companies. The minimum capital requirement on incorporating a stock company was also lifted. In addition, a new company form of LLC was introduced. General partnership companies, limited partnership companies and limited liability companies were considered to have similar organizational characteristics, and as such were grouped together as membership companies, governed by the same provisions in many parts of the Companies Act.

169. The regulations concerning company reorganizations were also reviewed to introduce, among others, flexibility in the consideration to be paid upon merger or other reorganizations and summary proceedings. Other amendments included a greater flexibility on the restrictions on transfer of shares as well as abolition of the restrictions on the number of occasions that dividends of surplus can be distributed in a business year and authority to determine dividends of surplus newly granted to the board of directors under certain conditions. The Companies Act also achieved consistency in the liability of directors in Companies with Committees and other companies.

170. On derivative actions, a plaintiff who lost the status of shareholder, for example, upon a share transfer (*kabushiki iten*), would not lose the standing to file a derivative action. Further, Large Companies are required to establish an internal control system. Also, primarily with small companies in mind, accounting advisors (either certified public accountants or certified public tax accountants) were introduced as a new company organ in an effort to ensure the properness of financial statements. All stock companies were allowed to have an accounting auditor. The special liquidation procedures were also reviewed.

171. The Companies Act bill was partially revised during deliberations of the Diet. First, an exception to the derivative actions in Article 847, paragraph 1, item 2 of the Companies: Act bill was deleted on the grounds that the following language was unclear:

> instances where filing a derivative action would significantly damage the legitimate interests of the stock company or excessive costs would be incurred by the stock company or other equivalent situations could be expected to occur with considerable certainty.

Second, with respect to the liability of directors involved in shareholder payoffs, liability of directors directly involved in shareholder payoffs were changed from negligence liability to strict liability. Third, provisions allowing the market sale of treasury shares under certain conditions were deleted.[71] This was due to the concern that it may encourage insider trading or manipulation of the market.

172. The Companies Act and the associated Arrangement Act entered into force on May 2006. The Companies Act allowed the surviving company of a merger to deliver properties other than the shares of the surviving company to the shareholders of the absorbed company (so-called 'flexibility in merger consideration'). The implementation of this provision was delayed by one year. This delay was aimed to give companies an opportunity to introduce hostile takeover measures that would require amendments to their articles of incorporation at the annual shareholders meeting.

XIX. 2014: Amendment to the Companies Act

173. There has been criticism from investors both in Japan and abroad that corporate governance in Japanese companies is inadequate, and that this is a factor that has contributed to lower profitability and lower stock prices compared to overseas companies. It has also been remarked that Japanese company law relating to parent companies has been inadequate. It was in the context of these criticisms that the Companies Act was amended in 2014 and entered into force on 1 May 2015.

174. In seeking to reinforce corporate governance, the amendment calls for companies to use the outside directors effectively. Specifically, the amendment includes (i) the introduction of a 'company with audit and supervisory committee' (*kansatou iinkai setchi kaisha*), (ii) a stricter duty to provide explanations to shareholders

71. Article 179, Companies Act bill.

meetings concerning outside directors, (iii) and the 'externality' criteria required to be met by outside directors and outside company auditors. With respect to the regulations concerning parent companies, (iv) 'multiple derivative actions' (*taju daihyo soshou*) were introduced. In respect of M&As, the amendment (v) expanded the shareholders' right to demand enjoinment of mergers, etc., and (vi) introduced a protection for the creditors from being harmed by fraudulent company splits.

§6. Sources of Company Laws

175. Company laws in practical terms consist of statutes, commercial customs (*shou kanshu*) and the articles of incorporation of each company, which provide the internal rules of the company. The Companies Act (Act No. 86 of 2005) is the general statutory law in Japan. There are also special laws and ordinances as follows:

- Act on the Book Transfer of Stocks and Bonds, etc. (Act No. 75 of 2002).
- Secured Bonds Trust Act (Act No. 52 of 1905).
- Commercial Registration Act (Act No. 125 of 1963).
- Commercial Registration Ordinance (Ordinance No. 23 of 1964).
- Ordinance for the Enforcement of the Companies Act (Ordinance No. 12 of 2006).
- Ordinance on Company Accounting (Ordinance No. 13 of 2006).
- Ordinance on Electronic Public Notice (Ordinance No. 14 of 2006).

176. The Financial Instruments and Exchange Act and the Act on Prohibition of Private Monopolization and Maintenance of Fair Trade (Anti-Monopoly Act) are also important for stock companies.[72] The Financial Instruments and Exchange Act entered into force on 30 September 2007 as a revision of the Securities and Exchange Act. Pursuant to the Act on Arrangement of Relevant Acts Incidental to Enforcement of the Companies Act (Arrangement Act), the following nine statutory laws, including the Limited Company Act, were abolished:

- Act on Instances where Signature is Required under the Commercial Code (Act No. 17 of 1900).
- Act on the Enforcement of Acts to Revise the Commercial Code (Act No. 73 of 1938).
- Limited Company Act (Act No.74 of 1938).
- Act on the Simplification of Banking Business Matters (Act No. 42 of 1943).
- Act on the Payment of Profit or Interest Distributed by Companies (Act No.64 of 1948).
- Act for Aligning Acts Related to the Establishment of the Legal Affairs Bureaus and the Regional Legal Affairs Bureaus (Act No. 137 of 1949).
- Act for the Implementation of Acts for the Partial Amendment of the Commercial Code (Act No. 210 of 1951).

72. Act No. 25 of 1948; Act No. 54 of 1947.

- Act on Special Measures for the Commercial Code concerning Audits of Stock Companies (Act No. 22 of 1974).
- Act on Special Measures for Merger Procedures Pertaining to Banks, etc., for the Creation of a Bank Holding Company (Act No. 121 of 1997).

These statutes were abolished as they were no longer necessary after the enactment of the Companies Act or the amendments to other laws pursuant to the Arrangement Act, or as the transitional measures for the previous amendments to the Commercial Code became unnecessary.

§7. Cross-Border Legal Issues

I. Conflict of Law Principles

177. Corporate transactions are not limited to the domestic market and are extended globally. Particularly in Japan, Japanese companies are actively developing their business in overseas markets and non-Japanese companies are also eager to enter into the Japanese market. In such situation, many legal issues arise which may involve not only domestic laws but also non-Japanese laws.

178. In the past, cross-border legal issues were generally dealt with by identifying the company's governing law to be uniformly applied to all legal issues relating to such company. Currently, however, the prevailing view differentiates the issues of conflict of law principles relating to a company and the legal status of a non-Japanese corporation in Japan.

II. Issues Relating to Conflict of Law Principles

179. There are no statutory provisions in Japanese conflict of law principles stipulating the laws to be applied (*juzokuhou*) to determine issues such as whether or not a company has legal personality, the type, nature and competences of company organs, company-shareholder relations and the rights and obligations of shareholders. Judicial precedents have not taken a clear stand either. Scholarly views are divided into the principle of law governing incorporation of the company (*setsuritsu junkyohou shugi*) and the principle of law governing the location of the company's principal office (*honkyochihou shugi*). The former is the generally accepted view. Previously, the Act on the Application of Laws in which the rules concerning conflict of law principles were provided, was mostly intended to identify the applicable laws in cross-border legal issues.[73] In 2006, the Act on the General Rules of Application of Laws was enacted to revise the rules under the said Act on the Application of Laws.[74]

73. Act No. 10 of 1898.
74. Act No. 78 of 2006.

180. It would be natural to apply the laws that granted legal personality to the company to the company's internal and external legal issues as companies are regulated by the laws of their respective countries. On the other hand, application of such laws may need to be restricted occasionally to ensure the security of the transactions in the country where it was implemented.

III. Regulations Governing 'Foreign Companies' (*Gaikoku Kaisha*)

A. *Overview*

181. The Companies Act defines a 'foreign company' (*gaikoku kaisha*) as a judicial person incorporated under the law of a foreign country or such other foreign organization that is of the same kind as, or is similar to, Japanese company.[75] In this regard, the Companies Act adopted the principle of applying the law governing incorporation of the company. While such foreign companies are naturally not subject to the Japanese Companies Act, it is necessary to prevent circumventing the Companies Act by setting up foreign companies under foreign laws while establishing their head office in Japan or conducting most of their operations in Japan. Before its amendment in 2005, the Commercial Code provided that such 'Pseudo-Foreign Companies' (*giji gaikoku kaisha*) are subject to the same provisions as domestic companies.[76] However, views were divided as to the meaning of the 'same provisions'. A judicial precedent and prevailing view construed the 'same provisions' to also include provisions pertaining to incorporation of the company, in which case such companies must be re-established under Japanese law before any commercial registration may be made as foreign companies.[77] It also meant that no legal personality of pseudo-foreign companies will be recognized, and therefore representatives will bear the liability pertaining to their company transactions.

182. The Companies Act replaced Article 482 of the Commercial Code prior to amendment, and provides that a foreign company that has its head office in Japan or whose main purpose is to conduct business in Japan may not carry out transactions continuously in Japan.[78] A person who has carried out transactions in violation of the foregoing will be liable, jointly and severally with the foreign company, to perform the obligations that have arisen from such transactions to the counterparty.[79] The Companies Act does not deny the legal personality of Pseudo- Foreign Companies to protect the counterparties of such companies' transactions. However, with an aim to prevent any circumvention of the Companies Act by using foreign companies, the Companies Act prohibits the Pseudo-Foreign Companies from carrying out transactions continuously in Japan.

75. Article 2, item 2, Companies Act.
76. Article 482, Commercial Code prior to amendment; Art. 76, Limited Company Act prior to amendment.
77. 16 Dec. 1918, Records of Great Court of Judicature Decisions on Civil Actions 24-2326.
78. Article 821, para. 1, Companies Act.
79. Article 821, para. 2, Companies Act.

*B. Capacity to Hold Rights (*Kenri Nouryoku*)*

183. The capacity to hold rights granted to a foreign company under the laws of its jurisdiction will be recognized under Japanese law. This means that a foreign company may hold the rights that are identical to the same kind of company established under Japanese law; provided, however, that such rights will not include any right which may not be held by a foreign national, or a right for which special rules are provided in a treaty.[80]

C. Application of Laws Other than the Companies Act

184. Although foreign companies are not subject to the Companies Act, reference to a 'company' under other laws, for example, the Tax Code and the Financial Instruments and Exchange Act, would in principle include foreign companies.[81]

*D. Appointment and Registration of Representative (*Daihyousha*) in Japan*

185. If a foreign company intends to carry out transactions continuously in Japan, it must specify its representative(s) in Japan and register the company by commercial registration.[82] At least one of the representatives must be domiciled in Japan.[83] The registration of a foreign company will be governed by the rules of the same kind of company or the most similar company in Japan.[84] If the foreign company established a business office in Japan, such business office will be deemed to be a branch office.[85] The commercial registration must include the law governing the incorporation of the foreign company as well as the name and domicile of the representatives in Japan.[86] A foreign company will not be permitted to carry out transactions continuously in Japan until the commercial registration is completed, and any person who has carried out a transaction in violation of such restriction will be liable, jointly and severally with the foreign company, to perform the obligations that have arisen from such transactions and may be subject to a certain non-penal fine.[87]

186. If all representatives in Japan intend to resign, the foreign company will be required to carry out the same creditor protection procedures as in the case of capital reduction.[88] The resignation will become effective upon commercial registration

80. Article 35, para. 2, Civil Code.
81. Article 823, Companies Act.
82. Articles 817, 933, Companies Act.
83. Article 817, para. 1, Companies Act.
84. Article 933, para. 2, Companies Act.
85. Article 933, para. 3, Companies Act.
86. Article 933, para. 2, Companies Act.
87. Article 818, paras 1 and 2; Art. 979, para. 2, Companies Act.
88. Article 820, para. 1, Companies Act.

of resignation after the completion of the above procedures.[89] This is intended to prevent circumventing the jurisdiction as a defendant in Japan by the foreign company while the foreign company still has outstanding obligations in Japan.

E. Disclosure of Financial Conditions

187. Foreign companies in Japan, for which the same kind of company or the most similar company in Japan is a stock company, will be under the same obligation as Japanese stock companies to disclose, by a public notice without delay, the last balance sheet in Japan or its closest equivalent, or a summary thereof, after its approval at the annual shareholders meeting or the nearest equivalent procedures.[90] The balance sheet or nearest equivalent may also be published via an internet website in lieu of public notice.[91] The method of public notice and the website address are part of the matters to be stated in the commercial registry.[92]

F. Order to Close Business Office of Foreign Company

188. In cases where there are certain statutory grounds (e.g., conducting business for an illegal purpose, failing to commence business within one year from registration), the court may, in response to a request by the Minister of Justice, shareholders, partners, creditors or any other interested parties, order the prohibition on a foreign company to carry out transactions continuously in Japan or the closure of its business office established in Japan.[93] In such cases, the court may also order commencement of liquidation of all of the company's properties in Japan.[94] This is intended to permit liquidation procedures in Japan to protect domestic creditors.

§8. Employee Participation and Corporate Organizational Structure of Companies

189. 'Joint decision-making' is a management system whereby certain employees participate in the management organization of the company as employee representatives and act as officers having the same rights and obligations as officers elected by the shareholders. The joint decision-making system adopted in Germany is a prime example and has been studied extensively in Japan. Some have suggested that this system should be introduced into public service companies and financial

89. Article 820, para. 3, Companies Act.
90. Article 819, para. 1, Companies Act.
91. Article 819, para. 3, Companies Act.
92. Article 933, Companies Act.
93. Article 827, para. 1, Companies Act.
94. Article 822, Companies Act.

institutions. The suggestion, however, has been strongly criticized and received negative reactions. The reasons are outlined below.

190. The first reason is lack of merits in the German system. In reality, the German joint decision-making system does not achieve the primary objective of the employee participation, which intends to enable employees to influence the decisions concerning basic company policies. However, its role has been limited to expansion of employee welfare, which can be sufficiently achieved through collective bargaining and union-management consultations.

191. Second, if joint decision-making were to be introduced in Japan, the following difficult legislative issues would need to be addressed:

(i) There will be an issue in relation to Article 2 of the Labour Union Act.[95] According to item 1 of the proviso to this article, officers are not permitted to join labour unions. Thus, under current law, an employee representative would have to abandon union membership to become a director or company auditor. A great degree of difficulty is expected even if new legislation were to be introduced.

(ii) It would also be problematic under the Companies Act. Paragraph 2, Article 335 of the Companies Act provides that an employee of a company or its subsidiary may not become company auditor. Thus, an employee or executive member of labour union may not be company auditor. The Companies Act does, however, permit such person to be a director. There are currently a large number of directors who are also employees, but, as stated above, the Labour Union Act prohibits employees who are members of labour unions from concurrently serving as directors.

(iii) It will be difficult to determine which company management organization the employee representatives should be allowed to participate in. In Germany, employee representatives participate in the auditing board. Auditing boards in Germany have the power to appoint and remove directors, as well as the right to give consent to the execution of company operations, which makes it effectively equivalent to the board of directors. An employee representative who is a member of the auditing board in a German company is comparable to a part-time director under the current Japanese corporate governance system. If employee representatives are to participate in the management of Japanese companies, further study will be necessary to examine whether they should be a director or company auditor.

(iv) As has been highly debated in Germany, there is also a difficult issue of confidentiality obligations of employee representatives who participate in company management as directors or company auditors.

(v) If a wrongful act of a representative director leads to the bankruptcy of a company or causes the company to suffer substantial damage, directors or company auditors who failed in their supervisory duties will be liable for damages to the company and the company's creditors. Whether there would be any

95. Act No. 174 of 1 Jun. 1949.

employees who would be willing to take on a position with such liabilities and whether it should be mandatory for an elected employee to take on such position would be difficult issues.

192. During the process of fundamental amendments to company law in Japan since 1975, no request has been made to introduce a joint decision-making system from business communities, labour unions or political parties supported by labour unions. In this regard, the social and economic situation in Japan does not require further studies relating to the introduction of this system.

193. Nevertheless, after winning the House of Representatives general election in 2009 (see paragraph 20), the DPJ proposed a system where some company auditors will be elected from among employee representatives. The intention was to introduce a mechanism to allow employee opinions to be reflected in company management policies. There is a view that this proposal was made to draw the attention of the labour union support base by the DPJ, along with its then coalition partner, the SDP. However, a system of this kind was ultimately not adopted in the 2014 amendment of the Companies Act.

§9. Privatization of Companies

I. Post-War Increase of Special Public Corporations (*Tokushu Houjin*)

194. Special public corporations are defined in Article 4, item 15 of the Ministry of Internal Affairs and Communications Establishment Act as corporations directly established by an act or corporations established by special juristic acts of incorporation under a special act (upon the introduction of the independent administrative agency system in 2001 (see paragraph 206), Independent Administrative Agencies (IAA) (*dokuritsu gyousei houjin*) were excluded from the scope of special public corporations). As special public corporations are defined broadly by forma standards, the names of special public corporations vary greatly, including public corporation (*kodan*), agency (*jigyo-dan*), bank (*kin-ko*) and organization (*kiko*). Their operations also vary, from roads and railways, finance and international exchanges to organizing bicycle and horse races. Some special public corporations obtain all of their funds from the government, while others are partially funded by private companies or local government. Some receive subsidies from the government to cover the costs of their operations, while others are supported by license or subscription fees, such as the Japan Broadcasting Corporation.

195. Many special public corporations were established in Japan during the post-war period of rapid economic growth. In an effort to rebuild the Japanese economy after the Second World War, there was a strong financing need to develop national land, to improve the public transportation network and to promote industry. However, it was not realistic for private companies to provide such financing due to their limited financing capacity and less expectations on the profitability of the investments by such financing. The only viable option was to carry out the work as State projects, while adopting private-sector approaches to the management of the operations, financial affairs and human resources. It was intended to run those projects efficiently by assigning the projects to the special public corporations having an independent legal personality separately from government agencies. There were as many as 113 special public corporations set up between 1965 and 1975.

II. Reorganization of Special Public Corporations

196. While there was a need to establish special public corporations as indicated above, their increase also expanded government spendings rapidly. This was due to their being given financial support such as government capital investment, loans, subsidies and tax exemptions. In the meantime, as rapid economic growth was achieved, social infrastructure was developed gradually and the private-sector gained financing capabilities, the existence of special public corporations was called into question. In other words, many special public corporations seemed to have completed their tasks and their operations could be handed over to a private company – or indeed operated better by a private company in many cases. In addition, officers of special public corporations were often retired governmental officers previously responsible for such corporations (*amakudari*) (see paragraph 24) or officers who 'migrated' between such corporations, which caused the general public to wonder if the purpose of special public corporations was simply to provide unfair preferential treatment to governmental officers.

197. Due to the tight control by the government, special public corporations have been criticized for their loss of independence and inefficient operations, lack of transparency in activities and unclear management accountability. Accompanied by the overall need to simplify and streamline government finances and administrations, it was asserted that special public corporations should undergo a reform as part of the total reform of the government. Later, in 1982, the Second Ad Hoc Commission on Administrative Reform strongly recommended the privatization of the three main inefficient special public corporations, namely, Japan National Railways, NTT Public Corporation and Japan Tobacco & Salt Public Corporation.

III. Privatization of Japan National Railways

198. Japan National Railways (JNR) started as a public corporation (*kousha*) in 1949 to take over the management of Japan's railways, an operation that had until then been directly managed by the government. It was a special public corporation that relied entirely on government funding and its accounts were booked independently. Although JNR was initially profitable due to its monopolistic position, its results of operations quickly deteriorated after recording a loss of JPY 30 billion in 1964 and later amassed an accumulated loss of JPY 2.45 trillion by 1985. This was attributed to the loss of independence in management and significantly low productivity due to its reliance on the government. On 1 April 1987, JNR was split into six regional passenger railway companies (JR) and one freight railway company (Japan

Freight Railway Company), which were established as special companies (*tokushu kaisha*) under the Act on Passenger Railway Companies and Japan Freight Railway Company.

199. The shares of the East Japan Railway Company, West Japan Railway Company, and Central Japan Railway Company were listed on the stock exchange in 1993, 1996 and 1997, respectively. Later, all of the 8.24 million government-owned shares in the three companies were gradually sold off.

200. In 1985, two years before the privatization of JNR, NTT Public Corporation and Japan Tobacco & Salt Public Corporation were established as special companies, NTT Corporation and Japan Tobacco Inc. (JT). The shares of NTT were listed on the stock exchange in 1987, followed by JT in 1994. NTT then became a pure holding company in 1999, with NTT East, NTT West, NTT Communications and NTT Docomo as its main subsidiaries.

IV. Further Reorganization of Special Public Corporations

201. While 1980s was the era of privatization of Japan's railway, communications and tobacco companies, 1990s was a decade when the reorganization of special public corporations such as the Japan Highway Public Corporation, the Honshu-Shikoku Bridge Authority, the Japan National Oil Corporation, the Government Housing Loan Corporation and the Urban Development Corporation became a major political issue. Further, the Cabinet resolution of 1 December 2000 outlining the administrative reforms set out plans for fundamental review of overall operations and structure of all special public corporations. This review turned into the cessation of operations for the Japan National Oil Corporation and the Government Housing Loan Corporation, as well as the enactment in June 2004 of the Act on the Privatization of the Four Highway-Related Public Corporations. This act dissolved the four public highway corporations, including the Japan Highway Public Corporation, replacing them with six new special companies, including the East Nippon Expressway Company to construct and manage roads, and the independent administration agency in Japan Expressway Holding and Debt Repayment Agency to take over the assets and JPY 40 trillion of debts of the four dissolved corporations.

202. The privatization of the postal services was another big issue. The basic strategy of its reform was outlined by the Council on Economic and Fiscal Policy on 6 August 2004. This basic strategy comprised a schedule of initially privatizing Japan Post in April 2007, and then, after allowing a transition period, implementing the final stages of the privatization process by 2017 at the latest. The final stage was to involve setting up a holding company and splitting the postal services into four independent stock companies, each individually responsible for mail services, postal savings, postal life insurance and counter services.

203. In 2005, the Diet passed the Postal Privatization Act, as well as the Act for the Alignment of Acts relating to the Enactment of the Privatization of the Postal

Service, and they were publicly announced on 21 October. Based on these acts, the fully government-funded Japan Post Holdings Company was established in October 2007, together with its four subsidiary stock companies, Japan Post Service Co., Ltd., Japan Post Network Co., Ltd., Japan Post Bank Co., Ltd. and Japan Post Insurance Co., Ltd. The plan was to initiate the preparatory phase in October 2005, then allow a transition period beginning in October 2007, and finally complete the privatization process by October 2017.

204. However, the situation changed when the DPJ won the 2009 House of Representatives election (see paragraph 20). In the run up to the election, the DPJ and its coalition partners, the Social Democratic Party and the People's New Party, had campaigned for a fundamental review of the postal privatization process. Accordingly, in the same year, they established the Act on the Suspension of the Disposal of Shares in Japan Post Holdings Company, Japan Post Bank Co., Ltd. and Japan Post Insurance Co., Ltd. With this act, the new government suspended the sale of shares in Japan Post Holdings Company, and also stopped Japan Post Holdings Company from selling the shares of Japan Post Bank Co., Ltd. and Japan Post Insurance Co., Ltd. until otherwise provided in a future act.

205. The situation changed again when in April 2012 the LDP came to power once more. An amendment bill for the Postal Privatization Act was passed by the Diet and came into law. Together with this, the Act on the Suspension of the Disposal of Shares in Japan Post Holdings Co. Ltd., Japan Post Bank and Japan Post Insurance was abolished, and the government moved to dispose of all shares in Japan Post Bank and Japan Post Insurance by the end of September 2017. The shares of holding company Japan Post Holdings Co., Ltd. will also be disposed of in a series of phases, but the government is obligated to maintain a holding of over one-third. Japan Post Holdings Co., Ltd. is also required to keep Japan Post (which is an operational company engaged in postal services) as its subsidiary with 100% ownership of the shares (no privatization will occur on postal services).

V. Reorganization of IAA (*Dokuritsu Gyousei Houjin*)

206. The system of IAA was introduced in April 2001 in response to a recommendation in the final report (dated 3 December 1997) of the Administrative Reform Council established under the Hashimoto Cabinet (see paragraph 17). Article 2 of the General Rule Act for IAA defines IAAs as corporations established under this act or other individual acts with the aim of effectively and efficiently implementing publicly necessary business or operations which do not need to be directly implemented by the government but may not be implemented if fully deferred to private businesses.

207. The first IAAs started with fifty-seven entities established separately from government agencies (so-called forerunner IAAs). Later, under administrative reforms strongly promoted by the Koizumi Cabinet (see paragraph 18), many special public corporations (see paragraphs 194–197) were converted to IAAs after

October 2003. As of 1 April 2010, there were 104 IAAs, incurring the government a cost of JPY 3.4227 trillion.

208. Since then, many problems came to light, including free contracts (*zuii keiyaku*) lacking transparency which were entered into with subsidiaries and other affiliated companies, such contract parties accepting *amakudari* re-employees from the IAA, and continuation of less needed business or operations. As a result, trust in the IAA system itself began to be questioned. One of the typical cases was the publicly-initiated cartel that was discovered to have been engaged in 2007 by the Japan Green Resources Agency, an IAA under the direction of the Ministry of Agriculture, Forestry and Fisheries. After this scandal, the 2007 Basic Policy for Economic and Financial Reform announced to set out a plan to reorganize and streamline Japan's IAAs by the end of the year, involving a full review into whether the existing IAAs are fulfilling the original purpose of the system.[96] Despite fierce resistance from government ministries and agencies, an IAA reorganization and streamlining plan was approved by the Cabinet on 24 December 2007. This plan went on to shut down the Japan Green Resources Agency and the National Institute of Multimedia Education as of the end of March 2008, and privatize the Nippon Automated Cargo Clearance System Operation in October later in the same year. It also aimed to merge sixteen IAAs into six IAAs, but ended up having five IAAs absorbed into two IAAs.[97]

209. In April 2008, the Cabinet approved a bill to amend the General Rule Act for IAA, which was then presented to the Diet. This amendment – although later quashed – included an open-recruitment of IAA chairpersons and auditors, prohibition on IAAs from arranging re-employment opportunities for their staff at affiliated companies, and an obligation of IAAs to return to the public purse those assets acquired using government money which turned out to be not necessary for the IAA's operations. After the DPJ came to power, the proposed amendment regarding the return of those assets to the public purse was enacted (21 May 2010).

96. Cabinet Decision of 16 Jun. 2007.
97. See Toshio Nishizawa, Status and Issues of Independent Administrative Agencies, House of Councillors report no. 293 (June, 2009).

Part I. Stock Companies

Chapter 1. Incorporation of Stock Companies (*Kabushiki Kaisha*)

§1. Incorporation Procedures

I. Incorporators (*Hokkinin*)

210. A stock company is incorporated by its incorporator(s). An incorporator is the person who has signed, or affixed their name and seal, as the incorporator in the articles of incorporation.[98] The incorporators are determined by such formalistic standard in order to make the responsible person for the incorporation of the company clear (see paragraph 278). Moreover, a pseudo-incorporator (*giji hokkinin*), who has not signed the articles of incorporation as an incorporator but has the external appearance of an incorporator, will also be subject to the same responsibilities as the incorporator (see paragraph 290).[99]

211. The prevailing theory is that there are no particular restrictions on who may incorporate a company, and therefore, a juridical person as well as a natural person is eligible to be an incorporator. This being the case, a company may act as incorporator to form its own subsidiary. There is no minimum incorporator requirement, as the minimum requirement of seven incorporators for a stock company was abolished by the amendment to the Commercial Code in 1990 (see paragraph 252).

212. In incorporating a company, each incorporator must subscribe for at least one share.[100] The procedures to incorporate a company are divided into two types, namely a 'promotive incorporation' (*hokki setsuritsu*), where the incorporators subscribe for all of the shares issued at the time of incorporation (simultaneous incorporation or simple incorporation), or a 'subscriptive incorporation' (*boshu setsuritsu*), where incorporators subscribe for part of the shares and solicit other shareholders for the remaining shares (gradual incorporation or complex incorporation).[101] Other than the method of subscription, the difference between promotive incorporation and a subscriptive incorporation includes the procedures to determine

98. Article 26, para. 1, Companies Act; 29 Jun. 1932, Great Court of Judicature Collection of Court Decisions on Civil Actions 11-1257.
99. Article 103, para. 2, Companies Act.
100. Article 25, para. 2, Companies Act.
101. Article 25, para. 1, items 1 and 2, Companies Act.

the members and establishing the organs of the company (see paragraphs 228, 234, 229 and 238).

213. Prior to the amendment to the Commercial Code in 1990, an investigation by a court-appointed inspector was required on the payment for shares in the promotive incorporation. It was therefore extremely rare for stock companies to undergo the promotive incorporation. The amendment to the Commercial Code in 1990 allowed the payment for shares to be made through a bank or trust company (so-called payment handling institution) in the promotive incorporation in the same way as the subscriptive incorporation, and the investigation by a court-appointed inspector was no longer required. In addition, the Companies Act abolished the requirement of certificate of deposit to be issued by the payment handling institution to verify the payment for shares in the case of promotive incorporation (see paragraph 229).

II. Companies under Incorporation and Incorporator Partnerships

214. A stock company will become a juridical person upon the registration of its incorporation.[102] Although there is no legal personality prior to the registration, the substance of a company will be created gradually to form the predecessor of the company, known as 'company under incorporation' (*setsuritsu chuno kaisha*). Since a company under incorporation does not have legal personality, it is generally considered an 'association without the capacity of rights' (*kenri nouryoku naki shadan*). Thereafter, upon incorporation of the company, the incorporators (subscribing for at least one share) and other subscribers become shareholders.

215. From a legal perspective, except for the legal personality, the company under incorporation and the company after incorporation are in substance the same entity. This theory is called the 'co-identity theory'. Therefore, the rights and obligations belonging to the company under incorporation will automatically become those of the company's after incorporation without any special acts of transfer or succession.

216. The scholarly views differ on when the company under incorporation comes into existence as follows:

- at the time the articles of incorporation have been prepared;
- at the time the articles of incorporation have been prepared and all of the shares to be issued upon incorporation of the company have been subscribed for;
- at the time the articles of incorporation have been prepared and each incorporator has subscribed for at least one share.

217. Most scholars support the third theory, citing the fact that the fundamental rules of the company under incorporation as an association are prescribed by the

102. Article 49, Companies Act.

articles of incorporation and the initial members of the association are determined at the time each incorporator subscribes for at least one share. The company under incorporation continues to exist until the completion of incorporation of the company, in other words, until the company has been registered.

218. Theoretically, the incorporation procedures, such as preparation of the articles of incorporation and subscription for the shares, will be carried out pursuant to the contract for incorporation of the company entered into by the incorporators. The relationship among the incorporators is known as an 'incorporators' partnership' which is legally a partnership under the Civil Code (see paragraph 1026).[103] The company under incorporation and the incorporators' partnership co-exist during the incorporation process of the stock company.

III. Preparation of the Articles of Incorporation

A. Preparation by Incorporators and Certification by Notary Public

219. Incorporators must prepare the articles of incorporation to form a stock company.[104] Preparing the articles of incorporation involves prescribing the fundamental rules of the stock company (substance) in writing (formality). On the other hand, Article 466 of the Companies Act provides for an amendment to the articles of incorporation, which will become effective without reflecting the amendment in writing to the articles as a matter of formality.

220. The articles of incorporation require signatures or names and stamped seals of all incorporators.[105] The articles of incorporation may be prepared by electromagnetic records, in which case certain measures to replace the signatures or names and stamped seals with an electronic signature must be taken in accordance with the applicable ordinance of the Ministry of Justice.[106]

221. The articles of incorporation will not be effective unless certified by a notary public.[107] This is intended to make the articles of incorporation clear through the review of the notary public and prevent future disputes and illegal acts.

222. The articles of incorporation prepared at the time of incorporation of the company are called the initial articles of incorporation. Only the initial articles of incorporation require certification by notary public. Amendments to the articles made after the incorporation of the company do not require certification.

103. Articles 667 et seq., Civil Code.
104. Article 26, para. 1, Companies Act.
105. Article 26, para. 1, Companies Act.
106. Article 26, para. 2, Companies Act.
107. Article 30, para. 1, Companies Act.

*B. Mandatory Description Matters (*Zettaiteki Kisaijikou*)*

223. Article 27 of the Companies Act provides the matters required to be specified or recorded in the articles of incorporation. Any omission of such matters will invalidate the articles of incorporation, which, in turn, invalidates the incorporation of the company. The following must be specified or recorded in the articles of incorporation:

- *Purpose of the company*: This means the business activities contemplated by the company. There are different views on whether the scope of the company's legal capacity (*kenri nouryoku*) will be restricted by the purpose of the company set forth in the articles of incorporation (see paragraph 299).
- *Trade name*: The trade name of a stock company must include the word '*kabushiki kaisha*' (stock company).[108] In addition, companies which engage in activities related to banking or trusts must include the word '*ginko*' (bank) or '*shintaku*' (trust) in their trade names.[109]
- *Location of head office*: This may be indicated by the smallest independent administrative area (municipality, or in the case of Tokyo, ward). Location of the head office is meaningful as the place where the minutes of the shareholders meetings and the board of directors meetings, articles of incorporation, shareholder registry and financial statements will be disclosed.[110]
- *Value of property to be contributed (or the lower limit)*: Prior to the amendment to the Commercial Code in 2005, the total number of shares authorized to be issued by the company and the total number of shares issued at the time of incorporation were required to be prescribed in the articles of incorporation (Article 166, paragraph 1, item 3 and item 6 of the Commercial Code prior to its amendment). Under the Companies Act, the value of the property to be contributed at the time of incorporation (or the lower limit thereof) must be provided in the articles of incorporation. On the other hand, the total number of authorized shares may be specified later in the articles of incorporation by the completion of incorporation procedures, after checking the number of shares subscribed for in the incorporation process of the company.[111]
- *Names and addresses of incorporators*: These details are required to confirm the identity of the incorporators. However, even in the absence of the names and addresses of the incorporators, the articles of incorporation are construed to be valid if the incorporators have signed the articles of incorporation and their addresses are appended.

108. Article 6, para. 2, Companies Act.
109. Article 6, para. 1, Banking Act; Art. 14, para. 1, Trust Business Act.
110. Article 318, para. 2; Art. 371, para. 1; Art. 31, para. 1; Art. 125, para. 1; Art. 442, para. 1, the Companies Act.
111. Articles 37 and 98, Companies Act.

C. *Relative Description Matters (*Soutaiteki Kisaijikou*) and Optional Description Matters (*Ninyiteki Kisaijikou*)*

224. The absence of relative description matters in the articles of incorporation does not affect the validity of the articles, but such relative description matters will not be effective unless prescribed in the articles. The matters provided in Article 28 of the Companies Act (irregular incorporation matters) are a typical example of the relative description matters (see paragraph 258–271).

225. The method of public notice is also a relative description matter. The Companies Act requires companies to give public notice in certain events, such as the record date, subscription requirements and balance sheet.[112] These public notices must be made through one of the following methods: publication in official gazette; publication in daily newspaper which publishes news on current affairs; or electronic public notice.[113] The third method which became available by the amendment to the Commercial Code in 2004 enabled public notices to be published on Internet websites. Companies giving an electronic public notice must state in the articles of incorporation that the method of public notice is an electronic public notice.[114] Either the first or second method may be prescribed as the alternative method in cases where the electronic public notice cannot be used due to an accident or other unavoidable circumstances. The website address will be registered in commercial registration.[115] Except for public notices on the settlement of accounts, electronic public notice must be reviewed by certain research providers to verify whether it was lawfully made.[116]

226. An absence of the optional description matters in the articles of incorporation will not invalidate the articles (which differs from the mandatory description matters) nor will it deny the effect of the optional description matters (which differs from the relative description matters). The optional description matters may be prescribed in the articles solely to make such matters explicit. Once prescribed in the articles, such matters can only be amended by amending the articles of incorporation (see paragraph 571). The procedures on name changes in the shareholder registry, the timing of convocation of annual shareholders meeting, the number of directors and auditors and the settlement period are frequently prescribed in the articles as optional description matters.

IV. Determination of Members (*Shain*) and Establishment of Organs (*Kikan*)

227. After the preparation of the articles of incorporation, the procedures for determining the members and establishing the organs will be carried out. At this

112. Article 124, para. 3; Art. 201, paras 3 and 4; Art. 440, para. 1, Companies Act.
113. Article 939, para. 1, Companies Act.
114. Article 939, para. 3, Companies Act.
115. Article 911, para. 3, item 29, Companies Act.
116. Articles 941–959, Companies Act; Arts 3 et seq., Electronic Public Notice Rules.

stage, the company undergoes either the 'promotive incorporation' or 'subscriptive incorporation'.

A. *Promotive Incorporation (*Hokki Setsuritsu*)*

1. Subscription for Shares

228. In a promotive incorporation, the incorporators subscribe for all shares issued at the time of incorporation of the company.

2. Performance of Contribution

229. Following their subscription for the shares, the incorporators must contribute fully without delay.[117] If an incorporator makes contribution in kind, such contribution must be made by the payment due date.[118] The contribution in money must be made at a payment handling institution specified by the incorporators, such as a bank, trust company or other similar institution.[119] Prior to the enactment of the Companies Act, the payment handling institution was required to issue a certificate of deposit for the payment. Namely, at the request of incorporator or director, such payment handling institution was obliged to prove that it had the paid-in amount in custody, and the payment handling institution may not assert either that the proven paid-in amount had not been paid or that a restriction existed on its return (e.g., a commitment by the incorporator that the incorporator would not withdraw the paid amount until a borrowing has been repaid). However, the Companies Act did not impose such obligation to prove the custody on the payment handling institutions because, in a promotive incorporation, there was little need for such proof of custody since the incorporators would be involved in the custody of the contributed property by themselves. In a promotive incorporation, it would be sufficient to prove the completion of payment using the bank account balance. If an incorporator does not make the payment, the right to become a shareholder will be forfeited following a notification from other incorporators to fulfil the performance of contribution.[120]

3. Appointment of Directors and Company Auditors

230. Once the performance of contribution is fulfilled, the incorporators will elect the directors and other officers at the time of incorporation.[121] The company's organs will be established by this appointment. Each incorporator will be entitled to

117. Article 34, para. 1, Companies Act.
118. Article 34, para. 1, Companies Act.
119. Article 7 of the Rules for Enforcement of the Companies Act; Art. 34, para. 2, Companies Act.
120. Article 36, Companies Act.
121. Article 38, Companies Act.

one voting right per subscribed share.[122] Such directors and officers at the time of incorporation will be elected by a majority of the votes of the incorporators.[123]

4. Investigation by Inspector (*Kensayaku*)

231. The directors appointed at the time of incorporation must seek the appointment of an inspector by the court to conduct an investigation if the matters provided in Article 28 of the Companies Act have been prescribed in the articles of incorporation (see paragraph 258).[124] Where the court finds from the report of the inspectors that the investigated matters are proper, the incorporation will be completed by registration. On the other hand, if the court finds the articles of incorporation to be improper based on the inspector's report, the court will make a ruling to amend the matters stipulated in Article 28 of the Companies Act.[125] If the incorporators agree to such ruling of the court, it may proceed with the incorporation procedures based on such ruling. However, if the incorporators disagree with such ruling, they may rescind their subscription for the shares.[126] The incorporators may, with the consent of all incorporators, amend the articles to repeal the provisions which have been amended by such order of the court.[127]

*B. Subscriptive Incorporation (*Boshu Setsuritsu*)*

1. Solicitation of Shareholders

232. In a subscriptive incorporation, the incorporators will subscribe for a portion of the shares and solicit subscribers for the remaining shares.[128]

233. Persons who intend to subscribe for shares must apply in writing, stating their names and addresses and the number of shares which they intend to subscribe for.[129] The incorporators must notify the persons intending to apply for the shares of certain statutorily required matters, such as the date of certification of the articles, the name of the notary public who effected such certification, certain matters prescribed in the articles, the value of the property contributed by the incorporators and the place designated for payment.[130]

234. If the subscribers are to be solicited widely from the general public, the shares may be regulated as an offering under the Financial Instruments and

122. Article 40, para. 2, Companies Act.
123. Article 40, para. 1, Companies Act.
124. Article 33, para. 1, Companies Act.
125. Article 33, para. 7, Companies Act.
126. Article 33, para. 8, Companies Act.
127. Article 33, para. 9, Companies Act.
128. Article 57, Companies Act.
129. Article 59, para. 3, Companies Act.
130. Article 59, para. 1, Companies Act.

Exchange Act (see paragraph 471). In practice, very few cases of incorporation involve the Financial Instruments and Exchange Act.

2. Allotment of Shares

235. After the applications are made for shares, the shares will be allotted at the discretion of incorporators.[131] The subscription will be completed and the members will be fixed upon the payment for the allotted shares by the applicants.[132]

236. It is common practice for companies to require an advance payment proportionate to the number of shares applied for. This advance payment will be appropriated to the payment of the allotted shares. If the applicant is not allotted any shares, then the advance on the subscription will be refunded to the applicant. In many cases, the full amount of issue price will be collected in the form of such advance payment and the solicitation will be ceased once the applications reach the total number of shares.

3. Performance of Contributions

237. Payment for the shares in a subscriptive incorporation will be made through the bank or trust company specified as the payment handling institution.[133] The payment handling institution must certify the amount of money paid (and is required to issue a certificate of deposit for payment).[134] The payment handling institution may not assert to the stock company after its incorporation any misstatement in the certificate or any restrictions regarding the withdrawal of the paid amount.[135] In a subscriptive incorporation, as the persons other than incorporators will perform the contribution before the stock company is established as a legal entity, the payment certification has been maintained to provide an assurance on the deposit of the property contributions.

4. Forfeiture

238. If a subscriber for the shares fails to make a payment, such subscriber's right to become a shareholder will be forfeited.[136] Additional subscribers must be solicited if the value of the property contributed by other subscribers does not meet the value specified in the articles of incorporation (see paragraph 223, property contributions).[137]

131. Article 60, para. 1, Companies Act.
132. Article 63, para. 1, Companies Act.
133. Article 63, para. 1, Companies Act.
134. Article 64, para. 1, Companies Act.
135. Article 64, para. 2, Companies Act.
136. Article 63, para. 3, Companies Act.
137. Article 27, item 4, Companies Act.

5. Organizational Meeting

239. If the total number of shares issued at the time of incorporation of the company has been subscribed for and the payments or contributions in kind have been made, the incorporators will hold an organizational meeting.[138] The organizational meeting involves those persons who have subscribed for shares (i.e., shareholders at the time of incorporation). The shareholders at the time of incorporation have one voting right per share.[139] The resolutions at the organizational meeting will be made by a majority of the votes of the total number of subscribed shares, being two-thirds or more of the votes of the shareholders present at the meeting.[140] The incorporators will report the matters pertaining to the incorporation of the company, and the directors at the time of incorporation will be elected.[141] The organs of the company will be established by the election of the directors and company auditors at the time of incorporation.

240. In addition, if the matters provided in Article 28 of the Companies Act are specified in the articles of incorporation, the incorporators must apply for an inspector to be appointed by the court for investigation of such matters.[142] The report of such inspector will be submitted by the incorporators at the organizational meeting.[143] If the organizational meeting finds the matters to be improper based on this report, the organizational meeting may make amendments to such matters.[144] In such case, subscribers dissenting to such amendments may rescind their subscription for the shares.[145]

241. If some or all the directors or company auditors at the time of incorporation are incorporators, an inspector may be elected at the organizational meeting to investigate the incorporation procedures and report the outcome of such investigation to the organizational meeting.[146]

V. Registration of Incorporation

A. *Principle of Standardized Rules (*Junsoku Shugi*)*

242. After the statutory incorporation procedures, including preparation of the articles of incorporation, determination of members and establishment of organs, the

138. Article 65, para. 1, Companies Act.
139. Article 72, para. 1, Companies Act.
140. Article 73, para. 1, Companies Act.
141. Article 87, para. 1; Art. 88 of the Companies Act.
142. Article 33, para. 1, Companies Act.
143. Article 87, para. 2, item 1, Companies Act.
144. Article 96, Companies Act.
145. Article 97, Companies Act.
146. Article 94, Companies Act.

company will be granted a legal personality upon the registration of its incorporation.[147] Under the 'principle of standardized rules' of the Companies Act, the incorporation of the company will be recognized without requiring particular permission from a government agency. There could be other principles, such as the 'principle of special permission' (*tokkyo shugi*) where an order of the monarch or national legislation is required for the incorporation of companies, or the 'principle of license' (*menkyo shugi*) where a license by a competent government agency for companies will be required. The principle of special permission will apply when authorizing the incorporation of particular companies through special laws, for example, NTT Corporation (NTT Corporation Act) and Japan Tobacco Inc. (Japan Tobacco Inc. Act). Under the 'principle of standardized rules' of the Companies Act, the examination conducted by a local bureau in the registration of incorporation only reviews the formality of the incorporation procedures.

243. In the meantime, companies engaged in business that are strongly tied with public interests are required by special laws to obtain a relevant business license (such as banking, insurance, trust, railway, electricity and gas companies). These business licenses are practically very similar to incorporation licenses.

B. Procedures for Registration

244. Registration of company incorporation must be made at the location of the head office. In a promotive incorporation, the registration must be made within two weeks from the completion of the investigation conducted by the directors or such other day specified by the incorporators, whichever day comes later. In a subscriptive incorporation, the registration must be made within two weeks from the conclusion of the organizational meeting or certain other prescribed day, whichever comes later.[148] The registration must also be made at the location of the branch offices within two weeks of the registration of its incorporation.[149] The matters to be registered include some of the details prescribed in the articles of incorporation, such as the purpose of the company and trade name, as well as the total number of authorized shares, the amount of stated capital, the names of directors, and the name and domicile of the representative director.[150]

245. The attachment documents to file the registration of incorporation include, among others, the articles of incorporation, a written document proving the application and subscription for the shares, an investigation report of directors at the time of incorporation or inspector and a certificate of deposit for payment of shares.[151] In addition, an amount corresponding to 0.7% of the stated capital (minimum of JPY

147. Article 49, Companies Act.
148. Article 911, paras 1 and 2, Companies Act.
149. Article 930, para. 1, item 1, Companies Act.
150. Article 911, para. 3, Companies Act.
151. Article 47, para. 2, Commercial Registration Act.

150,000) must be paid as the registration and license tax (Appended Table 1, item 24(1)(b) of the Registration and License Tax Act).

246. After the incorporation, any changes to the registered matters must be made within two weeks at the location of the head office (within three weeks at the location of branch offices).[152]

C. *Effect of Registration*

247. A stock company is incorporated upon the registration of its incorporation.[153] Upon the incorporation of the company, the subscribers become shareholders, and the directors and company auditors become the organs of the company. In addition, the paid-in money for shares and the property of contribution in kind belong to the company. On the other hand, there is a debate as to whom the effects of the 'act for preparation of business' (*kaigyo junbi koui*) performed by the incorporators and the expenses incurred by the incorporators belong (see paragraph 270).

248. Once the registration has been completed, the subscribers for shares may not assert that their subscription is invalid due to a mistake or rescind their subscription on the grounds of fraud or duress.[154] This is intended to secure the subscription of the shares and stabilize the foundation of the company. In addition, a transfer of 'rights to shares' (*kenri kabu*) prior to the incorporation of the company may not be asserted against the company (although such transfer will be valid between the parties) (see paragraph 383) because the incorporation procedures would become cumbersome if such potential shares were to be freely transferred.[155] Such restrictions on transfer of rights to shares will automatically extinguish upon incorporation of the company. Upon incorporation of a company, a share certificate issuing company must issue share certificates without delay.[156]

VI. Invalidation of Incorporation (*Setsuritsu Mukou*) and Failure to Form a Company (*Kaisha Fuseiritsu*)

A. *Invalidation of Incorporation*

249. Invalidation of incorporation of a stock company may be asserted only by filing an action disputing the defect in the incorporation procedures.[157] The grounds for invalidation may be asserted when there is a serious defect in the incorporation procedures, such as required matters missing in the articles of incorporation, the

152. Article 915, Companies Act.
153. Article 49, Companies Act.
154. Article 51, Companies Act.
155. Article 35, Companies Act.
156. Article 215, para. 1, Companies Act.
157. Article 828, para. 1, item 1, Companies Act.

articles of incorporation not having been certified, the organizational meeting not being held in accordance with the statutory requirements and the invalidity of the incorporation registration. An action for invalidation of incorporation may be filed only by a shareholder, director or liquidator (a shareholder, director, company auditor or liquidator in the case of Company with Company Auditor(s); and a shareholder, director, executive officer or liquidator in the case of Company with Nominating Committee, etc).[158] In addition, the action for invalidation of incorporation must be filed within a period of two years from the date of incorporation of the company.[159] Under the Companies Act, these restrictions are provided to ensure that the rights and obligations of third parties created based on the assumption that the company has been validly incorporated will not be significantly affected.

250. In addition, a final and binding judgment on invalidation of incorporation will be effective not only with regard to the parties to the action but also against third parties.[160] The judgment will not have a retroactive effect and the incorporation will become effective from then on to avoid the confusion on the rights and obligations existing at the time of such judgment.[161] Upon such judgment becoming final and binding, the company must go into liquidation and register in commercial registration.[162]

B. *Failure to Form a Company*

251. Invalidation of incorporation will be permitted if there is a ground for invalidation after the registration of incorporation. By contrast, failure to form a company will be permitted when the incorporation procedures ended before the registration of incorporation was completed and the company is deemed in both legal and practical terms not to have been established. In such cases, any person may assert such failure to form the company by any method.

§2. Financial Base of a Stock Company

I. Number of Incorporators and Single-Shareholder Companies

252. Each incorporator must subscribe for one or more shares issued by the company upon incorporation.[163] Prior to the amendment to the Commercial Code in 1990, a minimum of seven incorporators was required for incorporation of a stock company.[164] This was intended to assure the process of incorporation of a stock company by requiring a large number of incorporators who will be subject to the

158. Article 828, para. 2, item 1, Companies Act.
159. Article 828, para. 1, item 1, Companies Act.
160. Article 838, Companies Act.
161. Article 839, Companies Act.
162. Article 475, item 2, Companies Act.
163. Article 25, para. 2, Companies Act.
164. Article 165 of the Commercial Code prior to its amendment in 1990.

incorporators' responsibilities on incorporation. In practice, however, such statutory requirement was met as a formality only, as most incorporators listed in the articles of incorporation had no substance as an incorporator. Therefore, the minimum requirement on the number of incorporators was abolished by the amendment to the Commercial Code in 1990.

253. A stock company is an association (*shadan*) aimed at generating profits (see paragraph 114). Since an association is a collective group of individuals, traditionally, there was a debate as to whether a company should be dissolved if there was only one member. The Commercial Code prior to the amendment in 2005 provided that a general partnership company would be dissolved if the number of members of such general partnership company was reduced to one.[165] The Limited Company Act prior to its amendment in 1990 also provided the number of members being one as a ground for dissolution.[166] However, no such provision existed with regard to stock companies. In this regard, the court precedents and prevailing view construed that the stock company would not be dissolved even if the number of members – in other words, the shareholders – was reduced to one. The reasons were that the amendment to the Commercial Code in 1938 abolished the article which provided that the existence of only one shareholder will be a ground for dissolution, and the number of shareholders could be increased at any time through transfer of shares. A company which has only one shareholder is commonly referred to as a single-shareholder company (*ichinin kaisha*).

254. In Japan, companies are often incorporated as a wholly-owned subsidiary of its parent company. As each of the seven incorporators was previously required to subscribe for one or more shares upon incorporation, the parent companies had to acquire the shares from each of the incorporators after the incorporation was completed. However, as mentioned above, the minimum requirement of incorporators was removed by the amendment to the Commercial Code in 1990 and the Limited Company Act was also amended in 1990 to remove the relevant provision on dissolution grounds. In the Companies Act, membership companies (see paragraph 998) were also permitted to be single-member companies (see paragraph 117).

II. Abolition of Minimum Capital Requirement

255. Prior to the amendment to the Commercial Code in 1990, a minimum stated capital of JPY 10 million was required for stock companies.[167] This was intended to protect the creditors of the stock company because the shareholders will be liable only to the extent of the amount of their contribution in the company (see paragraph 312, Stated capital). In this regard, the amount of stated capital should be commensurate with the risks of the business. On the other hand, as it was difficult to create

165. Article 94, item 4, Commercial Code prior to amendment; in case of a limited partnership company, Art. 162, para. 1, Commercial Code prior to amendment.
166. Article 69, para. 1, item 5, Limited Company Act prior to amendment in 1990.
167. Article 168-4, Commercial Code prior to amendment.

a feasible mechanism, a fixed amount of JPY 10 million was set for stock companies. Another purpose to establish the minimum stated capital was to limit the stock companies to large-size companies only, but the figure of JPY 10 million was meaningless in achieving such purpose.

256. The minimum stated capital requirement was an obstacle to set up a venture company in Japan. Therefore, with an aim to proactively help small and medium-size enterprises 'take on the challenge' of new business activities, such as starting up a business or new ventures, the Act on Support for the Ventures of Small and Medium-Sized Enterprises (i.e., an act for partial amendment to the Small and Medium-Sized Enterprise Cooperatives Act to facilitate the new business activities of small and medium-sized enterprises), which was enacted in February 2003, provided an exemption to the minimum stated capital requirement of JPY 10 million (JPY 3 million in the case of limited companies) to start up a new business. This allowed the entrepreneurs starting up a new business (defined as an individual not engaged in business but who has a concrete plan to start the business within two months of forming the company) to incorporate a company with the stated capital of just JPY 1. However, as the exemption to the Commercial Code was available only for five years, such companies were forced to convert into general partnership companies or to dissolve if they were unable to satisfy the minimum stated capital requirement under the Commercial Code after five years.

257. While the minimum stated capital requires a certain amount of contributions at the time of incorporation of the company, it was more important for creditor protection purposes to properly retain the assets in the company after its incorporation and to disclose such amount properly. Globally, the minimum stated capital was not required in the states of Delaware or New York in the United States and there were a number of countries in Europe abolishing such requirement. It was also necessary to remove the obstacles to entrepreneurship. On these bases, the minimum stated capital requirement was abolished in the Companies Act. Instead, the Companies Act requires the preparation of accurate account books in a timely manner and also made changes related to preparation of proper financial statements, such as the appointment of accounting advisors (see paragraph 170).[168] In addition, certain measures were taken to prevent improper cash-out of company assets, such as prohibition of dividends of surplus if the amount of net assets falls below JPY 3 million.[169]

III. Regulations on 'Irregular Incorporation Matters' (*Hentai Setsuritsu Jikou*)

258. Article 28 of the Companies Act provides certain material matters in which the incorporators may possibly promote the interests of the incorporator itself or those of a third party. Therefore, the Companies Act provides that these matters will

168. Article 432, para. 1, Companies Act.
169. Article 458, Companies Act.

not be effective unless prescribed in the articles of incorporation (required matters) (see paragraph 224). In addition, an investigation must be implemented by the inspector appointed by the court (see paragraphs 231 and 240). The following matters that require such special procedures in the incorporation of a company are known as irregular corporation matters.

A. *Contribution in Kind (*Genbutsu Shusshi*)*

259. Contribution in kind is a contribution of properties other than money. In stock companies, contributions must be made by means of property and not by labour works or providing credit. The properties may be movable property, real property, claims or intangible properties, such as patent rights. However, unlike the contribution of money, there is a risk that the value of the property may be overestimated and harm the company's financial base. Therefore, contribution in kind is provided as one of the irregular incorporation matters under the Companies Act, setting forth certain restrictions to prevent any abusive use.

B. *Property Assumption (*Zaisan Hikiuke*)*

260. Property assumption is an agreement where the incorporator agrees to purchase from a third party certain property necessary for the newly incorporated company. This is an 'act for preparation of business' which is intended to secure the necessary assets during the company incorporation procedures so as to enable business to commence immediately after the company is incorporated. A property assumption does not differ from the aforementioned contribution in kind in that it contains the risk of overestimation at the time of incorporation of the company. Therefore, the Companies Act provides the same rules for property assumption as contributions in kind.

261. There are conflicting views on the rationale that an incorporator may implement property assumption because this is an act for preparation of business which may be beyond the scope of authority granted to incorporators. A judicial precedent (24 December 1963, Collection of Court Decisions on Civil Actions 17-1744) and majority view interpret that an act for preparation of business is outside the authority granted to the incorporators and therefore property assumption was permitted from the perspective of practicality, as an exception subject to certain conditions under the Companies Act. On the other hand, a contrary view interprets that acts for preparation of business is in general within the authority of the incorporators, but given the risk of abuse, the incorporators are limited to perform property assumption only.

262. In addition, there are conflicting views on whether the company may subsequently ratify the property assumption if it was implemented at the time of incorporation without the required description in the articles of incorporation. A negative view rejects ratification, arguing that it will not be in line with the strict statutory conditions provided for property assumption (3 December 1953, Supreme Court Collection of Court Decisions on Civil Actions 7-1299), whereas an affirmative view supports ratification from the perspective of enhancing the stated capital of the company. A majority view is in support of the ratification of property assumption.

263. Regulations on property assumption were established to prevent circumvention of the rules on contributions in kind in the form of sale and purchase. However, such regulations may be circumvented if similar discussions are held by the incorporator beforehand on the purchase of particular property, and then the incorporators enter into a contract to purchase such property after becoming a director following the incorporation of the company. Therefore, the Companies Act requires that a special resolution be passed by the shareholders meeting upon a so-called 'subsequent incorporation' (*jigo setsuritsu*) where a company enters into a contract, within two years of its incorporation, to acquire a property which has been in existence from prior to the incorporation and will be used continuously to operate the business at a value equivalent to at least 20% of the stated capital.[170]

C. Investigations on Contribution in Kind and Property Assumption

264. As an exemption to the rules regarding contribution in kind and property assumption, an investigation by court-appointed inspector will not be required in the following three cases:

(1) The total value of the property for contribution in kind or property assumption specified in the articles of incorporation does not exceed JPY 5 million (exemption for small amounts, Article 33, paragraph 10, item 1, Companies Act).
(2) In cases where the property for contribution in kind or property assumption is securities having a market value (as regulated under the Financial Instruments and Exchange Act), the value prescribed in the articles of incorporation does not exceed such market value (calculated through the method prescribed in the applicable ordinance of the Ministry of Justice (exemption pertaining to securities, Article 33, paragraph 10, item 2, Companies Act)).[171]
(3) Certification of an attorney, legal professional corporation, certified public accountant, auditing firm, tax accountant or tax accounting firm verifying the reasonableness of the articles of incorporation pertaining to the contribution in kind and property assumption (exemption pertaining to certification by expert, Article 33, paragraph 10, item 3, Companies Act); provided that an appraisal of a certified property appraiser will be required with regard to real property.

265. The expert certification or appraisal may not be provided by (i) incorporators, (ii) the assignor of property, (iii) directors or company auditors at the time of incorporation, (iv) a person who is subject to disposition ordering suspension of his or her business, (v) a legal professional corporation, auditing firm or tax accounting

170. Article 467, para. 1, item 5, Companies Act.
171. Article 6, Regulations on Enforcement of the Companies Act.

firm, a half or more of whose members fall under the persons in item (i) through (iii) above.[172] Such disqualification is intended to ensure fair verification.

266. Upon the exemption of investigation by an inspector with regard to contribution in kind or property assumption, the directors at the time of incorporation and certain other prescribed persons must investigate the reasonableness of the amount of property prescribed in the article of incorporation that is subject to the exemption for small amounts or the exemption pertaining to securities. In cases of the exemption through expert certification, the directors at the time of incorporation and certain other prescribed persons must investigate the appropriateness of the submitted certification.

D. Remuneration of Incorporators and Special Benefits

267. The remuneration of incorporators is usually paid-in a fixed amount as the expenses of the company. The company may also grant incorporators certain benefits, such as priority rights relating to the distribution of profits or use of company facilities. There is a risk that excessive or unfair special benefits may be granted if such benefits were to be decided simply by the discussions among the incorporators. There is no distinction between the remuneration and special benefits except for the timing of payment where the remuneration will be paid-in one lump sum after the incorporation of the company.

E. Incorporation Expenses

268. Incorporation expenses are the expenses paid for by the incorporators in the process of company incorporation. These expenses include office rent, staff salaries and the printing fees for share subscription forms. While the incorporators may naturally request the company to reimburse these expenses after the establishment of the company, certain rules exist to control the company's spendings.

269. Among the incorporation expenses to be borne by the company, the following expenses may be reimbursed by the company without specific reference in the articles of incorporation: stamp duty on the articles of incorporation, fees to be paid to banks or other institutions for handling the payment of shares, remuneration of inspector and registration and license tax for the registration of incorporation.[173] These exceptions are permitted as such expenses are objective and hold little risk of excessive payment.

270. The incorporators may seek reimbursement of the expenses paid for incorporation of the company after its incorporation, to the extent so provided in the articles of incorporation. There are different views as to whether any expenses

---

172. Article 33, para. 11, Companies Act.
173. Article 28, item 4, Companies Act; Art. 5, Regulations on the Enforcement of the Companies Act.

incurred by the incorporators that are unpaid at the time of incorporation will turn out to be the company's obligations after the incorporation. A judicial precedent interpreted that the obligations to pay such expenses belong to the company, to the extent of the amount provided in the articles of incorporation (4 July 1927, Great Court of Judicature Collection of Court Decisions on Civil Actions 6-428). However, many scholars criticize that it would be inappropriate from a creditor protection perspective to determine the scope of the company's obligations by the articles of incorporation, which are merely internal affairs of the company.

271. One of the scholarly views interprets that the unpaid obligations belong to the company and therefore the company may seek reimbursement from the incorporators for the unpaid expenses that were in excess of the amount provided in the articles of incorporation. Another scholarly view argues that the unpaid obligations still belong to the incorporators and the incorporators may seek reimbursement from the company after performing such obligations, to the extent of the amount provided in the articles of incorporation.

IV. Regulations on Fake Payments

272. The payment of contribution for the shares is strictly required upon incorporation of a stock company. There are some instances, however, where the payment for the shares may be fake with the result that no capital enhancement is achieved. In particular, such fake payments are sometimes found when sole proprietorships convert into a stock company.

*A. Borrowing and Depositing of Money (*Azukeai*)*

273. A fake payment using borrowing and depositing of money is when the incorporators borrow the funds from the payment handling institution in their capacity as incorporators to make the payment of contribution for the shares to the same payment handling institution using these funds (see paragraphs 229 and 237, Payment handling institutions). The incorporators agree not to cause the company to withdraw the paid amount after they become a director of the company until the incorporators have repaid the borrowings to the payment handling institution. This allows the payment of contribution for the shares required by the Companies Act to be made as a matter of formality.

274. In a subscriptive incorporation, the payment handling institution must certify that it has custody of the paid-in money. The payment handling institution cannot assert any misstatement in the certificate or the existence of restrictions regarding the withdrawal of the paid amount (see paragraph 237). As the certificate of deposit for the payment is required to be attached to the incorporation registration, the incorporation registration cannot be processed without such certificate.[174] As such, the fake payments are prevented by the registration requirement because the payment handling institutions will certify the deposit only when the actual payment has been made without any restriction. However, in a promotive incorporation, the amount of money paid-in at the time of incorporation may be verified by other available methods such as the balance statement of a bank account (see paragraph 229).

275. The fake payments are not valid (although there is a contrary view indicated by some governmental officials in charge of drafting the Companies Act interpreting that such payments are valid). Criminal punishment may be imposed if there is a conspiracy between the payment handling institution and the incorporators with regard to the faking of the payment.[175]

*B. Pretence Money (*Misegane*)*

276. Pretence money is when the incorporators repay their borrowings from an institution other than the payment handling institution, the proceeds of which were appropriated to the payment of shares, by withdrawing the paid money from the payment handling institution after the incorporation of the company. This type of fake payment is carried out to circumvent the abovementioned regulations on the borrowing and depositing of money. There has been an argument over whether such payment for shares is valid as, unlike the borrowing and depositing, pretence money involves the actual payment by transfer of funds, although it is just a matter of formality.

277. A judicial precedent and majority scholarly views construe that the payment for shares through pretence money is invalid because it is in substance a deliberate faking of payment.[176] There is also a scholarly view interpreting that while it is difficult to deny the validity of the actual payment, the issue may be resolved by imposing criminal punishments of misappropriation (*hainin*) or embezzlement in the course of business (*gyomujou oryo*) or special misappropriation (*tokubetsu hainin*) in the Companies Act (i.e., the incorporator (director) used the funds of the company to pay back his or her personal borrowings).[177] In addition, the application for incorporation registration based on the fake payment will constitute a crime of false entry in the original of notarial deed (11 October 1966, Supreme Court Collection of Court Decisions on Civil Actions 20-817).

174. Article 47, para. 2, item 5, Commercial Registration Act.
175. Article 965, Companies Act.
176. 6 Dec. 1963, Supreme Court Collection of Court Decisions on Civil Actions 17-1633.
177. Articles 247 and 253, Penal Code; Art. 960, Companies Act.

V. Liability upon Incorporation

A. *Liability of Incorporators, Directors and Company Auditors*

1. Liability for the Shortfall in the Value of Properties Contributed

278. If the value of the properties contributed by contribution in kind or property assumption is substantially short of the value prescribed in the articles of incorporation, the incorporators and directors upon incorporation will be jointly and severally liable for the payment of such shortfall.[178] However, if an investigation by the court-appointed inspector was carried out with regard to the matters pertaining to the contributions in kind or property assumption or where the incorporators or directors upon incorporation prove that they did not fail to exercise due care in the performance of their duties, they will not be liable for such shortfall.[179]

279. In case of a promotive incorporation, such liability is negligence liability. On the other hand, in case of a subscriptive incorporation, such liability is strict liability.[180] The difference is intended to ensure that the incorporators who made the contribution in kind will subscribe the same value as other subscribers who are, unlike incorporators, not permitted to make contribution in kind.

280. In Article 192 of the Commercial Code prior to amendment in 2005, the incorporators, directors and company auditors were liable for warranty in cases where there were unsubscribed shares after the incorporation of the company or shares for which payment had not been completed (warranty for subscription and warranty for payment).

281. In the past, the Commercial Code calculated the stated capital of a stock company as 'number of shares × par value'. In those days, the number of issued shares was required to be provided in the articles of incorporation at the time of incorporation of the company because it would determine the amount of stated capital. If the shares issued at the time of incorporation had not been subscribed or paid for in full, it would have been a violation of the articles and hence the incorporation became invalid. Therefore, it was intended in Article 192 of the Commercial Code to minimize such risk of invalid incorporation by creating the abovementioned liability on the incorporators, directors and company auditors.

282. Subsequently, the amount of stated capital and the number of shares became irrelevant (see paragraph 316). As such, the Companies Act did not establish a provision corresponding to Article 192 of the Commercial Code as there was no longer a need for the warranty of subscription or warranty of payment by the incorporators or other persons. Meanwhile, the minimum amount of contribution which needs to be secured in the incorporation of the company must be provided in

178. Article 52, para. 1, Companies Act.
179. Article 52, para. 2, Companies Act.
180. Article 103, para. 1; Art. 52, para. 2, Companies Act.

the articles of incorporation (see paragraph 223).[181] The number of shares to be issued upon incorporation of a company will be determined by the incorporators in the process of incorporation, and the shares for which contribution was not made will be forfeited. If the minimum amount of contribution provided in the articles of incorporation is not satisfied, the incorporation of such company will be invalid (as the warranty is not in place, such invalidation may not be cured).

2. Liability for Damages

a. Liability to the Company

283. If incorporators, directors or company auditors neglect their duties in the incorporation of the company, they will be jointly and severally liable for damages to the company.[182] This liability is negligence liability and may not be exempted unless the consent of all shareholders is obtained.[183] This liability corresponds to the liability of directors to the company (see paragraph 735).

b. Liability to Third Parties

284. If incorporators, directors or company auditors are with knowledge or grossly negligent in performing their duties pertaining to the incorporation of the company, they will be jointly and severally liable for damages to third parties.[184] A majority scholarly view interprets that this liability is a special statutory liability to enhance the protection of third parties which is separately provided from the tort liability in the Civil Code. (Therefore, if there is intent or negligence with regard to the infringement of the rights of a third party, a tort liability may also be sought pursuant to Article 709 of the Civil Code.) This liability corresponds to the liability of directors to third parties (see paragraph 749).

285. There is a question as to whether shareholders are included as third parties for purposes of this liability. A judicial precedent (10 February 1927, Great Court of Judicature Collection of Court Decisions on Civil Actions 6-428) and the majority scholarly view interpret the third parties to include shareholders. In addition, if the third party is negligent, a judicial precedent (30 March 1940, Great Court of Judicature Collection of Court Decisions on Civil Actions 19-639) and the prevailing scholarly view allow comparative negligence with regard to the damages.

3. Liability for Failure to Form the Company

286. If the procedures for incorporation of the company fail prior to the completion of incorporation registration, the incorporators will be jointly and severally

---

181. Article 27, item 4, Companies Act.
182. Article 53, para. 1; Art. 54, Companies Act.
183. Article 55, Companies Act.
184. Article 53, para. 2; Art. 54, Companies Act.

liable for the acts performed in the incorporation of the company.[185] In addition, the incorporators will assume the full amount of the expenses already paid in the incorporation process of the company.[186]

4. Liability Pertaining to Expert Certification

287. If the actual value of the property which is subscribed by contribution in kind or property assumption is substantially short of the value specified in the articles of incorporation, the attorney or other professionals who conducted the expert certification or appraisal (see paragraph 264) will be jointly and severally liable for payment of the shortfall to the company.[187] Such liability is negligence liability and the burden of proof lies with the expert who conducted the certification or appraisal.

5. Liability concerning Fake Contributions

288. If an incorporator makes fake payment of money or delivery of property to be contributed in kind in respect of shares, the incorporator has an obligation to pay to the company the entire amount of such fake contribution or deliver to the company the entirety of the property to be contributed.[188] If the company requests, in lieu of delivery of the property, payment of an amount of money equivalent to the value of the property, the incorporator is required to pay the full amount of such monies. This liability is strict liability. If a subscriber for shares in a subscriptive incorporation makes fake payments, the subscriber has an obligation to pay to the company the full amount of monies pertaining to the fake contribution.[189] This is also strict liability. An incorporator who is involved in faking the performance of contributions also bears a similar liability, but can avoid liability if able to prove that the incorporator did not fail to exercise due care.[190] This liability is jointly and severally held by the incorporator and the subscriber.[191]

289. An incorporator who faked performance of contributions or a subscriber who made a fake payment may not exercise any rights in respect of the shares for which such performance of contribution or payment was faked until the aforesaid liability is performed.[192] However, if shares (*kenri kabu*) are transferred, the transferee may exercise rights in respect of the shares, unless the transferee acted with

185. Article 56, Companies Act.
186. Article 56, Companies Act.
187. Article 52, para. 3, Companies Act.
188. Article 52-2, para. 1, Companies Act.
189. Article 102-2, para. 1, Companies Act.
190. Article 52-2, para. 2 and Art. 103, para. 2, Companies Act.
191. Article 52-2, para. 3 and main text of Art. 103, para. 2, Companies Act.
192. Article 52-2, para. 4 and Art. 102, para. 3, Companies Act.

knowledge or was grossly negligent.[193] These provisions were introduced with the 2014 amendment.

B. Liability of Pseudo-Incorporator

290. A pseudo-incorporator (*giji hokkinin*) is not an incorporator but has consented to his or her name being entered or recorded in advertising for the solicitation of shares or other documents or electromagnetic records pertaining to the solicitation of shares to the effect of supporting the incorporation of the company. The pseudo-incorporator will be subject to the same liability as the incorporators.[194] A prevailing scholarly view construes that the pseudo-incorporator should be held liable only for securing the capital (as described in (1) above) and failure to form the company (abovementioned as described in (3) above) because it does not have the authority as an incorporator and therefore should not be held liable for damages based on a failure to perform its duties.

§3. Legal Personality of Stock Companies

I. Doctrine of Piercing the Corporate Veil

A. Overview

291. In Japan, there are many sole proprietorships that are operated in the form of stock company and, in addition, many divisions of large corporations are operated as a subsidiary (stock company). In those cases, there are instances where it is unreasonable to treat such companies as an independent juridical person.

292. Therefore, judicial precedents and majority scholarly view adopt the doctrine of piercing the corporate veil where the company's independent legal personality is denied and the shareholders will be liable for the liabilities of the company. This doctrine may not be asserted by the company or the shareholders against a third party since it is intended to protect third parties, such as customers or business partners.

B. Criteria

293. The doctrine of piercing the corporate veil is based on the general principle of prohibiting the abuse of rights under Article 1, paragraph 3 of the Civil Code. According to a Supreme Court ruling, the doctrine of piercing the corporate veil requires that the legal personality is either: (i) abused to avoid the application of

193. Article 52-2, para. 5 and Art. 102, para. 4, Companies Act.
194. Article 103, para. 2, Companies Act.

laws or (ii) has no substance.[195] The majority scholarly view is in support of the interpretation of this judicial precedent.

294. According to this theory, the abuse of legal personality requires as its first element a control where legal personality is under full control of another party. The second element is a purpose that the legal personality is being used for an illegal or unjustifiable purpose. Some of the examples where judicial precedents recognized the abuse of legal personality are as follows:

(i) A person attempted to circumvent the duty of non-competition by forming a company to perform competing acts.
(ii) A company was dissolved with the purpose to dismiss a union activist. After all employees were dismissed, a new company was formed to rehire all employees except for such union activist.
(iii) A manager of a financially distressed small enterprise formed a new company and attempted to continue the business by transferring the assets of the old company to the new company to circumvent the payment of the company debts.

295. There is no clear standard as to the circumstances in which the legal personality is deemed to have no substance. Therefore, various facts and circumstances must be taken into account, in addition to the fact that the shareholders substantively control the company, such as whether the properties of the company and the shareholders are commingled; the business activities are continuously intermingled; the accounting books are not separately recorded; and the board of directors meetings and the shareholders meetings are actually held.

296. Some scholars criticize that the courts could have reached a reasonable conclusion in many cases by interpreting specific laws and regulations to be applied in each case rather than by using the general doctrine of piercing the corporate veil.

II. Restrictions on the 'Capacity to Hold Rights' (*Kenri Nouryoku*)

297. As a juridical person, a stock company will not be subject to the rights or duties that are unique to a natural person (e.g., right to life, parental right, duty of support). In addition, a stock company will be bound by the restrictions on 'capacity to hold' under the laws and regulations as well as the purpose of the company as prescribed in the articles of incorporation.

A. Restrictions under the Laws and Regulations

298. As stock companies are a juridical person created by the statutes, its capacity to hold rights is limited by laws and regulations. For example, companies in

195. 27 Feb. 1969, Supreme Court Collection of Court Decisions on Civil Actions 23-511.

dissolution or bankruptcy procedures may have rights and obligations only within the scope of the objective of liquidation or bankruptcy.[196] Therefore, companies in the process of liquidation will not be able to engage in new business activities.

B. Restrictions by the Prescribed Purpose in the Articles of Incorporation

299. Stock companies must specify their business purposes in the articles of incorporation and register in commercial registration.[197] Article 34 of the Civil Code provides that a juridical person will have rights and obligations to the extent of its purpose provided in the articles of incorporation (*ultra vires* doctrine). While this provision regulates public interest corporations, the judicial precedents and majority scholarly view interpret that it also applies by analogy to profit corporations.

300. In the past, the courts strictly interpreted the scope of companies' purposes prescribed in the articles of incorporation by focusing on the literal words used in the article of incorporation. However, the courts later expanded the scope of companies' purposes to include acts that are necessary in achieving the purpose prescribed in the articles of incorporation by interpreting the scope broadly and flexibly (25 December 1920, Great Court of Judicature Collection of Court Decisions on Civil Actions 18-1078). As to the standard to judge whether or not certain acts are necessary in achieving the purpose, the courts initially scrutinized the specific circumstances to find whether the act in question was actually necessary to achieve the purpose given in the articles of incorporation of the company. Subsequently, the courts turned to a more generic standard to review the nature of each act in general to protect the transactions entered into by the related parties.[198]

301. In recent years, an influential scholarly view has argued that the capacity to hold rights of a company should not be restricted by the purpose prescribed in the articles of incorporation. The rationale supporting this view includes: (i) although the purpose of the company is publicly available through the commercial registration, it is impractical for third parties to check such purpose upon entering into each transaction and (ii) the restrictions on the company's capacity based on its purpose may be used abusively as a way to avoid the company's liability in a transaction unfavourable to the company. Among the supporters of this view, there are some variations to the effect that: (i) the capacity of a company is nonetheless restricted by its common purpose to generate profits or (ii) the purpose of a company will instead limit the authority of the company's representative organs. There is also a different view that the capacity to hold rights of a company should not be subject to any restrictions. In any case, acts of directors which contravene the prescribed

196. Article 476, Companies Act.
197. Article 27, item 1; Art. 911, para. 3, item 1, Companies Act.
198. 7 Feb. 1938, Great Court of Judicature Collection of Court Decisions on Civil Actions 17-50; 15 Feb. 1952, Supreme Court Collection of Court Decisions on Civil Actions 6-77.

purpose of the articles of incorporation will be grounds for an enjoinment by the shareholders and liability for damages to the company.[199]

C. *Company Donations*

302. It is generally considered that the companies may lawfully make donations as donations may indirectly contribute to the company in achieving the prescribed purpose of the company or because companies are required to play a socially responsible role in modern society. In this regard, there is some debate over whether the donations to a particular political party or politician – in other words, political donations – similarly fall within the scope of the prescribed purpose in the articles of incorporation of the company.

303. The Supreme Court ruled that the political donations were lawful in the well-known case of Yahata Steel (one of the predecessors of the current Nippon Steel Corporation) stating the following reasons:[200]

(i) A company may engage in those activities that it is expected or requested to perform under conventional wisdom (*shakai tsunen*) even if such activities may not be relevant on its face to the prescribed purpose in the articles of incorporation.
(ii) These activities are necessary in achieving the prescribed purpose indirectly because the value and effect of such social activities may enhance the smooth development of the company as a corporate entity.

304. The majority scholarly view also construes that political donations made by stock companies do not contravene the prescribed purpose of the articles of incorporation, provided that they are reasonable in amount taking into consideration such factors as the size of the company and its results of operations. There is also a view, however, that political donations may be invalid under the Constitution or the Civil Code, unless such donations are made with the consent of all shareholders.[201]

305. In Japan, the Public Offices Election Act (Act No. 100 of 1950) prohibits political donations that accompany special interests. In addition, the Political Funds Control Act (Act No. 194 of 1948) restricts political donations by requiring fund management bodies (*shikin kanri dantai*) which thoroughly segregates the political funds from personal assets of the candidates running for elective public office (including those persons intending to run for elective public office and those currently in public office). Under this system, a candidate will designate one political body out of all political bodies that he or she represents as the political body to

199. Article 360, para. 1; Art. 355; Art. 423, para. 1, Companies Act.
200. Judicial precedent of the Supreme Court (Great Bench) 24 Jun. 1970, Court Collection of Court Decisions on Civil Actions 24-625.
201. Article 90, Civil Code.

receive all political donations so as to allow a review of the political funds of such candidate.[202]

306. Companies, labour unions, employee organizations and other organizations are prohibited from making a donation relating to political activities to any person other than the political party or fund management body.[203] This prohibition was established because the majority of political corruption cases were caused by the group donations of companies. A 'donation' here includes money, goods and any other property benefits provided or delivered other than payment of political party membership fees, association membership fees or other monetary obligations.[204] This also includes providing benefits, such as secretary services and car services. Any solicitation or request for such prohibited donations are also prohibited.[205] Any person in violation of the above will be punished with imprisonment without work for a period of up to one year or a fine of up to JPY 500,000 and may also be subject to suspension of civil rights.[206] Certain companies, such as companies receiving a government subsidy and companies which have continuously recorded a deficit for at least three fiscal years, are not permitted to make any donations relating to political activities.[207] The maximum amount of donation that a company may make to political parties or political funds management bodies is specified based on the size of its capital (ranging from JPY 7.5 million to JPY 30 million).[208]

202. Article 19, paras 1 and 2, Political Funds Control Act.
203. Article 21, para. 1, Political Funds Control Act.
204. Article 4, para. 3, Political Funds Control Act.
205. Article 21, para. 3, Political Funds Control Act.
206. Article 26, Political Funds Control Act; Art. 28, Political Funds Control Act.
207. Article 22-3, Art. 22-4, Political Funds Control Act.
208. Article 21-3, para. 1, item 2, Political Funds Control Act.

Model Articles of Incorporation (Company with Board of Auditors/Company with Accounting Auditors/company at which the board of directors determines the dividends of surplus)

22 August 2008
Resolution of the Board of Directors
National Federation of Stock Companies

CHAPTER 1 GENERAL PROVISIONS

Article 1 (Trade Name)

The name of this Company shall be 'xxx Kabushiki Kaisha' and shall be expressed 'xxx Co., Ltd.' in English.

Article 2 (Purpose)

The purpose of the Company shall be to engage in the following businesses:

(1) … … … … … .
(2) … … … … … .
(3) … … … … … ..
(4) All other business incidental or related to the preceding items.

Article 3 (Location of the Head Office)

The head office of the Company shall be located in xx ward, Tokyo.

Article 4 (Organs)

The Company shall have the following organs in addition to shareholders meeting and directors:

(1) Board of Directors;
(2) Company Auditors;
(3) Board of Auditors; and
(4) Accounting Auditors.

Article 5 (Method of Public Notice)

The method of public notice of the Company shall be electronic public notice; provided, however, that if the Company is unable to post an electronic public notice owing to an accident or other unavoidable reasons, the public notice may be posted in xxx Newspaper.

CHAPTER 2 SHARES

Article 6 (Total Number of Authorized Shares)

The total number of authorized shares by the Company shall be x shares.

Article 7 (Share Unit)

A share unit shall be composed of one thousand (1,000) shares.

Article 8 (Rights in Relation to Shares Less Than One Unit)

Company shareholders owning shares less than one unit may not exercise any rights other than those listed below:

(1) The rights given in any of the items of paragraph 2 of Article 189 of the Companies Act.
(2) The right to claims through the provision of paragraph 1 of Article 166 of the Companies Act.
(3) The right to receive the allotment of solicited shares or the allotment of share options corresponding to the number of shares owned by the shareholder.
(4) The right to claims through the provisions of the following Article.

Article 9 (Additional Purchases of Shares Less Than One Unit)

Shareholders of the Company holding shares less than one unit may demand the Company that the Company sell to the shareholder such number of shares which, when added to its shares less than one unit, constitute one share unit in accordance with the Regulations on the Handling of Shares.

Article 10 (Administrator of Shareholder Registry)

(1) The Company shall have an administrator of shareholder registry.

(2) The administrator of shareholder registry and its administration office shall be decided by a resolution of the Board of Directors, and public notice shall be given thereof.
(3) The preparation and maintenance of the shareholder registry and the share option registry, and other business pertaining to the shareholder registry and the share option registry shall be entrusted to the administrator of shareholder registry and shall not be handled by the Company.

Article 11 (Regulations on the Handling of Shares)

The handling of shares and handling fees of the Company shall, in addition to laws and regulations or these Articles of Incorporation, be governed by the Regulations on the Handling of Shares stipulated by the Board of Directors.

CHAPTER 3 GENERAL MEETING OF SHAREHOLDERS

Article 12 (Convocation of Shareholders Meeting)

The annual shareholders meeting of the Company shall be convened in June each year and an extraordinary shareholders meeting shall be convened from time to time whenever necessary.

Article 13 (Record Date of Annual Shareholders Meeting)

The record date of the voting rights to be exercised at annual shareholders meetings of the Company shall be March 31 of each year.

Article 14 (Convener and Chairperson)

(1) The president shall convene the shareholders meeting and act as the chairperson.
(2) If the president is unable to act, another director designated by the order of priority determined in advance by the Board of Directors, shall convene the shareholders meeting and act as the chairperson.

Article 15 (Provision of Reference Documents for Shareholders Meeting, Etc. through the Internet)

In convening a shareholders meeting, the Company shall be deemed to have provided the information to the shareholders required to be described or indicated in the reference documents for the shareholders meeting, business reports, non-consolidated financial statements and consolidated financial statements by the disclosure of such information through the Internet in accordance with the provisions stipulated in an ordinance of the Ministry of Justice.

Article 16 (Method of Resolutions)

(1) Except as otherwise provided in laws and regulations or by these Articles of Incorporation, all resolutions of the shareholders meetings shall be made by a majority of votes held by the attending shareholders entitled to exercise their voting rights.
(2) The resolutions provided in Article 309, paragraph 2 of the Companies Act shall be made by not less than two-thirds of the votes held by the attending shareholders who hold not less than one-third of the votes of shareholders entitled to exercise their voting rights.

Article 17 (Proxy Voting)

(1) A shareholder may entrust the voting rights to another shareholder who has voting rights of the Company as a proxy, and may exercise its voting rights.
(2) The shareholder or its proxy must submit a document verifying the right of representation in writing for each shareholders meeting.

CHAPTER 4 DIRECTORS AND THE BOARD OF DIRECTORS

Article 18 (Number of Directors)

The directors of the Company shall be within xx members.

Article 19 (Method of Election of the Directors)

(1) Directors shall be elected at the shareholders meeting.
(2) Resolutions for the election of directors shall be made by a majority of the votes of the attending shareholders holding not less than one-third of the voting rights of shareholders entitled to exercise their voting rights.
(3) No cumulative voting shall be allowed with respect to resolutions for the election of directors.

Article 20 (Directors' Term of Office)

(1) Directors' term of office shall continue until the conclusion of the annual shareholders meeting for the last business year which ends within one (1) year from the time of their election.

Article 21 (Representative Director and Other Directors)

(1) The representative director shall be elected by a resolution of the Board of Directors.
(2) The Board of Directors may by its resolution designate one (1) chairperson and president, and a number of vice-presidents, senior managing directors and managing directors.

Article 22 (Convener of the Board of Directors and Chairperson)

(1) The Chairperson of the Board of Directors shall convene the meetings of the Board of Directors except where otherwise provided in laws and regulations, and shall act as the chairperson.
(2) If the Chairperson is unable to act or there is a vacancy, the President shall convene the meetings of the Board of Directors and act as chairperson thereof, and if the President is unable to act, another director designated by the order of priority determined in advance by the Board of Directors shall convene the meeting of the Board of Directors and act as the chairperson.

Article 23 (Convocation Notice of the Board of Directors)

(1) A notice convening a meeting of the Board of Directors shall be sent to each director and company auditor at least three days prior to the meeting; provided, however, that in cases of urgency, such period may be shortened.
(2) If consent has been given by all of the directors and company auditors, the meeting of the Board of Directors may be held without the formality of convening procedures.

Article 24 (Omission of the Resolution of the Board of Directors)

If the Company satisfies the requirements of Article 370 of the Companies Act, a resolution of the Board of Directors shall be deemed to have been made.

Article 25 (Regulations of the Board of Directors)

The matters pertaining to the Board of Directors shall, in addition to laws and regulations and these Articles of Incorporation, be governed by the Regulations of the Board of Directors stipulated by the Board of Directors.

Article 26 (Remuneration)

The financial benefits such as remuneration, bonuses and other considerations for the execution of duties of the directors (hereinafter collectively referred to as 'Remuneration'), which are to be given by the Company, shall be determined by a resolution of the shareholders meeting.

Article 27 (Exemption of Liabilities of Directors)

(1) The Company may, pursuant to Article 426, paragraph 1 of the Companies Act, exempt directors (including persons who were formerly directors) from liability for the damages caused by a failure to perform their duties by a resolution of the Board of Directors within the extent permitted by laws and regulations.
(2) The Company may, pursuant to Article 427, paragraph 1 of the Companies Act, enter into a contract with outside directors, which limits the maximum amount of liability for the damages caused by a failure to perform their duties; provided, however, that the maximum limit based on such contract is whichever is the higher of an amount equal to or more than JPY X, which has been determined in advance, or an amount prescribed in laws and regulations.

CHAPTER 5 COMPANY AUDITORS AND THE BOARD OF AUDITORS

Article 28 (Number of Company Auditors)

The company auditors of the Company shall be within xx members.

Article 29 (Method of Election of the Company Auditors)

(1) The company auditors shall be elected at the shareholders meetings.
(2) Resolutions for the election of company auditors shall be made by a majority of the votes of the attending shareholders holding not less than one-third of the voting rights of shareholders entitled to exercise their voting rights.

Article 30 (Company Auditors' Term of Office)

(1) Company auditors' term of office shall continue until the conclusion of the annual shareholders meeting for the last business year which ends within four (4) years from their election.
(2) The term of office of a company auditor elected as the substitute for a company auditor who retired from office before the expiration of the term of office, shall continue until the time the term of office of the company auditor who retired from office expires.

Article 31 (Full-Time Company Auditors)

The Board of Auditors shall by its resolution elect full-time company auditors.

Article 32 (Convocation Notice of the Board of Auditors)

(1) A notice convening a meeting of the Board of Auditors shall be sent to each company auditor at least three days prior to the meeting; provided, however, that in cases of urgency, such period may be shortened.
(2) If consent has been given by all of the company auditors, the meeting of the Board of Auditors may be held without the formality of the convening procedures.

Article 33 (Regulations of the Board of Auditors)

The matters pertaining to the Board of Auditors shall, in addition to laws and regulations and these Articles of Incorporation, be governed by the Regulations of the Board of Auditors stipulated by the Board of Auditors.

Article 34 (Remuneration)

Remuneration of the company auditors shall be determined by a resolution of the shareholders meeting.

Article 35 (Exemption of Liabilities of Company Auditors)

(1) The Company may, pursuant to Article 426, paragraph 1 of the Companies Act, exempt company auditors (including persons who were formerly company auditors) from liability for the damages caused by a failure to perform their duties by a resolution of the Board of Directors within the extent permitted by laws and regulations.

(2) The Company may, pursuant to Article 427, paragraph 1 of the Companies Act, enter into a contract with outside company auditors, which limits the maximum amount of liability for the damages caused by a failure to perform their duties; provided, however, that the maximum limit based on such contract is whichever is the higher of an amount equal to or more than JPY X, which has been determined in advance, or an amount prescribed in laws and regulations.

CHAPTER 6 ACCOUNTS

Article 36 (Business Year)

The business year of the Company shall be for one (1) year commencing on April 1 of each year and ending on March 31 of the following year.

Article 37 (Decision-Making Organ for Dividends of Surplus, Etc.)

The Company may determine the matters provided in each item of Article 459, paragraph 1 of the Companies Act such as the dividends of surplus by a resolution of the Board of Directors without a resolution of a shareholders meeting, except where otherwise provided in laws and regulations.

Article 38 (Record Date of Dividends of Surplus)

(1) The record date for the distribution of year-end dividends of the Company shall be March 31 of each year.
(2) The record date for the distribution of interim dividends of the Company shall be September 30 of each year.
(3) In addition to the preceding two paragraphs, a record date may be established to distribute dividends of surplus.

Article 39 (Expiration Period of Dividends)

In cases where the dividends are paid in cash, the Company shall be exempted from the obligation to pay dividends if such dividends remain unreceived for three (3) years after the date of the commencement of payment thereof.

Chapter 2. Shares

§1. Capital and Shares

I. Shares

307. Shares represent the status of a shareholder as the constituent member of stock company and are equity interests that have been divided into small parts. By dividing the equity interests into small parts, the company may finance a significant amount of funds from a large number of investors. This also allows the investors to acquire such number of shares in accordance with their investment purpose or funding capacity. As such, each shareholder will have the rights as a shareholder in proportion to the number of shares that it holds. On the other hand, in a membership company, each member has one equity interest of differing sizes (see paragraph 1009).

308. Shares may not be subdivided into smaller parts to create partial shares. However, a share can be owned jointly by a number of persons.[209]

309. Shares include various types of rights against the company which may be classified into the following two groups based on their purpose:

(i) Rights to receive economic benefits from the company (right to self-interest): mainly the right to dividends of surplus and the right to distribution of residual assets.[210] Other rights to self-interest include an appraisal right which entitles the shareholders to request purchase of shares by the company.[211]
(ii) Rights to participate in the management and operations of the company (right to common benefits): mainly the right to vote at shareholders meetings.[212] Other rights to common benefits include, among others, the right to seek revocation of a shareholder resolution, the right to file derivative action, the right to enjoin acts of directors, etc., the shareholders' right to propose, the right to convene a shareholders meeting, the right to demand dismissal of directors, etc., the right to inspect accounting books and the right to demand dissolution.[213]

310. Certain shareholder rights, such as the right to dividends of surplus and voting rights, may be exercised by a shareholder holding just one share (sole shareholder right). On the other hand, there are other shareholder rights, such as the shareholders' right to propose, the right to convene a shareholders meeting and the right to inspect accounting books, that can only be exercised by shareholders who

209. see Art. 106, Companies Act.
210. Article 105, para. 1, items 1 and 2, Companies Act.
211. Article 116, para. 1; Art. 469, para. 1; Art. 785, para. 1, Companies Act.
212. Article 105, para. 1, item 3, Companies Act.
213. Article 831, para. 1; Art. 847; Art. 360, para. 1; Art. 303, para. 1; Art. 297, para. 1; Art. 854, para. 1; Art. 433, para. 1; Art. 833, para. 1, Companies Act.

hold at least a certain percentage of all shareholders' voting rights or a certain number of shares (minority shareholder right) (see paragraphs 563, 566, 586). The threshold of minority shareholder rights is intended to prevent any abusive use of the shareholder rights.

311. Under the principle of equal treatment of shareholders (*kabunushi byoudou no gensoku*), the shareholders must be treated equally in accordance with the features and number of shares that they hold, as far as the shareholders' capacity as a shareholder is concerned.[214] While different treatment may be permitted with regard to various classes of shares that have differing features, shares with the same features must be treated equally in accordance with the number of shares held by each shareholder; however, in certain limited circumstances where there are reasonable grounds to do so, certain different treatment may be permitted. For example, voting rights are not granted to the shareholders holding less than one unit (see paragraph 364).[215] Moreover, in non-Public Companies, it may be prescribed in the articles of incorporation that the shareholders' rights (see paragraph 309) will be treated differently on an individual shareholder basis because in such companies it is generally expected that the shareholders have a close relationship with one another and changes in the shareholders do not occur frequently.[216]

II. Stated Capital (*Shihonkin*)

312. In a stock company, the shareholders owe limited liability to the extent of the subscription price of the shares that they hold.[217] As a result, the company's creditors may recourse only against the company's assets for the payment of their claims. While the company's assets may fluctuate depending on the state of its business, the stock companies are generally expected to maintain a certain level of assets equivalent to the amount of the company's stated capital. The amount of the company's stated capital must be commercially registered.[218]

313. With an aim to ensure that the assets equivalent to the amount of stated capital are contributed in the company, the Companies Act provides strict regulations on contributions in kind and property assumption (see paragraph 259–266) and prohibition on the set-off of contributions by the subscribers.[219]

314. Legal reserves (*houtei junbikin*) also functions so that the amount of stated capital will be reserved in the company. The legal reserves which must be accumulated as required by law include the retained earnings reserve (*rieki junbikin*) and capital reserve (*shihon junbikin*). The retained earnings reserve will be accumulated based on the profits of the company. If the company generates profit, a portion of

214. Article 109, para. 1, Companies Act.
215. Article 189, para. 1, Companies Act.
216. Article 109, para. 2, Companies Act.
217. Article 104, Companies Act.
218. Article 911, para. 3, item 5, Companies Act.
219. Article 208, para. 3, Companies Act.

such profit will be accumulated to provide for future losses. On the other hand, the capital reserve will be accumulated based on funds other than the profits of the company. The legal reserves may be used for such purposes as supplementing deficits in the stated capital or inclusion into the stated capital. A deficit in the capital (*shihon no kesson*) means that the amount of net assets (i.e., assets minus liabilities) is less than the aggregate amount of stated capital and legal reserves. In this case, the deficit can be supplemented by reducing the amount of legal reserves equivalent to the shortfall. Either the capital reserve or the profits reserve may be used for this purpose. On the other hand, the company may transfer all or part of the legal reserves into the stated capital by an ordinary resolution at the shareholders meeting.[220] The legal reserves may also be reduced by an ordinary resolution at the shareholders meeting.[221] In addition, reduction of the reserves requires creditor protection procedures (see paragraph 370).[222]

315. A company is required to accumulate 10% of the amount to be distributed as dividends into the capital reserve or retained earnings reserve.[223] The amount of reserves may also be increased by transferring the surplus by a resolution at the shareholders meeting.[224]

III. Stated Capital and Shares

A. *Amount of Stated Capital and 'Total Amount of Shares' (*Kabukin Sougaku*)*

316. Under the Commercial Code prior to its amendment in 1950, the amount of the stated capital was required to be equal to the total amount of shares. The 'total amount of shares' is equal to the amount of the par value share certificate multiplied by the total number of issued shares. However, currently, par value shares have been abolished, and with regard to no-par value shares, the total paid-in amount (or in cases of contributions in kind, the amount of the contribution) will, in principle, be the amount of stated capital.[225]

317. Nonetheless, an amount not exceeding half of the total paid-in amount is not required to be recorded as stated capital (i.e., the amount of stated capital must be equal to or more than the total paid-in amount x 1/2).[226] In this case, the amount not included in stated capital must be recorded as capital reserve.[227] In practice, as a result of the large volume of equity finances in the 1980s, a large amount of capital reserves were accumulated. Therefore, the 2001 amendment to the Commercial

220. Article 448, para. 1, item 2; Art. 309, para. 1, Companies Act.
221. Article 448, para. 1, item 1, Companies Act.
222. Article 449, Companies Act.
223. Article 445, para. 4, Companies Act.
224. Article 451, Companies Act.
225. Article 445, para. 1, Companies Act.
226. Article 445, para. 2, Companies Act.
227. Article 445, para. 3, Companies Act.

Code allowed the amount of legal reserves to be reduced by a shareholder resolution so that such amount may be used as the dividend resources.[228] While the same amendment provided that an amount equivalent to 25% of the stated capital must be maintained as reserves, the Companies Act has no such restrictions (therefore, the entire amount of the reserves may be reduced).

*B. Share Split (*Kabushiki Bunkatsu*)*

1. Overview

318. A stock company may split its shares to create a larger number of outstanding shares in smaller units.[229]

319. Prior to the amendment to the Commercial Code in 1990, issuance of new shares without consideration (*shinkabu no mushou koufu*) and share dividends (*kabushiki haitou*) were provided separately from share splits. In issuance of new shares without consideration, it was funded by appropriating the amount exceeding the total amount of shares in stated capital or by transferring a certain amount of legal reserves into stated capital. Share dividends meant issuance of new shares by transferring the distributable earnings into stated capital. These were all recharacterized as share splits by the amendment to the Commercial Code in 1990.

320. In a share split, the net assets of the company will not increase and only the aggregate number of issued shares increases. Therefore, if one share is split into 1.1, one share will be issued for every ten shares.

321. If the split-ratio is large, for example, in cases where one share is split into two shares, the share price will be lowered and the liquidity of shares increases. On the other hand, if the split-ratio is small (e.g., one share is split into 1.1 share), the substantive effect of the share split will be to increase the dividends. This is because, in such cases, since Japanese companies tend to maintain the amount of annual dividends per share, shareholders will receive a larger amount of dividends if the number of shares they hold increases by the share split. In such case, the share price tends to instead increase.

2. Share Split Procedures

322. Share split may be implemented by a resolution of the board of directors, where the company has a board of directors (in other companies, by a resolution at shareholders meeting).[230] This is because the interests of the existing shareholders will not be harmed by a share split. If the aggregate number of issued shares after

228. Corresponding to Art. 448 in the Companies Act.
229. Article 183, para. 1, Companies Act.
230. Article 183, para. 2.

the share split will exceed the number of authorized shares (see paragraphs 437–439), the company may amend the articles of incorporation to increase the number of authorized shares in accordance with the ratio of the share split without a resolution at the shareholders meeting.[231]

323. The Companies Act requires the total number of authorized shares to be provided in the articles of incorporation to set a cut-off point for the disadvantages that may be suffered by the existing shareholders upon the dilution of shares to occur if new shares are issued. In a share split, since new shares are delivered to the existing shareholders in accordance with the number of shares that they hold, the shareholding ratio will not change. Therefore, an amendment to the articles of incorporation is permitted for this purpose without a special resolution at the shareholders meeting.

324. In a company issuing two or more classes of shares, a change in the number of authorized shares will affect the interests of the existing shareholders. For example, if preferred shares are split, the total amount of preferred dividends will increase. Therefore, the abovementioned amendment to the articles of incorporation may not be made by a resolution of the board of directors in such cases.[232]

325. Unless otherwise provided in the articles of incorporation, a company must give public notice of the record date and the details of the share split two weeks before the record date for such share split.[233] The number of shares held by shareholders that are listed in the shareholder registry as of the record date will increase in accordance with the split-ratio on the effective date specified by the company.[234] The number of treasury shares held by the company will also increase.

326. Prior to the amendment to the Commercial Code in 2001, the share split was not permitted if the amount of net assets per share after the share split was less than JPY 50,000. This was intended to avoid the unit of contribution by shareholders to be excessively subdivided by the share split. In the amendment to the Commercial Code in 2001, such restriction was abolished as the size of contribution unit was left to the discretion of the company.

327. Allotment of shares without consideration (*kabushiki musho wariate*) is where a company allots the shares to shareholders without requiring additional contribution from the shareholders.[235] Unless otherwise provided in the articles of incorporation, the allotment of shares without contribution may be implemented by a resolution of the board of directors in Companies with Board of Directors (in other companies, by a shareholder resolution).[236] In the allotment of shares without consideration, the shareholders of a certain class may be allotted not only the same class

231. Article 184, para. 2, Companies Act.
232. Article 184, para. 2, Companies Act.
233. Article 124, para. 3, Companies Act.
234. Article 184, para. 1, Companies Act.
235. Article 185, Companies Act.
236. Article 186, para. 3, Companies Act.

of shares that they hold but also different classes of shares (e.g., class A shareholders may be allotted class B shares).[237] In this regard, it is different from a share split, which increases the number of shares of the same class. Another differing point is that, in the allotment of shares without consideration, no shares will be allotted to the treasury shares and furthermore the existing treasury shares may be used as the shares to be delivered to the allotted shareholders.

C. *Consolidation of Shares (*Kabushiki No Heigou*) and Cancellation of Shares (*Kabushiki No Shoukyaku*)*

1. Consolidation of Shares

328. A stock company may consolidate two or more shares to one share so that there will be a smaller number of issued shares (e.g., two shares may be combined into one).[238] This is known as consolidation of shares (*kabushiki no heigou*). In a consolidation of shares, there is no change in the company assets or in the amount of stated capital. However, it may have a significant impact on the interests of the shareholders as the shares that they hold may be forced into fractional shares as a result thereof. Therefore, consolidation of shares requires a special resolution at the shareholders meeting.[239]

329. In consolidation of shares, a notice must be sent to the shareholders to inform them of (i) the ratio of consolidation, (ii) the effective date, and (iii) in case of a corporation with class shares, the classes of shares to be consolidated, at least two weeks before the effective date (a public notice may be used in lieu of such notice).[240] The directors must explain the reasons for the need to consolidate the shares at the shareholders meeting.[241] A share certificate issuing company must notify the shareholders one month in advance for the shareholders to submit their share certificates before the effective date of consolidation of shares (such procedures will not be required for companies other than share certificate issuing companies).[242] If a shareholder is unable to submit their share certificates, at the request of such shareholder, the company may give public notice to interested parties that an objection may be stated within a given period (at least three months). If no objection is stated within this given period, post-consolidation share certificates may be delivered to such shareholder.[243] Consolidation of shares does not automatically affect the total number of authorized shares.

330. A company may use consolidation of shares at its subsidiary as a means of removing minority shareholders of that subsidiary and making it a wholly-owned

237. See Art. 186, para. 1, item 1, Companies Act.
238. Article 180, para. 1, Companies Act.
239. Article 180, para. 2; Art. 309, para. 2, item 4, Companies Act.
240. Article 180, para. 2; Art. 181, Companies Act.
241. Article 180, para. 3, Companies Act.
242. Article 219, para. 1, Companies Act.
243. Article 220, Companies Act.

subsidiary. Specifically, a company may squeeze out minority shareholders by using consolidation of shares to change the number of shares held by the minority shareholders into fractions and then delivering cash to such shareholders (i.e., the proceeds from the sale of the number of shares equivalent to the aggregate of those fractions will be delivered to the shareholders in proportion to the fractions attributed to them).[244] However, such consolidation of shares could result in a large volume of shares in fractions, and there is a risk that adequate consideration may not be delivered due to circumstances such as sharp drop in the market share price. There is also a large impact on the rights of shareholders in that many of them lose their status as shareholders. Given the foregoing concerns, certain procedures aimed at shareholder protection are required to be undertaken in the process of a consolidation of shares.

331. The company must notify shareholders, etc., of matters relating to the consolidation of shares no later than two weeks prior to the date on which the consolidation takes effect (notice may instead be made by way of public notice).[245] Further, the company must keep documents or electronic records on which such matters are stated or recorded at its head office and make them available for inspection by shareholders.[246]

332. Shareholders who will be allocated fractions of shares as a result of the consolidation of shares may notify the company in advance of the resolution by the shareholders meeting to the effect that they are opposed to the consolidation of shares, and after voting against the resolution may demand the company to purchase their shares at a fair price.[247] Further, if such consolidation of shares violates the articles of incorporation of the company and there is a risk that the shareholders may suffer disadvantage, the shareholders may demand the company to cease the consolidation of shares.[248] These provisions were introduced with the 2014 amendment.

2. Cancellation of Shares

333. Cancellation of shares means to cancel particular shares. Conceptually, there is compulsory cancellation, which will be implemented regardless of the will of shareholders holding such cancelled shares, and voluntary cancellation, which will be carried out by repurchasing the shares from the shareholders. In addition, depending on whether or not the shareholders will be paid any consideration, there may be cancellation of shares with consideration and cancellation of shares without consideration.

244. Article 235, Companies Act.
245. Article 181, para. 1 and para. 2, Companies Act.
246. Article 182-2, Companies Act.
247. Article 182-4, para. 1 and para. 2, Companies Act.
248. Article 182-3, Companies Act.

334. Prior to its amendment in 2005, the Commercial Code allowed cancellation of shares in cases of (i) cancellation of treasury shares, (ii) reduction of stated capital and (iii) cancellation of shares using distributable profits.[249] In item (i) above, the company will repurchase the shares from the shareholders for subsequent cancellation, while in items (ii) and (iii) the shares held by the shareholders will be cancelled without the company repurchasing such shares. From the perspective of shareholders, however, the shareholders will in any event receive consideration in exchange for forfeiting their shares. As such, the Companies Act unified the concepts so that any cancellation of shares will take place after the shares are repurchased by the company as treasury shares.

335. As discussed above, the Companies Act only provides cancellation of treasury shares. To cancel treasury shares, the company must specify the number of treasury shares to be cancelled (for a corporation with class shares, the classes of the shares and the number of shares for each class).[250] In a Company with Board of Directors, cancellation of shares must be made by a resolution of the board of directors.[251]

IV. No-Par Value Shares (*Mugakumen Kabushiki*)

336. Prior to the amendment to the Commercial Code in 2001, companies could issue both par value shares and no-par value shares. Par value shares have a face value per share. In issuing par value shares, the face value was required to be specified in the articles of incorporation as well as on the share certificate.

337. On the other hand, no-par value shares have no face value. It was introduced by the amendment to the Commercial Code in 1950 modelling on the US law. While there was no difference between par value shares and no-par value shares with regard to the rights and obligations of the shareholders, no-par value shares could be issued at the current market price, whereas par value shares could not be issued at a price lower than the face value.

338. The face value of par value shares represented nothing more than the historical fact that an amount equivalent to the face value was paid into the capital at the time of issuance. It did not represent the then current market price. In addition, it does not represent the substantive value of the equity interest held by the shareholders. As such, the face value of the par value shares was not significant and therefore, by the amendment in 2001, the par value shares system was abolished. Nonetheless, the amendment did not prohibit the statement of face value on the share certificates.

249. Article 213, para. 1; Art. 222, para. 1, item 4 of the Commercial Code prior to amendment.
250. Article 178, para. 1, Companies Act.
251. Article 178, para. 2, Companies Act.

339. Under the Companies Act, a company may provide in the articles of incorporation that it will issue share certificates for its shares.[252] In other words, share certificates will be issued only if so provided in the articles of incorporation. A company which has provided in the articles of incorporation that it will issue share certificates is known as a 'share certificate issuing company' (*kabuken hakkou kaisha*). In a share certificate issuing company, to the extent that the company is not a Public Company, share certificates need not be issued until so requested by the shareholders.[253]

V. Features (*Naiyou*) and Classes (*Shurui*) of Shares

A. *Classes of Shares*

340. The Companies Act allows the diversification of shares under certain conditions. First, the company may establish the following special terms as the features of all issued shares: (i) the requirement to obtain approval of the company for acquisition of shares by assignment (i.e., shares with restrictions on transfer), (ii) the shareholder may demand that the company acquire such shares (shares with put option), and (iii) the company may acquire such shares upon certain grounds arising (shares subject to call).[254] In these cases, there are no classes of shares because the terms are identical for all shares.

341. Second, the Companies Act allows multiple classes of shares with different features (corporation with class shares).[255] The features of class shares have the following nine categories:

(i) dividends of surplus;
(ii) distribution of residual assets;
(iii) voting rights at shareholders meeting (shares with restricted voting rights);
(iv) requirement to obtain approval of the company for acquisition of class shares by assignment (shares with restrictions on transfer);
(v) the shareholders may demand that the company acquire such class shares (shares with put option);
(vi) the company may acquire such class shares on condition of certain grounds arising (shares subject to call);
(vii) the company may acquire all of such class shares by resolution of shareholders meeting (shares subject to wholly call);
(viii) requirement that certain prescribed matters be resolved by class meeting (shares with veto rights);
(ix) requirement that directors and company auditors be appointed by class meeting.[256]

252. Article 214, Companies Act.
253. Article 215, para. 4, Companies Act.
254. Article 107, para. 1, Companies Act.
255. Article 2, item 13, Companies Act.
256. Article 108, para. 1, Companies Act.

In addition, non-Public Companies are allowed to prescribe in the articles of incorporation that each shareholder will be treated differently with respect to dividends of surplus, distribution of residual assets and voting rights (see paragraph 311).[257] Such shares will be deemed as class shares with different features for purposes of the provisions on stock companies and entity conversion, etc., under the Companies Act.[258]

342. If a company has issued different classes of shares, there will be a need to balance the rights of shareholders having different classes of shares. For this purpose, the Companies Act has established a class meeting composed of the shareholders of each class (see paragraph 587).

B. Preferred Shares and Subordinated Shares

343. Preferred shares take priority over common shares in dividends of surplus and distribution of residual assets. The features of class shares and the total number of authorized shares in each class share must be prescribed in the articles of incorporation.[259] It may be provided in the articles of incorporation that the amount of preferred dividends will be determined by the resolution of the board of directors in Company with Board of Directors or at the shareholders meeting for all other companies so that the financing may be implemented in a timely manner, subject to the changes in interest rates.[260] In such case, the articles of incorporation must at least specify the outline of amount of dividends.

344. A so-called tracking stock will have its value linked to the performance of a particular business division or subsidiary operated by the company. The issuing company may obtain financing from the capital market on favourable terms that reflect the performance of particular business, while keeping such business within the company. While it is precisely not a 'preferred' share as the amount of dividends may be zero depending on the performance of such business, it will have different features on dividends of surplus and an outline of the amount of dividends must be prescribed in the articles of incorporation.

345. Cumulative preferred shares will have a shortfall in the dividends for a certain accounting period to be carried over to the following period, in cases where all or some of the preferred dividends have not been paid. Shares for which the shortfall is not to be carried over are known as non-cumulative preferred shares. In addition, the preferred shares may be categorized into participating preferred shares, pursuant to which, after the preferred shareholder has received preferred dividends, such preferred shareholder may receive further allocation of profit if there is any remaining profit to be distributed as dividends to the shareholders of common

257. Article 109, para. 2; Art. 309, para. 4, Companies Act.
258. Article 190, para. 3, Companies Act.
259. Article 108, para. 2, items 1 and 2, Companies Act.
260. Article 108, para. 3, Companies Act.

shares, and non-participating preferred shares, in which the preferred shareholder does not receive such further allocation.

346. Subordinated shares will be subordinated to common shares in the distribution of dividends and residual assets. They are also known as deferred shares. The features of subordinated shares must be provided in the articles of incorporation.[261]

C. Shares with Restricted Voting Rights

347. Companies may issue shares with different features on voting rights.[262] In the past, shares with no voting rights were allowed only where such shares had preferred dividends. In the Companies Act, companies may issue common shares without voting rights. However, in a Public Company, the total number of shares with restricted voting rights must not exceed half of the total number of issued shares.[263] Shares with no voting rights are typically issued to shareholders who expect to receive distribution of dividends of surplus but have no interest in exercising voting rights. The company may save on the cost of sending out convocation notices and, moreover, obtain financing without any change in control of the company. Furthermore, it is possible to grant voting rights on certain limited matters only. For example, shares having voting rights only for changes to the organization of the company, such as merger, is permitted.

*D. Shares with Put Option (*Shutoku Seikyuken Tsuki Kabushiki*)*

348. Companies may issue shares with put option which allows the shareholders to demand that the issuing company repurchase such shares.[264] Prior to its amendment in 2005, the Commercial Code allowed the shares which may be converted into another class of share (known as shares with conversion option. Prior to the amendment in 2001, these were known as convertible shares).[265] Under the Companies Act, a similar result may be achieved by the company acquiring class shares with put option in exchange for other class shares. The company may deliver bonds, share options or other property in exchange for the acquisition.

349. Prior to its amendment in 2005, the Commercial Code allowed shares which were scheduled to be cancelled by the profits of the company (redeemable shares). Where the consideration for the acquisition of shares with put option is cash, it will be an equivalent to redeemable shares.

261. Article 108, para. 2, item 1 and item 2, Companies Act.
262. Article 108, para. 1, item 3, Companies Act.
263. Article 115, Companies Act.
264. Article 2, item 18; Art. 107, para. 1, item 2; Art. 108, para. 1, item 5, Companies Act.
265. Article 222-2, para. 1, Commercial Code prior to amendment.

350. Companies may issue all of the shares as shares with put option.[266] Alternatively, it may issue a portion of its shares as shares with put option.[267] In the former case, because all shares of the company will have identical features, no shares of the company may be delivered in exchange for the acquisition of shares with put option, and in the latter case, as the company may issue classes of shares with different features, it may deliver shares having different features in exchange for the shares with put option.

*E. Shares Subject to Call (*Shutoku Joukou Tsuki Kabushiki*)*

351. Companies may issue shares subject to call which allows the issuing company to acquire the shares from the shareholders on condition of certain grounds arising.[268] While the company will acquire the shares upon the request of the shareholders in shares with put option, in shares subject to call, the shareholders will be forced to give up the shares. Prior to the amendment to the Commercial Code in 2005, the companies were permitted to issue shares which will be converted by the company into a different class of shares upon the occurrence of certain grounds prescribed in the articles of incorporation (known as shares subject to compulsory conversion).[269] In the Companies Act, the same result may be achieved by issuing shares subject to call pursuant to which such shares will be acquired by the company in exchange for the other shares of the company. For example, the preferred shares may be issued as shares subject to call which will be acquired by the company on condition of certain grounds arising in exchange for common shares. It may also be structured to compulsorily redeem the shares by providing that cash will be paid in exchange for acquiring such shares.

352. Companies may issue all of the shares as shares subject to call.[270] Alternatively, it may issue a portion of its shares as shares subject to call in the form of class shares.[271] Common shares may be changed to shares subject to call by amending the features of such shares prescribed in the articles of incorporation. Such amendment to the articles of incorporation requires the consent of all shareholders holding such shares because such shares will be acquired by the company upon the occurrence of certain events without the consent of the shareholders.[272]

*F. Shares Subject to Wholly Call (*Zenbu Shutoku Joukou Tsuki Kabushiki*)*

353. Shares subject to wholly call are shares pursuant to which the company may acquire all of such shares by a special resolution at the shareholders meeting

266. Article 107, para. 1, item 2, Companies Act.
267. Article 108, para. 1, item 5, Companies Act.
268. Article 2, item 19; Art. 107, para. 1, item 3; Art. 108, para. 1, item 6, Companies Act.
269. Article 222-8, first part, Commercial Code prior to amendment.
270. Article 107, para. 1, item 3, Companies Act.
271. Article 108, para. 1, item 6, Companies Act.
272. Article 110; Art. 111, para. 1, Companies Act.

(Article 108, paragraph 1, item 7, Companies Act). In general, if the company intends to acquire the shares of all shareholders, the consent of all shareholders will be required. However, in cases of 100% capital reduction of a near bankrupt company (i.e., cancellation of all existing shares to replace all shareholders), such a strict requirement will hinder the flexibility of voluntary capital restructuring arrangement. Therefore, the Companies Act did not require the consent of all shareholders to acquire shares subject to wholly call.

354. Amendment to the articles of incorporation by a special resolution at shareholders meeting will be required to change the terms of existing shares to shares subject to wholly call.[273] After such change, a special resolution at the shareholders meeting will also be required for the company to actually acquire the shares subject to wholly call.[274] In cases of acquiring shares subject to call (see paragraph 351), an ordinary resolution at shareholders meeting will suffice (a resolution of the board of directors in Companies with Board of Directors).[275] On the other hand, a special resolution will be required to acquire shares subject to wholly call. With regard to the former, the material terms of the company's call option, including consideration of the acquisition, are prescribed in the articles of incorporation. In contrast, in the latter, the terms of the wholly call may not be clear in the articles of incorporation as it is sufficient to prescribe only the method for determining the value of the acquisition price in the articles.[276] Therefore, a strict voting requirement is provided to acquire shares subject to wholly call to determine the acquisition price at the shareholders meeting. Dissenting shareholders will be granted the right to request the company to purchase his or her shares.[277]

G. *Shares with Veto Rights*

355. Companies may issue class shares which require a resolution of class meeting, in addition to the resolution at a shareholders meeting, with regard to particular matters as prescribed in the articles of incorporation (see paragraph 587, Class meeting).[278] Such class shares were introduced by the amendment to the Commercial Code in November 2001, in which veto rights were permitted to be granted to the shareholders of certain classes of shares with regard to the resolution matters at the shareholders meeting.

356. For example, in a financing transaction of a venture company from venture capital, the founder and venture capital may agree in a shareholders agreement that certain matters, such as organizational changes and share equity financings, may not be implemented by the company without the consent of the venture capital, who will

273. Article 309, para. 2, item 11; Art. 466, Companies Act.
274. Article 171, para. 1; Art. 309, para. 2, item 3, Companies Act.
275. Article 168, para. 1; Art. 169, para. 1, Companies Act.
276. Article 108, para. 2, item 7, Companies Act.
277. Article 116, para. 1, item 2, Companies Act.
278. Article 108, para. 1, item 8, Companies Act.

be the minority shareholder of the company. However, as a matter of corporate law, it may be difficult for the venture capital to invalidate such matters if such matters are approved by the shareholder resolution or resolution of the board of directors. Taking into account such concerns of venture capitals, the Companies Act permitted veto rights to be granted on a wide range of matters.

H. Shares with Rights to Elect Directors and Company Auditors

357. Traditionally, venture capital firms obtained a commitment from other shareholders in a shareholders agreement with regard to its right to designate a certain number of directors after the closing of their investment in the company. There was a concern, however, that if a resolution is passed by a majority of shareholders on appointment directors in contravention of such shareholder agreement, such resolution may not be invalidated. While shares with veto rights were allowed as described above, minority shareholders could only veto the proposal for appointment of such director at the class meeting (i.e., limited to passive resistance not to allow the appointment of the director). Therefore, in the amendment to the Commercial Code in 2002, companies having restrictions on share transfer were permitted to issue classes of shares with different features with regard to the appointment of directors and company auditors.[279] In such cases, the directors and company auditors will be appointed at the class meeting of such class shareholders.

358. Under the Companies Act, companies that are neither a Company with Nominating Committee, etc., nor Public Company may issue such class shares.[280] The issuing company must prescribe in the articles of incorporation the total number of authorized shares in such class share, as well as the number of directors and company auditors to be elected.[281] The directors and company auditors appointed at a class meeting may be dismissed at any time by a resolution at the class meeting that made the election.[282]

VI. Share Unit (*Tangen Kabu*)

A. Overview

359. The share unit is a unit of a certain prescribed number of shares that will be granted one voting right at sharcholders meeting or class meeting. This is intended to save the management costs incurred by the company by allowing the company to omit the sending of convocation notices to shareholders holding less than such number of shares constituting a share unit.

279. Article 222, para. 1, item 6, Commercial Code prior to amendment.
280. Article 108, para. 1, item 9, proviso to para. 1.
281. Article 108, para. 2, item 9, Companies Act.
282. Article 347, paras 1 and 2, Companies Act.

360. Prior to the amendment to the Commercial Code in 2001, round-lot shares (*tanyi kabu*), that rounded 1,000 shares for shares with a JPY 50 par value and 100 shares for shares with a JPY 500 par value as one rounded-lot were used to cut down on such costs. The rounded-lot shares were mandatory for listed companies, whereas non-listed companies could elect to prescribe the number of shares for one round-lot in the articles of incorporation. As the par value of shares was later abolished (see paragraph 338), the round-lot shares were eliminated and, in their place, share units were introduced. Unlike the round-lot shares which was an interim measure established in the supplementary provisions of the amendment to the Commercial Code, the share units were introduced as a permanent system.

361. Prior to the enactment of the Companies Act, the Commercial Code permitted fractional shares (*hakabu*).[283] At the time, the shareholders could occasionally end up with fractional shares under certain circumstances, such as implementation of consolidation of shares or share split. As the economic value of fractional shares may possibly be significant in companies having a large value on a per share basis, certain shareholder rights such as right to receive dividends of surplus was granted to fractional shares constituting the integral multiple of one hundredth of one share (subject to restrictions by the articles of incorporation). The share units and fractional shares commonly grant certain shareholders rights other than voting rights to the holders of such shares. On this basis, these two were integrated under the Companies Act into the share units by abolishing the fractional shares (the rights of unit holders may be specified in the articles of incorporation to be the same as the rights of the holders of fractional shares (see paragraph 364)). The reason given for continuing the share unit system rather than the fractional share system was that more companies employed the share unit system than the fractional share system.

362. Companies may voluntarily introduce a share unit system by the articles of incorporation.[284] In determining the number of shares constituting one unit, one unit of shares must not exceed 1,000 shares because prescribing an excessively large unit may be detrimental to small shareholders.[285] To amend the articles of incorporation and introduce a share unit system, directors must provide an explanation of the need for such alteration at the shareholders meeting.[286]

363. A share split may be carried out by a resolution of the board of directors in Companies with Board of Directors (see paragraph 318, Share split).[287] However, if a share split is carried out, the total number of voting rights will increase in the same proportion and the cost of administrating the shareholders will also increase. If the number of shares constituting one unit is set or increased at the same time in proportion to the share split, the changes to the total number of voting rights will not

283. Articles 220-2 et seq., Commercial Code prior to amendment.
284. Article 188, para. 1, Companies Act.
285. Article 188, para. 2, Companies Act; Art. 34, Ordinance for Enforcement of the Companies Act.
286. Article 190, Companies Act.
287. Article 183, para. 2, Companies Act.

occur. In such case, there is no change in the rights of the shareholders. Therefore, if the number of shares constituting one unit is set or increased at the same time as the share split, subject to certain conditions, the Companies Act allows an amendment to the articles of incorporation with regard to the number of shares constituting one unit to be effected without the shareholder resolution.[288] If the number of shares constituting one unit will be reduced or share units will be abolished, such amendment to the articles of incorporation may also be made without the shareholder resolution (a resolution of the board of directors in Companies with Board of Directors; a decision by directors in other companies) as there is no disadvantage for the shareholders.[289]

B. Rights of Shareholders Having Less than One Unit

364. Shareholders of shares of less than one unit are not permitted to vote at the shareholders meeting or class meeting.[290] In addition, such shareholders are not entitled to the rights to ask questions or make proposals, or other similar rights that presuppose voting rights. Yet, such shareholders may, in principle, exercise other rights as a shareholder of the company; provided, however, that the company may prescribe in the articles of incorporation that the rights of such shareholders may not be exercised. However, no restrictions may be imposed on: (i) the right to receive consideration for shares subject to wholly call, (ii) the right to receive consideration for shares subject to call, (iii) the right to receive allotment of shares without consideration, (iv) the right to request the purchase of shares of less than one unit, (v) the right to receive distribution of residual assets, and (vi) other rights provided by the applicable ordinances.[291] Under the Companies Act, fractional shares were abolished and integrated into share units. Previously, the holders of fractional shares could be subject to further restrictions by the articles of incorporation, including restriction on the right to receive dividends, in addition to the restrictions that may be similarly imposed on the rights of shareholders having less than one unit.[292] Under the Companies Act, the rights of shareholders having less than one unit may be provided by the articles of incorporation to be the same as the rights of holders having former fractional shares.

365. A share certificate issuing company may provide in the articles of incorporation that the company will not issue any share certificates for shares of less than one unit.[293] This will allow the companies to save the costs of issuing share certificates for small numbers of shares. Meanwhile, shareholders may request the company to purchase the shares of less than one unit held by such shareholders to recoup

288. Article 191, Companies Act.
289. Article 195, para. 1, Companies Act.
290. Article 189, para. 1, Companies Act.
291. Article 189, para. 2, Companies Act.
292. Article 220-3, Commercial Code prior to amendment.
293. Article 189, para. 3, Companies Act.

their investments.[294] Furthermore, if so prescribed in the articles of incorporation, shareholders having shares of less than one unit may request the company to sell to such shareholder the additional shares necessary for the shareholder to own one full unit.[295]

VII. Capital Reduction

A. *Reduction of Stated Capital*

366. Reduction of stated capital means reducing the amount of stated capital of the company. The amount of stated capital is booked to protect the company's creditors (see paragraph 312). As a fundamental change in the company, it will also have a large impact on the shareholders. Therefore, a reduction of stated capital requires strict procedures.[296] Similarly, reduction of reserves is also subject to similar procedural requirements.[297]

367. In case the company assets corresponding to the capital are returned to the shareholders, the assets of the company will be reduced in real terms. This is known as a substantive capital reduction. On the other hand, if there is a deficit in the company, the amount of stated capital may be reduced to enable distribution of profits by the company. In this case, the reduction of stated capital will not cause the company assets to be distributed. This is known as nominal capital reduction. In Japan, capital reduction is mostly implemented by the latter method.

368. In a reduction of stated capital, the number of shares issued by the company may also be reduced by cancellation or consolidation of shares.

B. *Procedures for Reduction of Stated Capital*

369. Reduction of stated capital must be carried out by a special resolution at shareholders meeting approving the amount of stated capital and reserves to be reduced.[298] There are no restrictions on the amount of stated capital and reserves to be reduced; provided, however, that the amount to be reduced may not exceed the amount of stated capital and reserve as of the effective date of such reduction (i.e., stated capital may not be minus but may be reduced to zero).[299] The procedural requirements will be eased in cases where the interests of shareholders are not harmed. Namely, if the amount of stated capital or reserves increases by issuing new shares concurrently with the reduction of State capital or reserves, the shareholder

294. Article 192, para. 1, Companies Act.
295. Article 194, para. 1, Companies Act.
296. Articles 447 et seq., Companies Act.
297. Article 448, Companies Act.
298. Article 447, para. 1; Art. 448, para. 1, Companies Act (Art. 309, para. 2, item 9, Companies Act; reduction of reserves requires an ordinary resolution).
299. Article 447, para. 2; Art. 448, para. 2, Companies Act.

resolution will not be required (resolution of the board of directors in Companies with Board of Directors; decision of directors in other companies).[300] In addition, if the reduced amount of stated capital does not exceed the amount of deficit as calculated in accordance with the ordinance of the Ministry of Justice (i.e., in cases where there will be no surplus for dividends after the reduction of stated capital), an ordinary resolution at the annual shareholders meeting will be sufficient to implement the reduction of stated capital.[301]

370. In addition, certain procedures will be required to protect the company's creditors. In the creditor protection procedure, the creditors may state objections to the reduction of stated capital or reserves.[302] The company must give public notice to the creditors and also notify the known creditors, in either case that the objecting creditors must state objections within a certain period of time (one month or more).[303] Notice to the known creditors will not be required if the company gives public notice not only in the official gazette but also in a daily newspaper which publishes news on current affairs or by an electronic public notice, as prescribed in the company's articles of incorporation.[304] If the creditors do not state objection within the prescribed period, such creditor will be deemed to have approved the reduction of stated capital.[305] If a creditor states objection, the company must: (i) pay its debt to such creditor, (ii) provide reasonable security or (iii) entrust reasonable assets with a trust company for the purpose of making a payment to such creditor; provided, however, that such measures will not be necessary if there is no risk of harming the creditors by the capital reduction (e.g., if a security interest has been created for such debt).[306] If there is a defect in the procedures or contents of the capital reduction, an action may be filed seeking invalidation of the capital reduction.[307]

§2. Transfer of Shares

I. Transfer Methods

371. In principle, shareholders may freely transfer the shares that they hold.[308] This is intended to ensure that the shareholders have the opportunity to recoup their capital investment. In a 'share certificate issuing company' (*kabuken hakkou kaisha*), transfer of shares become effective upon a delivery of the share certificates representing such shares.[309] In addition to actual delivery, the share certificates may

300. Article 447, para. 3; Art. 448, para. 3, Companies Act.
301. Article 309, para. 2, item 9, Companies Act.
302. Main clause of Art. 449, para. 1, Companies Act; items 1 and 2 of the same para.
303. Article 449, para. 2, Companies Act.
304. Article 449, para. 3, Companies Act.
305. Article 449, para. 4, Companies Act.
306. Article 449, para. 5, Companies Act.
307. Article 828, para. 1, item 5; para. 2, item 5, Companies Act.
308. Article 127, Companies Act.
309. Article 128, main text of para. 1, Companies Act.

be delivered by: (i) a 'summary transfer' (*kanyi hikiwatashi*),[310] (ii) a 'constructive transfer with retention of possession' (*senyu kaite*)[311] or (iii) a 'transfer of possession by instruction' (*sashizu ni yoru senyu iten*)[312] (see paragraph 418, Book-entry transfer system).

372. A possessor of share certificates will be presumed to be the lawful owner of the shares.[313] Therefore, in the event that (i) a company intends to refuse the request of name change in the shareholder registry by a person possessing the share certificates or (ii) a shareholder who lost the share certificates requests the return of share certificates from the possessor, such company or shareholder must prove that the possessor of the share certificates is not the lawful owner (presumption of lawful ownership). In addition, a company will be exempted from any liability if the company accepts a request of name change in the shareholder registry from a person possessing the share certificates, to the extent that the company was without knowledge and not grossly negligent in accepting such request (exemption of liability).

373. Prior to the amendment to the Commercial Code in 2005, companies were, in principle, required to issue share certificates.[314] While share certificates were required to be issued as securities (*yuka shouken*) to enhance the transferability of shares, in practice, many small stock companies had not issued share certificates as such companies were mostly privately owned companies and therefore did not need to ensure the transferability of shares. On the other hand, listed companies are currently subject to the securities deposit and book-entry transfer system (*hokan furikae seido*) (i.e., no share certificates are issued by listed companies) (see paragraph 418) and therefore no delivery of share certificates will be necessary to transfer the shares of listed companies. Given the above, the Companies Act does not require companies to issue share certificates unless otherwise prescribed in the company's articles of incorporation as a 'share certificate issuing company'.[315] In a share certificate issuing company, the company must, in principle, issue the share certificates without delay after the shares are issued.[316] In companies other than a share certificate issuing company, transfer of shares will not be perfected against the company

310. Article 182, Civil Code. For example, if a transfer is made to a securities firm with whom the share certificate is deposited, the transfer may be effected simply by the parties' agreement to transfer the possessory right pertaining to such share certificate without any actual delivery.
311. Article 183, Civil Code. For example, if the share certificates will continue to be possessed in deposit by the securities firm after the securities firm sold the shares, the delivery of share certificates may be made by the securities firm expressing an intention as the seller that it will possess the share certificates on behalf of the buyer.
312. Article 184, Civil Code. For example, if the share certificates sold to a third party are deposited with the securities firm, the delivery of share certificates may be made by the seller instructing the securities firm to possess the share certificates on behalf of such third party upon such third party's consent.
313. Article 131, para. 1, Companies Act.
314. Article 226, Commercial Code prior to amendment.
315. Article 214, Companies Act.
316. Article 215, para. 1, Companies Act.

or third parties unless the name and address of the transferee is stated or recorded in the shareholder registry (see paragraph 405, Shareholder registry).[317]

II. Restrictions on Transfer of Shares

A. *Restrictions by the Articles of Incorporation*

1. Overview

374. Prior to the amendment to the Commercial Code in 1950, companies were not permitted to prohibit or restrict the transfer of shares. In practice, however, most of the stock companies in Japan were privately owned small or medium-sized businesses (see paragraph 53) and they strongly lobbied for a legislation to allow the companies to prevent an unwanted third party from becoming a shareholder. As a result, the amendment to the Commercial Code in 1966 allowed the companies to prescribe in the articles of incorporation that transfer of shares will be subject to the approval of the company. The Companies Act also allows the companies to prescribe in the articles of incorporation that transfer of shares requires the approval of the board of directors in Companies with Board of Directors (for companies other than Company with Board of Directors, the shareholders meeting).[318] Under the Companies Act, such 'shares with restriction on transfer' (*jouto seigen kabushiki*) are categorized as a class share.[319]

375. Even in shares with restrictions on transfer, transfer of shares may not be prohibited completely because there must be an opportunity for the shareholders to recoup their capital investment (see paragraph 378). In addition, as the transfer restriction is intended to allow the companies to prevent an unwanted third party from becoming a shareholder, the approval requirement may not be established to restrict transfers not related to such purpose, for example, a transfer restriction based on the nature of the transferor or a transfer restriction based on the number of shares to be transferred (on the other hand, approval requirement on a transfer if the transferee is not a shareholder or employee is valid).

2. Amendment to the Articles of Incorporation

376. Restrictions on transfer of shares may be prescribed in the initial articles of incorporation (see paragraph 222) or by an amendment to the articles of incorporation. An amendment to the articles of incorporation requires a shareholder resolution. Unlike other amendments, a resolution on the restrictions on transfer of shares requires the approval of: (i) at least half of the shareholders entitled to exercise the votes at the shareholders meeting and (ii) two-thirds or more of the votes of

317. Article 130, para. 1, Companies Act.
318. Article 139, para. 1, Companies Act.
319. Article 107, para. 1, item 1; Art. 108, para. 1, item 4, Companies Act.

all shareholders.[320] Such strict procedural requirement is provided because the restrictions on transfer of shares have a substantial effect on the interests of shareholders. The dissenting shareholders may exercise an appraisal right to demand the company to purchase his or her shares at fair price.[321] Under the Companies Act, the restrictions may be prescribed on all or part of the classes of shares issued by the company.[322] In case of prescribing the restrictions on a certain class share, a special resolution at class shareholders meeting of such class share will also be required.[323]

377. As the restrictions on transfer of shares are subject to a strict procedural requirement, it is difficult for the companies having a large number of shareholders to newly introduce such transfer restrictions. On the other hand, once introduced, the transfer restrictions must be stated on the share certificate and must be registered in the commercial registration.[324]

3. Transfer of 'Shares with Restrictions on Transfer'

378. Shareholders who intend to transfer the shares with restrictions on transfer may request that the company make a determination as to whether or not to approve the transfer.[325] In such case, the shareholder must specify the number of shares intended to be transferred (in a corporation with class shares, the classes of the shares and the number of shares for each class), the name of the acquirer of shares, and, if the shareholder requests the company or certain purchaser to be designated by the company to purchase such shares when the company does not approve the transfer, a statement to such effect.[326] The acquirer of the shares may also make such request.[327] Upon the company's decision on whether or not to approve the transfer, the company must notify the person who made the request for approval of such decision.[328] If the company fails to give notice to the shareholder within two weeks from the day of the request, or the company fails to give notice of its statement to purchase such shares within forty days from the day of the notice on its decision, the company will be deemed to have given the approval on the transfer of such shares.[329]

379. If the company decides not to approve the transfer of shares, the company must, in principle, repurchase these shares, in which case such repurchase of shares

320. Article 309, para. 2, item 11; Art. 466; Art. 309, para. 3, Companies Act.
321. Article 116, para. 1, item 1, Companies Act.
322. Article 108, para. 1, item 4, Companies Act.
323. Article 324, para. 3, item 1, Companies Act.
324. Article 216, item 4; Art. 911, para. 3, item 7, Companies Act.
325. Article 136, Companies Act.
326. Article 138, item 1, Companies Act.
327. Article 137; Art. 138, item 2, Companies Act.
328. Article 139, para. 2, Companies Act.
329. Article 145, Companies Act.

as treasury shares will require a special resolution of the shareholders meeting.[330] In the shareholders meeting, the person requesting approval of the transfer of shares may not exercise voting rights.[331] Alternatively, the company may designate a third party to purchase some or all of the subject shares (designated purchaser).[332] Such designation of a designated purchaser must be made by a resolution of the board of directors, in a Company with Board of Directors (in other companies, a shareholders meeting), unless otherwise provided in the articles of incorporation.[333]

380. If the company decides to repurchase the shares, the company must notify the person requesting the approval of transfer and deposit an amount calculated by multiplying the amount of the company's net assets per share by the number of subject shares with the depositary located in the area where its head office is located, and deliver a document certifying such deposit to the person requesting the transfer.[334] In a share certificate issuing company, the shareholder will then be required to deposit the share certificates with the same depositary within one week from the receipt of such document from the company.[335] After the company (or the designated purchaser) has notified the shareholder of its decision to purchase the shares, the shareholder may not withdraw his or her request for approval of the share transfer unless an approval of the company is obtained.[336] This is because at this stage the company has already procured the funds for such repurchase intended to avoid.

381. Subsequently, if the parties are unable to agree on the sale price of the shares, the parties may file a petition to the court for determination of the sale price within twenty days from the notice by the company to purchase the shares.[337] The court will determine the sale price taking into consideration the financial conditions of the company at the time of the request for approval of share transfer as well as all other circumstances.[338] If no petition is made within the abovementioned period, the deposited amount will become the sale price.[339]

382. A transfer of the shares with restrictions on transfer which was implemented without the approval of the company's board of directors is not valid against the company but will be effective between the parties to the transfer (15 June 1973, Supreme Court Collection of Court Decisions on Civil Actions 27-700). Under the Companies Act, the companies may provide in the articles of incorporation that the company may demand that a person who has acquired the shares with restrictions

330. Article 140, para. 1; Art. 140, para. 2; Art. 309, para. 2, item 1, Companies Act.
331. Article 140, para. 3, Companies Act.
332. Article 140, para. 4, Companies Act.
333. Article 140, para. 5, Companies Act.
334. Article 141, para. 1; Art. 141, para. 2, Companies Act.
335. Article 141, para. 3, Companies Act.
336. Article 143, Companies Act.
337. Article 144, para. 2, Companies Act.
338. Article 144, paras 3 and 4, Companies Act.
339. Article 144, para. 5, Companies Act.

on transfer by general succession, including inheritance, sell such shares to the company.[340] The company will be required to obtain a resolution of the shareholders meeting to demand such sale of the shares to the company on each occasion.[341] If the parties are unable to agree on the sale price, the parties may file a petition to the court to determine the sale price.[342]

B. *Statutory Restrictions on Share Transfers*

1. Restrictions on Assignment of the 'Right to become a Shareholder' (*Kenri Kabu*)

383. Assignment of the subscriber's rights to become a shareholder prior to the incorporation of the company or the effective date of newly issued shares may not be validly asserted against the company.[343] This is intended to facilitate the administrative works of formation or issuance of new shares. The assignment, however, is effective between the parties.

2. Restrictions Prior to the Issuance of Share Certificates

384. A share certificate issuing company must issue share certificates without delay after the issuance of shares.[344] While the transfer of shares in a share certificate issuing company prior to the issuance of share certificates will in principle not be effective against the company, the shareholders may validly transfer the shares by the parties' agreement if the company is unduly delaying the issuance of share certificates (8 November 1972, Supreme Court Collection of Court Decisions on Civil Actions 26-1489).[345]

C. *Treasury Shares*

1. Overview

385. Prior to the amendment to the Commercial Code in 1994, stock companies were, in principle, not permitted to repurchase own shares (treasury shares). Treasury shares could harm the capital of the company as it would have the effect of refunding the contributions back to the shareholders. Other potential adverse effects would include the following: (i) it could violate the principle of equal treatment of shareholders if acquisitions are made from specific shareholders, (ii) the company

340. Article 174, Companies Act.
341. Article 175, para. 1, Companies Act.
342. Article 177, Companies Act.
343. Article 35; Art. 63, para. 2; Art. 208, para. 4, Companies Act.
344. Article 215, para. 1, Companies Act.
345. Article 128, para. 2, Companies Act.

will suffer double damages if the share price drops as a result of insufficient future operational results, (iii) it could potentially be used for market manipulation, (iv) there is a higher risk of insider trading (see paragraph 423) where the shares of the company are traded based on insider information known only to an insider in the company, and (v) it is conceivable that the current management team may purchase the shares of the company to preserve their own position. For these reasons, acquisition of treasury shares by the company had long been, in principle, prohibited in Japan.

2. Deregulation on Treasury Shares

386. In Japan, many companies had arranged a so-called crossholding of shares (*kabushiki mochiai*) to prevent corporate takeovers or buy up of shares (see paragraph 68). As such practice was criticized by non-Japanese companies as preventing them from entering into the Japanese market, Japanese industry leaders requested that treasury shares be deregulated as an alternative defence measure to prevent unjustifiable corporate takeovers. In other words, it was argued that if cross-shareholdings were to be reduced, it was necessary to ease the restrictions on treasury shares. In addition, it was argued that the deregulation of treasury shares would assist the companies to cancel the shares that had been excessively issued during the bubble economy and also to allow employee stock ownership schemes (*jugyouin mochikabukai*) to acquire the shares of the company in a flexible manner.

387. In response to the abovementioned arguments, the restrictions on treasury shares were eased by the 1994 and 1997 amendments to the Commercial Code. In these amendments, treasury shares were allowed under the following circumstances: (i) acquisition for the purpose of subsequent transfer to the company's officers and employees, (ii) acquisition for the purpose of subsequent cancellation of shares using the company's retained earnings (*kabushiki no rieki shoukyaku*) and (iii) acquisition of shares with restrictions on transfer from an heir due to the death of a shareholder. However, certain procedural requirements as well as restrictions on the volume and holding period were established to avoid the adverse effects associated with the treasury shares.

388. A further amendment to the Commercial Code was enacted in October 2001 to generally permit the treasury shares regardless of the purpose of the acquisition and without any restrictions on the holding period. Meanwhile, it was necessary to introduce new rules on the disposal of treasury shares which should be consistent with the rules on issuance of new shares. In the 2003 amendment to the Commercial Code, repurchase of own shares as treasury shares was allowed to be determined by a resolution of the board of directors, to the extent so permitted in the articles of incorporation. The Companies Act later reorganized the procedural rules governing treasury shares.

3. Repurchase of the Company's Shares as Treasury Shares

389. Under the Companies Act, companies must prescribe the following matters by a shareholder resolution in advance of repurchasing its shares for value by an agreement with its shareholders: (i) the number of shares to be acquired, (ii) the description and total amount of money or other consideration to be delivered in exchange for the acquisition of shares and (iii) the period during which the shares can be acquired (which must not exceed one year).[346] A shareholder resolution, in either the annual shareholders meeting, or extraordinary shareholders meeting, was required because acquisition of treasury shares is essentially a profit distribution. Based on such authorization by the shareholders, the board of directors (in Companies with Board of Directors) will, on each occasion, determine the following: (i) the number of shares to be acquired, (ii) the description, and the number or amount, or the method of calculation thereof, of money or other consideration per share to be delivered in exchange for the acquisition, (iii) the total amount of money or other consideration to be delivered in exchange for acquisition of the shares and (iv) the date on which the offer to transfer the shares will be made.[347] The conditions for the acquisition of shares must be identical for all shares to be acquired in such determination.[348] The company will be required to notify the above determined matters to the shareholders.[349] The company will be deemed to have accepted the sale offer from the shareholders if the shareholders who have received such notice offer to sell their shares to the company, and, if the total number of shares offered is in excess of the total number of shares to be acquired, the acquisition by the company will be carried out on a pro-rata basis.[350]

390. In addition to the above method, shares may be repurchased from specific shareholders by a special resolution at the shareholders meeting.[351] To ensure the fairness of the shareholder resolution, the specific selling shareholders may not exercise their voting rights in the shareholders meeting.[352] In addition, from the perspective of equal treatment of shareholders, other shareholders may request that they be added as the selling shareholder on or before five days prior to the date of the shareholders meeting; provided, however, that other shareholders will not be permitted to make such requests if, in cases where the shares to be acquired are shares with a market price, the purchase price per share does not exceed the market price per share, or if the acquisition is from general successors of the shareholders, including an heir.[353] Such request right of other shareholders will also not apply if

346. Article 156, para. 1, Companies Act.
347. Article 157, paras 1 and 2, Companies Act.
348. Article 157, para. 3, Companies Act.
349. Article 158, para. 1, Companies Act; in a Public Company, the notice may be substituted by a public notice (Art. 158, para. 2, Companies Act.).
350. Article 159, Companies Act.
351. Article 160, para. 1; Art. 309, para. 2, item 2, Companies Act.
352. Article 160, para. 4, Companies Act.
353. Article 160, para. 3, Companies Act; Art. 29, Ordinance for Enforcement of the Companies Act; Arts 161 and 162, Companies Act.

so permitted in the articles of incorporation by obtaining the consent of all shareholders.[354]

391. Repurchase of the company's shares as treasury shares from subsidiaries may be implemented by a resolution of the board of directors, in Company with Board of Directors (in other companies, a shareholder resolution).[355] In addition, if the shares are to be acquired in the market or through tender offers, they may be acquired simply by a resolution at the shareholders meeting; provided, however, that in a Company with Board of Directors, such acquisitions may be implemented by a resolution of the board of directors if so permitted in the articles of incorporation.[356]

392. As previously discussed, repurchase of shares as treasury shares are subject to certain financial restrictions. The total book value of money or other consideration to be delivered upon the repurchase of shares as treasury shares must not exceed the 'distributable amount' (*bunpai kanougaku*) (i.e., an amount obtained by subtracting the sum of certain prescribed items from the amount of surplus) as of the effective date of such acquisition (see paragraph 644).[357] If a deficit arises in the company's financial statements as of the end of the business year in which shares were repurchased as treasury shares, the directors or other officers who executed such repurchase will be jointly and severally liable to the company for payment of the company's deficit (or the total book value of money and other consideration in the repurchase of shares as treasury shares, if such total book value is less than the amount of deficit); however, no such liability arises if such executing director or other officers prove that they did not fail to exercise due care with respect to the performance of their duties.[358] This liability may not be exempted without the consent of all shareholders.[359] The financial restrictions do not apply in cases of the following: (i) acquisition of shares as treasury shares as a result of certain events, including merger, or (ii) shares repurchased as treasury shares as a result of the exercise of appraisal rights by the shareholders (however, the financial restrictions do apply in cases of (i) acquisition of shares with put option (*shutoku joukou tsuki kabushiki*), (ii) acquisition of shares subject to call (*shutoku seikyuken tsuki kabushiki*) and (iii) acquisition of class shares subject to wholly call (*zenbu shutoku joukou tsuki shurui kabushiki*)).[360] The financial restrictions also apply to an acquisition upon the company's demand for sale against heirs.[361]

---

354. Article 164, Companies Act.
355. Article 163, Companies Act.
356. Article 165, paras 1 and 2, Companies Act.
357. Article 461, paras 1 and 2, Companies Act.
358. Article 465, para. 1, Companies Act.
359. Article 465, para. 2, Companies Act.
360. Article 166, proviso to para. 1; Art. 170, para. 5; Art. 461, para. 1, item 4, Companies Act.
361. Article 461, para. 1, item 5, Companies Act.

4. Holding Treasury Shares

393. Treasury shares may be held by the company for an unlimited period. The company, however, may not exercise rights of common interest (*kyoueki ken*), such as voting rights.[362] In addition, dividends of surplus will not be distributed to the company.[363]

394. Prior to the amendment to the Commercial Code in October 2001, treasury shares were booked in the balance sheet of the company as an asset independently from shares of other companies owned by the company. However, after the amendment, treasury shares are booked by way of deduction in the shareholders' equity section.[364] This is because, given that the companies are no longer required to dispose the treasury shares, the amount of treasury shares repurchased should be construed to have flowed out of the company in the same way as dividends. As such, the total amount of treasury shares will not be counted in the calculation of the distributable amount.

5. Disposal of Treasury Shares

395. Disposal of treasury shares will, in principle, require the same procedures as the issuance of new shares (subscription procedures).[365] This is because these two have the same economic substance. In disposing of treasury shares, the company must prescribe at a meeting of the board of directors in a Public Company (in other companies, the shareholders meeting) the following:

(i) the class and number of the shares;
(ii) the amount to be paid for the shares or the method of calculating such amount;
(iii) if properties other than money are the subject of contribution, a statement to such effect and the description and value of such properties; and
(iv) the day or period for the payment of money in exchange for the shares or the contribution of the property given in item (iii) above.[366]

In non-Public Companies, the determination of subscription requirements may be delegated by a shareholder resolution to the board of directors in Companies with Board of Directors (in companies other than Companies with Board of Directors, the directors).[367] The company may also cancel the treasury shares by a resolution of the board of directors (where the company has a board of directors).[368]

362. Article 308, para. 2, Companies Act.
363. Article 453, Companies Act.
364. Article 76, para. 2, item 5, Ordinance for Company Accounts.
365. Article 199, para. 1, Companies Act.
366. Article 199, paras 1 and 2; Art. 201, para. 1, Companies Act.
367. Article 200, para. 1, Companies Act.
368. Article 178, Companies Act.

6. Disclosure of Repurchase and Disposal of Treasury Shares

396. Under the Commercial Code, the business reports contained a status report on the repurchase of shares as treasury shares authorized by the shareholder resolution to the company management.[369] In the Companies Act, the disclosure items of the business report were significantly simplified.

397. Under the Financial Instruments and Exchange Act, listed companies are required to submit to the relevant authorities, and provide it for public inspection, a treasury shares purchase status report each month following the resolution of annual shareholders meeting authorizing the repurchase of shares.[370]

7. Preventing Unfair Securities Trading

398. Regulations on market manipulation have been reinforced under the applicable Cabinet Office Ordinance of the Financial Instruments and Exchange Act, setting forth certain necessary and appropriate matters to ensure fair transactions. This is because the company management may be tempted under the deregulated rules on treasury shares in the Companies Act to increase the company's share price, or to prevent its decline, by the buying and selling of treasury shares using the company's funds.[371]

399. The Cabinet Office Ordinance provides the following restrictions on the repurchase of shares to be implemented during a trading day: (i) the number of securities firms (financial instrument business operators) to handle the purchase (i.e., limited to one company), (ii) the timing of purchase order (i.e., orders are prohibited within thirty minutes of the end of the trading session), (iii) the pricing of orders (e.g., orders at the opening of trading sessions may not be priced at a higher value than the closing price of the previous day), and (iv) the total volume of orders (e.g., an upper limit of 25% of the average trade volume).[372] Any violation of the above restrictions may be subject to administrative fines.[373]

400. In addition, an 'insider' having knowledge of the fact that the company has determined to acquire or dispose (or not to acquire or dispose) of the company's shares is prohibited from purchasing or selling the company's shares. This is because the company or its related parties may purchase or sell the shares of the company using inside information.[374]

369. Article 103, para. 12, item 9, Ordinance for Enforcement of the Commercial Code prior to amendment.
370. Article 24-6, Financial Instruments and Exchange Act.
371. Article 162-2, Financial Instruments and Exchange Act.
372. Article 17, Cabinet Office Ordinance Relating to the Regulations on the Trading of Securities.
373. Article 208-2, item 3, Financial Instruments and Exchange Act.
374. Article 166, para. 2, item 1(d), Financial Instruments and Exchange Act.

III. Bona Fide Acquisition by Third Parties

401. In general, transfer of shares should not be legally valid if the transferor has no legal title in the shares. However, a transferee who received the delivery of share certificates in such transfer will obtain a legally valid ownership in the shares if such transferee was without knowledge and not grossly negligent as to the defective title of the transferor.[375] This concept of bona fide acquisition (*zenyi shutoku*) is intended to protect the stability of share transfer transactions.

402. There is an issue as to whether or not the concept of bona fide acquisition applies not only when the transferor has no legal title in the shares but also when the transferor was an unauthorized agent. The prevailing view denies the protection under the bona fide acquisition on a purchase from unauthorized agent, unless the apparent agency doctrine of the Civil Code were to apply to protect the transferee.[376] On the other hand, there is also a view that purchases from unauthorized agents should also be protected by the bona fide acquisition principle, arguing that it is necessary to protect the agency transactions that have increased as a result of the development of the depositary system.

403. Shareholders who have lost their share certificates may make a request to the share certificate issuing company to register such loss of the share certificates, in which case the company will state or record such loss in the registry of lost share certificates.[377] The registry of lost share certificates will be made available for public inspection.[378] When the loss of share certificates is registered, no changes of registered holder in the shareholder registry or exercise of voting rights against the company (if the request was made by a person other than a registered holder in the shareholder registry) will be permitted.[379] Upon registration of the lost share certificate, the company will notify the shareholders registered in the shareholder registry and registered pledgees to such effect.[380] A person holding the share certificates that are subject to such registration of lost share certificate may file an application for the cancellation of such registration.[381] Upon such application, the company will notify the registrant of the lost share certificate and cancel the registration of the lost share certificate after two weeks have elapsed from such notice by the company.[382] Thereafter, the rights to the share certificate will be contested between the registrant of the lost share certificate and the holder of the share certificate. If such application for the cancellation is not made, the share certificate in the registry of lost share certificates will become invalid after one year has elapsed from the day immediately

375. Article 131, para. 2, Companies Act.
376. Article 109; Art. 110; Art. 112, Civil Code.
377. Article 223; Art. 221, Companies Act.
378. Article 231, Companies Act.
379. Article 230, Companies Act.
380. Article 224, para. 1, Companies Act.
381. Article 225, para. 1, Companies Act.
382. Article 225, paras 3 and 4, Companies Act.

following the day of such registration, in which case the registrant may obtain a reissued share certificate from the company.[383]

404. The Companies Act allows a non-possession of share certificates (*kabuken no fushoji*) where the shareholder makes an offer to the company that they do not wish to hold the share certificates.[384] This is intended to protect the shareholders from potentially losing their rights in the shares by losing the share certificates or through a bona fide acquisition. Upon receipt of such offer from the shareholders, the company must state or record in the shareholder registry, without delay, a statement that the company will not issue share certificates for such shares.[385] The offering shareholder must submit the share certificates to the company, in which case such share certificates will become invalid when the above statement is stated or recorded in the shareholder registry.[386] Once the offer is stated or recorded in the shareholder registry, the company may not issue the share certificates for such shares subject to the offer.[387] The shareholder who has made the offer of non-possession of share certificates may, at any time, demand that the company issue the share certificates for the shares subject to the non-possession.[388] The costs for issuing the share certificates will be borne by such shareholder.

IV. Change of Shareholder in Shareholder Registry

A. Shareholder Registry

405. Shareholder registry will be prepared by the company to state or record the following: (i) the names and addresses of shareholders, (ii) the number of shares held by each shareholder, (iii) the day when the shareholders acquired the shares, and (iv) the serial numbers of the share certificate in cases of a share certificate issuing company.[389] The shareholder registry will be kept at the head office of the company or the business office of the company's 'administrator of shareholder registry' (*kabunushi meibo kanrinin*) (see paragraph 410).[390] The shareholders and creditors may make a request to inspect or copy the shareholder register at any time during the business hours of the company; provided, however, that the reason for such request must be disclosed.[391] The company may not refuse the request except in one of the following cases: (i) if the request was made for a purpose other than for research on securing or exercising their rights, (ii) if the request was made with the purpose of interfering with the execution of operations of the company or prejudicing the common benefits of the shareholders, (iii) if the requestor operates or

383. Article 228, Companies Act.
384. Article 217, para. 1, Companies Act.
385. Article 217, para. 3, Companies Act.
386. Article 217, para. 2; Art. 217, para. 5, Companies Act.
387. Article 217, para. 4, Companies Act.
388. Article 217, para. 6, Companies Act.
389. Article 121, Companies Act.
390. Article 125, para. 1, Companies Act.
391. Article 125, para. 2, Companies Act.

engages in any business which is, in substance, in competition with the operations of the company, (iv) if the request was made in order to report the facts which may be acquired by inspecting or copying the shareholder registry to third parties for profit or (v) if the requestor has reported the facts which were obtained by inspecting or copying the shareholder registry, to a third party for profit in the immediately preceding two years.[392]

406. Transfer of shares may not be perfected against the company or third parties in a share certificate issuing company (in companies other than a share certificate issuing company, against the company) unless the name and address of the acquirer is stated or recorded in the shareholder registry.[393] In a share certificate issuing company, a pledge of shares requires delivery of the share certificate.[394] A share pledge will be effective as a registered pledge (*touroku shichi*) if the pledge has been stated or recorded in the shareholder registry. In such registered pledge, the pledgee may receive the money distributed as dividends of surplus or distribution of residual assets, and appropriate them to the payment to satisfy their claims in priority to other creditors.[395] In practice, however, a simplified pledge (*ryakushiki shichi*) is frequently used, whereby the pledge is created by the delivery of share certificate only (i.e., no registration is made in the shareholder registry), and registered pledges are rarely used. The Companies Act also prescribes the scope of pledgee's 'right of extension of the security interest to the proceeds of the collateral' (*butsujou daii ken*).[396]

407. It is sufficient for the company to send a notice or demand to shareholders to the addresses of such shareholders stated or recorded in the shareholder registry.[397] The company may also make the payment of dividends to the shareholders stated or recorded in the shareholder registry. In cases where notices or demands from the company do not reach a shareholder for at least five consecutive years at the address stated or recorded in the shareholder registry, the company will no longer be required to give notices or issue demands to such shareholder.[398]

408. While the company will be exempt from the obligation to send a notice or demand to the above shareholders, the company is still subject to the burdensome and costly administrative works for managing the shareholders. Therefore, the Companies Act allows the company to sell the shares held by a shareholder, whom the notices and demands have not reached for five consecutive years, by auction pursuant to a resolution of the board of directors (in a Company with Board of Directors) and tender the proceeds thereof to the shareholder of such shares.[399] In lieu of sale by auction, the company may also sell shares with market price at such market

392. Article 125, para. 3, Companies Act.
393. Article 130, para. 1, Companies Act.
394. Article 146, para. 2, Companies Act.
395. Article 154, para. 1, Companies Act.
396. Article 362, para. 2; Art. 350; Art. 304, Civil Code; Art. 151, Companies Act.
397. Article 126, para. 1, Companies Act.
398. Article 196, para. 1, Companies Act.
399. Article 197, Companies Act.

price, or shares without a market price using a method other than auction with the permission from the court.[400] In cases where the company effects an auction or sale in lieu of auction, the company must (i) give public notice that interested parties may state their objections during a period of time which may not be less than three months and (ii) issue separate demands seeking such objections (if any) to each shareholder and registered pledgee.[401] The company may elect to purchase some or all of the shares sold in the sale in lieu of auction.[402] In such case, the company will in general need to deposit the proceeds of the sale at the deposit office as the company will likely not be able to identify the location of the shareholder.

409. Transfer of shares will not be perfected against the company unless the name and address of the transferee is stated or recorded in the shareholder registry.[403] In a share certificate issuing company, the transfer of shares will be effective upon the delivery of share certificates, after which the transferee will present such share certificates to the company to request the name change.[404] As the possessor of the share certificates will be presumed to be the lawful owner of the shares, the company must accept such request from the possessor unless the company proves that the possessor is not the lawful owner of the shares.[405] In companies other than a share certificate issuing company, the transferee of the shares must request the name change jointly with the transferor stated or recorded in the shareholder registry as the shareholder (shareholder of record) (or inheritors or other general successors).[406] A transferee acquiring shares with restrictions on transfer may not request the name change unless the required approval for such transfer has been obtained.[407] In companies other than a share certificate issuing company, the name change in the shareholder registry will also be required to perfect the transfer of shares against third parties.[408] As such, the shareholders of companies other than a share certificate issuing company may request that the company deliver a written document stating the matters specified in the shareholder registry or to provide the electromagnetic records recording such matters.[409] Under the book-entry transfer system, ownership of shares is determined by the account book (see paragraph 422).[410]

410. Companies may appoint an 'administrator of shareholder registry' (*kabunushi meibo kanrinin*) if so provided in the articles of incorporation. The administrator of shareholder registry will prepare and keep, and handle other

400. Article 197, para. 2, Companies Act.
401. Article 198, para. 1, Companies Act.
402. Article 197, para. 3, Companies Act.
403. Article 130, para. 1, Companies Act.
404. Article 128, para. 1, Companies Act.
405. Article 131, para. 1, Companies Act.
406. Article 133, para. 2, Companies Act.
407. Article 134, Companies Act.
408. Article 130, para. 1, Companies Act.
409. Article 122, Companies Act.
410. Articles 140, and 141, Act on the Book-Entry Transfer of Company Bonds, Shares, etc.

administrative works of, the shareholder registry on behalf of the company.[411] While they were called a transfer agent (*meigi kakikae dairinin*) prior to the amendment to the Commercial Code in 2005, they were renamed under the Companies Act based on their broader scope of work as provided above. If a company appoints an administrator of shareholder registry, the name, address and business office of such administrator must be registered in the commercial registration.[412]

B. *Record Date (*Kijunbi*)*

411. While the rights of shareholders against the company will be based on the shareholder registry, the shareholder registry is constantly subject to entries of name changes. Therefore, a company may set a record date to fix the shareholders who will be entitled to exercise shareholder rights, such as voting rights at a shareholders meeting or rights to receive dividends of surplus. By setting the record date, the company may delineate the shareholders who may exercise their rights based on the shareholders stated or recorded in the shareholder registry on a certain date.[413] While companies must prescribe the rights which the shareholder on the record date may exercise (limited to those rights which will be exercised within three months from the record date), most companies provide in their articles of incorporation the last day of the business year as the record date concerning the annual shareholders meeting.[414] Previously, companies could also prohibit any entries or records in the shareholder registry for a period not exceeding three months (closure of the shareholder registry). For example, the shareholder registry could be closed from the day following the last day of the business year until the day of conclusion of the annual shareholders meeting. However, by the amendment to the Commercial Code in 2004, closure of the shareholder registry was abolished and integrated with the record date.

412. The company must give public notice of the record date two weeks prior to such record date, unless the articles of incorporation separately provides for such record date.[415] In practice, the record date for the annual shareholders meeting is often provided in the articles of incorporation.

413. As discussed above, a transferee of the shares may not validly assert his or her rights against the company if the transferee has not requested the entry of name change in the shareholder registry. There is a question as to whether or not the company may voluntarily treat such transferee as a shareholder. It would be unreasonable for the company to be forced to continue treating a shareholder of record as a shareholder if the company is aware that such shareholder of record has transferred his or her shares. In this regard, a Supreme Court ruling held that the company will

411. Article 123, Companies Act.
412. Article 911, para. 3, item 11, Companies Act.
413. Article 124, para. 1, Companies Act.
414. Article 124, para. 2, Companies Act.
415. Article 124, para. 3, Companies Act.

be permitted to treat the transferee as the shareholder at its own risk (i.e., the company will not be exempt if the transferee is not the lawful owner of the shares).[416] On the other hand, an opposing view argues that there may be a case where neither the transferor nor transferee will be permitted by the company to exercise shareholders rights if the company elects not to take such risk with the transferee. Another view points out a possible issue that the company may arbitrarily choose a company-friendly transferor or transferee to exercise the shareholder rights (there is also a view pointing out that the shareholders in record should be treated as the shareholder uniformly because it would be difficult for a large company to treat many possible transferees equally).

414. A similar issue may arise over whether the company may allow persons who acquired the shares after the record date to exercise their voting rights. The Companies Act allows the company, at its own discretion, to determine whether to permit persons who acquired the shares after the record date to exercise their voting rights at the shareholders meeting; provided, however, that the rights of the shareholders on the record date will not be prejudiced.[417] The Companies Act, however, is not construed to permit the directors to allow shareholders after the record date to exercise their voting rights with an aim to preserve the directors' own positions.

V. Listing of Shares

415. In Japan, listing of shares is mainly carried out by listing the shares on a market operated by a financial instruments exchange (stock exchange). The listing will be subject to certain screening procedures to ascertain its suitability as listed shares (Table 14). A listed company is different from the concept of Public Company (*koukai kaisha*) under the Companies Act (see paragraph 122). The listing will allow the shares to be traded on the market, thereby increasing the liquidity of the shares and facilitating the shareholders' need to recoup their capital investment. The listing will also facilitate the companies' financing from the capital market and enhance the market recognition and credibility of the company, thereby assisting the company to expand its business and also secure human resources. On the other hand, the listing will impose mandatory disclosure obligations and also create a risk that the company may be subject to an unsolicited takeover attempt or speculative trading of its shares.

416. 20 Oct. 1955, Supreme Court Collection of Court Decisions on Civil Actions vol. 9, item 11, 1657.
417. Article 124, para. 4, Companies Act.

Table 14 Outline of Listing Criteria (Tokyo Stock Exchange)

		Securities Listing Regulations (Formal Requirements of Main Exchange Rules)	*Designation on the First Section upon New Listing (Requirements for Listing Directly on the First Section)*	*Rules for Listing on the Securities Exchange (Formal Requirement for Mothers)*
		Following Criteria Must Be Met.	*Following Criteria Must Be Met.*	*Following Criteria Must Be Met.*
CRITERIA	(1) Number of shareholders (at the time of listing)	800 or more.	2,200 or more.	300 or more (public offering of at least 500 units of shares prior to the listing).
	(2) Tradable shares (estimated at time of listing)	(a) Number of tradable shares: 4,000 units or more. (b) Market capitalization of tradable shares: JPY 1bn or more. (c) Ratio of tradable shares to listed shares: 30% or more.	(a) Number of tradable shares: 20,000 units or more. (b) Market capitalization of tradable shares: JPY 1bn or more. (c) Ratio of tradable shares to listed shares: 35% or more.	(a) Number of tradable shares: 2,000 units or more. (b) Market capitalization of tradable shares: JPY 500mn or more. (c) Ratio of tradable shares to listed shares: 25% or more.
	(3) Market capitalization of listed shares (estimated at the time of listing)	JPY 2bn or more.	JPY 50bn or more.	JPY 1bn or more.

	(4) Number of years of business operation	No less than 3 years under the board of directors (calculating retroactively from the final day of the last business year prior to date of application for listing).	Same as on left	No less than 1 year under the board of directors (calculating retroactively from the date of application for listing).
	(5) Shareholders' equity (as of the end of the fiscal year immediately preceding the current fiscal year)	JPY 1bn or more on a consolidated basis (and not negative on a non-consolidated basis)	Same as on left	N/A
	(6) Pre-tax profit or total market capitalization (Pre-tax profit can be the lower of consolidated operating profits and current net income before taxes and other adjustments)	Must meet one of the following (*a* through *c*): (a) Annual total for each of the last 2 years: JPY 100mn or more in the first year; JPY 400mn or more in the second year. (b) Annual total for each of the last 3 years: JPY 100mn or more in the first year; JPY 400mn or more in the third year; 600mn or more in total for the three years.	Same as on left	N/A

		Securities Listing Regulations (Formal Requirements of Main Exchange Rules)	*Designation on the First Section upon New Listing (Requirements for Listing Directly on the First Section)*	*Rules for Listing on the Securities Exchange (Formal Requirement for Mothers)*
		Following Criteria Must Be Met.	*Following Criteria Must Be Met.*	*Following Criteria Must Be Met.*
		(c) Total market capitalization: JPY 100bn or more (except for when sales for the immediately preceding year is less than JPY 10bn).		
	(7) False statements or adverse opinion	(a) No false statements in securities reports, etc., for the last 2 years (3 years, where the criteria in *6(b)* is to be applied. Same applies to *(b)* below). (b) Auditor's opinions of financial statements, etc., for the last 2 years (excluding the most recent year) have been either unqualified opinion or qualified opinion.	Same as on left	a. Auditor's report (excluding the most recent year) attached to securities report for listing application contains unqualified opinion or qualified opinion with certain exceptions. b. Auditor's report (for the most recent year) attached to securities report for the applicant contains unqualified opinion.

<table>
<tr>
<td></td>
<td></td>
<td>(c) Auditor’s opinion of financial statements, etc., for the most recent year was, in principle, unqualified opinion.</td>
<td></td>
<td>c. If the applicant has share certificates listed on another Japanese securities exchange, neither of the following shall apply:
(a) Internal control report for the most recent year stating ‘unable to express evaluation results’.
(b) Internal control report for the most recent year stating ‘no opinion expressed’.
d. No false statements in securities reports, etc., in which financial statements, etc., are stated or referred to in the above auditor’s report or quarterly review report.</td>
</tr>
</table>

		Securities Listing Regulations (Formal Requirements of Main Exchange Rules)	*Designation on the First Section upon New Listing (Requirements for Listing Directly on the First Section)*	*Rules for Listing on the Securities Exchange (Formal Requirement for Mothers)*
		Following Criteria Must Be Met.	*Following Criteria Must Be Met.*	*Following Criteria Must Be Met.*
				e. If the share certificates subject to the listing application are listed on another Japanese securities exchange, neither of the following shall apply: (a) Internal control report for the most recent year stating 'unable to express evaluation results'. (b) Internal control report for the most recent year stating 'no opinion expressed'.

	(8) Appointment of share transfer agent	The applicant has commissioned a share transfer agent approved by the Tokyo Stock Exchange or has obtained consent that such share transfer agent will act as agent.	Same	Same
	(9) Share units and class of share certificates	Number of shares constituting one full share unit anticipated to be 100. Share certificates subject to the listing application must meet one of the following: (a) Shares with voting rights in a company issuing only one class of shares with voting rights (b) In a company issuing several classes of shares with voting rights, shares with voting rights in a class where the right to receive economic benefits is higher	Same	Same

		Securities Listing Regulations (Formal Requirements of Main Exchange Rules)	*Designation on the First Section upon New Listing (Requirements for Listing Directly on the First Section)*	*Rules for Listing on the Securities Exchange (Formal Requirement for Mothers)*
		Following Criteria Must Be Met.	*Following Criteria Must Be Met.*	*Following Criteria Must Be Met.*
		than at least one of the other classes of shares with voting rights. (c) Shares without voting rights		
	(10) Restrictions on transfer	There are in principle no restrictions on the transfer of shares subject to the listing application	Same	Same
	(11) Consent for handling by designated deposit and book-entry institution	Consent given or anticipated to be given for handling of share certificates by designated deposit and book-entry institution (Japan Securities Depositary Center, Inc.)	Same	Same

	(12) Anticipated merger, etc.	Neither of the following shall apply: (a) The applicant will not be the surviving company in substance as a result of merger, company split, subsidiary acquisition, subsidiary sell-off, or assignment or accepting of business, or any of the foregoing that the applicant intends to carry out within the next 2 years. (b) There are plans within the next 2 years whereby the applicant will dissolve as a result of merger, or become a wholly-owned subsidiary following share transfer (*kabushiki iten*) or share exchange (*kabushiki koukan*).	Same	N/A

Note: As of 24 August 2009.

416. A notification must be submitted to the prime minister to list the shares on a financial instruments exchange.[418] The listing will strengthen the company's status. There are 3,541 companies listed on the Japanese financial instruments exchanges (as of the end of March 2015), of which 3,491 companies are listed on the Tokyo Stock Exchange totalling an aggregate market capitalization (i.e., product of total number of issued shares and market price) of approximately JPY 569 trillion (as of 1 May 2015) (stocks listed on the First Section of the Tokyo Stock Exchange). In Japan, the mandatory rule that a purchase of listed shares must be carried out at the stock exchanges was abolished in December 1998. Hence, investors may implement the trading directly with securities firms (financial instruments business operators) outside of the financial instruments exchanges. In addition, the eight stock exchanges in different locations are progressing integration as a result of the wide-spread of computers that have reduced the need of stock exchanges in different regions. The JASDAQ market, an OTC marketplace established by the Japan Securities Dealers Association, obtained a license as a securities exchange in December 2004 and has commenced business operations as JASDAQ Securities, Inc. (later merged into Osaka Securities Exchange Company Limited). Currently in Japan, there is the Japan Exchange Group (comprising the Tokyo Stock Exchange and the Osaka Exchange) as well as the Sapporo Securities Exchange, the Nagoya Stock Exchange, and the Fukuoka Stock Exchange.

417. In the United States, the National Association of Securities Dealers (NASD) operates NASDAQ, an automated notification system of indicative prices in OTC securities, to provide investors with fair investment information. The shares of cutting-edge firms, such as those in the computer industry, are registered on the NASDAQ, and its aggregate market capitalization exceeds that of the New York Stock Exchange. Meanwhile, in December 1999, the Tokyo Stock Exchange established Mothers, a marketplace targeting companies in the new high-tech sector, in other words, venture companies. The Osaka Stock Exchange equivalent Hercules merged with JASDAQ in 2010.

VI. Book-Entry Transfer System

418. The deposit and book-entry transfer system for shares was established in 1984 under the Act on the Deposit and Transfer of Shares (Act No. 30 of 1984). On 27 May 1985, Japan Securities Depositary Centre Foundation was designated as the deposit and book-entry agency. The foundation implemented the deposit and book-entry system in several phases from October 1991, and started full operations for listed and OTC share certificates in October 1992. Thereafter, Japan Securities Depositary Centre, Inc. (the 'Depositary Centre'), a stock company version of the foundation, assumed the business of the foundation pursuant to the amendment to the Commercial Code in 2002.

418. Article 121, Financial Instruments and Exchange Act.

419. Under the deposit and book-entry transfer system, the shareholders deposited the share certificates with a 'participant' (*sankasha*) in the system (such as financial instrument business operators, banks, securities finance companies), who will then deposit such share certificates with the Depositary Centre. In other words, the shareholders opened an account with the participant by creating a customer account book (*kokyaku kouzabo*)[419] and the participant had an account with the Depositary Centre (participant account book (*sankasha kouzabo*).[420] For those share certificates deposited with the Depositary Centre, the Depositary Centre was the shareholder of record in the company's shareholder registry.[421] The companies were required to separately prepare a beneficial shareholder registry, which was based on the notices from the Depositary Centre, for example, as of the end of each business year, with regard to the owners of the share certificates that have been deposited therewith. As the entries in the beneficial shareholder registry had the same effect as the entries in the shareholder registry, companies treated the beneficial shareholders as their shareholders.[422]

420. Upon a share transfer, the beneficial shareholder requested an account transfer, in which case the entry of the account transfer in the participant account book and the customer account book in accordance with such request had the same effect as the delivery of the share certificates.[423]

421. In 2004, the Act for Partial Amendment of the Act on the Book-Entry Transfer of Bonds for the Streamlining of Settlements Relating to the Trading of Shares was established, and from 5 January 2009, all listed share certificates are uniformly managed electronically through the accounts opened at account management institutions, such as banks, trust banks and securities firms (financial instruments business operators). The new account transfer system (*kabushiki furikae seido*) primarily handles the transfer of listed shares. Upon the commencement of the management of share certificates under the new account transfer system on 5 January 2009, the share certificates subject to such system were automatically invalidated without the ordinary share certificate collection procedures.

422. Under the new account transfer system, ownership of shares are determined by the account books. Transfer of shares will be effective upon the entry of the record of increase in the transferee's account book based on the transferor's request.[424] In other words, the share transfer will not be valid without the record of increase in the account book. If the company sets a record date for the purpose of delineating which shareholders will exercise shareholder rights against the company, the deposit and book-entry agency will promptly notify the company of the names and other information of the shareholders recorded in the account book on

419. Article 15, Act on the Deposit and Transfer of Shares.
420. Article 17, para. 1, Act on the Deposit and Transfer of Shares.
421. Article 29, para. 1, Act on the Deposit and Transfer of Shares.
422. Article 33, para. 1, Act on the Deposit and Transfer of Shares.
423. Article 26, para. 1, Act on the Deposit and Transfer of Shares; Art. 27, para. 2, Act on the Deposit and Transfer of Shares.
424. Articles 140 and 141, Act on the Book-Entry Transfer of Company Bonds, Shares, etc.

that date (*sou kabunushi tsuchi*).[425] The company receiving such notice from the deposit and book-entry agency will state or record accordingly in the shareholder registry.[426] In such case, the name changes will be deemed to have been entered in the shareholder registry on the abovementioned record date, and the company must allow those shareholders as of the record date to exercise their rights.[427]

VII. Insider Trading Regulations

423. The company's insiders should be prohibited from buying or selling the company's shares using undisclosed information obtained in relation to his or her duties in the company, as such activities are unfair and interfere with the fairness of securities markets. Under the Japanese Financial Instruments and Exchange Act, Article 157 generally prohibits fraudulent acts related to the buying and selling of securities.[428] This was modelled on section 10(b) of the US Securities Exchange Act of 1934 and Rule 10(b)(5) promulgated by the US Securities and Exchange Commission. In the United States, insider trading is strictly regulated through these regulations. In Japan, instead of the general provision in Article 157 of the Financial Instruments and Exchange Act, specific regulations on insider trading were established in 1988 as there was a need to reinforce insider regulations in the more globalized capital market.

A. Regulations on Insider Trading

424. A 'company related person' (*kaisha kankeisha*) of a listed company will be prohibited from buying or selling the company's shares before any material facts relating to the business of such company, which such person obtained in the course of performing his or her duties, is publicly announced.[429] The company related persons include: (i) an officer or employee of the company, (ii) a shareholder exercising the right to inspect the company's account books, (iii) a person who has the authority based on laws and regulations against the company (e.g., politicians, governmental officers having the authority of permission or certification) and (iv) a person who has executed an agreement with the company (e.g., commercial banks, underwriters, lawyers and certified public accountants) or a person with whom the company is negotiating the execution of an agreement. In addition, persons who have received information from the aforementioned persons are also subject to the same regulations.[430]

---

425. Article 151, paras 1 and 7, Act on the Book-Entry Transfer of Company Bonds, Shares, etc.
426. Article 152, para. 1, Act on the Book-Entry Transfer of Company Bonds, Shares, etc.
427. Article 152, para. 1, Act on the Book-Entry Transfer of Company Bonds, Shares, etc.
428. Article 58 of the Securities Exchange Act prior to its amendment in 1992.
429. Article 166, para. 1, Financial Instruments and Exchange Act.
430. Article 433, Companies Act; Art. 166, para. 3, Financial Instruments and Exchange Act.

425. 'Material facts' include the following: (a) certain decisions made by the company, (b) occurrence of certain facts and (c) revisions in the forecast of net sales, current profits or net profits.

In item (a) above, the decisions include, among others, the following:

(i) issuance of shares, etc.;
(ii) reduction of stated capital;
(iii) reduction of capital reserve or retained earnings reserve;
(iv) acquisition of shares as treasury shares;
(v) disposal of treasury shares;
(vi) share split;
(vii) dividends of surplus and interim dividends which differ from the most recent methods;
(viii) share exchanges (*kabushiki koukan*);
(ix) share transfers (*kabushiki iten*);
(x) mergers;
(xi) company splits;
(xii) business transfers;
(xiii) dissolutions;
(xiv) commercialization of new products or new technologies;
(xv) business partnerships.[431]

In item (b) above, the facts include, among others, the following:

(i) damages arising from disasters or in the course of performing operations;
(ii) changes in major shareholders (shareholders holding at least 10% of the total number of issued shares);
(iii) facts which may be a ground for delisting or recession of registration.[432]

Item (c) above includes the occurrence of difference between the latest publicized forecast and the newly calculated forecast or results of settlement of accounts.[433]

In addition to items (a) through (c) above, the material facts also include, as a catch-all in item (d), material facts concerning the operations, business or property of such listed companies which would have significant influence on the investment decisions of investors.[434]

426. In addition to the rules under Article 166, Article 167 of the Financial Instruments and Exchange Act provides that, in cases where a company decides to implement a tender offer for listed shares or buy up 5% or more of listed shares, certain related persons of the acquiring company who obtained the information

431. Article 166, para. 2, item 1, Financial Instruments and Exchange Act.
432. Article 166, para. 2, item 2, Financial Instruments and Exchange Act.
433. Article 166, para. 1, item 3, Financial Instruments and Exchange Act.
434. Article 166, para. 1, item 4, Financial Instruments and Exchange Act.

concerning such decision in the course of performing his or her duties will be prohibited from buying the target company's shares (in cases where the company decided to suspend such tender offer or buy up, prohibited from selling the target company's shares) before such decision concerning the tender offer or buy up is publicly announced.[435]

427. The criminal liability concerning violation of insider trading regulations under the Financial Instruments and Exchange Act is a maximum of five years' imprisonment or a fine of not more than JPY 5 million.[436] In addition, the property obtained through the insider trading will be confiscated.[437]

B. *Short-Swing Rules (*Tanki Baibai Saeki*)*

428. If the officers of listed companies (directors, company auditors, etc.) or major shareholders (shareholders holding at least 10% of the total number of issued shares) sell the company's shares within six months of purchasing such shares, or purchase the company's shares within six months of selling such shares, the company may demand that such officers or major shareholders provide the company with the profits obtained through such sale or purchase.[438] If the company does not make such demand, the shareholders may make such demand on behalf of the company.[439]

429. While these short-swing rules are aimed to prevent insider trading, it used to be difficult for shareholders to obtain information concerning the buying and selling of company shares by company related persons. After the amendment in 1988, officers and major shareholders of the company who sold or purchased the company's listed shares are required to submit a report pertaining to such sale or purchase to the local finance bureau by the fifteenth day of the following month.[440] If the local finance bureau finds from the report that the officer or major shareholder obtained profits from a short-term sale or purchase, the portion of the report pertaining to the profits (profit-related documents) will be made available for public inspection following certain procedures.[441]

C. *Securities and Exchange Surveillance Commission (*Shouken Torihikitou Kanshi Iinkai*)*

430. In Japan, the Securities and Exchange Surveillance Commission was established in 1992 as an affiliated organization of the Ministry of Finance to prevent

435. Article 167, Financial Instruments and Exchange Act.
436. Article 197-2, item 13, Financial Instruments and Exchange Act.
437. Article 198-2, para. 1, item 1, Financial Instruments and Exchange Act.
438. Article 164, para. 1, Financial Instruments and Exchange Act.
439. Article 164, para. 2, Financial Instruments and Exchange Act.
440. Article 163, Financial Instruments and Exchange Act.
441. Article 164, para. 7, Financial Instruments and Exchange Act.

unfair securities trading. Subsequently, in 1997, upon the establishment of the Financial Supervisory Agency (*kinyu kantokucho*) as an external agency of the Prime Minister's Office, the Surveillance Commission was placed under the Financial Supervisory Agency. In July 2000, the Financial Supervisory Agency and the financial system planning bureau of the Ministry of Finance were integrated to establish the FSA (*kinyu cho*), which was established as an external agency of the Cabinet Office. At present, the Surveillance Commission is placed under the FSA.[442] The Surveillance Commission is composed of a chairperson and two commission members.[443] The Surveillance Commission may, in addition to implementing investigations of insider trading and other illegal acts on a voluntary basis, conduct mandatory investigations, such as searches and seizures, upon the permission of the court.[444] Based on the findings from such investigations, the Surveillance Commission may file an accusation with the public prosecutors' office.[445] In addition, the Surveillance Commission may implement on-site inspections against securities firms (financial instrument business operators) and self-regulatory organizations (associations of financial instrument business operators, financial instrument exchanges).[446] The Surveillance Commission may, based on the findings from such inspections, make a recommendation to the prime minister and the FSA commissioner seeking an administrative disposition.[447]

442. Article 6, Act on Establishment of the Financial Services Agency.
443. Article 10, Act on Establishment of the Financial Services Agency.
444. Article 210, Financial Instruments and Exchange Act; Art. 211, Financial Instruments and Exchange Act.
445. Article 226, para. 1, Financial Instruments and Exchange Act.
446. Article 194-7, para. 2, Financial Instruments and Exchange Act.
447. Article 20, Act on the Establishment of the Financial Services Agency.

Chapter 3. Financing of Stock Companies

§1. Overview

431. The funds of a company may be categorized into internal funds and external funds. Internal funds are generated by the company through its business activities and include the internal reserve of profits. The internal reserve will be accumulated each year by the amount of profits during the current business year minus the sum of dividends of surplus to be paid to the shareholders, directors' bonuses, taxes and other applicable costs.

432. External funds are obtained from outside the company, and include the proceeds from issuance of shares, bonds and other securities, and bank loans. The funds obtained by issuing securities are known as direct financing and the funds obtained through bank loans are known as indirect financing. External funds were traditionally overwhelmingly dependent on indirect financing. The reasons were that (i) the Japanese government took a low interest rate policy following World War II, (ii) a close relationship had been built between the banks and companies (so-called main bank system), and (iii) the stock market was underdeveloped. In addition, during the subsequent period of high economic growth, the demands for financing increased due to the strong motivation of companies for capital expenditures, and the shortages in funds were financed by loans from the banks. However, as the economy entered a period of stable growth, companies began to curb capital expenditures and aimed to increase business efficiency, which led to the diversification of financing methods. In particular, moves to obtain funds through domestic and international stock markets became more active. However, this was very much limited to large companies, and many small and medium-size enterprises still rely on bank loans.

433. In the 1980s, the stock market was booming: stock prices rose, and the cost of equity financing (financing by issuance of shares) was relatively low (Table 15). Therefore, companies were eager to issue shares, convertible bonds and bonds with warrants (Table 16). In addition, during this period, in order to fulfil the capital adequacy requirements (requirements of a certain level of equity capital/total assets) prescribed by the Bank for International Settlements (BIS), equity financing by banks was carried out robustly. The equity financing by the finance and insurance industries increased by JPY 3.8088 trillion accounting for 50.3% of the total. In addition, the Commercial Paper (CP) market, which was established in 1987, expanded rapidly, and companies began to use the capital markets even for their short-term loans. Under such circumstances, the companies' reliance on bank loans (leverage ratio) decreased.

434. On 29 December 1989, the Nikkei Index of the Tokyo Stock Exchange recorded a record high of JPY 38,915. However, the stock prices reversed in 1990, followed by a downward trend, and therefore the amount of equity financing in 1990 fell by 91.2% compared with the previous year. In addition, the Nikkei Index fell below JPY 20,000 on 16 March 1992. Since then, it continued to be difficult for companies to implement equity financing (Table 15).

Table 15 Share Prices

	Nikkei Average (225 TSE Companies)	*TOPIX (Tokyo Stock Price Index)*
	JPY	JPY
1989	38,915.87	2,881.37
1990	23,848.71	1,733.83
1991	22,983.77	1,714.68
1992	16,924.95	1,307.66
1993	17,417.24	1,439.31
1994	19,723.06	1,559.09
1995	19,868.15	1,577.70
1996	19,361.35	1,470.94
1997	15,258.74	1,175.03
1998	13,842.17	1,086.99
1999	18,934.34	1,722.20
2000	13,785.69	1,283.67
2001	10,542.62	1,032.14
2002	8,578.95	843.29
2003	10,676.64	1,043.69
2004	11,488.76	1,149.63
2005	16,194.61	1,649.76
2006	17,224.81	1,681.07
2007	15,307.78	1,475.68
2008	8,859.56	869.24
2009	10,546.44	907.59
2010	10,228.92	898.80
2011	8,455.35	728.61
2012	10,395.18	859.80
2013	16,291.31	1,302.29
2014	17.450.77	1,407.51

435. With regard to convertible bonds (currently, convertible bond-type bonds with share options), the companies' stock prices continued to be lower than the conversion price. As a result, the conversion rights were barely exercised, and the issuing companies were forced to redeem such convertible bonds upon maturity. In addition, with regard to bonds with warrants (currently, bonds with share options), the company stock prices were lower than the exercise price of the subscription rights. In such cases, the detachable subscription warrants became worthless and the losses incurred by retail investors who had bought bonds with warrants through the aggressive sales activities of the securities companies turned out to be a social problem. This led to a large number of lawsuits being filed against the securities companies.

436. In cases where stock prices are not expected to increase, there is no incentive to issue bonds with share options. This is evident from Table 16. Specifically, the amount of funding raised by issuing the company bonds originally called 'bonds with subscription rights' (*shinkabu hikiukeken shasai*) (currently called 'bonds with share options' (*shinkabu yoyakuken tsuki shasai*)) has remained low in recent years. In contrast, there have continued to be many issuances of straight bonds.

Table 16 Amounts of Straight Bonds and Bonds with Share Options (Convertible Bond-Type) (Unit: JPY 1,000)

Year	*Straight Bonds*		*Bonds with Share Options (Convertible Bond-Type)*	
	No. of Cases	*Amount*	*No. of Cases*	*Amount*
1998	769	12,642,900,000	5	73,000,000
1999	394	6,912,500,000	26	528,000,000
2000	411	7,975,060,000	19	275,000,000
2001	354	8,272,390,000	17	248,000,000
2002	282	7,151,205,000	15	280,000,000
2003	366	7,380,760,000	9	56,500,000
2004	296	5,766,500,000	20	211,000,000
2005	329	6,851,500,000	9	65,000,000
2006	323	6,544,500,000	15	553,000,000
2007	443	9,186,300,000	4	35,000,000
2008	324	8,842,800,000	1	150,000,000
2009	374	11,393,100,000	4	203,500,000
2010	456	9,558,900,000	6	122,500,000
2011	394	8,282,500,000	2	32,500,000
2012	416	8,209,900,000	2	8,500,000
2013	444	8,658,803,000	7	75,500,000
2014	463	8,396,950,000	7	44,000,000

Source: Japan Securities Dealers Association, Issuance price and redemption amount, etc., of public and corporate bonds.

§2. EQUITY FINANCING

I. Authorized Capital (*Juken Shihon*)

437. The total number of shares that a company is authorized to issue is provided in its articles of incorporation.[448] Upon incorporation of a Public Company, at least 25% of the total number of such authorized shares must be issued.[449] The remaining unissued shares may be issued, in principle, by a resolution of the board of directors at any time after the incorporation of the company (this system is known as the authorized capital system). The total number of authorized shares is known as authorized capital or authorized stock. The company may increase the total number of authorized shares by amending the articles of incorporation. However, in a Public Company, the total number of authorized shares after the amendment to the articles of incorporation may not exceed four times the total number of issued shares.[450]

438. Equity financing will often create a disadvantage to the existing shareholders through the dilution of shares. On the other hand, the management team of a company will want to raise funds by issuance of shares in a timely manner. The authorized capital system is designed to authorize the board of directors to issue new shares flexibly within the total number of authorized shares as provided in the company's articles of incorporation (setting a limit to the dilution of shares held by existing shareholders).

439. The abovementioned restriction on the total number of shares issued upon the incorporation of a company having to be at least 25% of the total number of authorized shares does not apply to non-Public Companies.[451] The restriction that the total number of authorized shares must not exceed four times the total number of issued shares also does not apply to those companies.[452] This is because, in non-Public Companies, issuances of new shares are, in principle, subject to a special resolution at the shareholders meeting and therefore there is little risk of an abusive issuance of shares by the board of directors (see paragraphs 442–444).

II. Determination of 'Subscription Requirements' (*Boshu Jikou*)

440. A company will issue new shares in exchange for receiving new funds from the subscribers. This will be the same in the disposal of treasury shares by the company. Therefore, the Companies Act provides the same rules on the issuance of new shares and disposal of treasury shares.

448. Article 37, paras 1 and 2, Companies Act.
449. Article 37, main text of para. 3, Companies Act.
450. Article 113, main text of para. 3, Companies Act.
451. Article 37, proviso to para. 3, Companies Act.
452. Article 113, proviso to para. 3, Companies Act.

441. If a company intends to solicit persons to subscribe for new shares or treasury shares, the company must determine certain matters relating to the subscribed shares (subscription requirements).[453]

A. *Procedures for Non-public Companies*

442. The company must determine the subscription requirements by a special resolution at the shareholders meeting.[454] The matters which need to be determined as the subscription requirements are as follows:

(i) The number of shares (in cases of class shares, the class and number).
(ii) The amount to be paid-in for the shares (i.e., the amount of monies to be paid-in exchange for one solicited share or the amount of the property other than money to be contributed) or the method for calculating such amount. In the event that the amount to be paid-in is particularly favourable for subscribers (so-called 'favourable issuance' (*yuri hakkou*)), the directors must explain the reason for the need to solicit shareholders for such amount at the shareholders meeting.[455]
(iii) If property other than money will be contributed, a statement to such effect and the description and value of such property.
(iv) The date or period for the payment of money in exchange for the shares or the contribution of property under item (iii) above.
(v) If shares are issued, matters regarding the stated capital and capital reserves to be increased.

443. When a company issues shares using the method of shareholder allotment (*kabunushi wariate*) where entitlement to the allotment of shares is granted to the existing shareholders (see paragraph 450), such matters may be determined by the directors or the board of directors, to the extent so permitted in the articles of incorporation (in such case, in addition to items (i) through (v), items (vi) a statement to the effect of granting shareholders the right to be entitled to the allotment of new shares and (vii) the day for the application of subscription will also be required).[456] In cases other than a shareholder allotment (e.g., third-party allotment), the determination of such matters may be authorized to the directors or the board of directors by a special resolution at shareholders meeting (this authorization may not be made by a provision in the articles of incorporation).[457] In such case, the upper limit of the above item (i) and the lower limit of the above item (ii) must be specified at the shareholders meeting. For non-Public Companies, the shareholder resolutions on favourable issuance and third-party allotment were integrated under the Companies

453. Article 199, para. 1, Companies Act.
454. Article 199, para. 2; Art. 309, para. 2, item 5, Companies Act.
455. Article 199, para. 3, Companies Act.
456. Article 202, para. 3, items 1 and 2; Art. 202, para. 5, Companies Act.
457. Article 200, para. 1; Art. 309, para. 2, item 5, Companies Act.

Act (i.e., the Commercial Code prior to the amendment in 2005 required shareholder resolutions (i) upon a favourable issuance, the classes and number of the shares and the minimum issue price and (ii) upon a third-party allotment, the classes and number of shares. Under the Companies Act, a shareholder resolution on (i) the number of shares and (ii) the lower limit of the amount to be paid-in is sufficient to authorize the issuance of shares to the directors or board of directors, as the case may be).

444. For a corporation with class shares (*shurui kabushiki hakkou kaisha*), if the class shares to be subscribed are 'shares with restrictions on transfer' (*jouto seigen kabushiki*), a resolution at the class meeting of such class shares will be required unless otherwise provided in the company's articles of incorporation, in addition to the shareholder resolution or the resolution of the board of directors (as the case may be) in which the subscription requirements will be determined.[458]

B. Procedures for Public Companies

445. The company must determine the subscription requirements by a resolution of the board of directors.[459] The matters to be prescribed as subscription requirements are the same as those mentioned above for non-Public Companies.[460] However, with regard to item (ii) above (see paragraph 442), if the paid amount is particularly favourable for the subscribers, a special resolution at shareholders meeting will be required.[461] In addition, if the shares are shares with a market price, the company may alternatively provide 'the method for determining an amount to be paid-in that is appropriate to realize payment in at a fair value'.[462] This envisages a so-called book building, a method of determining the price by surveying the demands of institutional investors.

446. After the board of directors determines the subscription requirements, the company must notify the shareholders of such subscription requirements, or post a public notice, at least two weeks before the date of payment.[463] This is to ensure that the dissenting shareholders are given the opportunity to file an enjoinment against the solicitation (see paragraph 484). In cases where a securities registration statement is filed at least two weeks in advance (see paragraph 472) or in certain cases prescribed by the applicable Ordinance of the Ministry of Justice as where it is unlikely that the protection of shareholders is at risk, such shareholder notice or public notice will not be required.[464]

458. Article 199, para. 4; Art. 200, para. 4, Companies Act.
459. Article 201, para. 1, Companies Act.
460. Article 199, para. 1, Companies Act.
461. Article 201, para. 1, Companies Act.
462. Article 201, para. 2, Companies Act.
463. Article 201, paras 3 and 4, Companies Act.
464. Article 201, para. 5, Companies Act; Art. 40, Ordinance for Enforcement of the Companies Act.

447. The Companies Act permits Public Companies to implement financing flexibly through board of directors resolutions under the authorized capital system. When a company issues shares through a method other than shareholder allotment, the ratio of shares held by existing shareholders changes. Under the authorized capital system, existing shareholders permit such changes if it is implemented within the range of the total number of authorized shares prescribed in the articles of incorporation. However, even within the authorized shares, there may be large-scale third-party allotments resulting in a change of control of the company.

448. The 2014 amendment requires a shareholder approval upon certain circumstances where Public Companies issue shares for subscription, etc., on a large-scale that would cause a change of control of the company. Specifically, if particular subscribers would hold more than half of all voting rights of the company after the shares are issued, all shareholders must be notified at least two weeks prior to either the date of the payment or the first day of the payment period. Within two weeks of that notification, if shareholders who hold 10% or more of the total voting rights of all shareholders notify the company of their disagreement, then in principle, the company must obtain approval by a resolution at the shareholders meeting.[465] Although an ordinary resolution at the shareholders meeting will suffice, the articles of incorporation cannot specify a quorum of less than one third.[466] This requirement is similar to that for the appointment and dismissal of officers (see paragraph 661). The reason for this requirement was that an issuance of shares resulting in a change of control is similar to the appointment of directors in the sense that both determine who controls the management of the company.

III. Form of Equity Financing

449. In cases where a stock company solicits shares for financing, there are three types of solicitation methods: shareholder allotment, public offering and third-party allotment (Table 17).

Table 17 Number and Volume of Capital Increases

Year	*Shareholder Allotment*		*Public Offering*		*Third-Party Allotment*	
	No. of cases	*Volume*	*No. of Cases (IPOs)*	*Volume (IPOs)*	*No. of cases*	*Volume*
1998	-	-	8	278,181	32	688,016
1999	-	-	28	349,715	75	2,347,286
2000	2	8,240	24	494,149	46	922,756

465. Article 206-2, Companies Act.
466. Article 206-2, para. 5, Companies Act.

Year	*Shareholder Allotment*		*Public Offering*		*Third-Party Allotment*	
	No. of cases	*Volume*	*No. of Cases (IPOs)*	*Volume (IPOs)*	*No. of cases*	*Volume*
2001	3	32,047	18	1,201,483	57	477,176
2002	-	-	19	153,312	62	484,350
2003	2	1,451	35	567,236	84	223,161
2004	1	2,729	78	750,232	129	572,627
2005	2	3,721	74	650,847	150	778,055
2006	-	-	69	1,447,724	145	416,476
2007	1	8,086	60 (23)	456,974 (70,900)	117	662,102
2008	1	139	27 (19)	341,697 (31,444)	93	395,840
2009	-	-	52 (9)	4,966,829 (22,490)	115	714,609
2010	1	689	50 (11)	3,308,906 (201,338)	88	535,606
2011	-	-	45 (20)	967,813 (111,243)	66	395,151
2012	1	414	53 (29)	451,766 (32,036)	71	159,327
2013	1	981	114 (47)	1,113,702 (373,549)	151	371,855
2014	-	-	129 (66)	1,377,995 (234,650)	190	392,844

Source: Website of Japan Exchange Group.

450. A shareholder allotment is where the shareholders will be entitled to the allotment of new shares in accordance with the number of shares each shareholder holds. In a shareholder allotment, in addition to the determination of the abovementioned subscription requirements (see paragraph 440), the company must prescribe a statement to the effect of granting shareholders the right to be entitled to the allotment of new shares and the day for application.[467] These matters will be prescribed by a resolution of the board of directors in case of Public Company.[468] Non-Public Companies require a shareholder resolution; provided, however, that this may be

467. Article 202, para. 1, Companies Act.
468. Article 202, para. 3, item 3, Companies Act.

authorized to the directors (in Company with Board of Directors, the board of directors) by the articles of incorporation.[469]

451. After prescribing the subscription requirements, the company must notify the shareholders of the determined matters to allow the shareholders to decide whether or not to apply for shares.[470] In a shareholder allotment, even if the paid amount is particularly favourable for the subscribers, this does not disadvantage existing shareholders (i.e., in case of a company whose total number of issued shares is 80,000 and the market price of each share is JPY 1,000, if 20,000 new shares were solicited at a price of JPY 500 per share, the market price of the shares will drop to JPY 900 (i.e., (80,000 shares x JPY 1,000 + 20,000 shares x JPY 500) ÷ (80,000 shares + 20,000 shares)). A shareholder who held forty shares before the solicitation will receive ten shares. Before the allotment, such shareholder owned a total of JPY 45,000 of assets, made up of (i) forty shares x JPY 1,000, which was the value of the shares held, and (ii) cash to purchase the ten allotted shares x JPY 500. After the allotment, this shareholder will have fifty shares valued at JPY 900 per share and the total value of the assets will remain unchanged at JPY 45,000). Therefore, a Public Company may implement shareholder allotment by a resolution of the board of directors. However, in non-Public Companies, the shareholder allotment still requires, in principle, a shareholder resolution (see paragraph 442). This is because shareholders in non-Public Companies normally have strong interest in maintaining the proportion of the shares they hold and therefore should not be subject to the risk of dilution without a shareholders meeting, as such shareholders may not afford to subscribe in the allotted shares upon the shareholder allotment. In addition, when soliciting certain class shares of a corporation with class shares, if it is likely to cause detriment to the class shareholders, a resolution at class meeting will be required unless otherwise provided in the company's articles of incorporation.[471]

452. Prior to the amendment in 2005, the shareholder allotment was implemented in the form of granting subscription warrants. A subscription warrant certificate was issued for the subscription warrant to ensure the liquidity of such subscription warrants (it was also 'securities' as defined under the then Securities Exchange Act). In the Companies Act, the terminology of subscription warrants was abolished, and the abovementioned procedures were established with regard to the allotment of shares to shareholders.

453. Public offering is generally known as a method to widely solicit subscription of new shares from investors. An 'offering' as defined in the Financial Instruments and Exchange Act is also sometimes referred to as public offering (see paragraph 472). In the past, many companies issued shares through a public offering (Table 17). The issue price of the public offering is determined based on the market price of the shares of the issuing company. Therefore, this kind of issuance is also known as market price public offering.

---

469. Article 202, para. 3, items 1, 2 and 4, Companies Act.
470. Article 203, para. 1, item 2, Companies Act.
471. Article 322, paras 1, 2 and 3, Companies Act.

454. In a third-party allotment, the shares will be allocated to one or more specific subscribers. Allocation of new shares to particular shareholders also constitutes a third-party allotment unless allocated to all existing shareholders in accordance with the number of shares they hold. A third-party allotment is often implemented to strengthen the company's business alliance with a specific third party to whom the new shares will be allocated. It is also sometimes used by a financially distressed company which will be acquired by another company through such third-party allotment. In addition, it may be used to defend against a hostile takeover attempt. In these cases, the paid-in value at the time of solicitation of the shares is often set at a price lower than the market price. In the Companies Act, if the paid-in amount is particularly favourable for the subscribers, a special resolution at shareholders meeting will be required and the directors must explain the reasons at the shareholders meeting.[472] As such, a question arises as to what exactly constitutes an 'amount which is particularly favourable'. In particular, if the market price of the shares are soaring due to speculative trading in the stock market, there may be a dispute on the fairness of the paid-in value in the third-party allotment (in a favourable issuance, a special resolution at shareholders meeting is required and, without such resolution, the third-party allotment may be enjoined for violation of laws and regulations (see paragraph 484)).

455. A court precedent has ruled that while the market price cannot be excluded from the basis of calculating the fair issue price even if the market price is soared, in the event that such shares are subject to an unusually high degree of speculative trading that the market price has soared significantly higher than the objective value of the company and this is a temporary phenomenon in the stock market, the market price may be excluded from the basis of calculating the fair issue price (Tokyo District Court, 25 July 1989, *Hanrei Jihou* No. 1317-28). In this regard, the Japan Securities Dealers Association has established certain voluntary rules. According to such voluntary rules, the standard for the issue price of new shares through a third-party allotment is provided as:

> 90% of the closing price of the day immediately preceding the resolution of the board of directors with regard to a capital increase in third-party allotment, or 90% of the average closing prices for a period taking such immediately preceding day as the last day with the first day chosen voluntarily as a retroactive day within six months from such immediately preceding day.

IV. Allotment of Shares

456. The company must notify those persons who intend to subscribe for shares the following: (i) trade name of the stock company, (ii) subscription requirements (see paragraph 440), (iii) place handling the payment if payment of money is

472. Article 199, para. 3; Art. 201, para. 1; Art. 309, para. 2, item 5, Companies Act.

required and (iv) any other matters provided in the applicable ordinance of the Ministry of Justice; provided, however, that if the company delivers a prospectus pursuant to the Financial Instruments and Exchange Act (see paragraph 478), such notification procedures will not be required as the required disclosure will have been made by the prospectus.[473] The applicants who apply for subscription in response to the solicitation by the company must deliver to the company, as an application for the shares, a document that specifies (i) name and address of the applicant and (ii) number of shares which it intends to subscribe for, or must provide such details by electromagnetic records (subject to the approval of the company).[474] In a shareholder allotment, the shareholder who does not submit the application to subscribe for the shares will lose the right to be entitled to the allotment of shares.[475]

457. After such application for shares is delivered by the applicants, the company will determine the allottees of shares from among the applicants.[476] The company may decide allottees at its discretion (in the context of hostile takeovers, if shares are allotted to persons supporting the management team of the company for the purpose of self-preservation by the management team, it would be an unfair issuance (see paragraph 486)). Upon allotment, the applicant becomes the subscriber of the allotted shares.[477] If the subscriber enters into a contract with the company for subscription of all shares in its entirety (*sougaku hikiuke*), the abovementioned application and allotment procedures may be omitted.[478]

V. Contributions

458. A subscriber for the shares must pay the entire paid-in amount or make the contribution in kind at the place for the handling of payment by the payment due date or within the payment period.[479] If the contribution is not performed, the right to become the shareholder of the shares will be lost.[480] A person who has made the payment (contribution) by the payment due date (in cases of contribution in kind, the contribution date) becomes the shareholder.[481] If the payment is not fully made, the issuance of new shares will come into effect only to the extent that the payment has been made.

459. With respect to a contribution in kind, as is the case upon incorporation of a company (see paragraph 264), an investigation by the court-appointed inspector will be required.[482] Contribution in kind is also permitted in cases of disposal of

473. Article 203, paras 1 and 4, Companies Act.
474. Article 203, paras 2 and 3, Companies Act.
475. Article 204, para. 4, Companies Act.
476. Article 204, para. 1, Companies Act.
477. Article 206, Companies Act.
478. Article 205, Companies Act.
479. Article 208, paras 1 and 2, Companies Act.
480. Article 208, para. 5, Companies Act.
481. Article 209, Companies Act.
482. Article 207, para. 1, Companies Act.

treasury shares (prior to the amendment in 2005, since there were no provisions on the investigation by inspector upon disposal of treasury shares, there was some debate as to whether contribution in kind was permitted). The following cases have been provided as the exemptions where the investigation by inspector will not be required:

(i) Where the total number of shares allotted to the subscribers does not exceed 10% of the total number of issued shares.
(ii) Where the sum of the value of the contribution in kind does not exceed JPY 5 million.
(iii) Where the value of the securities with a market price does not exceed the market price as calculated by the method prescribed in the applicable ordinance of the Ministry of Justice.
(iv) Where the verification by an attorney (legal professional corporation), certified public accountant (auditing firm) or tax accountant (tax accounting firm) is obtained with respect to the reasonableness of the amount of contribution in kind (verification and appraisal by a real property appraiser will be required with regard to real estate).
(v) Where the property of the contribution in kind is a monetary claim against the issuing company which has already fallen due, and its stated value does not exceed the book value of the debt representing such monetary claim.[483]

460. The Companies Act newly added item (v) as the appropriateness of valuation should not be at risk because, in cases where the claim has already fallen due, the amount that the company must pay has already been fixed. As a result, in a capital restructuring, the creditors may exchange its claim against the company with the shares of the company (so-called debt-equity swap) in a simplified manner.

VI. Share Options (*Shinkabu Yoyakuken*)

A. Overview

461. If a share option holder exercises his or her option against the company, the company has the obligation to deliver the shares by issuance of new shares or, in lieu, delivery of treasury shares held by the company.[484] Prior to its amendment in 2001, the Commercial Code used the term 'subscription rights' (*shinkabu hikiukeken*), for both the options granted as part of the issuance of new shares and those options granted separately from the issuance of new shares. Through the amendment to the Commercial Code, a distinction was made between the two, and the former came to be called 'subscription right' and the latter came to be called 'share option' (further, the Companies Act abolished 'subscription rights' (see paragraph 440)). Share options are used in cases where stock options are granted to the directors or employees of the company, or where they are issued together with

483. Article 199, para. 1, item 3, Companies Act.
484. Article 2, item 21, Companies Act.

bonds ('bonds with share options' (*shinkabu yoyakuken tsuki shasai*), formerly known as 'bonds with warrants' (*shinkabu hikiukeken tsuki shasai*)) (see paragraph 507). Recently, there has been a growing number of cases where the share options are issued as a defence measure against hostile takeovers (see paragraph 488). In any case, the holders of share options will acquire the shares of the company upon exercise of their options against the company. In this regard, they have been granted a call option to acquire company shares.

B. *Issuance Procedures*

462. If a company intends to issue share options, it must determine the following matters as the features of the share options:[485]

(i) The number of shares underlying the share options or the method of calculating such number.
(ii) The value of the property to be contributed at the time of exercising the share options or the method of calculating such value.
(iii) If property other than money will be the subject of contribution, a statement to such effect and the description and value of such property.
(iv) The period during which the share option may be exercised.
(v) Matters concerning the stated capital and capital reserve to be increased when shares are issued as a result of the exercise of such share options.
(vi) If an approval of the company is required for the acquisition of such share options by assignment, a statement to such effect. This item (vi) corresponds to the restrictions on assignment of shares.
(vii) If the company may acquire share options on condition of certain grounds arising, certain matters prescribed by the Companies Act.[486] If the company grants share options (stock options) to its employees, a provision may be established to the effect that the company may compulsorily acquire the share options upon resignation of such employee from the company (share options subject to call).
(viii) Upon certain business combinations such as merger or absorption-type company split, if the share options of the surviving company or succeeding company are to be delivered to the holders of the share options issued by the absorbed company, a statement to such effect and the conditions thereof (succession of share options).
(ix) If a fraction of less than one share to be delivered to the holders of the share options who exercised the share options is to be rounded off, a statement to such effect.
(x) If share option certificates are to be issued, a statement to such effect.
(xi) In cases of item (x) above, if the holders of share options cannot make in whole or in part the demand of the conversion between the registered securities and bearer securities, a statement to such effect.

---

485. Article 236, para. 1, Companies Act.
486. Article 236, para. 1, item 7 (a)–(h), Companies Act.

463. Exercise of the share options may be subject to certain exercise conditions. In such case, the exercise conditions constitute a feature of the share options (commercial registration required).[487] In the context of a hostile takeover defence, the exercise conditions may provide that if certain specified parties acquire at least certain threshold percentage of the total number of issued shares of the company, the holders of the share options other than such specified parties will be entitled to exercise their share options.

464. If the company intends to solicit subscribers for its share options, it must prescribe the following subscription requirements each time:[488]

(i) The features and number of the share options.
(ii) Where there is no requirement for the payment of money in exchange for the share options (i.e., issuance without consideration), a statement to such effect.
(iii) In cases other than item (ii) above, the amount to be paid-in for the share options or the method of its calculation.
(iv) The day on which the share options are to be allotted (allotment date).
(v) If a due date is prescribed for the payment of money in exchange for the share options, such due date.

465. In non-Public Companies, the subscription requirements will be determined by a shareholder resolution.[489] The determination of the subscription requirements may be authorized to the directors (in Company with Board of Directors, the board of directors).[490] In such authorizations, the following matters must be determined at the shareholders meeting: (i) the features and the maximum number of share options, (ii) a statement to such effect in case of issuance without consideration and (iii) in cases of issuance with consideration, the lower limit of the amount to be paid in for the share options. In a Public Company, the subscription requirements will be determined by a resolution of the board of directors.[491] Then, a notice on the subscription requirements must be sent to the shareholders, or a public notice must be posted, at least two weeks prior to the allotment date. These provisions are similar to those rules on the subscription of shares (see paragraph 446).

C. Favourable Issuance of Share Options

466. As in the case of shares, the favourable issuance of share options is subject to certain special rules. If share options that are issued without consideration is a particularly favourable condition for the holders of the share options, or the amount to be paid-in for share options is a particularly favourable price to the holders of the

487. Article 911, para. 3, item 12(c), Companies Act.
488. Article 238, para. 1, Companies Act.
489. Article 238, para. 2, Companies Act.
490. Article 239, para. 1, Companies Act.
491. Article 240, para. 1, Companies Act.

share options, a special resolution at shareholders meeting will be required.[492] The directors must explain the reason for such favourable issuance.[493] Whether or not such condition or price is particularly favourable will be judged by measuring the value of the share options (using valuation theories such as the Black-Scholes model).

D. Assignment of Share Options

467. Assignment of share options is effective upon the agreement of the parties; provided however, that the assignment may be subject to the approval of the company if so prescribed in the features of the share options.[494] While those rules similar to the stock transfer restrictions exist, there is no statutory mechanism for a 'request to designate the purchaser' (see paragraph 378).

468. The company may elect to issue share option certificates for the share options regardless of whether the company is a share certificate issuing company (share options with issued certificates).[495] The company must issue the share option certificates without delay after issuing such share options.[496] The trade name of the company, features and number of the share option and the serial number must be given on the share option certificate, and the representative director (the representative executive officer in Company with Committees) must sign them or affix his or her name and seal.[497] The assignment of share options with issued certificates will not take effect unless the share option certificates have been delivered.[498]

469. Unless the name and address of the person acquiring such share options is stated or recorded in the share option registry, the assignment of share options will, in principle, not be perfected against the company or third parties.[499] The company must prepare a share option registry without delay after the issuance of share options.[500] The share option registry is equivalent to the shareholder registry and the bond registry. An assignment of 'bearer' (*mukimei shiki*) share options takes effect upon the delivery of the certificate, and the certificate must be possessed to perfect the ownership of such bearer share options against the company or third party. Therefore, only the serial number of the certificates and the features and number of the share options will be stated in the share option registry (i.e., name of the assignee will not be stated).[501] In cases where 'registered' (*kimei shiki*) share option certificates are issued, the name of the holder the share option must be stated in the

492. Article 238, para. 2; Art. 309, para. 2, item 6, Companies Act.
493. Article 238, para. 3, Companies Act.
494. Article 236, item 6, Companies Act.
495. Article 236, para. 1, item 10, Companies Act.
496. Article 288, para. 1, Companies Act.
497. Article 289, Companies Act.
498. Article 255, para. 1, Companies Act.
499. Article 257, para. 1, Companies Act.
500. Article 249, para. 1, Companies Act.
501. Article 249, item 1, Companies Act.

share option registry in addition to the serial number of the certificates, the features and number of share options and the date of the acquisition.[502] The statement in the share option registry will be required to perfect the ownership of share options against the company.[503]

470. The Companies Act permits 'share options subject to call' (*shutoku joukou tsuki shinkabu yoyakuken*) where the company may acquire the share options on condition of certain grounds arising.[504] These are equivalent to 'shares subject to call' (*shutoku joukou tsuki kabushiki*) (see paragraph 351). In the event that the company acquires share options, the company may hold such share options as treasury share options (Unlike the acquisition of its own shares by the company, the grounds to acquire the share options are not specified in the Companies Act).[505]

VII. Financial Instruments and Exchange Act (*Kinyu Shouhin Torihikihou*)

471. In an equity financing transaction, the securities regulations under the Financial Instruments and Exchange Act will apply in addition to the Companies Act. The rules under the Financial Instruments and Exchange Act are established primarily from the perspective of protecting investors.[506] An outline of the rules under the Financial Instruments and Exchange Act relating to the issuance of securities is provided below.

A. *Public Offering*

472. Under the disclosure requirements of the Financial Instruments and Exchange Act, a securities registration statement must, in principle, be submitted to the local finance bureau upon a 'public offering' (*boshu*) or 'secondary distribution' (*uridashi*).[507] The 'public offering' here means to solicit applications for the acquisition of newly issued securities from a large number of persons (solicitation to fifty persons or more; provided, however, that the number of 'qualified institutional investors' possessing expert knowledge and experience relating to investment will be excluded but, on the other hand, the number of counterparties to the solicitation for securities issued within the past six months will be included).[508] It should be noted that cases where solicitation is aimed at a small number of persons (less than fifty), or cases where the solicitation is made only to qualified institutional investors may still constitute a public offering under certain circumstances. The cases that will not constitute a public offering are: (i) when the solicitation is aimed at a small number of persons and there is little risk, as prescribed in the applicable Cabinet Order

502. Article 249, item 3, Companies Act.
503. Article 257, para. 2, Companies Act.
504. Article 236, para. 1, item 7, Companies Act.
505. See Art. 155, Companies Act.
506. See Art. 1, Financial Instruments and Exchange Act.
507. Article 4, para. 1, Financial Instruments and Exchange Act.
508. Article 2, para. 3, Financial Instruments and Exchange Act.

ordinance, that such securities will be assigned to a large number of persons (fifty or more) or (ii) where the solicitation is aimed at qualified institutional investors and there is little risk, as prescribed in the applicable Cabinet Order ordinance, that such securities will be assigned to persons other than qualified institutional investors; provided, however, that the issuance of listed shares or over-the-counter shares will always constitute a public offering regardless of the number of persons solicited.[509]

473. As an exemption to the filing requirement of the securities registration statement, the securities registration statement will not be required upon a public offering or secondary distribution if the total issue price or the total distribution price is less than JPY 100 million; provided, however, that in cases where total issue price or total distribution price is a certain amount or more as prescribed in the applicable Cabinet Order ordinance, a securities notification statement (*yuka shouken tsuchisho*) must be submitted.[510]

*B. Securities Registration Statement (*Yuka Shouken Todokedesho*)*

474. The securities registration statement will contain, among others, the following details:[511]

(i) Matters pertaining to such public offering.
(ii) The trade name of the company, the financial conditions of the corporate group to which the company belongs and of the company, and other important matters concerning their business affairs.
(iii) Other matters prescribed in the applicable Cabinet Office ordinance as necessary and appropriate in public interests or for the protection of investors.

475. If certain changes to the descriptions or corrections of the contents are necessary after the filing of the securities registration statement, an amendment notification must be submitted.[512]

476. The securities registration statement or the amendment notification will take effect upon the elapse of fifteen days after acceptance by the local finance bureau.[513] An examination of the statement or notification will be conducted during this period, known as the examination period or waiting period. This period may be shortened in certain cases.[514] While the activities to solicit the acquisition of securities will be permitted upon the filing of the securities registration statement, such

509. Article 2, para. 3, Financial Instruments and Exchange Act; Arts 1–7, item 1, Order for Enforcement of the Financial Instruments and Exchange Act.
510. Article 4, para. 1, item 5, Financial Instruments and Exchange Act; Art. 4, para. 5, Financial Instruments and Exchange Act.
511. Article 5, para. 1, Financial Instruments and Exchange Act.
512. Article 7; Art. 9; Art. 10, Financial Instruments and Exchange Act.
513. Article 8, para. 1, Financial Instruments and Exchange Act.
514. Article 8, para. 3, Financial Instruments and Exchange Act.

securities registration statement must have taken effect before the securities are acquired by investors through public offering or secondary distribution.[515]

477. The securities registration statement will be made available for public inspection immediately upon its submission.[516] In addition, copies must be made available for public inspection at the head office and the principal branch offices of the issuing company, as well as at a financial instruments exchange or an association of financial instrument business operators.[517]

*C. Prospectus (*Mokuromisho*)*

478. Prospectus explains the business of the issuer of securities and other matters for public offering or secondary distribution of securities.[518] In a public offering or secondary distribution, prospectus must be delivered to investors either in advance of or simultaneously upon acquisition of the securities by the investors.[519] No person may use prospectus which contains any false statement or lacks any statement that should be stated for the purpose of public offering or secondary distribution.[520] In addition, in cases where drawings, sounds or other materials are to be used by any person, no false indirection or misleading indication may be made.[521]

D. Deregulation of Disclosure Requirements

1. Contents of Securities Registration Statement

479. Securities registration statement will contain the details of the features of securities to be issued (securities information) and of the company issuing the securities (company information). The disclosure of such information in the securities registration statement may be simplified through the use of the insertion format (*kumikomi houshiki*) or the reference format (*sanshou houshiki*).

480. First, companies which have continuously submitted the annual securities report for at least one year (see paragraph 917) are allowed to integrate a copy of the latest annual securities report into the securities registration statement (insertion format) with regard to the company's business information.[522] If important facts occurred after the latest annual securities report was submitted, supplementary information must be added in the securities registration statement.

---

515. Article 15, Financial Instruments and Exchange Act.
516. Article 25, para. 1, item 1, Financial Instruments and Exchange Act.
517. Article 25, paras 2 and 3, Financial Instruments and Exchange Act.
518. Article 2, para. 10, Financial Instruments and Exchange Act.
519. Article 15, para. 2, Financial Instruments and Exchange Act.
520. Article 13, para. 4, Financial Instruments and Exchange Act.
521. Article 13, para. 5, Financial Instruments and Exchange Act.
522. Article 5, para. 3, Financial Instruments and Exchange Act.

481. Next, if a company has continuously submitted the annual securities report for at least one year and its shares have been listed on the financial instruments exchange or as over-the-counter securities at an association of financial instrument business operators, and the company meets one of the following requirements, the company will be permitted to provide in the securities registration statement that the latest annual securities report should be referred to with regard to the company's business information (reference format):[523]

(i) With regard to the issued shares, the average trading amount and the average market capitalization per year at a financial instruments exchange over the last three years or announced by an association of financial instrument business operators is at least JPY 10 billion.
(ii) With regard to the issued shares, the average market capitalization over the last three years is at least JPY 25 billion.
(iii) The total face value of the bond certificates or the total amount of book-entry bonds issued or delivered through submission of the securities registration statement or the supplementary documents for shelf registration relating to the public offering or secondary distribution of such in Japan over the five years prior to the date of submission of the securities registration statement is at least JPY 10 billion.
(iv) Bonds having the right to receive preferential repayment guaranteed by laws and regulations (electric power bonds, NTT bonds, etc.) have already been issued.

2. Shelf Registration (*Hakkou Touroku*)

482. Companies which qualify for use of the abovementioned reference format may use the shelf registration.[524] Shelf registration will require submitting a shelf registration statement to the local finance bureau. The disclosure items are the same as for the reference format. Solicitation for the acquisition of securities will be permitted upon shelf registration; provided, however, that the securities cannot be acquired by the investors until the shelf registration has taken effect. If the securities are to be acquired through a public offering, the issuer must submit certain shelf registration supplement which provides information on the conditions of each particular issuance. It is also necessary to deliver a prospectus.

483. By using the shelf registration, the companies will be permitted to flexibly issue the securities within a period of two years going forward. In other words, after the shelf registration takes effect, the company may issue the securities immediately by simply submitting the shelf registration supplement, taking into account, among

523. Article 5, para. 4, Financial Instruments and Exchange Act; Art. 9-4, Ordinance on the Disclosure of Business Details.
524. Articles 23-3 to 23-12, Financial Instruments and Exchange Act.

others, interest rate trends. The waiting period upon the filing of securities registration statement is no longer required. Shelf registration is primarily used by electric power companies for their annual issuance of bonds.

VIII. Enjoinment of Share Issuance

484. In cases where the shareholders are likely to suffer disadvantage upon an issuance of shares or disposal of treasury shares which: (i) violates the applicable laws and regulations or the articles of incorporation or (ii) is effected by using an extremely unfair method, the shareholders may demand that the issuance of shares or disposal of treasury shares be ceased.[525] In addition, if a director engages in an act in violation of the laws and regulations or the articles of incorporation (or if there is such risk) and such act is likely to cause substantial detriment to the company, certain shareholders may demand that the director cease such act.[526] The latter is intended to protect the interests of the company and the former is intended to protect the interests of the shareholders themselves.

485. In a Public Company, if the board of directors has determined the subscription requirements (see paragraph 445), the company must notify the shareholders of the details of the subscription requirements at least two weeks before the payment due date (if a payment period has been set, the first day of such period).[527] This allows the shareholders to know the features of the shares beforehand and make a demand to enjoin the issuance, if necessary. In cases where shares were allotted at a particularly favourable price to persons other than shareholders without obtaining a special resolution at shareholders meeting, the court precedents do not typically allow such allotments to be invalidated after the issuance of shares. This is because emphasis is laid on protecting the safety of subsequent distribution transactions as well as enhancement of the company's capital. Therefore, the demand for enjoinment of issuance of shares has great significance in the protection of shareholders.

486. There are no particular restrictions on the method of demanding an enjoinment. In practice, a provisional injunction is sought in many cases based on a claim for enjoinment of issuance of shares. For instance, where the management of a company that has had its shares bought up by a hostile investor decides to issue shares by a third-party allotment with an aim to dilute the shares held by such hostile investor (see paragraph 454), the demand for enjoinment may be petitioned by such hostile investor or other shareholders. In such case, the shareholders may enjoin the issuance of shares by reason of the use of extremely unfair method. In addition, as mentioned above, demands for enjoinment are sometimes petitioned where a third-party allotment is conducted at a price lower than the market value but the special resolution at shareholders meeting has not been obtained. In such case, if the third-party allotment constitutes a favourable issuance (see paragraph 454), the court will

525. Article 210, Companies Act.
526. Article 360, Companies Act.
527. Article 201, para. 3, Companies Act.

accept the demand for enjoinment on the grounds of violation of laws and regulations.

487. Except for the shareholder allotment, issuance of shares will change the ratio of shares held by the existing shareholders of the company (see paragraph 450). As previously discussed, the Companies Act balances the company's need to raise funds in a timely manner with the interests of existing shareholders to maintain their shareholding ratio by requiring the companies to prescribe the total number of its authorized shares in the articles of incorporation. Therefore, to the extent that there is an actual need to raise funds, the allotment of new shares to those subscribers who support the company's management, thereby causing dilution in the number of shares held by the company's hostile shareholders, will not be deemed as an extremely unfair method (court ruling of the Tokyo District Court, 5 September 1989, *Hanrei Jihou* no. 1323-48). The courts have established a so-called 'primary purpose rule' (*shuyou mokuteki rule*) which scrutinizes the primary purpose of the issuance of shares in judging whether or not an extremely unfair method was used.

488. Recently, there have been some cases where demand for enjoinment was petitioned against the share options that were issued as a measure to counter a hostile takeover attempt. Unlike the issuance of shares, it is difficult to justify the company's need to raise funds upon issuance of share options because until and unless the share options are exercised no funds will be raised by the company. Upon issuance of share options, the fairness of the issuance will be decided based on whether or not the hostile takeover attempt will enhance or damage the corporate value of the company (*Nippon Broadcasting System v. Livedoor*).[528] The Tokyo High Court ruled that if new share options are issued with the purpose of maintaining or ensuring the control of the company by the management or particular shareholder at a time there exists an actual dispute in that regard, the demand for enjoinment should be permitted as unfair issuance unless the company demonstrates prima facie evidence or verifies a special circumstance justifying the issuance of such share options to be protecting the interests of shareholders as a whole.

IX. Effect of New Shares and Responsibility of Directors

A. *Effect of New Shares*

489. The subscribers become a shareholder of the newly issued shares: (i) if the day for the payment of money or contribution in kind was prescribed in the subscription requirements, on such day, (ii) if a period for the payment of money or contribution in kind was prescribed, on the date of the performance of contribution.[529] If the contribution was made only with regard to a part of the shares intended for issue, the issuance of shares will take effect only to the extent of those shares for which contribution was made. The rights of those subscribers who did

528. Tokyo High Court, 23 Mar. 2005, *Kinyu Shoji Hanrei* no. 1214-6.
529. Article 209, Companies Act.

not perform the contribution will be forfeited (i.e., the company will not be deemed to have issued the number of unissued shares corresponding to such rights).

490. After the issuance of shares, the company must register the changes in the total number of shares issued by the company and the amount of increase in its stated capital.[530]

B. Responsibility of Directors, Etc.

491. If a subscriber who is in collusion with a director (in Company with Nominating Committee, etc., a director or executive officer) subscribes for the shares at an extremely unfair payment price, such subscriber will be liable to the company for the amount of difference between such payment price and the fair value of the shares.[531] In a contribution in kind, if the value of the contributed property is extremely short of the value as provided in the subscription requirements, the subscriber will be liable for the amount of such shortfall; provided, however, that if the subscriber is without knowledge and is not grossly negligent, such subscriber may rescind its application for shares.[532] The Companies Act abolished the joint and several liability of the directors under the Commercial Code prior to the amendment in 2005 which had required the directors to make the contribution for the shares by themselves if such shares were for whatever reason registered in the abovementioned commercial registration even though no application had been made or the application had been cancelled prior to the issuance of shares.[533]

492. As to the directors' liability, in the abovementioned cases where the value of the contributed property is extremely short of the value as provided in the subscription requirements, the executive director who carried out the duties regarding the solicitation of the subscribers (in Company with Committees, the executive officer) and other persons prescribed in the applicable Ordinance of the Ministry of Justice as those persons who were involved will be liable to the company for the amount of such shortfall (*kakaku tempo sekinin*).[534] In addition, even if the value of such property was determined by the shareholders meeting or the board of directors, the director who submitted such proposal, will also be liable for the amount of such shortfall; provided, however, that the directors, etc., will not be liable if an investigation had been carried out by the inspector with respect to the value of the contributed property or such directors, etc., prove that they did not fail to exercise care with respect to the performance of their duties.[535]

530. Article 911, para. 3, items 5 and 9; Art. 915, paras 1 and 2, Companies Act.
531. Article 212, para. 1, Companies Act.
532. Article 212, para. 2, Companies Act.
533. Article 280-13; Art. 203, para. 1, Commercial Code prior to amendment.
534. Article 213, para. 1, item 1, Companies Act.
535. Article 213, para. 1, items 2 and 3; Art. 213, para. 2, Companies Act.

493. A subscriber who makes a fake payment for shares is obliged to pay the entire amount of the faked payment.[536] This is strict liability. For contributions in kind, the subscriber has an obligation to deliver the property to be contributed. However, if the company requests monetary payment of an amount equivalent to such property, then the subscriber has an obligation to pay that entire amount. The consent of all shareholders is necessary to exempt the subscriber from these obligations.[537] Directors, etc., involved in such fake payments will be jointly and severally liable with the subscriber to fulfil the same payment obligations.[538] If the directors, etc., prove that they did not fail to exercise due care in performing their duties, however, they will be exempt from this liability, unless they faked the performance of the contribution themselves.[539]

494. A subscriber who makes a fake payment cannot exercise any shareholder rights in relation to the relevant shares until after the payment obligation has been performed by the subscriber or director, etc., stated above.[540] However, a person who receives shares that were subject to a faked payment may exercise shareholder rights if they are without knowledge and not grossly negligent.[541]

495. Liability in relation to faked payments was prescribed in the 2014 amendment, and the same rules apply upon incorporation of a company (see paragraph 288-289).

X. Invalidation of New Share Issue

496. Even after the issuance of new shares has taken effect, such issuance should be invalidated if there is any serious defect. The same logic applies to disposal of treasury shares and issuance of share options. However, it is also important to secure the legal status of such share issuance because many transactions would have been in place subsequently on the assumption that the share issuance is valid. Therefore, the Companies Act restricts the actions seeking invalidation of new share issue, requiring the actions to be filed within six months from the effective date of such new share issue (if the company is not a Public Company, within one year from the effective date) by the shareholders, directors or liquidators of the company (in Company with Company Auditor(s), the shareholders, directors, company auditors or liquidators; in Company with Committees, the shareholders, directors, executive officers or liquidators) (with regard to the invalidation of issuance of share options, including share option holders).[542]

536. Article 213-2, para. 1, Companies Act.
537. Article 213-2, para. 2, Companies Act.
538. Article 213-3, main text of para. 1 and para. 2, Companies Act.
539. Article 213-3, proviso to para. 1, Companies Act.
540. Article 209, para. 2, Companies Act.
541. Article 209, para. 3, Companies Act.
542. Article 828, para. 1, items 2 and 3; para. 2, items 2 and 3, Companies Act.

497. The causes for invalidation of new share issue include, among others, issuance of new shares exceeding the total number of the company's authorized shares and the issuance of class shares that are not prescribed in the articles of incorporation. However, the court precedents have ruled that the causes for invalidation of new share issue do not include: (i) issuance of new shares by the representative director without a resolution of the board of directors, or (ii) issuance of new shares without a resolution of the required shareholders meeting (or if such resolution was later revoked).[543] The courts' narrow interpretation of the causes for invalidation of new share issue is based on the need to secure the stability of subsequent transactions based on the new share issue.

498. The courts did, however, rule that the issuance of new shares carried out-in breach of provisional disposition enjoining such issuance will be invalid because otherwise the provisional disposition would be worthless.[544] There are some scholarly views that emphasize the need to secure the stability of subsequent transactions and do not consider such issuance invalid. Another issue is whether or not a share issuance which lacks the required shareholder notice or public notice (see paragraph 446) will be invalid. On this issue, the courts agreed with the scholarly views that such issuance will, in principle, be a cause for invalidation of new share issue because otherwise the shareholders will not be afforded with the opportunity to demand enjoinment of such new share issue; provided, however, that such new share issue will not be invalidated if the company can prove that there were no grounds for enjoinment other than lack of the procedural shareholder notice or public notice.[545]

499. Upon a final and binding judgment invalidating the new share issue, the new share issue will become ineffective from then on.[546] Such final and binding judgment will also be effective against third parties.[547] The company must pay to the shareholders of the invalidated shares monies equivalent to the amount of payment received from such shareholders or the value of the property delivered by such shareholders as of the time of delivery.[548]

500. In addition to the actions seeking invalidation of new share issue, the Companies Act provides an action for declaratory judgment of an absence of new share issue, disposal of treasury shares and share option issuance.[549] While such actions were not expressly prescribed in the Commercial Code prior to the amendment in 2005, such actions had been permitted by the court rulings.[550] Unlike the actions

543. 31 Mar. 1961, Supreme Court Collection of Court Decisions on Civil Actions 15-645; 8 Oct. 1965, Supreme Court Collection of Court Decisions on Civil Actions 19-1745.
544. 16 Dec. 1993, Supreme Court Collection of Court Decisions on Civil Actions 47-5423.
545. 28 Jan. 1998, Supreme Court Collection of Court Decisions on Civil Actions 51-71.
546. Article 839, Companies Act.
547. Article 838, Companies Act.
548. Article 840, para. 1, Companies Act.
549. Article 829, Companies Act.
550. 28 Jan. 1997, Supreme Court Collection of Court Decisions on Civil Actions 51-1-40; 27 Mar. 2003, Supreme Court Collection of Court Decisions on Civil Actions 57-3-312.

seeking invalidation, there are no time limitations on the filing of the actions for declaratory judgment of absence.

§3. BOND FINANCING

I. Overview

501. Unlike shares, bonds are a debt of the company and therefore the funds raised by a bond finance must be repaid upon the maturity of the bonds. In addition, the company will be required to pay the interests, normally at a fixed rate, to the bondholders regardless of the profits of the company. As the creditors of the company, bondholders will not have the right to participate in the company's management.

502. Bonds are a stable source of funds for companies as the bonds generally have a long-term maturity. Stock companies in Japan used to proactively engage in bond finances overseas. This was because various expenses to be incurred by domestic bond finances were relatively greater than those in overseas bond finances, and the financial covenants and other rules were stricter in Japan (see paragraph 514). However, amid the sluggish deposit interest rates and moves to lift bans on payoffs, the straight bonds aimed at domestic retail investors are increasingly issued.

503. Companies may issue preferred shares, pursuant to which dividends of surplus and distribution of residual assets will take priority over the shareholders of common stocks (see paragraph 343).[551] As part of the features of the preferred shares, the company may provide no voting rights of shareholders (see paragraph 347), cumulative preferred dividends, where a shortfall in the payment of preferred dividends in a business year will be accumulated in the next business year (cumulative preferred shares) (see paragraph 345), and a condition that the shares are subject to call. Such preferred shares are very similar in nature to the bonds. Alternatively, as an intermediate form of bonds and stocks, there are bonds with share options, which grant the right to acquire shares in the future (see paragraph 507).

504. In addition to the Companies Act, the bonds may be subject to the regulations under the Securities Bonds Trust Act and the Financial Instruments and Exchange Act. In the Commercial Code prior to the amendment in 2005, the provisions on bonds applied only to stock companies and not to limited companies. General partnerships companies and limited partnership companies were also not allowed to issue bonds. In the Companies Act, membership companies are also allowed to issue bonds (see paragraph 998). The bonds are prescribed independently in Part IV of the Companies Act, following Part II (Stock Companies) and Part III (Membership Companies) of the Companies Act.

551. Article 108, para. 1, items 1 and 2, Companies Act.

II. Types of Bonds

A. *Public Offering Bonds and Private Placement Bonds*

505. Upon an 'offering'*(boshu)* of securities, the Financial Instruments and Exchange Act requires certain corporate disclosures to protect the investors (see paragraph 471). Bonds issued by an 'offering' are called public offering bonds and bonds issued through other methods are called private placement bonds.

506. Private placement bonds will involve intermediary dealers who will sell the bonds to investors on behalf of the issuer. A dealing in private placement of securities is a 'financial instruments business' (*kinyu shouhin torihiki gyo*) under the Financial Instruments and Exchange Act.[552] Therefore, financial instruments business operators may engage in such dealings as their primary business.[553] Meanwhile, banks may also engage in such dealings because a dealing in private placement bonds is exempted from the general prohibition on banks in engaging in the 'securities-related business' under paragraph 1 of Article 33 of the Financial Instruments and Exchange Act. Therefore, banks may engage in such dealings as their ancillary business.[554] In practice, while banks and financial instruments business operators both engage in such dealings, most of the private placement bonds are dealt by banks.

B. *Bonds with Share Options (*Shinkabu Yoyakuken Tsuki Shasai*)*

507. Bonds that may be converted into the shares of the bond issuing company under certain conversion conditions and within a prescribed conversion period are generally known as convertible bonds.

508. In consideration for granting the conversion rights, the interest rates are normally lower in convertible bonds. In addition, the increase in the costs of dividends will normally correspond to the company's profit growth because the convertible bonds are likely to be converted gradually upon the growth of the company's profits.

509. Under the Companies Act, convertible bonds will be characterized as bonds with share options, pursuant to which the share options may not be detached from the bonds for transfer of share options only (see paragraph 461, Share options). The exercise price of the share options will be equivalent to the issue price of the bonds and the bonds will be deemed to have been redeemed upon exercise of the share options as the bonds will be appropriated to the payment of exercise price. The term 'convertible bonds' is still used in practice although such terminology is not expressly referred to in the Companies Act.

---

552. Article 2, para. 8, item 6, Financial Instruments and Exchange Act.
553. Article 28, Financial Instruments and Exchange Act.
554. Article 10, para. 2, item 6, Banking Act.

510. Separately, bonds pursuant to which the bondholders will have the right to subscribe for the shares of the bond issuing company within a certain period at a pre-determined issue price are known as 'bonds with warrants' (*shinkabu hikiukeken tsuki shasai*).

511. Bonds with warrants have similar economics with the convertible bonds in a sense that, in consideration for the warrants granted, the terms of bonds with warrants will be more favourable to the bond issuing company than the terms of a straight bond. However, bonds with warrants differ from convertible bonds as the bonds will continue to exist after the warrants are exercised (provided, however, that this difference does not exist in cases of bonds with warrants in a payment substitution type). One of the benefits of bonds with warrants is that if the company owns a long-term financial commodity denominated in a foreign currency, the company may avoid the risk of currency exchange rate fluctuations by issuing the bonds with warrants with a long-term maturity in such foreign currency. This is different from the convertible bonds as the bonds will not remain in convertible bonds after the exercise of the share options.

512. In bonds with warrants, the bonds and share options will be offered and allotted together as one set of securities. There are two types of bonds with warrants, namely, (i) bonds where the share options and the bonds may be transferred separately (detachable-type) and (ii) bonds where the share options may not be transferred separately from the bonds (non-detachable type). The detachable-type bonds with warrants will be subject to the rules of both bonds and share options under the Companies Act. The non-detachable type bonds with warrants will be characterized as bonds with share options under the Companies Act, in which case certain rules specific to the non-detachable type is provided in Article 292 of the Companies Act.

C. Secured Bonds and Unsecured Bonds

513. In secured bonds, a security interest will be created for the benefit of bondholders to secure the repayment of such bonds. The types of security interest are provided in the Secured Bond Trust Act. As it will be practically difficult for each bondholder to preserve or exercise the security interest, a trustee company will intermediate the bond issuing company and the bondholders (see paragraph 520).[555] On the other hand, in unsecured bonds, there will be no security interest created and the bondholders will be subject to the credit risk of the bond issuing company.

514. In the past, most of the bonds issued in Japan were secured bonds to protect the bondholders. However, unsecured convertible bonds were first issued in 1979, and later in 1985 unsecured straight bonds were issued through a public offering. In these cases, however, unsecured bonds were subject to certain 'issue standards' (*tekisai kijun*). The issue standards were gradually deregulated and were

555. Article 2, Secured Bond Trust Act.

completely abolished on 1 January 1996. In addition, as the previously mandated uniform financial covenants, such as restrictions on creation of security interest, maintenance of certain amount of net assets, restrictions on dividends and maintenance of profits, were later eliminated, the terms of financial covenants may be freely determined by the parties in each transaction.

D. Bond Credit Ratings

515. After the issue standards were abolished (see paragraph 514), the investors are responsible to assess the credit risks of the bond issuers by themselves. However, as it is difficult for the investors to assess such credit risks, certain investment information is published by the private credit rating agencies assessing the credit worthiness of the bonds – in other words, the degree of certainty in the repayment of the bonds. At the request of the bond issuing companies, the credit rating agencies provide the ratings based on the materials provided by such companies in consideration for the fees to be paid for such services. There are also some agencies that provide the ratings based on their own assessment without being so requested by the company.

516. In principle, a AAA (triple A) rating indicates the highest degree of safety, and BBB (triple B) or higher ratings are considered to be investment-grade bonds, while anything below BBB is considered to be speculative.

III. Protection of Bondholders

A. Removal of Limitations on Bond Issuance

517. Prior to the amendment to the Commercial Code in 1993, the amount of bonds issued by a company could not exceed the amount of net assets (i.e., assets minus liabilities) of the company based on the last balance sheet.[556] Such limitation was eased by the Act on Interim Measures for the Issuance of Bonds to twice the amount of such limitation provided in the Commercial Code, although any amount in excess of the limitation under the Commercial Code was permitted in the forms of secured bonds, convertible bonds, bonds with warrants or overseas bonds only. In addition, the limitations were further deregulated on the bonds issued by long-term credit banks (bank bonds) or electric power companies (electric power bonds).[557]

518. The limitations on issuance of bonds were established to control the amount of outstanding bonds within the company's financial capacity on a net asset

556. Article 297, para. 1, Commercial Code prior to amendment.
557. Article 8, Long-Term Credit Bank Act; Art. 2, Act on Special Measures Relating to the Limits on Issuance of Bonds of General Electric Power Companies.

basis. However, such limitations were abolished by the amendment to the Commercial Code in 1993, accepting a strong demand from the industry and the argument that the limitations are not meaningful given that there are no limitations on the amount of indebtedness, such as loans from banks or other institutions.

*B. Trustee Companies (*Jutaku Kaisha*)*

519. Traditionally, there were two types of services in the trust of bonds: (i) the trust services on offering and (ii) the trust services on security interest. The trust services on offering are where the trustee will be entrusted by the issuer with the offering of the bonds, and involve the preparation of the bond application forms, allotment of bonds and collection of payment on behalf of the bond issuing company. The trustee companies were also permitted to perform all acts relating to the redemption of bonds for the bondholders. While it was not mandatory to do so, the trustee companies were in practice retained in all bond issuances. The trustee company for offering was required to be a bank or trust company. The securities companies were prohibited from providing the trust services on offering under the then effective Securities and Exchange Act to explicitly split the banking business and the securities business. Thereafter, the trust companies for offering were replaced by the bond management companies (bond managers under the Companies Act) as described below pursuant to the amendment to the Commercial Code in 1993 (see paragraph 522).

520. The trust services on security interest are management services of the security interests for the secured bondholders. The trustee companies will be subject to the obligation to preserve and enforce the security interests for all bondholders pursuant to the trust agreement.[558] Unless otherwise specifically provided in the Secured Bond Trust Act, the trustee companies will have the same power and obligation as the bond managers concerning the rights of secured bonds (see paragraph 522).[559] Accordingly, the trustee companies must perform the administration of bonds in a fair and sincere manner, and must manage the bonds with the due care of a prudent manager to the bondholders.[560] As the beneficiaries under the trust agreement, the bondholders will benefit from the security interests equally in proportion to the amount of bonds held by each bondholder.[561] The trustee company must obtain a governmental license to perform the trust services on security interest.[562]

521. In the past, there was a very unique customary practice where the trustee companies would purchase all of the bonds at par value from the bondholders upon

558. Article 35, Secured Bond Trust Act.
559. Article 35, Secured Bond Trust Act.
560. Article 704, paras 1 and 2, Companies Act.
561. Article 37, para. 12, Secured Bond Trust Act.
562. Article 3, Secured Bond Trust Act.

a default of the bond issuing company. Currently, however, there is no such practice as the bondholders must be fully responsible for their investment in the bonds.

*C. Bond Managers (*Shasai Kanrisha*)*

522. In the amendment to the Commercial Code in 1993, appointment of trustee companies for offering (later renamed to bond management companies) was made mandatory when issuing unsecured bonds. In the Companies Act, it was further renamed as bond manager because the bond administration services could also be performed by juridical persons other than companies (e.g., Norinchukin Bank). The bond managers will not be required if (i) the amount of each bond is at least JPY 100 million or (ii) the total amount of bonds divided by the minimum amount of bonds is less than fifty.[563] The bond manager must be a bank, trust company or a company which has obtained the governmental license of a trustee company of security interest, etc. (see paragraph 520).[564]

523. Bond managers will have the authority to do all judicial and non-judicial acts on behalf of the bondholders that are necessary to receive payment of the bonds or to secure the collection of the claims relating to the bonds.[565] If necessary to carry out the acts as a bond manager, the bond managers may, with the permission of the court, investigate the status of the business and assets of the bond issuing company.[566]

524. The bond managers must perform the administration of the bonds on behalf of the bondholders in a fair and sincere manner and manage the bonds with due care of a prudent manager to the bondholders.[567] In addition, the bond manager will, in principle, be liable to compensate bondholders for losses if the bond issuing company falls into a default within three months after the bond manager received payment for its own claim against the bond issuing company.[568] This is because, in Japanese practice, the main banks of the bond issuing company often act as the bond manager, in which case there is a need to regulate the acts of those banks which may possibly prioritize the collection of their own loan claims by using the information on the bond issuing company that such banks obtained as the main bank. However, the bond manager will not be subject to such liability if it proves that it did not fail to manage the bonds with due diligence or that such losses were not caused by its acts.[569]

525. Bond manager will not be required in cases where the amount of each bond is at least JPY 100 million. After the bonds were issued by Softbank in 1995 without

563. Article 702, Companies Act; Art. 169, Ordinance for Enforcement of the Companies Act.
564. Article 703, Companies Act; Art. 170, Ordinance for Enforcement of the Companies Act.
565. Article 705, para. 1, Companies Act.
566. Article 706, para. 4, Companies Act.
567. Article 704, paras 1 and 2, Companies Act.
568. Article 710, main text of para. 2, Companies Act.
569. Article 710, proviso to para. 2, Companies Act.

appointing a bond management company (bond manager), an increasing number of companies have issued bonds without appointing the bond management company. While the commission fees may be saved by not appointing the bond management company, a fiscal agent is often retained to handle the administrative procedures such as payment of principal and interest to the bondholders.

D. Bondholders' Meeting

526. Bondholders' meeting may be convened for each class of bonds to determine certain matters which are critical for the interests of the bondholders.[570] Bondholders' meetings will be held to protect the common interests of the bondholders. This will also allow the bond issuing company to avoid having to deal with each individual bondholder as a counterparty. The bondholders' meeting is an organization outside of the company and is not an organ of the company; provided, however, that the costs of bondholders' meeting will be borne by the company.[571] The bondholders' meeting may not resolve any matters other than the matters provided in the Companies Act as the purpose of the bondholders' meeting.[572]

527. Bondholders' meeting may be convened from time to time by the bond issuing company, the bond manager or the bondholders who hold at least 10% of the total amount of bonds of a certain class, and the trustee company of secured bonds.[573] At the bondholders' meeting, each bondholder will have voting rights in proportion to the total amount of bonds that it holds. The resolution of the bondholders' meeting will not be effective unless the approval of the court is obtained.[574]

528. In Japan, most bonds are issued in the form of bearer bonds (*mukimei shiki*), in which case it is practically difficult to convene bondholders' meetings. Hence, the amendment to the Commercial Code in 1993 changed the voting requirement of a resolution of bondholders' meeting, in principle, to an ordinary resolution without any quorum; provided, however, that a resolution to grant extension for the payment of all bonds, or releasing or settling liability arising from the failure to perform the obligations of all bonds requires the consent of bondholders holding not less than 20% of the total amount of voting rights of all bondholders entitled to exercise voting rights, being not less than two-thirds of the total amount of voting rights of such bondholders present at the meeting.[575]

570. Article 715, Company Act.
571. Article 742, para. 1, Companies Act.
572. Article 724, para. 3, Companies Act.
573. Article 717, para. 2; Art. 718, para. 1, Companies Act.
574. Article 734, para. 1, Companies Act.
575. Article 724, paras 1 and 2, Companies Act.

IV. Procedures to Issue Bonds

A. Decision to Issue Bonds

529. Issuance of bond will be determined by the board of directors in Companies with Board of Directors.[576] The resolution of the board of directors must decide not only to the effect of issuing the bonds, but also certain material matters, such as the amount of bonds, interest rate and the method of redemption.[577] In Company with Committees, the decision may be delegated to the executive officers.[578]

530. The directors may be authorized by the board of directors with a predetermined total amount of bonds to make the decisions to issue a series of bonds in multiple occasions (series issuance). Unlike the share issuance, issuance of straight bonds will not require a public notice or notices to the shareholders on the details of bond issuance.

B. Method to Issue Bonds

531. In issuing secured bonds, a trust agreement will be entered into with the trustee company for the bonds.[579]

532. Upon public offering of bonds in a significant amount, an underwriter may be retained by the issuing company. Underwriting is an agreement to purchase all of the securities issued by the issuing company for sale to third parties at its own risk (*sougaku hikiuke* or *kaitori hikiuke*), or to buy up any remaining securities unsold after the efforts made to sell such securities to third parties (*zangaku hikiuke*). The underwriting business may be handled only by the securities companies (financial instruments business operators) as it is a financial instruments business regulated by the Financial Instruments and Exchange Act.[580] When a company issues secured bonds, the operations will be divided where the securities company will handle the underwriting and the bank will engage in the trust services (see paragraph 506, Private placement bonds, and 961, Financial system reform).

533. In 1987, the 'proposal issuance method' was introduced with regard to the execution of an underwriting agreement to surge the straight bond issuance market. In this method, a lead manager of the underwriting securities companies (representing the underwriting syndicate) will be designated by the bond issuing company based on the terms and conditions of underwriting presented by a number of securities companies as potential underwriters. In May 1987, NTT bonds were issued using this method for the very first time.

576. Article 362, para. 4, item 5, Companies Act.
577. Article 676, Companies Act.
578. Article 416, main text of para. 4, Companies Act.
579. Article 2, Secured Bond Trust Act.
580. Article 2, para. 8, item 4; Art. 29, Financial Instruments and Exchange Act.

534. Thereafter, a problematic drop in the prices of bonds occurred as a result of fierce competition between securities companies and escalated discount sales. As such, the 'uniform price sales method' (*kinyitsu kakaku hanbai houshiki*) was adopted where the terms and conditions, such as the issue price, will be predetermined based on the discussions with the lead managers.

C. *Solicitation of Bonds*

535. The company must notify persons who intend to subscribe for bonds certain details, such as the company's trade name and subscription matters.[581] A person who intends to apply for the subscription of bonds must deliver a document to the company specifying certain matters, such as the name and address of the applicant, the amount of bonds which he or she intends to subscribe and the number of bonds for each amount.[582] The bonds will then be allotted to the applicants.[583] The payment for bonds must be made by the due date for payment.[584] If the total amount of applications to subscribe for the bonds is less than the total amount of bonds planned for issuance, the bonds may be issued at such total amount of applications, to the extent so prescribed in the subscription matters.[585]

536. The applications for bonds are customarily handled in practice by the securities company in its own name at the account of the applicants, although in formality the applications are made by each applicant. In addition to the rules under the Companies Act, the bonds solicited to a large number of investors are also regulated by the Financial Instruments and Exchange Act as the bonds are 'securities' as defined thereunder (see paragraph 472).[586]

D. *Bond Certificates*

537. The bond issuing company must issue bond certificates if so specified in the subscription matters.[587] Under the book entry-transfer system, the company is prohibited to issue bond certificates.[588]

V. Commercial Papers

538. CP are issued by companies to obtain short-term financing. CPs are unsecured and legally characterized as promissory notes. The details of CPs are provided

581. Article 677, para. 1, Companies Act.
582. Article 677, para. 2, Companies Act.
583. Article 678, para. 1, Companies Act.
584. Article 676, item 10, Companies Act.
585. Article 676, item 11, Companies Act.
586. Article 2, para. 1, item 5, Financial Instruments and Exchange Act.
587. Article 676, item 6, Companies Act.
588. Artcile 67, para. 1, Act on Book-Entry Transfer of Bonds, Shares, etc.

in the applicable cabinet order. The Japanese CP market was established in November 1987 (Initially, twenty-five companies issued JPY 800 billion worth of CPs). Since then, the domestic CP market expanded steadily and has become an integral part of the short-term finance market.

539. There will be an intermediary between the issuing company and investors in the issuance transaction of CPs, which are 'securities' as defined under the Financial Instruments and Exchange Act.[589] Therefore, financial instruments business operators may be involved in the dealings of CPs as their primary business. On the other hand, CPs are exempted from the prohibition on banks to engage in securities-related business.[590] Therefore, banks may handle CPs as an ancillary business.[591]

VI. Legislation on Settlement of Bonds, Etc.

540. In the process of developing the securities market, it was necessary to build a safe and highly effective settlement system, such as a new book-entry transfer system, which will not require any certificates, as well as certain clearing agencies to enable effective settlement of securities transactions. In May 2001, the Act on the Transfer of Short-Term Bonds enabled the paperless form of CPs and a book-entry transfer system relating to CPs. In June 2002, the Act on the Establishment of Relevant Acts for the Development of the Securities Market through Reform of the Securities Settlement System (Securities Payment System Reform Act) was enacted to realize a more comprehensive securities settlement system. Under this act, the scope of the unified book-entry transfer system, which does not require any certificates, was expanded to include company bonds and government bonds, thereby renaming the Act on the Transfer of Short-Term Bonds to the Act on Book-Entry Transfer of Company Bonds, etc.

541. In this book-entry transfer system, ownership of the rights to the company bonds will be determined by the records of the transfer account registry.[592] The issuer will notify the relevant book-entry transfer institution once the issuance procedures, including the payments, are completed.[593] Then, the book-entry transfer institution records the notified information in the transfer account registry. Bond certificates will not be issued for the book-entry transfer bonds.[594]

542. The book-entry transfer institutions are those stock companies designated by the competent authorities. It will be necessary to become a participant in the book-entry transfer institution or account management institution to own the bonds, etc., that are traded through this system. As a lower-level agency of the book-entry transfer institution, the account management institution opens an account on behalf

589. Article 2, para. 1, item 15; Art. 2, para. 2, Financial Instruments and Exchange Act.
590. Article 33, para. 2, item 1, Financial Instruments and Exchange Act.
591. Article 10, para. 2, item 5-3, Banking Act.
592. Article 66, Act on Book-Entry Transfer of Company Bonds, etc.
593. Article 69, Act on Book-Entry Transfer of Company Bonds, etc.
594. Article 67, Act on the Registration of Bonds, etc.

of the participants to implement the book-entry transfer of the bonds, etc.[595] Financial instrument business operators, banks and certain others will be eligible to become the account management institution. In the transfer account registry, the account management institution must distinguish its personal account, which records the book-entry transfer bonds held by itself, and the customers' account, which records the book-entry transfer bonds held by the participants.[596] Separately, the deposit and book-entry transfer system had been used with regard to the settlement of share certificates. However, such system was moved to the new book-entry transfer system for the settlement of share certificates as amended by the 2004 amendment of the act, pursuant to which such act was renamed to the Act on the Book-Entry Transfer of Company Bonds, Shares, etc. (see paragraphs 421–422).

595. Article 44, Act on the Registration of Bonds, etc.
596. Article 68, Act on the Registration of Bonds, etc.

Chapter 4. Organization and Management of Stock Companies

§1. ORGANS (*KIKAN*)

I. Overview

543. Stock company is a juridical person (see paragraph 119).[597] Naturally, the decisions or acts of a company in the capacity of such juridical person will be made or taken by certain natural persons (or a group of natural persons) who are authorized as the organs of the company to make such decisions or take certain acts.

544. Traditionally, the shareholders are considered as the beneficial owners of the company. However, it would not be practical for the large group of shareholders in large-size companies to directly participate in the company management. As such, under the Companies Act, the shareholders will elect directors at shareholders meeting to delegate the management of the company to such directors; provided, however, that the authority to make decisions on certain fundamental matters of the company will remain with the shareholders. Shareholders will participate in these decisions through the exercise of voting rights at the shareholders meeting.

545. Under the Commercial Code, the ownership and management of stock companies were systematically segregated as the form of stock company was originally expected to be used by large-size companies. Hence, a stock company could not provide in its articles of incorporation that the directors must be elected from among the company's shareholders.[598] In practice, however, most of the stock companies in Japan are small-size companies, which are based on personal trust relations where no segregation of ownership and management can be found (see paragraphs 51–53). On this basis, under the Companies Act, non-Public Companies are permitted to limit the eligibility of director to the company's shareholders by the articles of incorporation.[599]

546. The board of directors is an organ consisted of the company's directors (see paragraphs 680–698). The board of directors will make decisions on the company's execution of operations and appoint one or more representative directors. The representative director will make day-to-day operational decisions and execute the company's operations (see paragraphs 699–710). The shareholders may correct the acts of directors through derivative actions and exercise of the right to enjoinment, as well as the election and dismissal of directors at shareholders meetings (see paragraphs 754–766). The shareholders will also elect company auditors who will

597. Article 3, Companies Act.
598. Article 254, para. 2, Commercial Code prior to amendment; this rule still applies to a Public Company under the Companies Act (Art. 331, main text of para. 2).
599. Article 331, proviso to para. 2, Companies Act.

monitor the activities of directors (see paragraphs 767–798). The board of auditors is an organ consisted of company auditors (see paragraphs 782 and 783). In addition to these organs, 'accounting auditors' (*kaikei kansanin*) are also appointed at the shareholders meetings as the accounting experts (although there is some debate over whether the accounting auditors are an organ of the company) (see paragraphs 799–813). The amendment to the Commercial Code in 2002 allowed the companies to become Company with Committees (renamed to 'Company with Nominating Committee, etc.' in the 2014 amendment) in which the company will establish three committees (nominating committee, compensation committee and audit committee) and elect executive officers, in lieu of having company auditors (see paragraphs 816–842). The Companies Act also allows the companies to appoint 'accounting advisors' (*kaikei sanyo*), who will prepare the company's financial statements together with the directors, as an organ of the company (see paragraph 613).

II. Organizational Structure under the Companies Act

547. The Companies Act abolished limited companies (*yugen kaisha*) which was integrated into stock companies (see paragraph 112, Special limited companies). Therefore, the simple organizational structure of traditional limited companies was introduced for stock companies. In addition, the Companies Act permits a greater flexibility for the companies in selecting their organizational structures by the articles of incorporation. At a minimum, stock companies must establish a shareholders meeting and at least one director. On this basis, the companies may add board of directors, accounting advisors, company auditors, board of auditors, accounting auditors, audit and supervisory committees, or nominating committees, etc., by their articles of incorporation (commercial registration will be required), subject to the following restrictions.[600]

548. Companies are categorized into (i) Public Company (*koukai kaisha*) or (ii) non-Public Company, and (iii) Large Company (*dai kaisha*) or (iv) non-Large Company. Therefore, companies can be divided into the following four types (Table 18):

- (i) and (iii) as Category 1;
- (ii) and (iii) as Category 2;
- (i) and (iv) as Category 3; and
- (ii) and (iv) as Category 4.

600. Article 326, para. 2; Art. 911, para. 3, items 15 and 22, Companies Act.

Table 18 Organizational Structure under the Companies Act

	(i) Public Companies	*(ii) Non-Public Companies*
(iii) Large Companies	(Category 1) (a) Board of directors + board of auditors + accounting auditor (b) Board of directors + three committees + accounting auditor (c) Board of directors + audit and supervisory committee + accounting auditor	(Category 2) (a) Board of directors + board of auditors + accounting auditor (b) Board of directors + three committees + accounting auditor (c) Board of directors + audit and supervisory committee + accounting auditor (d) Board of directors + company auditors + accounting auditor (e) Directors + company auditors + accounting auditor
(iv) Non-Large Companies	(Category 3) (a) Board of directors + board of auditors + accounting auditor (b) Board of directors + three committees + accounting auditor (c) Board of directors + audit and supervisory committee + accounting auditor (d) Board of directors + company auditors + accounting auditor (f) Board of directors + board of auditors (g) Board of directors + company auditors	(Category 4) (a) Board of directors + board of auditors + accounting auditor (b) Board of directors + three committees + accounting auditor (c) Board of directors + audit and supervisory committee + accounting auditor (d) Board of directors + company auditors + accounting auditor (f) Board of directors + board of auditors (g) Board of directors + company auditors (h) Board of directors + accounting advisors (i) Directors + company auditors (j) Directors

In a Public Company, board of directors must be established.[601] This is because, in a Public Company which will normally have a large group of shareholders due to the free assignability of shares, the shareholders often have less interest in participating in the management of the company and therefore it is essential to establish an organ executing the company's operations as well as an organ to monitor such operations. In addition, a Company with Board of Auditors, Company with Audit and Supervisory Committee, and Company with Nominating Committee, etc., must establish a board of directors.[602] In a Company with Board of Directors, there is a risk of abusive operations by the representative directors or executive officers as the authority of the shareholders meeting is narrowed by the broad authority granted to the board of directors.[603] Therefore, Company with Board of Directors will be monitored by the company auditors, etc. In a Large Company (excluding non-Public Companies, Companies with Audit and Supervisory Committee, and Companies with Nominating Committee, etc.), a board of auditors will be required.[604] On the other hand, in non-Public Companies, it would be sufficient to have accounting advisors in place of the company auditors, to the extent that the company is not a Large Company.[605] However, a Company with Audit and Supervisory Committee and Company with Nominating Committee, etc., would have either an audit and supervisory committee or audit committee, so they must not have company auditors.[606]

549. As Large Companies are expected to involve a large number of stakeholders, Large Companies must have accounting auditors for the purpose of preparing the financial statements for these stakeholders properly.[607] Companies with Accounting Auditors (excluding Companies with Audit and Supervisory Committee and Companies with Nominating Committee, etc.) must have company auditors.[608] This is because it would be necessary to have company auditors, who have the right of consent for proposals regarding the appointment or dismissal of accounting auditors, to ensure independence of accounting auditors from the company management so that the auditing will be implemented appropriately.

550. All companies may elect to have accounting auditors regardless of the size of the company.[609] In order to have accounting auditors, the company must establish either the company auditors/board of auditors (having the authority to audit the company's operations) or the three committees.[610] As to the committees, the company may not have the committees unless it has an accounting auditor.[611] A

601. Article 327, para. 1, item 1, Companies Act.
602. Article 327, paras 2–4, Companies Act.
603. Article 295, para. 2, Companies Act.
604. Article 328, para. 1, Companies Act.
605. Article 327, proviso to para. 2, Companies Act.
606. Article 327, paras 5 and 6, Companies Act.
607. Article 328, Companies Act.
608. Article 327, para. 3, Companies Act.
609. Article 326, para. 2, Companies Act.
610. Article 327, paras 3 and 5, Companies Act.
611. Article 327, para. 5, Companies Act.

Company with Audit and Supervisory Committee and Company with Nominating Committee, etc., must have accounting auditors.[612] In these companies, there must be monitoring on the operations of executive officers by the accounting auditors from a financial point of view through the preparation of proper financial statements because the matters to be resolved by the board of directors are largely delegated to executive officers.

551. Based on the above, companies in Category 1 (i.e., companies that are both a Public Company and Large Company) may select the following: type (a) shareholders meetings plus board of directors plus board of auditors plus accounting auditors, type (b) shareholders meetings plus board of directors plus the three committees plus accounting auditors (for a Company with Nominating Committee, etc.), or type (c) shareholders meeting plus board of directors plus audit and supervisory committee plus accounting auditors (for a Company with Audit and Supervisory Committee). With regard to companies in Category 2 (i.e., Large Company that is not a Public Company), there is no need to establish a board of directors and neither a board of auditors or the three committees will be required. Accordingly, such companies may select the following: type (d) shareholders meetings plus board of directors plus company auditors plus accounting auditors, or type (e) shareholders meetings plus directors plus company auditors plus accounting auditors. In addition, as such companies may elect to have a board of auditors or the three committees voluntarily, they may also select types (a), (b) or (c). In either case, accounting advisors may be established voluntarily.[613]

552. Companies in Category 3 (i.e., Public Company that is not a Large Company) must have board of directors. In addition, unless the three committees are established, the company must have one or more company auditors, in which case a board of auditors may be established.[614] On the other hand, since they are not a Large Company, such companies will not be required to have accounting auditors or board of auditors. Therefore, companies in this category may select, in addition to type (d), either type (f) shareholders meetings plus board of directors plus board of auditors or type (g) shareholders meetings plus board of directors plus company auditors, and moreover, may also select types (a), (b), or (c), which is available to companies in Category 1. In this case, accounting advisors may also be appointed voluntarily.[615]

553. Finally, companies in Category 4 (i.e., companies that are neither a Public Company nor Large Company) may choose a simpler organizational structure than other companies. First, the board of directors is not mandatory because they are not a Public Company. Hence, the shareholders can participate directly in the management of those companies that have few changes in the shareholders, as such shareholders have a long-term stake in the company (no statutory restrictions in the scope

612. Article 327, para. 5, Companies Act.
613. Article 326, para. 2, Companies Act.
614. Article 327, para. 2, Companies Act.
615. Article 326, para. 2, Companies Act.

of shareholder resolution).[616] In addition, accounting auditors will not be required as there are relatively small number of creditors, such as customers or business partners, in these companies that are not a Large Company. In addition, company auditors will not be required.[617] As such, the companies in Category 4 may introduce the type of organizational structure of limited companies prior to the amendment in 2005. However, companies not having the board of directors are not permitted to have board of auditors as there should be little need for companies having such simple organizational structure to establish a complicated and elaborate structure in board of auditors solely with respect to the company auditors.[618]

554. On this basis, companies in Category 4 may, in addition to the aforementioned types (a) through (g), select type (h) shareholders meetings plus board of directors plus accounting advisors, type (i) shareholders meetings plus directors plus company auditors, or type (j) shareholders meetings plus directors. In addition, in types (i) and (j), the company may voluntarily appoint accounting advisors.[619]

§2. Shareholders Meeting

I. Overview

555. Shareholders meeting will be participated by all shareholders and determines the fundamental matters of the stock company. Shareholders meetings include the annual shareholders meeting and extraordinary shareholders meeting. The annual shareholders meeting must be convened at a certain time after the end of each business year.[620] In addition, extraordinary shareholders meetings may be convened whenever necessary.[621] The shareholders meeting is the highest decision-making organ of a company as the shareholder resolution will bind the management of the company by the directors, and moreover, the shareholders meeting has the authority to elect or dismiss the directors.

556. In fact, however, shareholders meetings in Japan had long been a mere formality until recently when the shareholders meetings have become more of a venue for investor relations. In other words, particularly in large-size companies, individual shareholders did not have significant influence over the shareholders meeting as the corporate shareholders that had a much higher shareholding ratio (see paragraph 68) generally tended to support the proposals made by the company management. In most stock companies, only a small number of shareholders attended the shareholders meetings and the meetings tended to end relatively quickly as no substantive discussions were held (Figure 5) (see paragraph 69).

616. Article 295, para. 1, Companies Act.
617. Article 327, para. 2, Companies Act.
618. Article 327, para. 1, item 2, Companies Act.
619. Article 326, para. 2, Companies Act.
620. Article 296, para. 1, Companies Act.
621. Article 296, para. 2, Companies Act.

Figure 5 Length of Shareholders Meetings

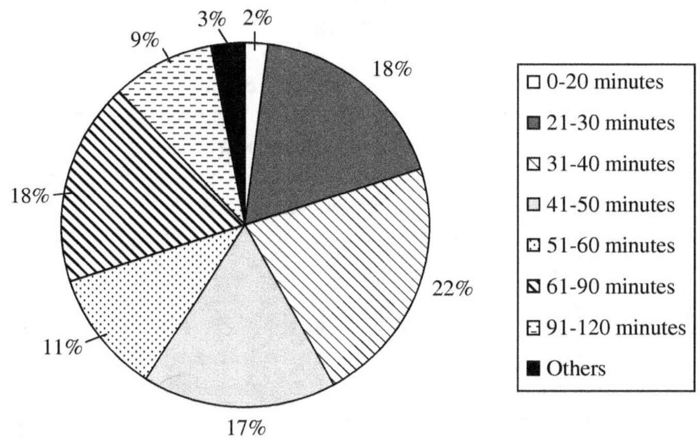

Source: 2014 White Paper on General Meetings of Shareholders (*Shojihomu*, issue number 2051).

557. In addition, there used to be a unique presence of corporate extortionists (*sokaiya*) who would receive money in exchange for cooperating with the smooth proceedings of the shareholders meeting led by the chairperson. As these corporate extortionists would interfere with, and distract, the management of shareholders meeting if they are not paid a substantial amount of money from the company, many large-size companies in Japan used to pay money to such corporate extortionists.

558. The amendment to the Commercial Code in 1981 prohibited such payments by prohibiting any payoffs in connection with the exercise of shareholder rights and imposed civil liability on the directors, etc., who violated this rule as well as the criminal charges.[622] This amendment was intended to eliminate the activities of such corporate extortionists, which were considered to be one of the reasons that the shareholders meetings in Japan had lost substance.

559. Annual shareholders meetings in Japan had a tendency to be held on the same day at the end of June each year (Table 19). This was because companies tried to dilute the attendance of corporate extortionists at annual shareholders meetings. Such practice, however, was criticized as it also prevented other shareholders from attending as many shareholders meetings as they may have wanted otherwise.

560. In 1997, an amendment to the Commercial Code was enacted to reinforce criminal punishments which has now been carried over into the Companies Act. If a director gives property benefits on the account of the company or its subsidiary in relation to the exercise of the right of a shareholder, such director will be punished

622. Article 294-2, Commercial Code at the time of enactment and later became Art. 295, Commercial Code, and Art. 120 of the Companies Act; Art. 497 at the time of enactment, Art. 970 of the Companies Act.

by imprisonment with work for a maximum period of three years or a maximum fine of JPY 3 million.[623] A criminal punishment will also be imposed if a person knowingly received the benefits or caused such benefits to be given to a third party, or requested such benefits.[624] If a person who received or requested such benefits intimidated with regard to the provision of the benefits, such person will be punished with imprisonment with work for a maximum period of five years or a maximum fine of JPY 5 million.[625] Any person who commits these crimes, depending on the circumstances, may be punished by the cumulative imposition of both imprisonment with work and fine.[626] However, if the person who gave the benefits surrenders, the punishment may be reduced or such person may be exempted from punishment.[627]

561. The activities of corporate extortionists declined as a result of the above reinforcement of criminal punishments. Such decline has, to some extent, contributed to the recent trend of decentralizing the dates that the annual shareholders meetings are held (see Table 19). The number of shareholders attending the shareholders meetings shows an increasing trend mainly with regard to well-known companies (Table 20).

Table 19 Dates of Shareholders Meetings

	1995	*2000*	*2005*	*2010*	*2014*
Number of shareholders meetings (June)	1,822	2,003	2,050	2,455	1,871
Date most shareholders meetings were held	29 June	29 June	29 June	29 June	27 June
Number of meetings held on this date	1,710	1,680	1,273	863	844
Percentage of all meetings	93.8	83.3	62.1	35.1	34.3

Source: Documents edition, *Shojihomu*.

623. Article 970, para. 1, Companies Act.
624. Article 970, paras 2 and 3, Companies Act.
625. Article 970, para. 4, Companies Act.
626. Article 970, para. 5, Companies Act.
627. Article 970, para. 6, Companies Act.

Table 20 Number of Shareholders in Attendance at Shareholders Meetings

Shareholders / *Capital*	*1–20*	*21–40*	*41–60*	*61–80*	*81–100*	*101–150*	*151–200*	*201–300*	*Over 300*	*Total*
JPY <500mn	10	24	4	8	2	5	6	1	4	64
JPY <1bn	30	61	39	17	10	10	6	6	9	188
JPY ≤2bn	38	93	81	39	26	28	19	14	25	363
JPY ≤3bn	25	60	55	27	22	22	11	15	16	253
JPY ≤5bn	14	61	67	44	28	53	6	22	32	327
JPY ≤10bn	9	60	106	60	41	57	24	24	45	426
JPY ≤30 bn	5	24	50	53	64	76	52	38	94	456
JPY ≤50bn	-	2	7	9	6	26	18	15	35	118
JPY ≤100bn	-	2	1	4	2	5	5	13	68	100
JPY > 100bn	-	1	-	1	-	1	2	9	94	108
Total	131	388	410	262	201	283	149	157	422	2403

Source: 2014 White Paper on Shareholders Meetings.

II. Convocation of Shareholders Meeting

A. Timing of Convocation

562. At the annual shareholders meeting, financial statements will be approved or reported after the settlement of accounts ends for each business year.[628] In many Japanese stock companies, the account closing dates are set on 31 March of each year (March settlement companies). Companies typically establish a record date to fix the shareholders who will attend the shareholders meeting (e.g., 31 March).[629] In such case, the shareholders who are listed or recorded in the shareholder registry on the record date will be entitled to exercise the shareholder rights. As the record date must be set at a date within three months before the day on which the shareholder rights will be exercised, the companies are practically required to hold a shareholders meeting within three months of the record date, and, therefore, the March settlement companies tend to hold their annual shareholders meetings at the end of June.[630]

B. Authority to Convene

563. Convocation of shareholders meeting will be determined by a resolution of the directors in companies other than Company with Board of Directors and by the board of directors in Company with Board of Directors.[631] The directors convene the shareholders meeting in companies other than Company with Board of Directors, while the representative director convenes the shareholders meeting in Company with Board of Directors.[632] In addition, shareholders who have consecutively held at least 3% of the voting rights of the shareholders for the preceding six months or more may demand that the company convene a shareholders meeting by indicating the purpose of the meeting and the reasons for such convocation.[633] Upon such demand, if the convocation procedure is not effected without delay after such demand, or a notice for convocation which designates, as the day of the shareholders meeting, a day falling within the period of eight weeks from the date of the demand, the shareholder who made the demand may convene the shareholders meeting with the permission of the court.[634] The abovementioned requirements of at least 3% of the voting rights or six months or more may be eased by the articles of incorporation.[635] Moreover, the six months requirement does not apply to non-Public Companies.[636] In addition to such demand by the shareholders to convene a shareholders meeting, the court may order the directors to convene a shareholders

628. Articles 438 and 439, Companies Act.
629. Article 124, para. 1, Companies Act.
630. Article 124, para. 2, Companies Act.
631. Article 298, paras 1 and 4, Companies Act.
632. Article 296, para. 3, Companies Act.
633. Article 297, para. 1, Companies Act.
634. Article 297, para. 4, Companies Act.
635. Article 297, para. 1, Companies Act.
636. Article 297, para. 2, Companies Act.

meeting if the court finds it necessary, after a report is submitted by the inspector specifying the results of his or her investigation on the convocation procedure of, and the method of resolutions at, a shareholders meeting.[637]

C. Convocation Notice

564. Convocation notice must be sent to each shareholder in writing at least two weeks before the date of the shareholders meeting (the notice does not need to be sent to shareholders who are not entitled to exercise voting rights).[638] Such notice period is one week for non-Public Companies, and may be further shortened by the articles of incorporation in companies other than Company with Board of Directors.[639] This is because there is little need to send out a convocation notice well in advance in privately owned companies where the shareholders are normally limited in numbers and have close relationships. The convocation notice may be sent by an electromagnetic method, in lieu of a written notice, upon the consent of shareholders.[640] The convocation notice must specify or record the purpose (subject matters) of the meeting as well as the date, time and place of the meeting.[641] The subject matters of the meeting also include the reporting matters, such as the business reports.[642] However, if the consent of all shareholders who are entitled to exercise voting rights at the shareholders meeting is obtained, the shareholders meeting may be held without following the convocation procedures.[643]

565. In Company with Board of Directors, the financial statements and business reports (including audit reports in Companies with Company Auditor(s) and accounting audit reports in Companies with Accounting Auditors) must be provided to the shareholders when giving the convocation notice to convene annual shareholders meetings.[644] In addition, in companies that the number of shareholders having voting rights is at least 1,000, in which case it would be mandatory to allow written votes (*shomen touhyou*), and the companies which voluntarily opted to allow written votes to the shareholders, the documents stating matters of reference for the exercise of votes (reference documents) and voting forms must be provided to the shareholders.[645] Such reference documents and voting forms may be provided by an electromagnetic method to the shareholders who have consented to receiving the convocation notice by such method; provided, however, that if requested by the shareholder, such documents must be delivered to the shareholder

637. Article 307, para. 1, item 1, Companies Act.
638. Article 299, para. 1, Companies Act.
639. Article 299, para. 1, Companies Act.
640. Article 299, para. 3 Companies Act.
641. Article 299, para. 4; Art. 298, para. 1, items 1 and 2, Companies Act.
642. Refer to Art. 438, para. 1, Companies Act.
643. Article 300, Companies Act.
644. Article 437, Companies Act.
645. Article 301, para. 1, Companies Act.

in written form.[646] In companies which allow the exercise of votes by an electromagnetic method (electromagnetic voting) (see paragraph 583), the reference documents must also be provided to the shareholders when dispatching the convocation notice of the shareholders meeting.[647]

*D. Shareholders' Right to Propose (*Kabunushi Teianken*)*

566. In Company with Board of Directors, the shareholders who have consecutively held at least 1%, or at least 300, of the voting rights of the shareholders for the preceding six months or more may demand that certain matters be included in the purpose of the shareholders meeting.[648] In addition, such shareholder may demand that a summary of the proposals with respect to the matters that are the purpose of the shareholders meeting be notified to the shareholders.[649] For example, 'appointment of A as a director' is a proposal with respect to the matter 'appointment of directors' which is a purpose of the shareholders meeting. The requirements of at least 1%, or at least 300, of the voting rights or the holding period of six months may be reduced by the articles of incorporation.[650] In Company with Board of Directors which is not a Public Company, the six-month holding period requirement will not apply.[651] Moreover, in companies other than Company with Board of Directors, the shareholders' right to propose is a right of single-share shareholders.[652] In Company with Board of Directors, these demands must be made no later than eight weeks (if a shorter period is provided by the articles of incorporation, such shorter period) prior to the date of the shareholders meeting.[653]

567. The company may refuse the abovementioned demand of a shareholder that a summary of such shareholder's proposals be notified to the shareholders if: (i) the proposals are in violation of the laws and regulations or the articles of incorporation or (ii) three years have not lapsed from the day on which, with respect to a proposal which is essentially identical to such proposals, affirmative votes not less than 10% of the votes of all shareholders were not obtained.[654] Shareholders may also submit proposals at the shareholders meeting with respect to the matters that are the purpose of the shareholders meeting; provided, however, that such proposals at the shareholders meeting may not be made in the event of items (i) or (ii) above.[655]

646. Article 301, para. 2, Companies Act.
647. Article 302, Companies Act.
648. Article 303, para. 2, Companies Act.
649. Article 305, proviso to para. 1, Companies Act.
650. Article 303, para. 2; Art. 305, para. 1, Companies Act.
651. Article 303, para. 3; Art. 305, para. 2, Companies Act.
652. Article 303, para. 1; Art. 305, main text of para. 21, Companies Act.
653. Article 303 para. 2; Art. 305, para. 1, Companies Act.
654. Article 305, para. 4, Companies Act.
655. Article 304, Companies Act.

III. Resolutions at Shareholders Meeting

A. Authority

568. In general, the shareholders meeting may resolve the matters provided in the Companies Act, as well as the organization, operations, administration and all other matters regarding the stock company.[656] In Company with Board of Directors, however, the shareholders meeting may resolve only the matters provided in the Companies Act and the matters provided in the articles of incorporation because other matters will be determined by the board of directors so that the company's business may be operated in a flexible manner.[657] Matters other than the statutory matters may be resolved by the shareholders meeting if so prescribed in the articles of incorporation. On the other hand, as to the matters requiring a shareholder resolution under the Companies Act, it will not be valid to provide in the articles of incorporation that such matters may be determined by the directors, executive officers, board of directors or any organ other than the shareholders meeting.[658] In Company with Board of Directors, the shareholders meeting may only resolve those proposals regarding the matters that are provided in the convocation notice as the purpose of the shareholders meeting.[659] In contrast, in companies other than Company with Board of Directors, the shareholders meeting may also resolve those matters for which prior notice was not given.

B. Types of Resolutions

569. Resolutions at shareholders meetings include ordinary resolutions (*futsu ketsugi*), special resolutions (*tokubetsu ketsugi*) and several other extraordinary resolutions (*tokushu no ketsugi*).

570. An ordinary resolution will be made by the majority of the votes of the shareholders present at the meeting where the shareholders holding a majority of the votes of the shareholders are present (quorum).[660] Ordinary resolutions will be required on matters such as appointment of officers, determination of remuneration of officers and approval of financial statements.[661] As the voting quorum and requirements of ordinary resolutions may be changed by the articles of incorporation, many companies have abolished the quorum by the articles of incorporation.[662] In such case, ordinary resolutions will be passed by a majority of the votes of the shareholders present; provided, however, that the quorum may not be less

656. Article 295, para. 1, Companies Act.
657. Article 295, para. 2, Companies Act.
658. Article 295, para. 3, Companies Act.
659. Article 309, para. 5, Companies Act.
660. Article 309, para. 1, Companies Act.
661. Article 329, para. 1; Art. 361, para. 1; Art. 379, para. 1; Art. 387, para. 1; Art. 438, para. 2, Companies Act.
662. Article 309, para. 1, Companies Act.

than one-third of the votes of the shareholders with regard to the appointment or dismissal of officers.[663]

571. A special resolution will be made by two-thirds or more of the votes of the shareholders at the meeting where the shareholders holding a majority of the votes of the shareholders (if a proportion of one-third or more is provided in the articles of incorporation, such proportion or more) are present (quorum).[664] The two-thirds requirement may be increased by the articles of incorporation. In addition, a company may also prescribe in the articles of incorporation that the approval of at least a certain threshold number of shareholders will be required. This was carried forward from the head-count requirement permitted in the special resolutions of former limited companies. Special resolutions will be required to resolve matters such as dismissal of company auditors, amendment to the articles of incorporation, business transfers and certain business reorganizations.[665]

572. Extraordinary resolutions have strict requirements where one of the extraordinary resolutions, including an amendment to the articles of incorporation requiring the approval of the company upon transfer of the company's shares as part of the features of all shares issued by the company, must be made by at least half of the shareholders entitled to exercise their votes at the shareholders meeting, being a majority of two-thirds or more of the votes of such shareholders.[666] A higher proportion may be provided as the threshold by the articles of incorporation. In addition, in non-Public Companies, it may be provided in the articles of incorporation that each shareholder will be treated differently with respect to the rights to receive dividends of surplus, the rights to receive distribution of residual assets and the voting rights at shareholders meetings.[667] A shareholder resolution on such amendment to the articles of incorporation is another type of extraordinary resolution which must be made by at least half of all shareholders, being a majority equating three quarters or more of the votes of all shareholders.[668] A higher proportion may also be provided as the threshold for this type of extraordinary resolution if so provided in the articles of incorporation.

C. *Voting Rights*

573. Voting right is a right to exercise votes in the resolution at shareholders meetings. In principle, the shareholders are entitled to one vote for each share they hold.[669] This is known as the principle of one vote per share (see paragraph 307). However, this principle does not apply in the following cases:

---

663. Article 341, Companies Act.
664. Article 309, para. 2, Companies Act.
665. Article 309, para. 2, all items, Companies Act.
666. Article 309, para. 3, Companies Act.
667. Article 109, para. 2, Companies Act.
668. Article 309, para. 4, Companies Act.
669. Article 308, main text of para. 1, Companies Act.

(i) Shares with restrictions on voting rights[670] (see paragraph 347).
(ii) Shares of less than one unit[671] (see paragraph 359).
(iii) Treasury shares[672] (see paragraph 385).
(iv) Certain cross-shareholding (*sougo hoyu kabushiki*) (i.e., shareholders prescribed by the applicable ordinance of the Ministry of Justice as the entity in a relationship that may allow the company to have substantial control of such entity through the holding of one quarter or more of the votes of all shareholders of such entity or for other reasons)[673] (see paragraph 962).

*D. Diverse Exercise of Votes (*Giketsuken No Futouitsu Koushi*)*

574. A shareholder holding two or more shares may diversely exercise their voting rights.[674] In cases of shares held in securities investment trusts, share management trusts or American depositary receipts, there will be multiple beneficial shareholders even though the shareholder in record may be one shareholder. In such case, a diverse exercise of votes may be necessary to reflect the intentions of such beneficial shareholders at the shareholders meeting.

575. In Company with Board of Directors, a shareholder who intends to exercise its voting rights diversely must notify the company to that effect and the reason no later than three days prior to the day of the shareholders meeting.[675] Advance notice will not be required in companies other than Company with Board of Directors because it would not be practical to require the shareholders of such companies to provide such advance notice as, in such companies, it is not necessary to state or record the subject matters of the meeting in the convocation notice, in which case the shareholders may not know the subject matters until the day of the meeting. However, there is no need to allow the diverse exercise of voting rights to general shareholders. Therefore, if the shareholders are not the persons who hold the shares on behalf of others, such as a trust, the company may refuse the diverse exercise of the votes held by such shareholders.[676]

E. Exercise of Voting Rights by Proxy

576. Shareholders may exercise their votes by proxy.[677] The grant of authority of proxy must be made for each shareholders meeting.[678] Companies may limit the number of proxies who may attend the shareholders meeting.[679]

---

670. Article 108, para. 1, item 3, Companies Act.
671. Article 308, proviso to para. 1, Companies Act.
672. Article 308, para. 2, Companies Act.
673. Article 308, para. 1, Companies Act.
674. Article 313, para. 1, Companies Act.
675. Article 313, para. 2, Companies Act.
676. Article 313, para. 3, Companies Act.
677. Article 310, para. 1, Companies Act.
678. Article 310, para. 2, Companies Act.
679. Article 310, para. 5, Companies Act.

577. The Companies Act does not specifically provide any qualification requirements of proxies. In practice, many companies limit the qualification of proxies by the articles of incorporation to shareholders of the company. Judicial precedents have affirmed the validity of such qualification in the articles of incorporation, ruling that it is intended to prevent the shareholders meeting from being disrupted by persons other than the shareholders and protect the interests of the company.[680] There is an influential contrary view, arguing that: (i) given the free transferability of shares, such limitation is meaningless and (ii) the limitation in fact deprives the opportunity to exercise votes as it would be difficult for the shareholders of large-size companies to find other shareholders to act as their proxies. In this regard, there is a judicial precedent, ruling that the denial by the company of a proxy voting by an attorney who was not a shareholder was construed to be illegal (28 March 2000, judicial precedent of the Amagasaki branch of the Kobe District Court, *Hanrei Jihou* 1580-53).

578. Voting rights may be exercised by proxy at a shareholders meeting through the solicitation of power of attorney by the company itself. Many companies obtain a general power of attorney to handle motions from the shareholders (see paragraph 596). In practice, it would normally be sufficient to obtain such general power of attorney from one or two major shareholders, as motions can be handled by a majority of the votes present at the shareholders meeting. In addition, shareholders who have submitted specific proposals to the company for the shareholders meeting may also solicit power of attorney seeking to exercise the voting rights by proxy, in which case it will develop into a proxy fight with the company. In cases where power of attorney is solicited with regard to the shares listed on the financial instruments exchange, such solicitation will be subject to the proxy rules under Article 194 of the Financial Instruments and Exchange Act and the Order for Enforcement of the Financial Instruments and Exchange Act.

F. *Written Votes (*Shomen Touhyou*)*

579. Where the number of shareholders having voting rights is 1,000 or more, shareholders who do not attend the shareholders meeting will be permitted to exercise their voting rights in written votes.[681] In such case, the company must provide to the shareholders in the convocation notice the documents stating matters of reference for the exercise of votes (reference documents) and voting forms.[682] In written votes, the shareholders will enter their voting forms and submit such voting forms to the company no later than the day before the shareholders meeting.[683] The

680. 1 Nov. 1968, Supreme Court Collection of Court Decisions on Civil Actions 22-2402.
681. Article 298, para. 1, item 3; Art. 298, para. 2, Companies Act.
682. Article 301, para. 1, Companies Act.
683. Article 311, para. 1, Companies Act; Art. 69, Ordinance for Enforcement of the Companies Act.

number of voting rights exercised through the voting forms will be included in the votes of the shareholders present at the meeting (quorum).[684]

580. The companies may, under certain circumstances, elect whether to follow the proxy rules on the exercise of voting rights through power of attorney pursuant to the Financial Instruments and Exchange Act or the rules on written votes (Table 21). Namely, where the written votes are required on a listed company, the written votes will nonetheless not be required if such listed company solicits the shareholders to exercise their voting rights through third-party proxy by attaching a power of attorney form to the convocation notice.[685]

Table 21 Use of Voting Cards versuss Proxies

	Voting Card (Mandatory)	*Paper Votes (Optional)*	*Proxies*	*No Response*	*Total*
JPY <500mn	27	7	1	–	35
	(77.1%)	(20.0%)	(2.9%)		(100%)
JPY <1bn	72	28	5	-	105
	(68.6%)	(26.7%)	(4.8%)		(100%)
JPY ≤2bn	192	39	7	2	240
	(80.0%)	(16.3%)	(2.9%)	(0.8%)	(100%)
JPY ≤3bn	140	12	3	2	157
	(89.2%)	(7.6%)	(1.9%)	(1.3%)	(100%)
JPY ≤5bn	226	9	1	2	238
	(95.0%)	(3.8%)	(0.4%)	(0.8%)	(100%)
JPY ≤10bn	316	1	-	1	318
	(99.4%)	(0.3%)		(0.3%)	(100%)
JPY ≤30bn	360	5	2	1	368
	(97.8%)	(1.4%)	(0.5%)	(0.3%)	(100%)
JPY ≤50bn	106	1	-	1	108
	(98.1%)	(0.9%)		(0.9%)	(100%)
JPY ≤100bn	86	–	–	–	86
	(100%)				(100%)

684. Article 311, para. 2, Companies Act.
685. Article 298, para. 2, Companies Act; Art. 64, Ordinance for Enforcement of the Companies Act.

	Voting Card (Mandatory)	*Paper Votes (Optional)*	*Proxies*	*No Response*	*Total*
JPY > 100bn	100 (99.0%)	–	–	1 (1.0%)	101 (100%)
Total	1,625 (92.5%)	102 (5.8%)	19 (1.1%)	10 (0.6%)	1,756 (100%)

Source: 2014 White Paper on Shareholders Meetings (*Shojihomu*).

581. The abovementioned written votes are shareholders' rights in companies having 1,000 or more shareholders with voting rights. In such companies, it will be necessary to provide their shareholders, who are likely to be territorially-distributed and unable to attend the shareholders meetings, with an opportunity to exercise their voting rights.

582. For companies that are not required to allow the written votes, such companies may also voluntarily opt to permit the written votes by a resolution of directors (in case of companies other than Company with Board of Directors) or a resolution of the board of directors (in case of Company with Board of Directors).[686] In such cases, the companies will be subject to the same regulations as the companies for which written votes are mandatory.

G. *Exercise of Votes by Electromagnetic Method*

583. The companies may decide that the shareholders not attending the shareholders meeting may exercise their voting rights by an electromagnetic method.[687] In such case, the company must provide the voting form by an electromagnetic method to those shareholders who have agreed to receive the convocation notice by an electromagnetic method.[688] If a shareholder who had not agreed to receive the convocation notice by an electromagnetic method requests the provision of the matters to be specified in the voting form by an electromagnetic method no later than one week prior to the day of the shareholders meeting, the company must provide such matters to such shareholder promptly by an electromagnetic method.[689] The exercise of voting rights using an electromagnetic method will be made by providing the matters to be entered on the voting form to the company by an electromagnetic method no later than the day immediately preceding the date of the shareholders meeting.[690]

686. Article 298, para. 1, item 3, Companies Act.
687. Article 298, para. 1, item 4, Companies Act.
688. Article 302, para. 3, Companies Act.
689. Article 302, para. 4, Companies Act.
690. Article 312, Companies Act; Art. 70, Ordinance for Enforcement of the Companies Act.

H. Written Shareholder Resolutions

584. Shareholders meeting must be held to pass the resolutions regardless of whether or not the company adopted written votes or exercise of voting rights by an electromagnetic method. These methods simply allow the shareholders to exercise their voting rights without physically attending the shareholders meeting. However, shareholders meetings should not be required if all shareholders have agreed on certain proposals. In this regard, the resolution to approve such proposals at the shareholders meeting will be deemed to have been made if all shareholders who may exercise their votes agree to such proposal in writing (or by means of electromagnetic records).[691] This will allow a so-called round-robin resolution. A shareholders meeting may also be omitted with regard to the matters to be reported to the shareholders meeting.[692] Such written documents (or electromagnetic records) must be kept at the company's head office for a period of ten years for inspection or copying by the shareholders or members of the parent company.[693] While written resolutions may be used by any company under the Companies Act, given the requirement to obtain the consent of all shareholders, the use of written resolutions is practically limited to those small companies with only a small number of shareholders.

I. Survey of Shareholders

585. The shareholders will need to know the precise status of the company to exercise their voting rights properly at the shareholders meeting. Shareholders may inspect and copy the articles of incorporation, the minutes of the shareholders meetings and the board of directors meetings, the shareholder registry, the financial statements and annexed schedules.[694] In Companies with Company Auditor(s) or Companies with Committees, however, the inspection or copying of the minutes of the board of directors meetings will be subject to the permission from the court.[695]

586. In addition, shareholders having not less than 3% of the votes of all shareholders, or of the outstanding issued shares, may inspect or copy the account books and related materials.[696] If these are prepared by electromagnetic records, the data recorded in such electromagnetic records may be inspected or copied.[697] In such cases, the reasons for such requests must be disclosed.[698] The Companies Act also

691. Article 319, para. 1, Companies Act.
692. Article 320, Companies Act.
693. Article 319, paras 3 and 4, Companies Act.
694. Article 31, para. 2; Art. 318, para. 4; Art. 371, para. 2; Art. 125, para. 2; Art. 442, para. 3, Companies Act.
695. Article 371, para. 3, Companies Act.
696. Article 433, para. 1, item 1, Companies Act.
697. Article 433, para. 1, item 2, Companies Act.
698. Article 433, para. 1, Companies Act.

prescribes certain events where the company may refuse such requests to inspect or copy the account books and related materials.[699]

J. Class Meetings

587. If the company has issued different classes of shares, there must be a mechanism to address the conflicts among the rights of class shareholders. In certain circumstances, the Companies Act requires class meetings which may resolve those matters that are specifically prescribed in the Companies Act or articles of incorporation.[700]

588. The types of resolutions at a class meeting are divided into ordinary resolutions, special resolutions and extraordinary resolutions. Unless otherwise provided in the articles of incorporation, ordinary resolutions will be approved by the majority of the votes of the class shareholders present at the meeting where the shareholders holding a majority of the votes of such class shareholders are present.[701] Special resolutions will be approved by two-thirds or more of the votes of the class shareholders present at the meeting where the shareholders holding a majority of the votes of the shareholders (if a proportion of one-third or more is provided in the articles of incorporation, such proportion or more) who are entitled to exercise their votes are present.[702] The two- thirds requirement may be increased by the articles of incorporation (it is also possible to require the approval of at least a certain threshold number of the shareholders). Extraordinary resolutions will be made by at least half of the shareholders entitled to exercise their votes at the class meeting, being a majority of two-thirds or more of the votes of such shareholders.[703] The quorum and resolution requirements may require a higher proportion if so provided in the articles of incorporation.

589. If the following acts of the company are likely to cause detriment to the class shareholders of certain class shares, such acts will not become effective unless a resolution is made at a class meeting composed of such class shareholders:

(i) creation of new class of shares, change in the features of the shares or increase of the total number of authorized shares or the total number of authorized shares in a class;
(ii) consolidation of shares or share split;
(iii) allotment of shares without contribution;
(iv) solicitation of subscribers for shares through a shareholder allotment;

699. Article 433, para. 2, Companies Act.
700. Article 321, Companies Act.
701. Article 324, para. 1, Companies Act.
702. Article 324, para. 2, Companies Act.
703. Article 324, para. 3, Companies Act.

(v) solicitation of subscribers for share options through a shareholder allotment;
(vi) allotment of share options without contribution;
(vii) merger;
(viii) absorption-type company split;
(ix) succession by absorption-type company split to all or part of the rights and obligations held by another company with respect to such company's business;
(x) incorporation-type company split;
(xi) share exchange (*kabushiki koukan*);
(xii) acquisition of all issued shares of another company by share exchange; and
(xiii) share transfer (*kabushiki iten*).[704]

These resolutions require a special resolution.[705]

590. The company may eliminate the requirement of a resolution at class meeting with regard to items (ii) through (xiii) above if so provided in the articles of incorporation.[706] For item (i) above, while the company may in principle not eliminate the requirement of a resolution at class meeting, such elimination is permitted with regard to an amendment to the articles of incorporation relating to the number of shares constituting one unit.[707] After the class shares are issued, an amendment to the articles of incorporation eliminating the requirement of a resolution of class meeting relating to such class shares will require the consent of all class shareholders of such class shares.[708]

591. In addition, a resolution at the class meeting will also be required on the following acts:

(i) amendment to the articles of incorporation to introduce restrictions on transfer of shares[709]
(ii) amendment to the articles of incorporation where the class shares will become class shares subject to wholly call[710]
(iii) issuance of shares with restrictions on transfer (or any delegation thereof)[711]
(iv) issuance of share options, the underlying shares of which are shares with restrictions on transfer (or any delegation thereof)[712]

704. Article 322, para. 1, all items, Companies Act.
705. Article 324, para. 2, item 4, Companies Act.
706. Article 322, paras 2 and 3, Companies Act.
707. Article 322, proviso to para. 3, Companies Act.
708. Article 322, para. 4, Companies Act.
709. Article 111, para. 2, Companies Act.
710. Article 111, para. 2, Companies Act.
711. Article 199, para. 4; Art. 200, para. 4, Companies Act.
712. Article 238, para. 4; Art. 239, para. 4, Companies Act.

(v) appointment or dismissal of directors or other officers if 'shares relating to the right to appoint or dismiss directors or other officers' has been issued[713]
(vi) approval of absorption-type merger, etc., by the surviving company[714]
(vii) approval of absorption-type merger, etc., by the absorbed company or approval of consolidation-type merger, etc., by the absorbed company.[715]

In these cases, the requirement of a resolution at class meeting may not be eliminated by the articles of incorporation. With regard to items (ii) through (vi) (in (v), limited to the resolution to dismiss company auditors), a special resolution will be required.[716] With regard to items (i) and (vii), an extraordinary resolution will be required.[717]

592. Separately, the companies may also issue class shares pursuant to which certain specified matters requiring the shareholders meeting or board of directors meeting will also require a resolution at the class meeting of such class shares, provided however, that such requirement must be so prescribed in the articles of incorporation.[718] To the extent that such requirement is prescribed in the articles of incorporation, the specified matters will not become effective unless an ordinary resolution at the class meeting (voluntary class meeting) is passed.[719]

IV. Proceedings of Shareholders Meetings

A. Chairperson

593. The shareholders meeting will be administrated by the chairperson. The chairperson will be appointed at the shareholders meeting if not determined in the articles of incorporation. In many companies, the president of the company is prescribed to be the chairperson in the articles of incorporation (Figure 6a). The chairperson will administrate, maintain the order of and organize the proceedings of the shareholders meetings.[720] The chairperson may order an exit from the meeting room to those persons who disrupt the order of the meeting by not following the chairperson's orders to organize the proceedings of the shareholders meeting.[721]

713. Article 347, Companies Act.
714. Article 795, para. 4, Companies Act.
715. Article 783, para. 3; Art. 804, para. 3, Companies Act.
716. Article 324, para. 2, items 1–3, items 5–6, Companies Act.
717. Article 324, para. 3, Companies Act.
718. Article 108, paras 1 and 2, item 8, Companies Act.
719. Article 323, Companies Act.
720. Article 315, para. 1, Companies Act.
721. Article 315, para. 2, Companies Act.

Figure 6a Person Chairing Shareholders Meeting

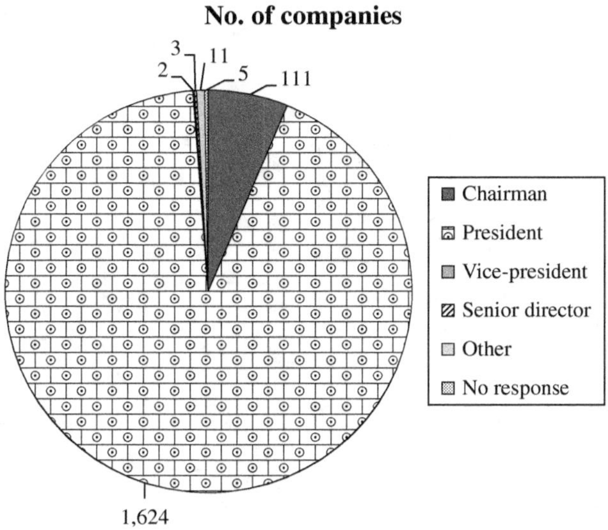

Note: 1,756 companies surveyed.

Figure 6b Person Answering Questions at Shareholders Meeting

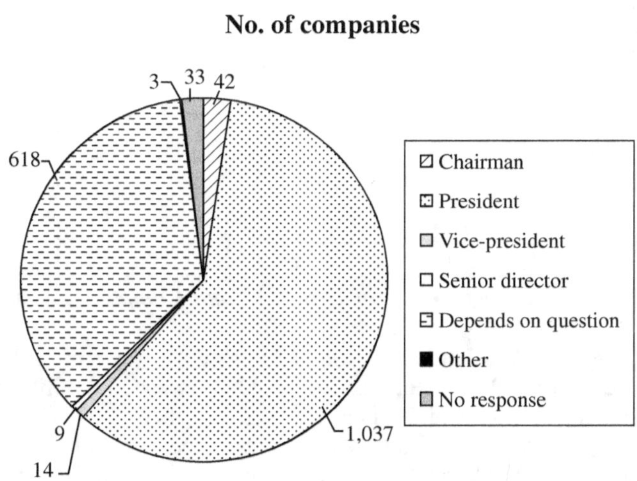

Note: 1,756 companies surveyed.

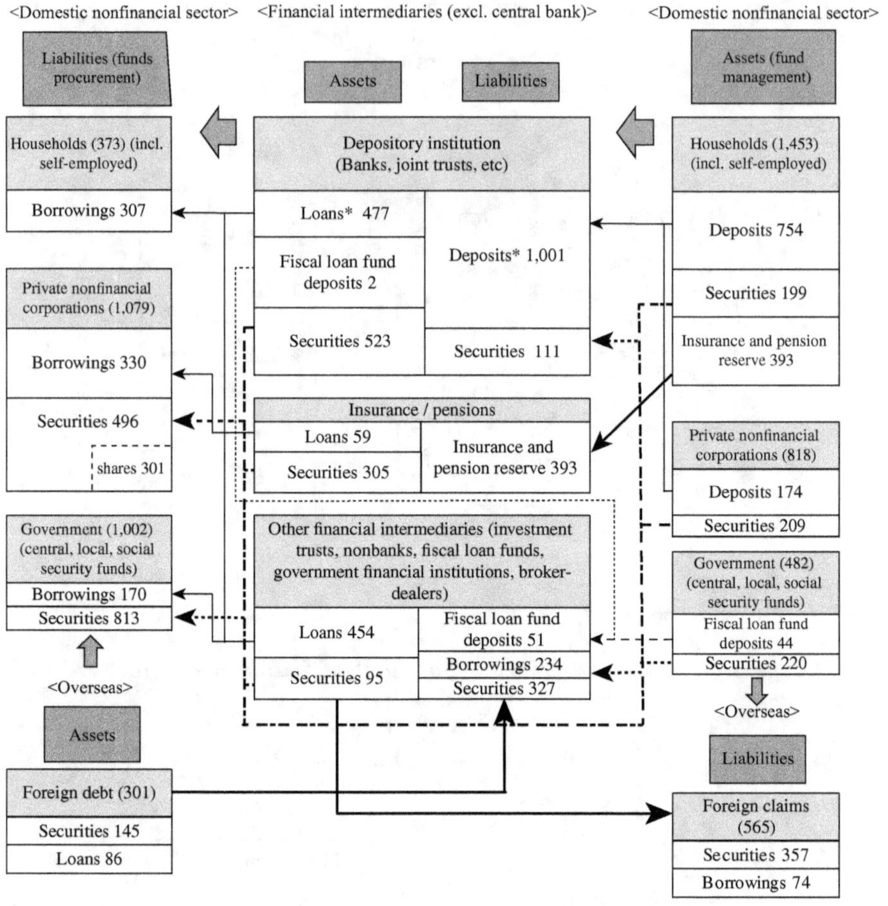

*B. Accountability (*Setsumei Gimu*) of Directors and Company Auditors*

594. The rights of shareholders to inquire questions concerning the agenda or proposals at the shareholders meeting are provided as accountability of directors, accounting advisors, company auditors and executive officers.[722] If the directors and others unlawfully refuse to give an explanation to the questions inquired by the shareholders, the relevant shareholder resolutions may be revoked; provided, however, that the directors and others may lawfully refuse to answer in the following cases:[723]

722. Article 314, Companies Act.

723. Article 831, para. 1, item 1; proviso to Art. 314, Companies Act; Art. 71, Ordinance for Enforcement of the Companies Act.

(i) The matters are not relevant to the subject matters of the shareholders meeting.
(ii) The explanations will cause serious detriment to the common interests of the shareholders.
(iii) An investigation will be necessary to provide explanation on the matters (except for cases where the shareholder had notified the matters to the company reasonably prior to the date of the meeting or cases where the necessary investigation is extremely easy to conduct).
(iv) The explanations would infringe the rights of the company or any other person.
(v) If the shareholder is repeatedly seeking explanation on essentially identical matters at the same shareholders meeting.
(vi) In addition to items (i) through (v), if there is a justifiable reason for not being able to explain the matters.

595. Upon a question raised by the shareholders, the chairperson will designate the person to answer the question (discretion of chairperson). While the questions are sometimes answered by several respondents, most questions will be answered by the president (chairperson) (figure 6b).

*C. Shareholders' Right to Submit Motions (*Dougi*)*

596. Shareholders may request at the shareholders meeting that certain matters be resolved by the shareholders. In other words, shareholders may submit motions to revise the proposals or certain procedural motions, such as termination of discussions, break, postponement or continuation of the shareholders meeting.

D. Votes

597. The voting will take place once the proposals have been deliberated. As the Companies Act does not require a particular voting method, the votes will not necessarily require a ballot and may be implemented by raising hands or standing.

598. The disclosure requirement on the results of the exercise of voting rights came into effect starting from the shareholders meeting relating to the settlement of accounts for the business year ending in March 2010 (June shareholders meeting). Namely, listed companies must file an extraordinary report setting forth the following matters upon the resolution of the proposals at the shareholders meeting: (i) the date of shareholders meeting, (ii) the contents of the proposals, (iii) the number of voting rights exercised as affirmative vote, dissenting vote and abstention, the resolution requirements and the results of such resolution.[724] The extraordinary reports are publicly available through the EDINET of the FSA.

724. Article 24-5, para. 4, Financial Instruments and Exchange Act; Art. 19, para. 2, item 9-2, Cabinet Order Ordinance for Disclosure of Business Contents.

E. Minutes

599. Minutes of the shareholders meeting must be prepared in accordance with the applicable ordinance of the Ministry of Justice.[725] The minutes must be kept at the head office of the company for ten years (copies at branch offices for five years).[726] The shareholders and creditors may request to inspect or copy the minutes during business hours.[727] If it is necessary for the purpose of exercising their rights, the members of the parent company of such company may also request to inspect or copy the minutes after obtaining permission of the court.[728]

F. Postponement and Adjournment

600. In cases where the quorum is not met on a particular matter at shareholders meeting, a resolution on postponement of the meeting may be passed (resolution for postponement). In companies that have eliminated the quorum for ordinary resolutions by the articles of incorporation (see paragraph 570), the ordinary resolution to approve the postponement may be passed by a majority of the votes of the shareholders present at the meeting. In addition, in cases where the proceedings of the shareholders meeting have not been completed, a resolution on adjournment of the meeting may be passed by ordinary resolution to continue the proceedings at a later date (resolution for adjournment). The shareholders meetings to take place on a later date after the postponement or adjournment may be held without taking another convocation procedures.[729]

*G. Shareholders Meeting Inspectors (*Soukai Kensayaku*) and Investigators (*Chousa Sha*)*

601. The company or shareholders satisfying certain requirements may file a petition with the court, before the shareholders meeting, for the election of an inspector to investigate the convocation procedures and method of resolutions.[730] This inspector will be appointed, in cases such as where any confusion of the shareholders meeting is expected, to preserve the evidence in preparation for an action to be filed at a later date arguing any procedural defect of the resolution. Shareholders who may request the election of an inspector are those who hold at least 1% of the votes of all shareholders.[731] In a Public Company, the shareholders will be required to have held the shares consecutively for at least six months.[732] Based on the reports submitted by the inspector, if the court finds it necessary, the court may order the

725. Article 318, para. 1, Companies Act.
726. Article 318, para. 2, Companies Act; also refer to para. 3.
727. Article 318, para. 4, Companies Act.
728. Article 318, para. 5, Companies Act.
729. Article 317, Companies Act.
730. Article 306, Companies Act.
731. Article 306, para. 1, Companies Act.
732. Article 306, para. 2, Companies Act.

convocation of a shareholders meeting.[733] The court may also order that the shareholders be notified of the results of the investigation.[734] The shareholders may, upon the notification of the results of such investigation, file an action seeking revocation of the resolution if they believe that there was a defect in the resolution of the shareholders meeting.

602. At the shareholders meeting, a resolution may be made to elect a person to investigate the materials submitted or provided to such shareholders meeting by the directors, accounting advisors, company auditors, board of auditors and accounting auditors.[735] At a shareholders meeting which was convened by minority shareholders, the resolution may be made to elect a person to investigate the status and property of the company.[736]

V. Defect in Shareholder Resolution

603. While a defective resolution at the shareholders meeting should in principle have no valid legal effects, the shareholder resolutions have significant influence on a large number of stakeholders. Therefore, depending on the extent of the defect, the Companies Act provides for defects constituting the grounds for revocation of the resolution and defects constituting the grounds for invalidation or absence of the resolution. The same rules apply to the resolutions at class meetings.

*A. Revocation (*Torikeshi*) of Resolutions*

604. If any of the following defects exists in a resolution at the shareholders meeting, such defect becomes grounds for revocation of the resolution.[737] Namely, a once valid resolution will be retroactively nullified if a judgment is granted on the revocation of the resolution:

(i) Violation of laws and regulations or the articles of incorporation with regard to the convocation procedures: e.g., cases where the convocation was not resolved by the board of directors, cases where the convocation notice was not sent to some of the shareholders, cases where the notice period of convocation was insufficient.

(ii) Violation of laws and regulations or the articles of incorporation with regard to the resolution method: e.g., cases where a resolution was passed without meeting the quorum provided by the laws and regulations or the articles of incorporation, cases where persons other than shareholders or their proxies

733. Article 307, para. 1, item 1, Companies Act.
734. Article 307, para. 1, item 2, Companies Act.
735. Article 316, para. 1, Companies Act.
736. Article 316, para. 2, Companies Act.
737. Article 831, para. 1, Companies Act.

participated in the resolution, cases where explanations given by the directors or company auditors at the shareholders meeting were insufficient.

(iii) Significantly unfair convocation procedures or resolution method: e.g., cases where the venue of shareholders meeting was changed on the actual day of the meeting, cases where a resolution was passed in a situation that was difficult for the shareholders to attend, cases where a resolution was passed by threat or assault.

(iv) Violation of the articles of incorporation with regard to the contents of the resolutions: This was a ground for invalidation of the resolution under the Commercial Code prior to the amendment in 1981. In a broad sense, however, this could be considered as a procedural defect because the resolution would not have been a violation of the articles of incorporation if the articles of incorporation was amended prior to such resolution so that such resolution would not constitute a violation thereof. In addition, as the articles of incorporation is an internal rule of the company, the standing to assert such violation should be limited to the constituent members of the company and therefore should be governed by the rules on the standing of actions for revocation of resolutions. As such, such resolutions were distinguished from violation of laws and regulations and became a ground for revocation of resolutions by the amendment to the Commercial Code in 1981.

(v) Significantly improper resolutions as a result of the exercise of voting rights by special interested parties: This has been added as a ground for revocation of resolution as the special interested parties were made eligible to exercise their voting rights by the amendment to the Commercial Code in 1981. For example, resolutions approving business transfer or merger may constitute grounds for revocation of resolution if the resolutions were approved at a significantly unfair price or merger ratio as a result of the exercise of voting rights by the counterparties to the company in such business transfer or merger (see paragraphs 910 and 889).

605. Action seeking revocation of a resolution at the shareholders meeting may be filed solely by the shareholders, directors or liquidators (in Company with Company Auditor(s), the shareholders, directors, company auditors or liquidators; in Company with Committees, the shareholders, directors, executive officers or liquidators).[738] The filing period for the action seeking revocation of a shareholder resolution is limited to three months to stabilize the status of, and avoid the significant influence to, the company stakeholders. A final and binding judgment on the revocation of a shareholder resolution will be effective not only against the parties to the action but also against third parties so that all stakeholders will be affected uniformly.[739]

606. In the event that the grounds for revocation of a shareholder resolution are violation of laws and regulations or the articles of incorporation on the convocation procedures or resolution method (i.e., in cases of items (i) and (ii) above), the court

738. Article 831, para. 1, Companies Act.
739. Article 838, Companies Act.

may, at its discretion, dismiss the claim for revocation of such shareholder resolution if it finds that the facts in violation thereof are not serious and will not affect the resolution.[740] Such discretion of the court is called discretionary dismissal (*sairyou kikyaku*).

*B. Invalidation (*Mukou*) and Absence (*Fusonzai*) of Resolutions*

607. Declaratory judgment for invalidation of shareholder resolution may be sought if the contents of the resolution were in violation of laws and regulations.[741] This includes, for example, a resolution passed on dividends in violation of the financial restrictions under Article 461 of the Companies Act (fraudulent accounts) (see paragraph 626).

608. In addition, declaratory judgment for absence of shareholder resolution may be sought separately in cases where a shareholders meeting was not held at all, or even if it was held, there was a significant procedural defect that no resolution may be considered to exist.[742] The examples would include those cases where most of the shareholders did not receive the convocation notice.

609. The Companies Act does not restrict the standing to assert invalidation or absence of shareholder resolution. There is also no time limitation for filing an action. While these points differ from the revocation of shareholder resolution, the effect of the judgment is the same that the declaratory judgment of invalidation or absence of shareholder resolution will be effective against third parties.[743]

§3. SETTLEMENT OF ACCOUNTS (*KESSAN*) AND DIVIDENDS (*HAITOU*)

I. Procedures for Settlement of Accounts

A. Preparation of Financial Statements

610. The purpose of a stock company is to distribute profits from its business to the shareholders. However, the assets of the stock company are the only source of recourse for the company creditors. Therefore, stock companies must follow certain procedures to demonstrate the financial conditions and results of operations to protect both the shareholders and creditors.

611. For each business year, the company must prepare financial statements, business report and supplementary schedules.[744] The financial statements include

740. Article 831, para. 2, Companies Act.
741. Article 830, para. 2, Companies Act.
742. Article 830, para. 1, Companies Act.
743. Article 838, Companies Act.
744. Article 435, para. 2, Companies Act.

the balance sheet, profit and loss statement, statement of changes in net assets and a separate table of annotations.[745] These documents may be prepared in the form of an electromagnetic record.[746]

612. Balance sheet is a table which describes the assets, liabilities and capital as of a specific point in time, and profit and loss statement is a table which describes the details of profit or loss during a specific business period. Statement of changes in net assets describes the changes in the capital section that are not reflected in profit and loss transactions included in the profit and loss statement (prior to the enactment of the Companies Act, such changes were described at the end of profit and loss statement). Business report describes material matters relating to the status of operations of the company. Supplementary schedules supplement the contents of the financial statements. Balance sheet and other statements will be prepared in accordance with the applicable ordinance of the Ministry of Justice (i.e., Ordinance on Company Accounting). The company may, at its option, set a certain temporary closing date during the business year and settle its accounts to find the financial status of the company.[747]

613. Stock companies may appoint an accounting advisor (*kaikei sanyo*) if so prescribed in the articles of incorporation.[748] The accounting advisor must be a certified public accountant (or auditing firm) or certified tax accountant (or tax accounting firm).[749] The accounting advisor prepares the financial statements jointly with the directors (in the Companies Act, an accounting auditor is included in the defined term of 'Officers').[750] As an accounting expert, the accounting advisor is expected to ensure the properness of the financial statements of small and medium-sized enterprises. While the appointment of accounting advisor is voluntary (except that the Companies with Board of Directors which elected not to have company auditors are required to appoint an accounting advisor), it may become more common if banks or other financial institutions require the borrowers to submit financial statements prepared by an accounting advisor.[751]

B. Audit of Financial Statements

614. The draft of the financial statements and other documents prepared by directors or responsible executive officers must be audited.

745. Article 435, para. 2, Companies Act.
746. Article 435, para. 3, Companies Act.
747. Article 441, para. 1, Companies Act.
748. Article 326, para. 2, Companies Act.
749. Article 333, para. 1, Companies Act.
750. Article 374, para. 1; Art. 329, para. 1, Companies Act.
751. Article 327, para. 2, Companies Act.

615. Company with Company Auditor(s) will be subject to an audit by the company auditors with regard to the financial statements, business reports and supplementary schedules.[752] Upon receipt of these documents, the company auditors must prepare an audit report (see paragraph 793).[753] In Company with Board of Auditors, the board of auditors will also prepare an audit report based on the audit report prepared by the company auditors.[754]

616. In Company with Accounting Auditors, the financial statements will be submitted to the accounting auditors and company auditors.[755] In Company with Committees, these documents will be submitted to the auditing committee member designated by the company's auditing committee. The accounting auditor must prepare an accounting audit report (see paragraph 793).[756] The company auditors of Company with Company Auditor(s) and the auditing committee of Company with Committees will then prepare their audit reports based on such accounting audit report.[757]

617. After receiving the financial statements and supplementary schedules, the company auditors and accounting auditors must notify the designated director (i.e., director whose duties concern preparing the financial statements required for audit or other directors designated to receive such notifications) of the audit report by the latest of: (i) the day on which four weeks have elapsed since the date of receipt of all financial statements, (ii) the day on which one week has elapsed since the date of receipt of the supplementary schedules accompanying the financial statements or (iii) the day agreed by the designated director (as described above) and the company auditors (accounting auditors).[758] The day on which such notification is received will be deemed to be the day that the audit took place.[759]

618. In Company with Company Auditor(s), the company auditors must audit the business reports and supplementary schedules and prepare the audit report.[760] In Company with Board of Auditors, the board of auditors will prepare its audit report, based on the audit report of the company auditors.[761] In Company with Committees, the audit committee prepares the audit report.[762] As with the audit report relating to the financial statements, the deadline for reporting the audit reports are set forth by the applicable ordinances.[763]

752. Article 436, para. 1, Companies Act.
753. Article 122, para. 1, Ordinance on Company Accounting.
754. Article 123, para. 1, Ordinance on Company Accounting.
755. Article 125, Ordinance on Company Accounting.
756. Article 126, para. 1, Ordinance on Company Accounting.
757. Articles 127 and 129, Ordinance on Company Accounting.
758. Article 124, para. 4; Art. 130, para. 4; Art. 124, para. 1, item 1; Art. 130, para. 1, item 1, Ordinance on Company Accounting.
759. Article 124, para. 2; Art. 130, para. 2, Ordinance on Company Accounting.
760. Article 129, para. 1, Ordinance for Enforcement of the Companies Act.
761. Article 130, para. 1, Ordinance for Enforcement of the Companies Act.
762. Article 131, para. 1, Ordinance for Enforcement of the Companies Act.
763. Article 132, para. 1, Ordinance for Enforcement of the Companies Act.

C. Approval of Financial Statements

619. In Company with Board of Directors, the financial statements, business report and their supplementary schedules must be approved by the board of directors after the abovementioned audits (in companies where an audit is not mandatory, only the approval of the board of directors is required).[764]

620. The financial statements and business report will be submitted or provided at the shareholders meeting.[765] The business report will be reported at the annual shareholders meeting.[766] With regard to the financial statements, an approval at the annual shareholders meeting will be required; provided, however, that, in Company with Accounting Auditors, such requirement does not apply and the financial statements will be reporting matters if financial statements which have been approved by the board of directors satisfy the requirements prescribed by the applicable ordinance of the Ministry of Justice as accurately indicating the status of the assets and profits and losses of the company in compliance with applicable laws and regulations.[767] Under the ordinance of the Ministry of Justice, the financial statements must comply with all of the following: (i) unqualified proper opinion in the accounting audit report, (ii) no opinion has been expressed in the audit report of the company auditors (board of auditors) or the audit committee with regard to the accounting audit report in item (i) above that the method or results of the audit of the accounting auditors is not reasonable, and (iii) a board of directors has been established.[768]

D. Disclosure of Financial Statements

621. In Company with Board of Directors, the financial statements and business report which have been approved by the board of directors must be provided to the shareholders in the convocation notice of the annual shareholders meeting.[769] The audit reports and accounting audit reports must also be provided in a similar manner. Such obligations do not apply to companies other than Company with Board of Directors.

622. A company must keep the financial statements, business reports and supplementary schedules (including audit reports and accounting audit reports) at the head office from one week before the date of the annual shareholders meeting for a period of five years.[770] In Company with Board of Directors, the disclosure must be made at least two weeks before the annual shareholders meeting. These documents must also be made available for disclosure for a period of three years at the branch offices

764. Article 436, para. 3, Companies Act.
765. Article 438, para. 1, Companies Act.
766. Article 438, para. 3, Companies Act.
767. Article 438, para. 2; Art. 439, Companies Act.
768. Article 163, Ordinance on Company Accounting.
769. Article 437, Companies Act.
770. Article 442, para. 1, Companies Act.

(the financial statements and other documents may also be prepared and disclosed in the form of electromagnetic records).[771]

623. The shareholders and creditors may request to inspect, or to provide a transcript or extract of, such documents at any time during the business hours of the company (or through electromagnetic records).[772] If it is necessary for the members of a parent company to exercise their rights, the members may obtain the permission of the court to request those matters to the company.[773]

624. The company must give public notice of its balance sheet without delay after obtaining the approval at the shareholders meeting.[774] A Large Company must give public notice of the balance sheet and profit and loss statement. For companies specifying the method of public notice in the articles of incorporation as publication in the official gazette or publication in a daily newspaper which publishes news on current affairs, public notice of a summary of the balance sheet (in a Large Company, a summary of the balance sheet and profit and loss statement) will be sufficient.[775]

625. Companies which specify in the articles of incorporation that public notice will be given using the method of electronic public notice may give public notice of the financial statements by an electronic public notice.[776] In such case, it is necessary to continue posting the financial statements for five years from the conclusion of the annual shareholders meeting.[777] In addition, companies which specified the method of public notice as the official gazette or a daily newspaper which publishes news on current affairs may also make the information contained in the balance sheet available to the general public through electromagnetic method for five years from the conclusion of the annual shareholders meeting.[778] In these cases, the public notice may not be a summary.

626. As an exception to the above, the companies which have submitted the annual securities report pursuant to the Financial Instruments and Exchange Act will not be required to give public notice under the Companies Act.[779] This is because the information regarding the financial statements has already been disclosed in detail.

771. Article 442, para. 2, Companies Act.
772. Article 442, para. 3, Companies Act.
773. Article 442, para. 4, Companies Act.
774. Article 440, para. 1, Companies Act.
775. Article 440, para. 2, Companies Act.
776. Article 939, para. 1, item 3, Companies Act.
777. Article 940, para. 1, item 2, Companies Act.
778. Article 440, para. 3, Companies Act.
779. Article 24, para. 1, Financial Instruments and Exchange Act; Art. 440, para. 4, Companies Act.

II. Temporary Financial Statements and Consolidated Financial Statements

A. Temporary Financial Statements

627. Companies may set a certain date during the business year as a temporary account closing date. Through the temporary settlement, the profits and losses of the business year through such temporary account closing date may be included in the calculation of distributable amount for dividends of surplus (see paragraph 638). For such purpose, temporary financial statements will be prepared to ascertain the financial status of the company as of the temporary account closing date.[780] The temporary financial statements comprise of (i) the balance sheet as of the temporary account closing date and (ii) the profit and loss statement for the period from the first day of the business year through such temporary account closing date.

628. In Company with Company Auditor(s) or Company with Accounting Auditors, an audit by the company auditors or accounting auditors will be required (in Company with Committees, the audit committee and the accounting auditors).[781] In Company with Board of Directors, the audited temporary financial statements must be approved by the board of directors.[782] The temporary financial statements must, in principle, be approved at the shareholders meeting.[783] As with the financial statements, it will become a reporting matter at the shareholders meeting if the temporary financial statements accurately indicate the status of the assets and profits and losses of the company in compliance with applicable laws and regulations and the articles of incorporation.[784]

B. Consolidated Financial Statements

629. Consolidated financial statements will be prepared to comprehensively report the financial status of the corporate group as a whole. Traditionally, the main disclosure method was through the financial statements prepared by individual companies. However, as a result of Japanese companies spinning off branches and business divisions (i.e., establishment of subsidiaries) to diversify their business activities or to develop business overseas, it has become difficult to ascertain the state of a corporate group by the individual financial statements, thereby requiring disclosure of the corporate group as a whole. The consolidated financial statements are also effective to prevent companies from using its subsidiaries for profit manipulation, whereby the parent company inflates its sales by sales to its subsidiaries.

---

780. Article 441, para. 1, Companies Act.
781. Article 441, para. 2, Companies Act.
782. Article 441, para. 3, Companies Act.
783. Article 441, main text of para. 4, Companies Act.
784. Article 441, proviso to para. 4, Companies Act.

630. The Ordinance on Consolidated Financial Statements was enacted in 1976, introducing the consolidated financial statements as a disclosure under the Securities Exchange Act (carried forward in the Financial Instruments and Exchange Act). Companies must provide their consolidated financial statements to disclose the status of the corporate group in the securities registration statements and securities reports.[785]

631. Consolidation of financial statements under the Commercial Code was required by the amendment in 2002. The consolidated financial statements must be prepared pursuant to the applicable ordinance of the Ministry of Justice, as an item necessary and appropriate in indicating the status of the assets and profits and losses of the corporate group, comprising the company, its subsidiaries and consolidated subsidiaries.[786]

632. Under the Companies Act, a similar mechanism was adopted. In Company with Accounting Auditors, consolidated financial statements may be prepared for each business year pursuant to the applicable ordinance of the Ministry of Justice.[787] Preparation in electromagnetic records is also permitted.[788] For Large Companies (as of the last day of the business year) which are required to submit the annual securities report under the Financial Instruments and Exchange Act, it will be mandatory to prepare consolidated financial statements.[789]

633. Consolidated financial statements must be audited by company auditors (in Company with Committees, the audit committee).[790] If the company has a board of directors, the audited consolidated financial statements must also be approved by the board of directors.[791] Thereafter, the shareholders must be provided with such consolidated financial statements at the annual shareholders meeting.[792] The directors must report on the consolidated financial statements and the results of the audit at the shareholders meeting.[793]

634. While the consolidated financial statements enhance the disclosure to the shareholders, the regulations on dividends of surplus will be calculated based on the individual financial statements.

785. Article 193, Financial Instruments and Exchange Act; Art. 8 (Form No. 2) and Art. 15 (Form No. 3), Ordinance on the Disclosure of Corporate Details.
786. Article 19-2, para. 1, Act on Special Measures for the Commercial Code prior to amendment.
787. Article 444, para. 1, Companies Act.
788. Article 444, para. 2, Companies Act.
789. Article 444, para. 3, Companies Act.
790. Article 444, para. 4, Companies Act.
791. Article 444, para. 5, Companies Act.
792. Article 444, para. 6, Companies Act.
793. Article 444, para. 7, Companies Act.

III. Dividends of Surplus (*Jouyokin No Haitou*)

A. *Overview*

635. Profits of the company will be distributed to the shareholders as dividends. The right to demand dividends of surplus is one of the most important rights of a shareholder.

636. On the other hand, due to the limited liability of the shareholders in stock companies, the company assets will be the only recourse for the claims of company creditors. Accordingly, it is necessary to set a limit on dividends of surplus to balance the interests of the company creditors and the shareholders.

637. In the Commercial Code prior to the enactment of the Companies Act, distribution were made to the shareholders not only in the form of dividends and interim dividends, but also in the form of repurchase of the company's shares, which was regulated separately. In the Companies Act, however, these two activities are subject to the same financial restrictions on of 'dividends of surplus' because the assets of the company will in either case flow to the shareholders in advance of the payment to company creditors.[794]

638. Companies may distribute dividends of surplus at any time during the business year. The distributable amount may be calculated taking into account the changes in the surplus after the end of previous business year through the time of distribution.[795] For this purpose, temporary settlement using the temporary financial statements is permitted.[796] Dividend in kind, which was previously highly debated, is permitted under the Companies Act.[797]

B. *Resolutions at Shareholders Meeting*

639. An ordinary resolution at the shareholders meeting is required to distribute dividends of surplus.[798] The resolution will include: (i) the kind and total book value of the dividend property, (ii) matters regarding the distribution of dividend property to shareholders and (iii) the effective date of the dividends of surplus.

640. Distribution of dividends of surplus in item (ii) above is, in principle, required to be proportionate to the number of shares held by the shareholders.[799]

794. Article 461, Companies Act.
795. Article 461, para. 2, Companies Act.
796. Article 461, para. 2, items 2 and 5, Companies Act.
797. Article 454, para. 4, Companies Act.
798. Article 454, para. 1, Companies Act.
799. Article 454, para. 3, Companies Act.

However, if class shares have different features on dividends, it is possible to provide a statement that each class of shares will be treated differently in accordance with the terms of such class shares.[800]

641. If the dividend property is a property other than money, a special resolution at the shareholders meeting will be required; provided, however, that an ordinary resolution will be sufficient if each shareholder is granted a right to demand distribution of money in lieu of such dividend property.[801]

642. Dividends of surplus may be determined by the board of directors if a company meets all of the following requirements: (i) Company with Board of Auditors, (ii) Company with Accounting Auditors, (iii) a company where the term of office of directors is one year, (iv) such authority of the board of directors is prescribed in the articles of incorporation and (v) whose financial statements relating to the most recent business year fulfil the requirements prescribed in applicable ordinance of the Ministry of Justice as accurately indicating the status of the assets and profits and losses of the company in compliance with laws and regulations and the articles of incorporation.[802] Item (iii) above is intended to exclude directors who are not supported by the shareholders from determining dividends of surplus.

643. In companies not meeting the above requirements, Company with Board of Directors may nonetheless distribute interim dividends by a resolution of the board of directors pursuant to the articles of incorporation.[803]

*C. Distributable Amount (*Bunpai Kanougaku*)*

644. The company is subject to certain financial restrictions in distributing dividends of surplus. The total book value of money and other property to be distributed to the shareholders must not exceed the 'distributable amount' as of the day of the distribution.[804] The financial restrictions are established not only regarding dividends of surplus but also for the repurchase of company's shares and the refunds due to reduction of stated capital and reserves.

645. In the Commercial Code prior to the enactment of the Companies Act, the calculation of distributable amount adopted a method of deducting the amount of certain statutory items from the amount of net assets. In the Companies Act, the distributable amount is calculated by aggregating the amount of the relevant items. Namely, the distributable amount will be calculated as follows:

---

800. Article 454, para. 2, Companies Act.
801. Article 454, para. 4; Art. 309, para. 2, item 10, Companies Act.
802. Article 155, Ordinance on Company Accounts; Art. 459, paras 1 and 2, Companies Act.
803. Article 454, para. 5, Companies Act.
804. Article 461, Companies Act.

Distributable amount = A – B.
A = (i) surplus + (ii) a sum of the profits recorded in the temporary financial statements (if any) and the value received upon disposal of treasury shares on or prior to the temporary account closing date.
B = (iii) the book value of treasury shares + (iv) the value of such treasury shares in cases of disposal of treasury shares after the last day of the most recent business year + (v) the losses recorded in the temporary financial statements (if any) + (vi) other than those listed in items (iii) through (v) above, a sum of the amounts recorded in each account title prescribed by the applicable ordinance of the Ministry of Justice (enumerated in Article 158 of the Ordinance on Company Accounts).[805]

646. Even if distributable amount exists as a result of the abovementioned calculation, if the amount of the net assets falls below JPY 3 million, no dividends of surplus may be distributed.[806] While the minimum stated capital requirement was abolished in the Companies Act (see paragraph 255), the interests of the shareholders and the creditors are balanced to same extent by this restriction.

D. *Illegal Dividends*

647. If illegal dividend is distributed, the Companies Act provides for the obligation of the executing persons (i.e., executive directors or executive officers) who distributed the illegal dividends and the directors who submitted the proposal on the illegal dividends to the shareholders meeting or board of directors to jointly and severally pay the book value of the illegally distributed money.[807] The governmental officers who drafted the legislation of the Companies Act explained that the abovementioned special obligations were established based on the understanding that the dividends of surplus is still valid even if it was distributed in excess of the distributable amount (they argue that it is apparent that such act is valid as the term 'on the day on which such act takes effect' is used in Article 463, paragraph 1 of the Companies Act. However, traditionally, dividends in excess of the distributable profits were deemed to be invalid, and therefore there has been strong criticism from scholars on such interpretation).

648. If a person subject to such liability – other than a shareholder – proves that he or she did not fail to exercise due care with respect to the performance of his or her duties, such person will not be liable.[808] Such liability may not be exempted by the consent of all shareholders with respect to the portion in excess of the distributable amount, because such regulations are intended to protect the creditors.[809]

805. Article 461, para. 2, Companies Act.
806. Article 458, Companies Act.
807. Article 462, para. 1; para. 1, item 6 Companies Act.
808. Article 464, para. 2, Companies Act.
809. Article 462, para. 3, Companies Act.

649. If a director or other officer has paid off an illegal dividend, such director or other officer may request a remedy from the shareholders who received such dividends with knowledge.[810] Shareholders without knowledge will not be liable for such remedy.

650. Creditors of the company may make a direct request to the shareholders for payment of the amount of illegal dividends.[811] The creditors are allowed to make the request as their inherent rights as creditors and not on behalf of the company. In such case, whether or not the shareholders were with or without knowledge is not an issue. The amount which may be claimed for return is limited to the amount of the claim which such creditor has against the company.

651. In cases where illegal dividends were distributed, the accounting advisors, company auditors and accounting auditors will also be liable for the damages to the company for neglecting their duties.[812] Liability to third parties is also provided.[813]

652. In addition, if there is a deficit at the end of the period, the executing persons will be liable to the company to jointly and severally pay the amount of the deficit; provided, however, that such persons will not be liable if they prove that they did not fail to exercise due care in the performance of their duties.[814]

§4. Management of Stock Companies

I. Overview

653. Prior to the enactment of the Companies Act, stock companies were required to establish board of directors. The purpose of requiring the board of directors was to ensure appropriate company management by mobilizing the directors' talents through their discussions at the board meeting. However, some large stock companies had established a voluntary executive board, composed of specific directors separate from the board of directors with an aim to expedite the decision-making process. In cases where the board of directors only serves the function of approving the decisions of the executive board as a formality, the board of directors could become a mere façade.

654. Even after the enactment of the Companies Act, certain companies are required to establish board of directors (see paragraph 548). In Company with Board of Directors, the decisions relating to the business operations of the company are made, in principle, by the board of directors. The actual execution of such decision will be carried out by the representative director appointed by the board of directors

810. Article 463, para. 1, Companies Act.
811. Article 463, para. 2, Companies Act.
812. Article 423, para. 1, Companies Act.
813. Article 429, para. 1, Companies Act.
814. Article 465, para. 1, Companies Act.

or by the director in charge of executing the operations.[815] In addition, the decisions on daily business operations are delegated to the representative director. The representative director has the authority to represent the company.

655. In addition to the above, the board of directors could also lose its substance in cases where a specific person such as the representative director (president) wields the power of the company. In most Japanese companies, the members of the board of directors are usually composed of internal directors who have been promoted from the employees. As a result, it is difficult for these directors to control the president's authority. On the other hand, it is also noteworthy that such internal directors do facilitate the process of establishing consensus among the directors and furthermore incentivize the employees by providing the opportunity for promotion.

656. Recently, companies have increasingly introduced the 'corporate officers' (*shikkou yakuin*). As it is not statutorily provided in the Companies Act, many variations were observed in the companies introducing corporate officers. In many cases, corporate officers are positioned as employees to whom the representative director or executive directors entrust certain execution of operations. Typically, the employees who had concurrently served as directors are appointed as corporate officers with an aim to reduce the number of directors. By reducing the number of directors, it would be easier for the board of directors to make important decisions expeditiously. Meanwhile, corporate officers can focus on execution of operations. It is also expected that the supervisory function of the board of directors will be enhanced as a result of appointing only those individuals who are capable of supervising the business operations of the company as directors.

657. In recent years, higher attention has been paid on outside directors. As mentioned above, many Japanese directors are internal directors who have been promoted from the employees (see paragraph 655). It is expected, however, that the outside directors will be in a better position to scrutinize the company's operations, and moreover, will firmly state their opinions to the representative director. In order to fulfil the latter role, the outside director needs to be 'independent' from the representative director (i.e., not merely 'external'). However, it is not easy to find an appropriate individual having the capability of an outside director who is not related to the company at all. In fact, the dilemma is that the more independent candidates are less likely to be familiar with the ongoing business of the company.

658.

(i) the Companies Act defines an 'outside director' as a director of a stock company who satisfies all of the following requirements:[816] a person who is not an executive director of the company (or any of its subsidiaries) and has not served as an executive director of the company (or any of its subsidiaries) within ten years prior to assuming office;

815. Article 363, para. 1, Companies Act.
816. Article 2, item 15, Companies Act.

(ii) a person who, if having served as a director, accounting advisor or company auditor of the company (or any of its subsidiaries) within ten years prior to assuming office, did not serve as an executive director of the company (or any of its subsidiaries) within ten years prior to that;

(iii) a person who is not a 'parent company, etc.' (*oyakaisha tou*) of another company (in case of a natural person) or a director, executive officer, manager or other employee of a parent company, etc.;

(iv) a person who is not an executive director of a subsidiary of a parent company, etc., of the company (a sister company); and

(v) a person who is neither the spouse nor a relative within the second degree of kinship of a director, manager, other important employee or parent company, etc. (in case of a natural person) of the company.

659. The 2014 amendment tightened the requirements for establishing a director's externality (*shagaisei*) by adding requirements that a person not be connected to a parent or sister company (items (iii) and (iv) above) and not be a close relative of certain people connected to the company (item (v) above). However, the amendment also loosened requirements by allowing a person with certain ten-year blank period to become an outside director (items (i) and (ii) above), whereas prior to the amendment, any service as a company director was deemed a loss of externality.

II. Appointment and Retirement of Directors

A. Appointment of Directors

660. Directors are appointed by an ordinary resolution at the shareholders meeting.[817] A substitute director may be appointed in preparation for the cases where there are no directors or where there is a vacancy resulting in a shortfall in the number of directors prescribed in laws and regulations or the articles of incorporation.[818] The names of the directors who have assumed the office will be registered in commercial registration.[819]

661. In many Japanese companies, the quorum for ordinary resolution of the shareholders meeting is eliminated by the articles of incorporation (see paragraph 570). However, in the resolution on appointment of directors, the quorum may not be lowered to less than one-third of all voting rights even through the articles of incorporation.[820]

662. If a resolution is to be passed on the appointment of two or more directors at the same shareholders meeting, unless otherwise provided in the articles of

817. Article 329, para. 1, Companies Act.
818. Article 329, para. 2, Companies Act.
819. Article 911, para. 3, item 13, Companies Act.
820. Article 341, Companies Act.

incorporation, it is possible to adopt the cumulative voting.[821] Cumulative voting is where the shareholders are entitled to such number of votes equal to the number of directors to be appointed for each share that the shareholder holds. In this method, shareholders may choose whether to focus all voting rights on one candidate or divide the votes among several candidates.[822] The shareholders may make a request for cumulative voting in writing until five days before the shareholders meeting.[823] In practice, however, most companies have eliminated the cumulative voting by the articles of incorporation.

663. If a company that is a Company with a Board of Auditors (and is a Public Company and a Large Company) as of the final day of the business year and that is required to submit annual securities reports does not have any outside directors, then the directors must explain at the annual shareholders meeting 'the reason why it is not appropriate to have an Outside Director'.[824] Companies that are Public Companies and Large Companies have frequent changes in shareholder composition and are large in scale, so there is a higher degree of necessity for supervision of executing officers by outside directors, and it was considered that such large-scale companies can afford to bear the cost of having outside directors. Furthermore, companies that are required to submit annual securities reports typically list their shares on a stock exchange or have 1,000 or more shareholders[825] and are therefore likely to have a large number of unspecified shareholders. Hence, it was considered that there is an especially high need for supervision of executing officers by outside directors. These provisions were prescribed in the 2014 amendment to the Companies Act.

664. In addition to the above obligation to provide an explanation, companies must also state the reason why it is not appropriate to have Outside Directors in their business reports or in the reference materials for shareholders meetings.[826] The Tokyo Stock Exchange has also amended its listing regulations and established a provision that listed companies must make an effort to secure at least one independent officer as a director.[827]

B. Director Qualification

665. Directors are not required to be shareholders of the company. In addition, a Public Company may not restrict the qualification to become director to its shareholders even through the articles of incorporation.[828] This is because the companies

821. Article 342, para. 1, Companies Act.
822. Article 342, para. 3, Companies Act.
823. Article 342, para. 2, Companies Act.
824. Article 327-2, Companies Act.
825. Article 24, para. 1, Financial Instruments and Exchange Act.
826. Article 124, para. 2, and Art. 74-2, Ordinance for the Enforcement of the Companies Act.
827. Rule 445-4, TSE Securities Listing Regulations.
828. Article 331, para. 2, Companies Act.

should seek directors from a wide range of candidates. On the other hand, in non-Public Companies, the shareholders rarely change and moreover directors are often elected from its large shareholders. On this basis, under the Companies Act, the previous rules were maintained with regard to the Public Companies, while non-Public Companies are now permitted to restrict the qualification to become director to their respective shareholders by the articles of incorporation (in these companies, ownership and management overlap). In addition, the company auditors are not permitted to serve concurrently as directors of the same company or its subsidiaries.[829]

666. On the other hand, the grounds for disqualification are provided in the Companies Act. The grounds for disqualification are as follows:[830]

(i) A juridical person.
(ii) An adult ward or a person under curatorship, or a person who is similarly treated under foreign laws and regulations.
(iii) A person who has been sentenced to a penalty for having violated the Companies Act or the Act on General Incorporated Association and General Incorporated Foundation, or for having committed certain crime proscribed in the Financial Instruments and Exchange Act, the Civil Rehabilitation Act, the Act on Recognition of and Assistance for Foreign Insolvency Proceedings, the Corporate Reorganization Act or the Bankruptcy Act, for whom two years have not elapsed since the day on which the sentence was completed or the sentence no longer applied.
(iv) A person who was sentenced to imprisonment or more severe penalty due to violation of laws and regulations other than those prescribed in item (iii) above and has not completed the execution of the sentence or to whom the sentence still applies; provided, however, that the persons for whom the execution of sentence is suspended are exempted.

667. Traditionally, it was interpreted that juridical persons could not become directors. The Companies Act made this point clear in item (i) above. In addition, the Commercial Code provided as grounds for disqualification 'persons who were declared bankrupt and has not been reinstated'.[831] However, this ground for disqualification was removed from the Companies Act as it was considered beneficial to provide the debtors with an opportunity for economic rehabilitation at an early date.

C. Term of Office of Directors

668. The term of office of directors continues until the conclusion of the annual shareholders meeting for the last business year ending within two years from the

829. Article 335, para. 2, Companies Act.
830. Article 331, para. 1, Companies Act.
831. Article 254-2, item 2, Commercial Code prior to amendment.

time of their election (in principle, two years).[832] This term may be shortened by the articles of incorporation or resolution of the shareholders meeting.[833] The term of office of directors in Company with Committees continues in the same manner except that the length of term is 'within one year from the time of their election'.[834]

669. In non-Public Companies (excluding Company with Committees), the term of office of directors may be extended by the articles of incorporation up to until the conclusion of the annual shareholders meeting for the last business year ending within ten years from the time of their election.[835] Prior to the enactment of the Companies Act, the term of office of a director of stock company was two years, and there was no term of office specified for directors of limited companies. Upon the enactment of the Companies Act in which limited companies and stock companies were integrated, a question was raised as to how the discrepancy on the term of office should be handled. In non-Public Companies, there is little need to frequently question the shareholders' confidence in the directors because changes in shareholders do not occur often in such companies. Therefore, while the term of office of directors was in principle kept at two years, non-Public Companies were permitted to extend the term of office to a maximum of ten years by the articles of incorporation.

D. Retirement of Directors

670. A director will retire from his or her position upon the expiration of the term of office or by resignation. In addition, the term of office of directors will terminate upon the death of the director, a court order for the commencement of guardianship or a court ruling on commencement of bankruptcy proceedings of the company.[836]

671. The directors may be dismissed at any time by an ordinary resolution at the shareholders meeting; provided, however, that if a director is dismissed at a shareholders meeting before the expiration of his or her term of office without a justifiable ground, such director may demand damages arising from the dismissal from the company.[837]

672. Prior to the enactment of the Companies Act, the dismissal of directors required a special resolution of the shareholders meeting.[838] The reason for requiring special resolution while their appointment required only ordinary resolution was to stabilize the position of the company's management. In the Companies Act,

832. Article 332, main text of para. 1, Companies Act.
833. Article 332, proviso to para. 1, Companies Act.
834. Article 332, para. 3, Companies Act.
835. Article 332, para. 2, Companies Act.
836. Article 330, Companies Act; Art. 653, Civil Code.
837. Article 339, para. 1; Art. 339, para. 2, Companies Act.
838. Article 257, para. 1 and para. 2, Commercial Code prior to amendment.

emphasis was laid on reinforcing the supervision of management by the shareholders and therefore the dismissal of directors came only to require ordinary resolution. However, the Companies Act permits the companies to tighten the resolution requirement by the articles of incorporation.[839] Therefore, it is possible to provide a resolution requirement which is equivalent to or stricter than special resolution by the articles of incorporation. In such cases, the aforementioned purpose of the legislation to reinforce the supervisory powers of the shareholders is no longer ensured.

673. Moreover, with regard to the directors who have been elected by the cumulative voting (see paragraph 662), dismissal by ordinary resolution is not permitted and the requirement of special resolution was maintained due to the purpose of cumulative voting to take into account the wishes of minority shareholders in the appointment of the directors.[840]

674. If the shareholders intend to dismiss a director, those shareholders who have continuously held shares of at least 3% of the voting rights of all shareholders for the immediately preceding six months have the right to convene a shareholders meeting (see paragraph 563).[841] Furthermore, if a proposal for the dismissal of a director is rejected at the shareholders meeting despite the fact that such director committed misconduct or there are material facts in violation of laws and regulations or the articles of incorporation in connection with the performance of his or her duties, such shareholders may file an action to the court for the dismissal of the director within thirty days after such shareholders meeting.[842] Upon such filing, both the company and the director become defendants.[843] In non-Public Companies, the abovementioned requirement of having held the shares for six months does not apply.[844]

675. With regard to the directors who have been elected by a class meeting (see paragraph 357), if the proposal for dismissal of a director is rejected at a class meeting despite the fact that such director committed misconduct or there are material facts in violation of laws and regulations or the articles of incorporation, shareholders who have continuously held shares of at least 3% of the voting rights of all shareholders for such particular class for the immediately preceding six months may file an action to the court for the dismissal of the director within thirty days after such class meeting.[845] The right of dismissal of a director elected by a class meeting remains with such class meeting and the director may not be dismissed by a resolution of the shareholders meeting of all shareholders.[846] However, those shareholders who have continuously held shares of at least 3% of the voting rights of all

839. Article 341, Companies Act.
840. Article 342, para. 6; Art. 309, para. 2, item 7, Companies Act.
841. Article 297, para. 1, Companies Act.
842. Article 854, para. 1, Companies Act.
843. Article 855, Companies Act.
844. Article 854, para. 2, Companies Act.
845. Article 854, para. 3, Companies Act.
846. Article 347, para. 1, Companies Act.

shareholders for the immediately preceding six months, may file an action for dismissal, if a shareholder resolution to dismiss the director fails to become effective, as a result of the lack of such resolution by the class meeting.[847]

676. If, upon the expiration of the term of office of a director, there is a shortfall in the number of members required in the Companies Act or the articles of incorporation, the retiring director continues to have the rights and obligations as director until a new director assumes his or her office.[848] However, upon a petition by interested persons, such as shareholder, director or employee and if the court finds it necessary, the court may elect a person to temporarily perform the duties of the director (temporary director).[849]

677. However, if the company has issued certain class shares that contain different features with regard to the election of directors (see paragraph 357), the election or dismissal of directors must be made in accordance with the terms of such class shares prescribed in the articles of incorporation.[850]

III. Directors (Companies Other than Company with Board of Directors)

A. *Execution of Operations*

678. In a company other than Company with Board of Directors, the number of directors may be just one. Unless otherwise provided in the articles of incorporation, each director executes the company's operations.[851] If there are two or more directors, the operations of the company will be decided by a majority of the directors.[852] In addition, the following matters may not be delegated to individual directors:[853]

(1) Election and dismissal of managers.
(2) Establishment, relocation and abolition of branch offices.
(3) Convocation of shareholders meeting.
(4) The system necessary to ensure that the execution of the duties of the directors complies with laws and regulations and the articles of incorporation and any other systems prescribed by the applicable ordinance of the Ministry of Justice as systems necessary to ensure the properness of the company's operation.
(5) Exemption of the liability of directors pursuant to the articles of incorporation.

847. Article 854, para. 1, Companies Act.
848. Article 346, para. 1, Companies Act.
849. Article 346, para. 2, Companies Act.
850. Article 347, Companies Act.
851. Article 348, para. 1, Companies Act.
852. Article 348, para. 2, Companies Act.
853. Article 348, para. 3, Companies Act.

B. Representatives of the Company

679. The directors may individually represent the company.[854] If a representative director or other persons who represent the company are otherwise designated, such person will represent the company.[855] If there are two or more directors, each director may represent the company individually.[856] A representative director may be appointed from among the directors by the articles of incorporation or through the appointment by the directors from among themselves pursuant to the articles of incorporation, or by resolution of a shareholders meeting.[857]

IV. Board of Directors

A. Overview

680. Company with Board of Directors must have at least three directors.[858] The board of directors will be composed of all directors.[859] The reference to 'board of directors' is sometimes made to refer to the organization of board of directors as an assembly of directors and at other times the meeting held by such organization. The board of directors makes decisions of the company in relation to the execution of operations.[860] In addition, the board of directors appoints and removes the representative director, and is also responsible for supervising the representative director and executive directors.[861]

B. Convocation of the Meeting of Board of Directors

681. The meeting of the board of directors (board meeting) may be convened by any director, unless the director to convene the board meeting is designated in the articles of incorporation or by the board of directors.[862] In Japan, many companies designate certain directors, such as the president, by the articles of incorporation or the rules of board of directors to limit the authority to convene the board meeting.[863]

682. Even if certain directors are designated to have the authority of convocation, other directors may also request the convocation of board meeting by indicating the subject matters of the meeting.[864] If the convocation notice of board

854. Article 349, para. 1, Companies Act.
855. Article 349, proviso to para. 1, Companies Act.
856. Article 349, para. 2, Companies Act.
857. Article 349, para. 3, Companies Act.
858. Article 331, para. 4, Companies Act.
859. Article 362, para. 1, Companies Act.
860. Article 362, para. 2, item 1, Companies Act.
861. Article 362, para. 2, item 2 and item 3, Companies Act.
862. Article 366, main text of para. 1, Companies Act.
863. Article 366, proviso to para. 1, Companies Act.
864. Article 366, para. 2, Companies Act.

meeting which sets the date of board meeting to be held within two weeks of such request is not dispatched within five days of the request, the director who requested that the board meeting be convened may convene the board meeting.[865]

683. When convening the board meeting, a notice must be sent to all directors at least one week before the day of the meeting (in Company with Company Auditor(s), each director and each company auditor).[866] However, this period may be shortened by the articles of incorporation. In addition, if the consent of all directors (in Company with Company Auditor(s), all directors and company auditors) is obtained, a board meeting may be held without the convocation procedures.[867] Therefore, to the extent that a company holds the board meeting on a scheduled day consented by all directors and company auditors, convocation procedures will not be necessary for each board meeting.

684. If a company auditor finds that a director has engaged in or is likely to engage in misconduct, or that there are facts in violation of laws and regulations or the articles of incorporation or grossly improper facts, such company auditor may request the convocation of a board meeting.[868] In companies other than Company with Company Auditor(s), if a shareholder recognizes that the director engages, or is likely to engage, in an act outside of the scope of purpose of the company or an act in violation of the laws and regulations or the articles of incorporation, such shareholder may request the convocation of a board meeting.[869]

C. *Resolution of the Board of Directors*

685. Resolution of the board of directors will be passed by a majority of the directors present at a meeting where the majority of the directors entitled to participate in the vote are present (quorum).[870] This resolution requirement may be made stricter by the articles of incorporation. However, the requirement may not be eased. Voting rights may not be exercised by proxy in resolution of the board of directors. These points differ from the resolutions at shareholders meeting (see paragraph 576).

686. If a director has special interest in the resolution of the board of directors, such director may not participate in the resolution (for comparison, see paragraph 604(v)).[871] In cases where a director carries out transactions which compete with the company or where a conflict of interests occur between the director and the company, such director must obtain approval of the board meeting (see paragraphs 729

865. Article 366, para. 3, Companies Act.
866. Article 368, para. 1, Companies Act.
867. Article 368, para. 2, Companies Act.
868. Article 383, para. 2, Companies Act.
869. Article 367, para. 1, Companies Act.
870. Article 369, para. 1, Companies Act.
871. Article 369, para. 2, Companies Act.

and 731).[872] In such board meeting, the director carrying out the transaction will be a special interested party. A court precedent has ruled that where a dismissal of representative director is proposed, such representative director is interpreted to be the special interested party.[873]

687. The minutes of board meetings must be kept at the head office for ten years.[874] If it is necessary for a shareholder to exercise its rights, the shareholder may make a request to inspect or copy the minutes at any time during the company's business hours; provided, however, that in Companies with Company Auditor(s) or Companies with Committees, such request will be subject to the permission of the court.[875]

688. Before the enactment of the Companies Act, it was interpreted that written resolutions or round-robin resolutions were not permitted in board meetings. This was because mutual discussions of directors would help them bring together their knowledge and experience and make better managerial decisions. However, if discussions could be held in a form comparable to in-person meeting as a result of the development of communications technology (e.g., by permitting video conferencing), then the directors do not necessarily need to meet in-person. On this basis, the Companies Act permitted the resolutions of in-person board meeting to be omitted. In other words, to the extent so permitted in the articles of incorporation, if all directors entitled to participate in the vote agree to the proposal in writing (or by means of electromagnetic records), it will be deemed that a resolution of the board of directors has been passed.[876] In Company with Company Auditor(s), such omission will not be permitted if a company auditor raises objection.

689. Matters to be reported to the board of directors may also be omitted by sending a notice to all directors (in Company with Company Auditor(s), the directors and company auditors).[877] However, the statutory periodic reports to be made by the representative director and the executive directors to the board of directors once every three months may not be omitted (see paragraph 696).[878] This is because such reporting is essential for the supervision by the board of directors. Therefore, Company with Board of Directors will be required to hold a board meeting at least once every three months.

690. In the event that there is any defect in the resolution of board meeting, unlike the shareholder resolution, such resolution will be invalid.

872. Article 356, para. 1, Companies Act.
873. 28 Mar. 1969, Supreme Court Collection of Court Decisions on Civil Actions 23-645.
874. Article 371, para. 1, Companies Act.
875. Article 371, paras 2 and 3, Companies Act.
876. Article 370, Companies Act.
877. Article 372, para. 1, Companies Act.
878. Article 372, para. 2, Companies Act.

D. Powers of the Board of Directors

691. Except for the matters provided in the Companies Act or the articles of incorporation as the matters to be decided by the shareholders meeting, the decisions regarding execution of the company's operations will be made by the board of directors.[879]

692. In addition, the Companies Act provides that the decisions on the following matters and other important matters regarding the execution of operations must be resolved by the board of directors and therefore may not be delegated to individual directors:

(i) Disposal or acceptance of assignment of important assets.
(ii) Borrowing in a significant amount.
(iii) Election or dismissal of managers or other important employees.
(iv) Establishment, changes or abolition of important structures including branch offices.
(v) Matters prescribed by the applicable ordinance of the Ministry of Justice as important matters regarding the solicitation of subscribers for bonds.
(vi) Development of systems necessary to ensure that the execution of duties by the directors complies with laws and regulations and the articles of incorporation and other systems prescribed in the applicable ordinance of the Ministry of Justice as systems necessary to ensure the properness of the operations of the company as well as the operations of the corporate group composed of the company and its subsidiaries.
(vii) Partial exemption of the liability of directors and other officers pursuant to the articles of incorporation.

693. Item (vi) above is namely an internal control system which is mandatorily required in Large Companies having board of directors.[880] The following items are prescribed in the applicable ordinance of the Ministry of Justice (see paragraph 815, Internal control system under the Financial Instruments and Exchange Act):[881]

(i) System to preserve and manage information relating to the performance of duties by the directors.
(ii) Systems, including internal rules, relating to the management of risk of loss.
(iii) System to ensure the efficient performance of duties by the directors.
(iv) System to ensure that the performance of duties of the employees complies with laws and regulations and the articles of incorporation.
(v) System to ensure appropriate operation of business by the corporate group composed of the company and its parent company and subsidiaries.

879. Article 362, para. 2, item 1, Companies Act.
880. Article 362, para. 5, Companies Act.
881. Article 100, para. 1, Ordinance for Enforcement of the Companies Act.

694. In companies other than Company with Company Auditor(s), the required internal control system includes a reporting system to ensure the reporting of directors to the shareholders.[882] In Company with Company Auditor(s), the required internal control system includes the following:[883]

(i) System relating to those employees who will assist the company auditors to perform their duties at the request of such company auditors.
(ii) Independence of the employees in item (i) above from the directors.
(iii) System for the reporting to company auditors (in Companies with Board of Auditors, the board of auditors or company auditors) by directors or employees.
(iv) Other systems, etc., to ensure the efficiency of audit by company auditors.

695. The board of directors supervises the execution of operations by the representative director and executive directors in charge of operations.[884] This power of supervision includes not only supervision on the legality of the operations, but also supervision on the appropriateness of the operations.

696. To ensure that such supervision is carried out effectively, the directors must report the status of operations to the board of directors at least once every three months.[885]

*E. Resolutions by Special Directors (*Tokubetsu Torishimariyaku*)*

697. There is a statutory framework where three special directors may be appointed in advance from the members of the board of directors to determine certain matters to be decided by the board of directors.[886] The matters that may be delegated by the board of directors to such special directors are (i) disposal and acceptance of assignment of important assets and (ii) borrowing in a significant amount. The board of directors did not seem to function well in companies which had a very large number of directors. Such companies typically established so-called executive board (*joumu kai*), composed of a smaller number of executive directors. The special directors system, which is designed to provide a legal basis to such executive board, is available for companies having six or more directors and at least one outside director as a member of the board of directors to ensure the board's supervisory roles.

882. Article 100, para. 2, Ordinance for Enforcement of the Companies Act.
883. Article 100, para. 3, Ordinance for Enforcement of the Companies Act.
884. Article 362, para. 2, item 2, Companies Act.
885. Article 363, para. 2, Companies Act.
886. Article 373, para. 1, Companies Act.

698. A person who is appointed by the special directors from among themselves must report the contents of the resolution by the special directors to the board of directors without delay after such resolution.[887]

V. Representative Director

A. Appointment and Removal of Representative Director

699. Representative director will be appointed and removed by the board of directors.[888]

700. There is no restriction on the number of representative directors. It may be one or more. As representative director must be appointed from among the directors, the term of office of a representative director may not exceed the term of office of the director.[889] In addition, if the representative director loses his or her position as a director, such person will also lose the status as representative director. If, upon the retirement of representative director there is a shortfall in the number of representative directors prescribed in laws and regulations or the articles of incorporation, the same interim measures as for the shortfall of directors will be permitted.[890] The appointment or removal of representative directors must be registered in commercial registration.[891]

B. Power of Representative Director

701. Representative director has the power to represent the company. For example, transactions entered into by Representative Director X on behalf of Company A will bind Company A (but not X).

702. Representative director has the authority to do all judicial or non-judicial acts relating to the operations of the company.[892] The acts relating to the operations of the company include not only the acts conducted as part of the company's business but also those acts conducted for the benefit of the company's business. Any limitation on the authority of representative director by the articles of incorporation or resolution of the board of directors may not be asserted against a third party without knowledge of such limitation.[893]

703. Representations by the representative director is internally an execution of the company's business. This means that the representative director has the power

887. Article 373, para. 3, Companies Act.
888. Article 362, para. 2, item 3, Companies Act.
889. Article 362, para. 3; Art. 332, para. 1, Companies Act.
890. Article 351, Companies Act.
891. Article 911, para. 3, item 14, Companies Act.
892. Article 349, para. 4, Companies Act.
893. Article 349, para. 5, Companies Act.

to execute the operations of the company based on his or her abovementioned authority. The representative director, however, does not have the power to make decisions with regard to the matters which require a resolution of the shareholders meeting or the board of directors pursuant to laws and regulations or the articles of incorporation.

704. Except for the representative director, directors do not have the authority to execute the company's operations per se. The directors may, however, be assigned by a resolution of the board of directors to execute certain operations of the company.[894] Directors other than the representative director who are in charge of the execution of the company's internal operations not accompanying external relationships are known as 'directors in charge of operations' (*gyoumu tantou torishimariyaku*). In the Companies Act, the defined term 'Executive Director' is used collectively for representative directors, directors in charge of operations and other directors who have executed the operations of the company.[895]

705. If the representative director abuses his or her power to represent the company by representing the company for the benefit of himself/herself own or a third party, the company may refuse to be bound by such representation by the principle of abuse of rights toward the counterparty, only if such counterparty was aware of such abuse of right of representation.

706. A question also arises if the representative director entered into a transaction without the required resolution of the board of directors. For example, in cases where the representative director issued new shares without obtaining the resolution of the board of directors, whether or not the issue of new shares is valid will be an issue. Such issuance of new shares is certainly not within the scope of the right of representation of the representative director. However, with a view to protect the security of subsequent transactions, it is interpreted that the company cannot assert the invalidity of such issuance of new shares against a bona fide third party. However, to the extent that the transaction is a purely internal act that is not related to the security of subsequent transactions, such as capitalization of reserve without issuance of new shares, such transactions will be invalid.

*C. Apparent Representative Director (*Hyouken Daihyou Torishimariyaku*)*

707. In cases where a director who is not the representative director conducts an act using a title that would be viewed as having the authority to represent the company, such as president or vice-president, if the counterparty did not know that the act was conducted by such director, the company will be liable to the extent that the company was attributable for giving such title to the director.[896] Such directors are known as apparent representative directors.

894. Article 363, para. 1, item 2, Companies Act.
895. Article 2, item 15, Companies Act.
896. Article 354, Companies Act.

708. The names of representative directors must be registered in commercial registration.[897] Therefore, whether or not a director is representative director should not be difficult for third parties to judge. However, if a director uses one of the abovementioned titles, there is a higher risk that the director will be mistaken as representative director and, furthermore, it is practically difficult for third parties to check the counterparty's commercial registration on each occasion. Therefore, the concept of apparent representative director is introduced to protect the security of transactions.

709. In apparent representative director theory, it is necessary for the company to have permitted the use of a title that was viewed as having the authority to represent the company. Therefore, the apparent representative director theory does not apply if the director used the title without any permission of the company. On the other hand, the company will be attributable not only when the company has proactively granted permission, but also where the company was aware of the use of the abovementioned title and yet tolerated without taking appropriate measures.

710. Moreover, the Supreme Court applied the theory of apparent representative directors by analogy to the acts where an employee of the company who is not a director used the title of executive managing director under the permission of the representative director.[898]

VI. Remuneration of Directors

A. Overview

711. If directors' remuneration is determined by the directors themselves, the directors may set an excessive amount of remuneration and promote their own interests at the expense of the shareholders' interests. Therefore, unless the amount of directors' remuneration is provided in the articles of incorporation, it must be determined at a shareholders meeting.[899]

712. With regard to remunerations in a fixed amount, such amount must be resolved at the shareholders meeting; provided, however, that such resolution or the company's articles of incorporation may provide the maximum amount of total remuneration for all directors, in which case there is no need to fix the amount of remuneration for each director at the shareholders meeting.[900] The allocation of total remuneration to each director may be delegated to be determined by the board of directors (26 March 1985, Supreme Court, *Hanrei Jihou* 1159-150) and most companies in Japan follow such allocation method. An increase of the maximum amount of total remuneration may be determined at the shareholders meeting if necessary to

897. Article 911, para. 2, item 14, Companies Act.
898. 14 Oct. 1960, Supreme Court Collection of Court Decisions on Civil Actions 14-2499.
899. Article 361, para. 1, Companies Act.
900. Article 361, para. 1, item 1, Companies Act.

expand the cap of directors' remuneration. In the resolution of the board of directors to allocate the remuneration to each director, the directors receiving the remuneration will not be considered as special interested parties (see paragraph 686). This is because there is no conflict of interest between the company and directors as the total remuneration of all directors is already capped by the shareholders' resolution. In addition, determination of the actual amount of remuneration for each director may be further delegated to the representative director by a resolution of the board of directors. In practice, many companies set a remuneration formula based on the titles of its directors.

713. With regard to remunerations which are not fixed in amounts, such as performance-based compensation, the specific method for calculating such amount must be passed at the shareholder resolution.[901] For remunerations that are not monetary, the specific contents must be resolved by the shareholders meeting.[902] The remunerations that are not monetary would include an offer of physical facilities such as company housing at a less than market price.

714. Stock options may also be granted as remuneration for directors. In stock options, if the performance of the company improves by the efforts of directors and as a result the share price increases, the directors will be able to gain profits by exercising the stock options at a pre-determined exercise price and selling the shares at the increased share price. In this regard, stock options are a typical example of performance-based remuneration, which is used as an incentive to improve the performance of the company. Stock options are granted in the form of share options (see paragraph 461). The value of share options will be calculated at the time of issuance and therefore stock options are categorized as 'remunerations in a fixed amount' in Article 361, paragraph 1, item 1 of the Companies Act, as well as 'remunerations that are not monetary' in item 3 of the same paragraph.

715. The directors submitting a proposal regarding the establishment or revision of remunerations other than fixed amount remuneration must explain the reasons for the reasonableness of such remunerations at the shareholders meeting.[903]

716. If a director concurrently serves as employee, it may be possible to circumvent the foregoing rules on directors' remuneration by increasing the amount of compensation as employee. In this regard, a Supreme Court ruling held that a shareholders resolution that is exclusive of the amount of compensation as employee is valid as long as a formula of employee compensation is explicitly established and the payment of employee compensation is made in accordance with such formula.

717. The reference documents to be attached to the convocation notice of shareholders meeting (see paragraph 565) must provide a formula for calculating directors' remuneration, reasons for any changes to the formula and, in cases of payment

901. Article 361, para. 1, item 2, Companies Act.
902. Article 361, para. 1, item 3, Companies Act.
903. Article 361, para. 2, Companies Act.

of remuneration to two or more directors, the number of directors.[904] In Public Companies, the description on outside directors must be distinguished from the description on internal directors.[905] Beginning from the business year ending March 2010, the names of officers and amount of remuneration for those officers receiving remuneration of JPY 100 million or more must be disclosed individually (see paragraph 42).

B. Retirement Benefits

718. Retirement benefits will be paid to directors upon their retirement. In general, it is interpreted that the above rules on directors' remuneration apply to the retirement benefits because the retirement benefits are a deferred remuneration, namely, compensation for the acts of duties of directors. If the retirement benefits are considered as directors' remuneration, then at the very least, the total amount of retirement benefits to be paid should be determined by a shareholder resolution. However, in many companies, the shareholder resolution authorizes the board of directors to determine the amount of the retirement benefits to be paid to the directors. This is because in practice there is a tendency to avoid the amount of retirement benefits to be paid to individual directors to become widely known, particularly when there are only a few retirees. Another reason is that because the retirees are no longer members of the board of directors at the time such determination is made, there is no risk that the retirees would add more remuneration for themselves.

719. It is not permissible to authorize the board of directors or representative director to determine directors' remunerations without any conditions. The Supreme Court rulings have held that a shareholder resolution authorizing the board of directors to determine the retirement benefits to be paid to directors will be valid if the actual amount, payment date and method of payment are to be determined by the board of directors in accordance with certain formula that is explicitly or implicitly presented at the shareholders meeting.[906]

720. If a proposal at the shareholders meeting authorizes a director, company auditor or other third party to determine the amount of retirement benefits in accordance with certain formula, such formula must be provided in the reference documents; provided, however, that such formula will not be required if appropriate measures have been taken to allow shareholders to know the formula.[907] On this basis, the company may elect to either (i) prescribe the total amount at the shareholders meeting or in the articles of incorporation, (ii) provide the formula in the

904. Article 82, para. 1, Ordinance for Enforcement of the Companies Act.
905. Article 82, para. 3, Ordinance for Enforcement of the Companies Act.
906. 11 Dec. 1964, Supreme Court Collection of Court Decisions on Civil Actions 18-2143; 26 Nov. 1973, Supreme Court, *Hanrei Jihou* 722-94.
907. Article 82, para. 2, Ordinance for Enforcement of the Companies Act.

reference documents or (iii) keep the formula at the head office of the company and make it available for inspection by the shareholders.

721. A Supreme Court ruling held in the case where a director who also served as employee of the company retired simultaneously from director and employee that, while such director may not seek the retirement benefits of a director as there was no such provision in the articles of incorporation or a shareholder resolution to such extent, such director may legally request the payment of retirement benefits as employee.[908]

722. However, there are many companies that are reviewing the retirement benefits of their officers (Table 22). As mentioned above, the retirement benefits are deferred remuneration and requires shareholder resolution, but such resolution may not be passed particularly if the company has been involved in a scandal. In addition, there is a trend, particularly among the institutional investors, to vote against such proposals at the shareholders meeting on the basis that the practice of authorizing the board of directors or others to determine the retirement benefits is procedurally vague. As such, there is an increasing trend among the companies to abolish the retirement benefits. Among the companies which have abolished the retirement benefits for officers, some companies have adjusted the amount of regular remunerations or have adopted a performance-linked remuneration structure, including stock options.

Table 22 Companies Abolishing Retirement Benefits for Officers

	Companies Offering Retirement Benefits			*Companies Not Offering Retirement Benefits*		*No Response*	*Total*
	No plan to Abolish	*Abolished at Last Shareholders Meeting*	*Plan to Abolish in the Future*	*Abolished*	*Never Offered Retirement Benefits*		
JPY <500mn	9	-	1	20	4	1	35
	(25.7%)		(2.9%)	(57.1%)	(11.4%)	(2.9%)	(100%)
JPY <1bn	43	1	4	47	9	1	105
	(41.0%)	(1.0%)	(3.8%)	(44.8%)	(8.6%)	(1.0%)	(100%)
JPY ≤2bn	87	6	9	116	19	3	240
	(36.3%)	(2.5%)	(3.8%)	(48.3%)	(7.9%)	(1.3%)	(100%)

908. 11 May 1981, Supreme Court, *Kinyu Shojihanrei* 624-18.

	Companies Offering Retirement Benefits			*Companies Not Offering Retirement Benefits*		*No Response*	*Total*
	No plan to Abolish	*Abolished at Last Shareholders Meeting*	*Plan to Abolish in the Future*	*Abolished*	*Never Offered Retirement Benefits*		
JPY ≤3bn	38	7	8	97	7	-	157
	(24.2%)	(4.5%)	(5.1%)	(61.8%)	(4.5%)		(100%)
JPY ≤5bn	63	5	9	145	15	1	238
	(26.5%)	(2.1%)	(3.8%)	(60.9%)	(6.3%)	(0.4%)	(100%)
JPY ≤10bn	59	4	9	232	14	-	318
	(18.6%)	(1.3%)	(2.8%)	(73.0%)	(4.4%)		(100%)
JPY ≤30bn	41	4	5	300	18	-	368
	(11.1%)	(1.1%)	(1.4%)	(81.5%)	(4.9%)		(100%)
JPY ≤50bn	6	3	1	94	4	-	108
	(5.6%)	(2.8%)	(0.9%)	(87.0%)	(3.7%)		(100%)
JPY ≤100bn	4	2	-	74	6		86
	(4.7%)	(2.3%)		(86.0%)	(7.0%)		(100%)
JPY > 100bn	5	1	1	91	3	–	101
	(5.0%)	(1.0%)	(1.0%)	(90.1%)	(3.0%)		(100%)
Total	355	33	47	1216	99	6	1756
	(20.2%)	(1.9%)	(2.7%)	(69.2%)	(5.6%)	(0.3%)	(100%)

Source: 2014 White Paper on Shareholders Meetings (*Shojihomu*).

C. Bonuses

723. Bonuses are paid to reward directors for generating the company's profits. Bonuses are also a form of remuneration, but under the Commercial Code prior to enactment of the Companies Act, in which the base remuneration was deductible expenses, bonuses were treated as distribution of profits subject to shareholder resolution.[909] In this regard, it was considered that no shareholder resolution under Article 269 of the Commercial Code prior to amendment was required.

909. Article 281, para. 1, item 4; Art. 283, para. 1, Commercial Code prior to amendment.

724. From a shareholder perspective, however, there is no difference among the various remunerations so long as the payments are made to the directors as consideration for the execution of the company's operations. Therefore, the Companies Act defines all such financial benefits as 'remunerations' requiring shareholder resolution pursuant to Article 361 of the Companies Act. Article 361 of the Companies Act. defines 'remunerations' as 'the financial benefits received from the stock company as consideration for the execution of duties, such as remunerations and bonuses', and requires a shareholder resolution unless such remunerations are prescribed in the articles of incorporation.

VII. Duties of Directors

A. *Duty of Due Care (*Zenkan Chui Gimu*) and Duty of Loyalty (*Chujitsu Gimu*)*

725. The contractual relationship between the directors and the company is governed by the rules on 'mandate' (*inin*).[910] Therefore, the directors are subject to the duty of due care towards the company.[911] This means that the directors must perform his or her duties on a level of care that would be ordinarily required for a person in the position of director, regardless of the skills and attentiveness of each individual director. The directors are also subject to the duty of loyalty in performing his or her duties for the company in compliance with laws and regulations, the articles of incorporation and shareholder resolutions (duty of loyalty).[912]

726. There are different views on the interactions between duty of due care and duty of loyalty of directors. The first view is that the duties are identical and duty of loyalty establishes duty of due care in a more specific and confirmatory manner. In contrast, the second view considers that duty of loyalty is different from duty of due care and establishes the directors' duty to prioritize the company's interests in cases where there is a conflict between the interests of the company and the director.

727. The directors would be intimidated and hesitate to pursue aggressive business plans if they are to be held liable for breach of the duty of due care automatically upon a failure of the company's business resulting in a loss of the company. The judicial precedents in the United States have ruled that the directors should not be held liable for failure of their performances to the extent that their decisions were made in good faith based on sufficiently gathered information. This principle is known as the business judgment rule. In Japan, some scholarly views in support of such principle have been asserted.

728. The business judgment rule adopted by courts in Japan is applied in respect to whether or not a director's business judgment breached the duty of due care. This

---

910. Article 330, Companies Act.
911. Article 644, Civil Code.
912. Article 355, Companies Act.

means that if there was no error due to lack of care in the factual awareness (research, analysis, etc.) that served as the grounds for the business judgment and no extremely unreasonable error in the decision-making process or the details of the decision based on those facts, then it is often found that there was no breach of the duty of due care (or the duty of loyalty) (this point differs from the US rule in that Japanese courts will be involved in the judgment of errors in the business judgment to a certain extent). Lower courts had already adopted the business judgment rule, and the Supreme Court has in recent years also made clear their adoption of such rule (Supreme Court, 15 July 2010, *Hanrei Jihou* No. 2091-90).

B. Competing Transactions

729. In Company with Board of Directors, if a director intends to carry out for himself/herself or for a third party any transactions in the line of the company's business, such director must obtain the approval of the board of directors.[913] In companies other than Company with Board of Directors, such transactions are subject to the shareholder approval.[914] These are intended to protect the interests of the company from unfair competing transactions by the directors (see paragraph 735, Liability of directors).

730. When a director seeks approval for competing transactions, such director must disclose the material facts relating to the competing transactions.[915] In addition, after the director has implemented the competing transaction, the director must report material facts concerning such transaction to the board of directors without delay.[916] This is intended to verify whether the actual transaction was within the scope of the approved transaction.

C. Conflict of Interest Transactions

731. In Company with Board of Directors, if a director intends to carry out any transactions with the company for himself/herself or for a third party, such director must obtain approval from the board of directors.[917] In companies other than Company with Board of Directors, such transactions are subject to the shareholder approval.[918] These rules are intended to avoid the inherent risk that the directors may prioritize his or her own interests or those of a third party over the interests of the company when they enter into transaction with the company.

913. Article 356, para. 1, item 1; Art. 365, para. 1, Companies Act.
914. Article 356, para. 1, item 1, Companies Act.
915. Article 356, para. 1, Companies Act.
916. Article 365, para. 2, Companies Act.
917. Article 356, para. 1, item 2; Art. 365, para. 1, Companies Act.
918. Article 356, para. 1, item 2, Companies Act.

732. The examples of conflict of interest transactions include the purchases of the company's products or other properties by directors, sale of directors' own products or other properties to the company and loans from the company to directors. In addition to these direct transactions between the company and the directors, indirect transactions between the company and a third party where there is a conflict of interest between the company and the director, such as a guarantee of directors' obligations by the company, is also subject to the approval requirement.[919]

733. In carrying out such conflict of interest transactions, the director must report material facts concerning such transaction to the board of directors without delay.[920] A conflict of interest transaction which is carried out without the approval of the board of directors is, in principle, invalid; provided, however, that the Supreme Court held that the company may not dispute the validity of the transaction unless the company can prove that the counterparty to the transaction knew that the approval of the board of directors had not been obtained (knowledge requirement).[921] Given that the rules on conflict of interest transactions are intended to protect the interests of the company, the directors may not dispute the validity of such transactions.

D. Lawsuits between the Company and Director

734. In the event that the company files an action against director or if director files an action against the company, there will be a conflict of interest between the company and the director. In such case, in Company with Company Auditor(s), the company will be represented by its company auditors.[922]

VIII. Liability of Directors

A. Liability to the Company

735. The directors are subject to duty of due care and duty of loyalty to the company (see paragraph 725). If a director neglects these duties, such director will be liable for the damages incurred by the company for his or her breach of contract.[923]

736. As the duties of directors will be determined not only by the terms of the mandate agreement (*inin keiyaku*) but also by operation of laws regardless of the intention of the parties, the Companies Act provides that if the directors neglect their duties, such directors will be liable to the company for the damages arising as a

919. Article 356, para. 1, item 3, Companies Act.
920. Article 365, para. 2, Companies Act.
921. 25 Dec. 1968, Supreme Court Collection of Court Decisions on Civil Actions 22-3511.
922. Article 386, para. 1, Companies Act.
923. Article 415, Civil Code.

result thereof.[924] Upon breach of statutory duties, the liability of directors will be determined by the existence or absence of negligence (liability for negligence).

737. The company may pursue damage claims against a director who carried out competing transaction without obtaining the approval from the board of directors (in companies other than Company with Board of Directors, the approval by shareholder resolution).[925] While the damages of the company will be the amount of profits that the company would have gained had there not been such competing transactions, it is difficult to prove such damages. Therefore, the amount of profits obtained by the director or third party as a result of such transaction is presumed to the amount of damages incurred by the company.[926]

738. The company may also pursue damage claims against the director who carried out conflict of interest transaction without the approval of the board of directors (in companies other than Company with Board of Directors, the approval by shareholder resolution) for the damages arising as a result of the director's failure to perform his or her duties.[927] In addition, even if the approval of the board of directors (or shareholder resolution) was obtained, the director may be held liable for the damages arising as a result of any unfair consideration or breach of contract.[928] Under the Companies Act, if the company has suffered damages as a result of conflict of interest transaction, the burden of proof will be on the directors to prove that such directors did not fail to perform his or her duties. This is because, as compared to ordinary transactions of the company, it is highly likely that the company's interests will be harmed in conflict of interest transactions. Here, the directors who are presumed to have neglected their duties will include not only the director who was the party to the transaction but also the directors who decided to implement such transaction (representative director) and the directors who agreed to the board of directors' resolution to approve such transaction.[929]

739. As noted above, under the Companies Act, directors' liability for failure to perform their duties requires negligence of such director; provided, however, that a director who carried out the direct conflict of interest transaction with the company for himself/herself will be liable even if such director was not negligent in the failure to perform his or her duties.[930] In other words, given that it would not be appropriate to allow the director to retain any profits from the direct transaction, such director is subject to strict liability.

740. In the event that any property benefits were given regarding the exercise of shareholder rights, the directors who were involved in giving such benefits will be jointly and severally liable to the company for payment of an amount equivalent to

924. Article 423, para. 1, Companies Act.
925. Article 423, para. 1, Companies Act.
926. Article 423, para. 2, Companies Act.
927. Article 423, para. 1, Companies Act.
928. Article 423, para. 3, Companies Act.
929. Article 423, para. 3, Companies Act.
930. Article 428, Companies Act.

the value of the benefits so given; provided, however, that the directors who have proven that they did not fail to exercise due care in performing their duties will be exempted.[931] However, such exemption does not apply to the director who gave such benefits.[932] Similar liability also applies to directors who have distributed illegal dividends (see paragraph 647).[933]

741. Liability of directors to the company may not, in principle, be exempted without the consent of all shareholders.[934]

742. In December 2001, a lawmaker-initiated bill that allows partial exemption of directors' liability to the company was passed by the Diet and enacted as an amendment to the Commercial Code. Under the Companies Act which basically prescribes the same partial exemption, liability of directors other than outside directors may be limited under certain circumstances to a maximum of his or her remunerations for four years.[935] With regard to the representative director, such limitation is set at a maximum of his or her remunerations for six years.[936] A further limitation is available for outside directors at a maximum of his or her remunerations for two years.[937]

743. In cases where the remuneration is given in the form of share options, the partial exemption is available at a maximum of the amount calculated by the method prescribed in the applicable ordinance of the Ministry of Justice as the amount equivalent to the amount of property benefits regarding such share options.[938]

744. The above partial exemption which requires special resolution at the shareholders meeting will not be permitted if the directors were with knowledge or grossly negligent in performing their duties.[939] In the shareholders meeting approving such resolution, the following details must be disclosed: (i) the facts that caused the liability and the amount of liability for damages, (ii) the maximum amount for which exemption may be given and the grounds supporting such calculation and (iii) the reasons for which exemption from liability is to be given and the amount for which exemption is to be given.[940] In addition, in a Company with Company Auditor(s), the consent of company auditors must be obtained if the directors wish to submit such proposal to the shareholders meeting.[941] If there are two or more

931. Article 120, para. 4, Companies Act.
932. Article 120, proviso to para. 4, Companies Act.
933. Article 462, Companies Act.
934. Article 424; Art. 120, para. 5; Art. 462, para. 3, Companies Act.
935. Article 425, para. 1, item 1(b), Companies Act.
936. Article 425, para. 1, item 1(a), Companies Act.
937. Article 425, para. 1, item 1(c), Companies Act.
938. Article 425, para. 1, item 2, Companies Act.
939. Article 425, para. 1; Art. 309, para. 2, item 8, Companies Act.
940. Article 425, para. 2, Companies Act.
941. Article 425, para. 3, item 1, Companies Act.

company auditors, the consent of each company auditor will be required (in a Company with Audit and Supervisory Committee, the consent of the audit and supervisory committee members must be obtained, and in a Company with Nominating Committee, etc., the consent of the audit committee members must be obtained).

745. Under the Companies Act, to the extent so permitted in the articles of incorporation, the partial exemption may be given by the board of directors if it is found particularly necessary and the directors were without knowledge and not grossly negligent.[942] Here, whether or not the partial exemption is particularly necessary will be decided taking into account the relevant circumstances, including the details of the facts that caused the liability and the status of execution of duties by the directors. As such, the partial exemption in connection with breach of duty of due care may be given by the managerial decision of the board of directors. In companies having only one director, however, the director may not be partially exempted without a shareholder resolution. This is intended to avoid any partial exemption to be given by an arbitrary discretion of such sole director.

746. To submit a proposal to amend the articles of incorporation to introduce the partial exemption of liability at the shareholders meeting or a proposal regarding the partial exemption of liability to the board of directors, the consent of all company auditors will be required (in a Company with Audit and Supervisory Committee, the consent of the audit and supervisory committee members must be obtained, and in a Company with Nominating Committee, etc., the consent of the audit committee members will be required).[943] If the board of directors passes a resolution on the partial exemption of liability, a public notice must be posted, or a notice must be sent to the shareholders without delay to the effect that any objections must be stated within a specific period of time (at least one month).[944] If shareholders having not less than 3% of the voting rights of all shareholders state objections, such partial exemption may not be effected by the company.[945]

747. The company may, pursuant to the provisions of the articles of incorporation, enter into an agreement with any directors other than executive directors to determine their maximum amount of liability in advance.[946] Initially, this type of limitation of liability agreement was allowed for outside directors with the aim of securing more suitable individuals for outside director positions. The 2014 amendment expanded the scope of these agreements in the way stated above and made it possible for directors who are not outside directors to enter into limitation of liability agreements. To submit a proposal at the shareholders meeting to amend the articles of incorporation to allow such agreements, the unanimous consent of all company auditors is required (in Companies with Audit and Supervisory Committee, the consent of each audit and supervisory committee member must be obtained,

942. Article 426, para. 1, Companies Act.
943. Article 426, para. 2, Companies Act.
944. Article 426, para. 3, Companies Act.
945. Article 426, para. 5, Companies Act.
946. Article 427, para. 1, Companies Act.

and in Companies with Nominating Committee, etc., the consent of each audit committee member is required).[947]

748. The partial exemption is not permitted with regard to the liability of directors who carried out the conflict of interest transaction for himself/herself (see paragraph 739).[948]

B. Liability to Third Parties

749. Under the Companies Act, the directors will be liable to third parties under certain circumstances to protect the interests of third parties harmed by the operations of the directors. Namely, the directors will be jointly and severally liable to a third party for the damages arising as a result of the failure to perform their duties by wilful misconduct or gross negligence.[949]

750. There are different views regarding the nature of such liability as follows: (i) the special tort theory which considers such liability as a type of tort liability and (ii) the special statutory liability theory which views such liability as a liability specially provided by the Companies Act. According to the special tort theory, the liability of directors to a third party is a special tort liability, for which the rules governing tort liability in Article 709 of the Civil Code (i.e., a tort requires wilful misconduct or negligence of the defendant in connection with the damages incurred by the third party) will not apply and therefore the director will be liable only upon his or her wilful misconduct or gross negligence. This theory eases the general principle under the Civil Code as the director will not be liable for mere negligence. The rationale for such easing is that the directors are required perform cumbersome duties in a timely manner.

751. On the other hand, the special statutory liability theory interprets that the liability of directors to a third party is a special statutory liability outside the regime of tort liability under the Civil Code and therefore directors are subject to this liability under the Companies Act in addition to the tort liability under the Civil Code. Under this theory, directors will be liable for their knowledge or gross negligence solely in connection with the performance of their duties, regardless of their knowledge or negligence with regard to the damages to be incurred by the third party required in general tort liability. In addition, if directors were with knowledge or negligent in causing the damages of a third party, such directors will also be liable for general torts. In this regard, this theory would increase the liability of directors. The Supreme Court supported the special statutory liability theory.[950] The policy

947. Article 427, para. 3, Companies Act.
948. Article 428, para. 2, Companies Act.
949. Article 429, para. 1; Art. 430, Companies Act.
950. 26 Nov. 1969, Supreme Court Collection of Court Decisions on Civil Actions 23-2150.

behind this increase of liability is to protect the business partners of small companies having weak financial resources. Many of the proponents supporting the special statutory liability theory construe that the damages would include not only the direct damages incurred by the third party but also the indirect damages caused to a third party through the damages incurred by the company.

752. In addition to the abovementioned liabilities, the directors will be liable to third parties on the following matters unless the directors prove that they did not fail to exercise due care with respect to the performance of their duties: (i) the giving of false notice with respect to important matters when soliciting persons to subscribe for shares, share options, bonds or bonds with share options, or the making of false statements or records with respect to materials used for explanation regarding the business of the company and other matters for the purpose of such solicitation, (ii) the making of false statements or records with respect to important matters to be specified or recorded in financial statements, business reports and temporary financial statements, (iii) the false registrations or (iv) the false public notice.[951]

753. Meanwhile, there are cases so-called nominal director (*meimoku torishimariyaku*) where a person may be appointed as representative director or director in form only and the actual operations of the company are executed by other directors. The Supreme Court held that such nominal directors will also be liable for the damages incurred by the third parties as a result of the failure to perform their duties to supervise other directors.[952]

C. Derivative Actions

754. Liability of directors to the company should generally be pursued by the company itself. However, in many cases, the company may not pursue such liability due to the close relationship among the officers within the company. Therefore, the Companies Act allows the shareholders to pursue the liability of directors and other officers on behalf of the company through a derivative action.

755. Derivative actions may be filed against the directors, accounting advisors, company auditors, executive officers and accounting auditors. First, a shareholder having the shares consecutively for the preceding six months or more may demand the company, in writing or by any other method prescribed in the applicable ordinance of the Ministry of Justice, to file an action to pursue the liability of directors or other officers.[953] To the extent so permitted under the articles of incorporation, a shorter period may be provided or the holders of shares less than one unit may be

951. Article 429, para. 2, Companies Act.
952. See *supra* n. 932.
953. Article 847, para. 1, Companies Act.

disqualified from derivative actions. The requirement to have the shares consecutively for the preceding six months will not apply in non-Public Companies.[954] Subsequently, if the company does not file an action within sixty days from the day of the demand, the shareholders who have made such demand may file an action on behalf of the company.[955] However, in cases where the company is likely to suffer irreparable harm before the elapse of such period, the shareholders may file an action immediately.[956] In cases where the company does not file an action within sixty days from the day of the demand, if requested by the shareholder who made such demand, the company must without delay notify the shareholders the reason for not filing an action in writing or by any other method prescribed in the applicable ordinance of the Ministry of Justice.[957]

756. The prevailing scholarly view construes that the scope of directors' liability in derivative actions would include all liabilities owed by the directors to the company. In the past, the derivative actions which were introduced by the amendment to the Commercial Code in 1950 based on a similar system in the United States were not frequently used in Japan. This was because there was little incentive for the shareholders to file derivative action due to its nature that the damages will be paid to the company rather than the plaintiff shareholder, as well as the financial burden of litigation costs to be borne by the plaintiff shareholder. Such trend, however, has changed dramatically thereafter. One of the reasons for such change was that the filing cost (*soshou hiyou*) to be paid by the plaintiff to the court has been reduced to just JPY 13,000 regardless of the amount of claim in the action, as the derivative actions are now deemed to be an action relating to claim not based on property right and, therefore, the value of the subject-matter of the action is calculated uniformly as JPY 1.6 million.[958]

757. The plaintiff shareholder will not lose the standing in the derivative action even if such shareholder ceases to be a shareholder during the pending litigation, to the extent that: (i) such shareholder acquires the shares of the parent company of the company through share exchange or share transfer or (ii) such shareholder acquires in merger the shares of the surviving company or the company newly incorporated as a result of such merger.[959] This theory will also apply to the subsequent share exchanges/share transfers or mergers implemented thereafter.[960] Under the Commercial Code prior to the amendment in 2005, if shareholder X who filed derivative action against Director Y of Company A becomes a shareholder of the parent company (Company B) through share exchange or share transfer, it was difficult for X to continue such derivative action against Company A (the court rulings had held that since X has become a shareholder of Company B, X may no

954. Article 847, para. 2, Companies Act.
955. Article 847, para. 3, Companies Act.
956. Article 847, para. 5, Companies Act.
957. Article 847, para. 4, Companies Act.
958. Article 847, para. 6, Companies Act; Art. 4, para. 2, Act. on Costs of Civil Procedure.
959. Article 851, para. 1, items 1 and 2, Companies Act.
960. Article 851, paras 2 and 3, Companies Act.

longer pursue the liability of Y as an officer of Company A). As abovementioned, this issue has been resolved under the Companies Act.

758. The derivative actions may possibly be used abusively, for instance, in harassing litigations filed by the shareholders. In this regard, the derivative actions may not be filed if the purpose of the action is to seek unlawful gains of such shareholders or a third party or to inflict damages on the company.[961] In addition, if the defendant director makes a prima facie showing that the action has been filed in bad faith, the court may order the plaintiff shareholders to provide reasonable security.[962] If the shareholders who filed the derivative action win the lawsuit, such shareholders may demand the company to pay reasonable and necessary costs (excluding filing cost) or attorney fees.[963] On the other hand, if the shareholders lose the lawsuit, the company may claim compensation of damages from such shareholders, to the extent that such shareholder was in bad faith.[964]

759. Intervention (*soshou sanka*) or action for retrial (*saishin*) is available in derivative actions to prevent any collusion. The company or shareholders other than the plaintiff shareholder may intervene in pending actions as a co-party.[965] Upon a filing of derivative action, the plaintiff shareholders must give notice of the action to the company without delay.[966] If the company files derivative action or receives the abovementioned notice of action, the company must give public notice to such effect or give notice to its shareholders without delay.[967] In non-Public Companies, the company must notify the shareholders.[968] If a settlement is reached in derivative action where the company is not a party, the court must notify the company of the terms of the settlement and give the company a notice that the company should state its objection to such settlement, if any, within two weeks.[969] If the company does not raise any objections in writing within such period, the company shall be deemed to have approved the settlement.[970] Finally, in cases where the plaintiff shareholders and the defendant director caused the court to render a judgment for the purpose of prejudicing the rights of the company, such as cases where the plaintiff shareholders intentionally lost the lawsuit or they intentionally won the case with a small claim, the company or other shareholders may enter an appeal against the final judgment that became final and conclusive by filing an action for retrial.[971]

760. In derivative actions, there were contrary scholarly views on whether the company could intervene in the action to assist the defendant director. The Supreme

961. Article 847, proviso to para. 1, Companies Act.
962. Article 847, paras 7 and 8, Companies Act.
963. Article 852, para. 1, Companies Act.
964. Article 852, para. 2, Companies Act.
965. Article 849, para. 1, Companies Act.
966. Article 849, para. 3, Companies Act.
967. Article 849, para. 4, Companies Act.
968. Article 849, para. 5, Companies Act.
969. Article 850, para. 2, Companies Act.
970. Article 850, para. 3, Companies Act.
971. Article 853, para. 1, Companies Act.

Court took the view to allow such intervention by the company.[972] Under the Companies Act, the intervention by the company as an assistant (*hojo sanka*) is explicitly permitted.[973] In order for the company to intervene in derivative action for the purpose of assisting the defendant director, the consent of all company auditors will be required (in Company with Committees, each audit committee member).[974]

*D. Multiple Derivative Actions (*Taju Daihyou Soshou*)*

761. In Japan, corporate group management under a holding company structure is becoming more common. In this type of structure, it is not unusual for the main business activities of the corporate group to be carried out by the subsidiaries. Parent companies control the management of the subsidiaries through such means as holding a majority of their voting rights. On this basis, if a parent company incurs damages due to a subsidiary's director being negligent in his or her duties regarding the management of the subsidiary, the parent company is able to enforce that liability. However, due to the close relationship among directors in the parent company and directors in the subsidiaries, there is a risk that the parent company would not seek to enforce the liability of a subsidiary's director. Therefore, the 2014 amendment introduced a new rule called the 'Rules for actions to enforce specific liabilities' (*tokutei sekinin tuikyu soshou seido*) where in certain situations, the shareholders of the parent company can directly enforce the liability of a subsidiary's director.

762. The right to file a derivative action is a right exercisable by single-share shareholders. In contrast, the standing to file an action to enforce a specific liability is limited to shareholders with at least 1% of all voting rights or issued shares of the 'Ultimate Wholly Owning Parent Company, etc.' (*saishu kanzen oyakaisha tou*) (minority shareholder right).[975] Under the Rules for actions to enforce specific liabilities, the relationship between the parent company's shareholders and the subsidiary's directors against whom such action is filed is indirect, passing through the subsidiary itself. It was therefore considered that certain significant ownership stake of the shareholders of the parent company should be required in enforcing such specific liability.

763. The shareholders permitted to file the action to enforce a specific liability are those of the Ultimate Wholly Owning Parent Company, etc. An Ultimate Wholly Owning Parent Company, etc., is defined to be a 'Wholly Owning Parent Company, etc.' (*kanzen oyakaisha tou*) of its subsidiaries but it must not have its Wholly Owning Parent Company, etc. It is the parent company at the top of the parent-subsidiary hierarchy. Because it is possible to seek enforcement of specific liabilities even if there are multiple levels of parent-subsidiary relationships, actions to pursue

972. 30 Jan. 2001, Supreme Court Collection of Court Decisions on Civil Actions 1740-3.
973. Article 849, para. 1, Companies Act.
974. Article 849, para. 2, Companies Act.
975. Article 847-3,para. 1, Companies Act.

specific liabilities are also called multiple derivative actions. A Wholly Owning Parent Company, etc., is defined to be the sole shareholder of a subsidiary. If there are other shareholders, then the liability of directors is expected to be pursued by those shareholders, so the shareholders of a Parent Company, etc., would not be permitted to seek enforcement. If the Ultimate Wholly Owning Parent Company is a Public Company, then the shareholders filing the action must have held shares continuously for six months prior to the request for filing the litigation.[976]

764. Furthermore, in order to enforce the specific liability, the book value of the shares of the relevant subsidiary must exceed one-fifth of the total assets of the Ultimate Wholly Owning Parent Company, etc. The one-fifth threshold is based on the criteria to omit a shareholder resolution upon business transfers or company splits. Enforcement of the specific liabilities is prescribed as a minority shareholder right and is furthermore limited to the liability of directors of material subsidiaries of a certain scale; in reality, therefore, cases where this liability would be enforced are likely to be limited.

E. *Enjoinment of Acts of Directors by Shareholders*

765. In cases where a director engages, or is likely to engage, in an act outside the scope of the purpose of the company or other acts in violation of laws and regulations or the articles of incorporation, if such act is likely to cause substantial detriment to the company, shareholders having the shares consecutively for the preceding six months or more may demand that such director cease such act.[977] This is known as the shareholders' right to enjoin illegal acts. The six-month period requirement may be shortened by the articles of incorporation. In non-Public Companies, such six-month period requirement does not apply. In Company with Committees, the acts of executive officers may also be enjoined.[978]

766. Whereas the derivative action is an ex post facto remedy for directors' illegal acts, the right to enjoin illegal acts is a means to prevent in advance.

§5. Audit of Stock Companies

I. Overview

767. Stock companies must carry out settlement procedures to ascertain the financial conditions and results of operations of the company (see paragraph 610). In addition to accounting audit, the Companies Act also provides for operational audit to audit the operations by directors. The accounting audit and operational audit of stock companies will be carried out by the company auditors. However,

976. Article 847-3, para. 1, Companies Act.
977. Article 360, para. 1, Companies Act.
978. Article 422, para. 1, Companies Act.

non-Public Companies may limit the scope of audit by the company auditors solely to the accounting audit by the articles of incorporation.[979]

768. Moreover, Large Companies are subject to accounting audit by accounting auditors.[980] Companies with Committees will also need to have accounting auditor.[981] Other companies may voluntarily have accounting auditors if so provided in the company's articles of incorporation.[982] In companies having accounting auditors, accounting audit will be handled primarily by the accounting auditors.

769. There are different views on the scope of operational audit by company auditors. The first view is that operational audit should be limited to the legality of operations. The second view is that the scope of operational audit should be extended to the appropriateness of operations. However, in cases where an act of director is significantly improper, such act will be illegal as the director would be in breach of duty of loyalty to the company (see paragraph 725). Therefore, to this extent, the company auditor will end up auditing the appropriateness of operations regardless of the two above views.

770. While the Companies Act provides such auditing mechanism to ensure that the operations and accounting of stock companies are carried out properly, such mechanism had not functioned effectively in practice. There has been a number of misconducts by stock companies uncovered in recent years that were not detected by the company auditors. One of the reasons that the company auditors had not functioned effectively is the customary practice of appointing the company auditors from within the company. As with the directors, the company auditors are elected at the shareholders meeting but the proposals that are submitted by the representative director are rarely rejected at the shareholders meeting (see paragraph 69). This explains why the company auditors were not able to correct the misconducts of the company management. In addition, there were only a small number of company auditors appointed by each company that the company auditors could not fully implement internal investigations. To overcome these issues, certain statutory amendments have been enacted to extend the term of office of company auditors or introduce outside auditors and board of auditors.

II. Appointment and Retirement of Company Auditors

A. Appointment of Company Auditors

771. Company auditors, like directors, are appointed by an ordinary resolution at shareholders meeting.[983] In appointing the company auditors, the quorum of

979. Article 389, para. 1, Companies Act.
980. Article 328, Companies Act.
981. Article 327, para. 5, Companies Act.
982. Article 326, para. 2, Companies Act.
983. Article 329, para. 1, Companies Act.

shareholder resolution may not be reduced to less than one-third of the voting rights of all shareholders.[984] Unlike the appointment of directors, cumulative voting (see paragraph 662) is not permitted.

772. In principle, a company is required to appoint a minimum of one company auditor (part-time permitted). However, in Public Companies that are categorized as Large Company, there must be at least three company auditors and at least half of these company auditors must be outside company auditors.[985] An outside company auditor must be a person who has neither served in the past as director, accounting advisor or executive officer, nor as employee, including manager, of the company or any of its subsidiaries.[986] In such Large Companies, a board of auditors must be composed of all company auditors.[987] The board of auditors must appoint one or more full-time company auditors from among the company auditors.[988]

B. *Qualification of Company Auditors*

773. The grounds for disqualification of company auditors are identical to those provided for directors (see paragraph 666).[989] The company may not provide in the articles of incorporation that the company auditors must be shareholders; provided, however, that this does not apply to non-Public Companies.[990] Company auditors may not concurrently serve as director or employee, including manager, of the company or its subsidiaries and may not act as accounting advisor or executive officer of its subsidiaries.[991]

774. There is also an issue as to whether a person who was appointed as a company auditor immediately after retiring director (so-called sliding auditors) will be able to audit the affairs of the company which occurred during his or her term of office as director. The Supreme Court held that such audit would not be in appropriate per se.[992]

C. *Term of Office of Company Auditors*

775. The term of office of company auditors continue until the conclusion of the annual shareholders meeting for the last business year ending within four years from the time of their election.[993] The term of office of company auditors, unlike that of

984. Article 341, Companies Act.
985. Article 335, para. 3, Companies Act.
986. Article 2, item 16, Companies Act.
987. Article 390, para. 1, Companies Act.
988. Article 390, para. 3, Companies Act.
989. Article 335, para. 1; Art. 331, para. 1, Companies Act.
990. Article 335, para. 1; Art. 331, para. 2, Companies Act.
991. Article 335, para. 2, Companies Act.
992. 21 Apr. 1987, judicial precedent of the Supreme Court, *Shojihomu* 1110-79.
993. Article 336, para. 1, Companies Act.

the directors, may not be shortened by the articles of incorporation. This is intended to ensure the independence of company auditors. In non-Public Companies, the term of office of company auditors may be extended up to ten years by the articles of incorporation.[994]

D. Retirement of Company Auditors

776. The grounds for retirement of a company auditor include the expiration of term of office, grounds for disqualification and resignation. A company auditor may also be dismissed at any time by the special resolution at shareholders meeting.[995] As with the directors, a temporary company auditor may be appointed upon the occurrence of a shortfall in the number of company auditors (see paragraph 676).[996] It is also possible to elect a substitute company auditor at the shareholders meeting in preparation for such shortfall.[997]

777. Company auditors may state their opinions on the election and dismissal of company auditors at the shareholders meeting.[998] In addition, a company auditor who has resigned from his or her office may attend the first shareholders meeting convened after his or her resignation, and state the fact of the resignation and the reason thereof.[999]

III. Remuneration of Company Auditors and Audit Costs

A. Remuneration of Company Auditors

778. Unless otherwise prescribed in the articles of incorporation, the remuneration of company auditors will be fixed by a shareholder resolution. The remuneration of company auditors must be fixed separately from the remuneration of directors which will also be determined by a shareholder resolution.[1000]

779. If there are two or more company auditors, the remuneration of each auditor may be fixed by mutual discussion of the company auditors, within the total amount of remunerations determined in the shareholder resolution or articles of incorporation.[1001] In addition, the company auditors may state their opinions on the remunerations at the shareholders meeting.[1002]

994. Article 336, para. 2, Companies Act.
995. Article 339, para. 1; Art. 309, para. 2, item 7, Companies Act.
996. Article 346, para. 2, Companies Act.
997. Article 329, para. 2, Companies Act.
998. Article 345, para. 4, Companies Act.
999. Article 345, para. 4, Companies Act.
1000. Article 387, para. 1, Companies Act.
1001. Article 387, para. 2, Companies Act.
1002. Article 387, para. 3, Companies Act.

B. Audit Costs

780. The contractual relationship between the company auditors and the company will be governed by the rules on 'mandate' (*inin*) under the Civil Code.[1003] Therefore, the company auditors may request the company to reimburse the audit expenses and interests thereon, as well as to make an advance payment of such audit expenses; provided, however, that the company auditor proves that such audit expenses are necessary for his or her audit.[1004]

781. The Companies Act facilitates such requests of the company auditors that, unless the company proves that the expenses are not necessary for the performance of duties of the company auditors, the company may not refuse the following requests of the company auditors: (i) requests for advancement of expenses, (ii) requests for reimbursement of expenses paid and the interests thereon from and including the day of the payment or (iii) requests to pay the payables incurred to the creditors.[1005]

IV. Power of Board of Auditors and Company Auditors

A. Power of Board of Auditors

782. A board of auditors meeting may be convened, as may be necessary, by any of the company auditors.[1006] In convening the board of auditors meeting, the company auditor must dispatch a notice to each company auditor at least one week in advance.[1007] The period of one week may be shortened by the articles of incorporation. The board of auditors meeting may be held without such convocation procedures if the consent of all company auditors is obtained to such extent.[1008] A resolution of the board of auditors meeting, which may not be made by written consents (cf. board of directors, see paragraph 688), may be made by a majority of the company auditors.[1009] The minutes of the board of auditors meeting must be prepared and signed, or affixed the names and seals thereto, by the company auditors present at the meeting (electromagnetic records are also permitted under Article 393, paragraph 3, Companies Act).[1010] Company auditors who participated in the resolution of the board of auditors meeting and did not have their objections recorded in the minutes of such meeting are presumed to have agreed to such resolution.[1011] If a director or other officers notified all company auditors of the matters

1003. Article 330, Companies Act.
1004. Article 649; Art. 650, paras 1 and 2, Civil Code.
1005. Article 388, Companies Act.
1006. Article 391, Companies Act.
1007. Article 392, para. 1, Companies Act.
1008. Article 392, para. 2, Companies Act.
1009. Article 393, para. 1, Companies Act.
1010. Article 393, para. 2, Companies Act.
1011. Article 393, para. 4, Companies Act.

that should be reported, it will not be necessary for such director or other officers to report such matters at the board of auditors meeting.[1012]

783. The board of auditors of a Public Company that is also categorized as Large Company is a collegial body and will decide the audit policy, methods for investigating the operations and financial status of the company and other matters regarding the performance of the duties of company auditors; provided, however, that such decisions may not preclude each company auditor from exercising his or her authority individually.[1013]

B. Power of Company Auditors

1. Attending Board Meetings and Stating Opinions

784. The company auditors are required to attend the board meetings and state their opinions if they find it necessary.[1014] Therefore, the convocation notice of board meeting must also be sent to the company auditors.[1015] The attendance of company auditors to the board meetings is intended to prevent any illegal or significantly inappropriate resolutions to be made at the meetings. If the company has established the votes by special directors (see paragraph 697), a specific company auditor may be appointed by the company auditors from among themselves to attend the board meetings by such special directors.[1016]

2. Convocation of Board Meetings

785. Company auditors may demand that the directors convene a board meeting.[1017] If a notice of convening the board meeting within two weeks from the day of the demand is not dispatched within five days of such demand, the company auditor who made such demand may convene the board meeting.[1018]

3. Reporting at Board Meetings

786. If company auditors find that the directors engaged in misconduct, or are likely to engage in misconduct, or that there are facts in violation of laws and regulations or the articles of incorporation or grossly improper facts, the company auditors must report to the directors without delay (in Company with Board of Directors,

1012. Article 395, Companies Act.
1013. Article 390, para. 2, item 3; Art. 390, proviso to para. 2, Companies Act.
1014. Article 383, main text of para. 1, Companies Act.
1015. Article 368, para. 1, Companies Act.
1016. Article 383, proviso to para. 1, Companies Act.
1017. Article 383, para. 2, Companies Act.
1018. Article 383, para. 3, Companies Act.

the board of directors).[1019] This is intended to encourage the board of directors to exercise its authority to supervise the operations of the directors (see paragraph 695). If the company auditor knew any illegal acts of directors but did not report to the board of directors, such company auditor will be held liable for neglecting his or her duties.[1020]

4. Investigation on the Company and Its Subsidiaries

787. Company auditors may at any time request reports on the business from the directors, accounting advisors, managers and any other employees or investigate the status of operations and financial status of the company.[1021] If a director detects any fact likely to cause substantial detriment to the company, the director must immediately report such fact to the company auditors (in Company with Board of Auditors, to the board of auditors).[1022]

788. Company auditors may, if it is necessary for the purpose of performing their duties, request reports on the business from the company's subsidiaries (for definitions of parent company and subsidiary, see paragraph 964), or investigate the operations and financial status of the subsidiaries.[1023] However, to protect the interests of the subsidiaries from any abusive use of such investigations, the subsidiaries may refuse the report or investigation if there are justifiable grounds.[1024]

5. Investigation on Documents to Be Submitted to Shareholders Meetings and Reporting

789. Company auditors are required to investigate proposals and documents that the directors intend to submit to the shareholders meeting and, if they find any violation of laws and regulations or the articles of incorporation or a grossly improper fact, they must report the results of the investigation to the shareholders meeting.[1025] This is intended to prevent any such proposals from being passed or approved at shareholders meeting. In addition, the company auditors may dismiss accounting auditor by the unanimous consent of all company auditors.[1026] In this case, the company auditor (in cases where there are two or more company auditors, a company auditor appointed by the company auditors from among themselves) must report such dismissal and the reason thereof at the first shareholders meeting

1019. Article 382, Companies Act.
1020. Article 423, para. 1, Companies Act.
1021. Article 381, para. 2, Companies Act.
1022. Article 357, paras 1 and 2, Companies Act.
1023. Article 381, para. 3, Companies Act.
1024. Article 381, para. 4, Companies Act.
1025. Article 384, Companies Act.
1026. Article 340, paras 1 and 2, Companies Act.

convened after the dismissal.[1027] In Company with Board of Auditors, the company auditor appointed by the board of auditors will be reporting such matters.[1028]

6. Demand for Enjoinment of Illegal Acts

790. Where a director engages, or is likely to engage, in an act outside the scope of the purpose of the company or other act in violation of laws and regulations or the articles of incorporation, if such act is likely to cause substantial detriment to the company, the company auditors may demand that the director cease such act.[1029] If the court orders the director to cease such act by provisional disposition, the court will not require the provision of security (*tanpo*).[1030]

7. Audit Reports

791. Company auditors must prepare an audit report in accordance with the applicable ordinance of the Ministry of Justice.[1031] The audit report on business reports must be prepared on the following matters:

(i) The method and contents of the audit.
(ii) An opinion on whether the business reports and supplementary schedules accurately describe the status of the company in accordance with laws and regulations and the articles of incorporation.
(iii) If a misconduct or material fact of violation of laws and regulations or the articles of incorporation regarding the duties of directors is found, such fact.
(iv) If an investigation necessary for the audit could not be conducted, a statement to such effect and the reason thereof.
(v) If the matters listed in Article 118, item 2 of the Ordinance for Enforcement of the Companies Act (i.e., contents of decisions and resolutions with regard to the development of internal control system) exist and such contents are found to be unreasonable, a statement to such effect and the reason thereof.
(vi) If the matters listed in Article 127 of the Ordinance for Enforcement of the Companies Act (i.e., basic policy on the control of stock companies) are provided in the business report, an opinion on such matters.
(vii) The date on which the audit report was prepared.[1032]

792. The board of auditors must prepare the audit report (audit report of the board of auditors) based on the audit report prepared by the company auditors.[1033]

1027. Article 340, para. 3, Companies Act.
1028. Article 340, para. 4, Companies Act.
1029. Article 385, para. 1, Companies Act.
1030. Article 385, para. 2, Companies Act.
1031. Article 381, para. 1, Companies Act.
1032. Article 129, para. 1, Ordinance for Enforcement of the Companies Act.
1033. Article 130, para. 1, Ordinance for Enforcement of the Companies Act.

In cases where the contents of the audit report of the board of auditors and the audit report of the company auditors differ, a note to such effect may be appended to the audit report of the board of auditors.[1034] The board of auditors must discuss the audit report of the board of auditors at least once by in-person meeting or a method that enables exchange of opinions simultaneously through the transmission and receipt of information.[1035]

793. The audit reports differ on the financial statements depending on whether or not the company has accounting auditors. In companies other than Company with Accounting Auditors, the audit report must include the following matters:[1036]

(i) The method and contents of the audit.
(ii) An opinion on whether the financial statements accurately reflect the financial status and profits and losses of the company in all material respects.
(iii) If an investigation necessary for the audit could not be conducted, a statement to such effect and the reason thereof.
(iv) Appended information (i.e., matters regarding the company's going concern, changes in the accounting policies on justifiable reasons, material contingencies, material subsequent events).
(v) The date on which the audit report was prepared.

In Company with Accounting Auditors, the audit report must be prepared to include the following matters after receiving the accounting audit report:[1037]

(i) The method and contents of the audit by the company auditors.
(ii) If it is found that the method or results of the audit by the accounting auditors is inappropriate, a statement to such effect and the reason thereof.
(iii) Material subsequent events.
(iv) Matters regarding the framework to ensure that the duties of accounting auditors will be properly performed.
(v) If an investigation necessary for the audit could not be carried out, a statement to such effect and the reason thereof.
(vi) The date on which the audit report was prepared.

As with the business reports, the board of auditors will prepare audit report of board of auditors based on such audit report prepared by the company auditors.[1038]

8. Others

794. Company auditors may file an action for revocation of the resolution at shareholders meeting and actions for, among others, invalidation of share issuance

1034. Article 130, para. 2, Ordinance for Enforcement of the Companies Act.
1035. Article 130, para. 3, Ordinance for Enforcement of the Companies Act.
1036. Article 122, para. 1, Ordinance on Company Accounting.
1037. Article 127, Ordinance on Company Accounting.
1038. Article 123; Art. 128, Ordinance on Company Accounting.

and mergers.[1039] In addition, the company auditors may petition for a court order to investigate the company's status of business and assets.[1040] In cases where the company files an action against its director or a director files the action against the company, the company auditors will be representing the company in such action.[1041]

V. Liability of Company Auditors

A. Liability to the Company

795. As the contractual relationship between company auditors and the company are governed by the rules on 'mandate' (*inin*), company auditors are subject to duty of due care as a prudent manager to the company.[1042] If company auditors fail in their duties, they will be liable for the damages arising as a result thereof.[1043] In this case, the liability of company auditors will be joint and several with directors and other officers.[1044]

796. As is the case for directors, derivative actions may be brought against company auditors (see paragraph 754).[1045] Similarly, partial exemption of liability or limitation of liability of company auditors is also permitted (see paragraphs 742–748).[1046]

B. Liability to Third Parties

797. If the company auditors are with knowledge or grossly negligent in performing their duties, such company auditors will be liable to third parties for the damages arising as a result thereof.[1047] The liability of company auditors will be joint and several with the directors.[1048]

798. The company auditors will be liable to third parties for damages arising as a result of the making of a false statement or records with respect to important matters to be specified or recorded in audit reports;[1049] provided, however, that this liability will not apply if the company auditor proves that such company auditor did not fail to exercise due care with respect to the performance of his or her duties.[1050]

1039. Article 831, para. 1; Art. 828, para. 2, Companies Act.
1040. Article 522, para. 1, Companies Act.
1041. Article 386, para. 1, Companies Act.
1042. Article 330, Companies Act; Art. 644, Civil Code.
1043. Article 423, para. 1, Companies Act.
1044. Article 430, Companies Act.
1045. Article 847, para. 1, Companies Act.
1046. Articles 425–427, Companies Act.
1047. Article 429, para. 1, Companies Act.
1048. Article 430, Companies Act.
1049. Article 429, para. 2, item 3, Companies Act.
1050. Article 429, proviso to para. 2, Companies Act.

VI. Accounting Auditors

A. Appointment of Accounting Auditors

799. Large Companies, Companies with Audit and Supervisory Committee, and Companies with Nominating Committee, etc., must appoint accounting auditors.[1051] Other companies may also have accounting auditors voluntarily by prescribing to such effect in the articles of incorporation.[1052] The accounting auditors will be elected by an ordinary resolution at shareholders meetings.[1053] In Companies with Company Auditor(s), the company auditors determine the contents of resolutions regarding the election of accounting auditors to be presented at the shareholders meeting. If there are two or more company auditors, then they decide by majority. In a Company with Board of Auditors, those decisions are made by the board of auditors.[1054] Before the 2014 amendment, resolutions to elect accounting auditors required the consent of the company auditors (or board of auditors), meaning that the company auditors were only given a veto right. In order to heighten the level of independence of accounting auditors, the 2014 amendment granted company auditors (and board of auditors) the right to determine the contents of the resolutions. Resolutions to elect accounting auditors are determined by audit and the supervisory committee in Companies with Audit and Supervisory Committee and by the audit committee in Companies with Nominating Committee, etc.[1055]

B. Qualification of Accounting Auditors

800. Accounting auditors must be a certified public accountant or an audit firm.[1056] This qualification requirement is intended to ensure effective accounting audit.

801. The grounds for disqualification of accounting auditors are as follows:[1057]

(i) A person who may not audit the financial statements under the Certified Public Accountant Act.
(ii) A person who is in continuous receipt of remuneration from a subsidiary of the company, or from a director or other officers of such subsidiary, for operations other than the operations of the certified public accountant or audit firm, or the spouse of that person.
(iii) An audit firm half or more of the members of which are persons listed in the preceding two items.

1051. Article 327, para. 5; Art. 328, Companies Act.
1052. Article 326, para. 2, Companies Act.
1053. Article 329, para. 1, Companies Act.
1054. Article 344, para. 1, item 1; Article 344, para. 3, Companies Act.
1055. Article 399-2, para. 3, item 2; Article 404, para. 2, item 2, Companies Act.
1056. Article 337, para. 1, Companies Act.
1057. Article 337, para. 3, Companies Act.

C. *Term of Office of Accounting Auditors*

802. The term of office of an accounting auditor continues until the conclusion of the annual shareholders meeting for the last business year which ends within one year from the time of their election.[1058] Unless otherwise resolved, the accounting auditor will be deemed to have been re-elected at such annual shareholders meeting.[1059] A consent of the board of auditors will be required in Company with Board of Auditors if the directors intend to include refusal to re-elect the accounting auditor in the purpose of the shareholders meeting.[1060] In Company with Company Auditor(s), the consent of company auditors (where there are two or more company auditors, its majority) will be required for such action.[1061] The company auditors (or the board of auditors) may also request that the directors include a refusal to re-elect the accounting auditor in the purpose of the shareholders meeting.[1062] These are intended to enhance the position of accounting auditors as well as to prevent any collusion between the directors and accounting auditors.

D. *Retirement of Accounting Auditors*

803. Accounting auditors may be dismissed during their term of office by an ordinary resolution at shareholders meeting.[1063] As with the appointment of accounting auditors, in Company with Company Auditor(s), the consent of company auditors (where there are two or more company auditors, its majority; in Company with Board of Auditors, the board of the auditors) will be required for the representative director to include dismissal of the accounting auditor in the purpose of shareholders meeting.[1064] The company auditors (the board of auditors, in Company with Board of Auditors) may also request that the directors include dismissal of accounting auditors in the purpose of shareholders meeting.[1065] In such case, the accounting auditor may state its opinions on the dismissal at the shareholders meeting.[1066] The dismissed accounting auditor may demand damages arising from the dismissal from the company, except in cases where there are justifiable grounds for such dismissal.[1067]

804. Accounting auditors may also be dismissed by the unanimous consent of all company auditors.[1068] The grounds for dismissal are as follows:

1058. Article 338, para. 1, Companies Act.
1059. Article 338, para. 2, Companies Act.
1060. Article 344, para. 1, item 3; Art. 344, para. 3, Companies Act.
1061. Article 344, para. 1, item 3; Art. 344, para. 3, Companies Act.
1062. Article 344, para. 2, item 3; Art. 344, para. 3, Companies Act.
1063. Article 339, para. 1, Companies Act.
1064. Article 344, para. 1, item 2; Art. 344, para. 3, Companies Act.
1065. Article 344, para. 2, item 2; Art. 344, para. 3, Companies Act.
1066. Article 345, paras 1 and 5, Companies Act.
1067. Article 339, para. 2, Companies Act.
1068. Article 340, paras 1 and 4, Companies Act.

(i) If the accounting auditor breached or neglected its duties.
(ii) If the accounting auditor has engaged in a misconduct inappropriate for accounting auditor.
(iii) If the accounting auditor has difficulty in, or is unable to cope with the execution of its duties due to mental or physical disability.

805. If the accounting auditor is dismissed, the company auditors must report such fact and the reason for dismissal at the first shareholders meeting after the dismissal.[1069] The dismissed accounting auditor may state its opinions on the dismissal at such shareholders meeting.[1070]

806. In cases where there is a vacancy which results in a shortfall in the number of accounting auditors due to events such as resignation, death, dismissal or grounds for disqualification, if an accounting auditor is not elected without delay, the company auditors (or board of auditors) must elect a person who is to temporarily perform the duties of accounting auditor.[1071]

E. Remuneration of Accounting Auditors

807. The remuneration of accounting auditors will be determined by the company, subject to the consent of company auditors (where there are two or more company auditors, its majority; in Company with Board of Auditors, the board of auditors).[1072] This consent requirement was newly established under the Companies Act to enhance the independence of accounting auditors.

F. Power of Accounting Auditors

808. Accounting auditors will audit the financial statements and supplementary schedules and temporary financial statements, as well as the consolidated financial statements of the company.[1073] Based on such audit, the accounting auditors will prepare accounting audit reports.[1074]

809. Accounting auditors have the following authority:

(i) To inspect or copy the accounting books or materials relating thereto of the company.[1075]

1069. Article 340, para. 3, Companies Act.
1070. Article 345, paras 1 and 5, Companies Act.
1071. Article 346, paras 4 and 6, Companies Act.
1072. Article 399, para. 1, Companies Act.
1073. Article 396, first part of para. 1, Companies Act.
1074. Article 396, latter part of para. 1, Companies Act.
1075. Article 396, para. 2, Companies Act.

(ii) To request reports on accounting from directors, accounting advisors, managers or other employees.[1076]
(iii) To investigate the status of operations and financial status of the company.[1077]
(iv) To request reports on accounting from the subsidiaries of the company and to investigate the status of operations and financial status of the subsidiaries.[1078] The subsidiaries may refuse the report or investigation if there are justifiable grounds.[1079]

810. Accounting auditors must prepare an accounting audit report on the following matters:

(i) The method and contents of the audit.
(ii) An opinion on whether the financial statements accurately reflect the financial status and profits and losses of the company in all material respects (unqualified opinion, qualified opinion, adverse opinion).
(iii) If the opinion in (ii) above is not given, a statement to such effect and the reason thereof.
(iv) Supplementary matters.
(v) The date on which the accounting audit report was prepared.[1080]

811. In addition, accounting auditors must report to company auditors (or board of auditors) any misconduct or material facts in violation of laws and regulations or the articles of incorporation in connection with the execution of the duties of directors, if they detect such misconduct or facts during the performance of their duties.[1081]

G. Liability of Accounting Auditors

812. If accounting auditors neglect their duties, they will be liable to the company for the damages arising as a result thereof.[1082] The liability of accounting auditors will be joint and several with other officers and may be subject to derivative actions of the shareholders (see paragraphs 754–760).[1083] Limitation of liability for accounting auditors is available as with the directors and other officers (see paragraphs 742–748).[1084]

1076. Article 396, para. 2, Companies Act.
1077. Article 396, para. 3, Companies Act.
1078. Article 396, para. 3, Companies Act.
1079. Article 396, para. 4, Companies Act.
1080. Article 396, latter part of para. 1, Companies Act; Art. 126, para. 1, Ordinance on Company Accounting.
1081. Article 397, paras 1 and 4, Companies Act.
1082. Article 423, para. 1, Companies Act.
1083. Article 430; Art. 847, para. 1, Companies Act.
1084. Articles 425–427, Companies Act.

813. Accounting auditors will be liable to third parties for damages arising as a result of making false statements or records with respect to important matters to be specified or recorded in accounting audit reports, unless they prove that they did not fail to exercise due care with respect to the performance of their duties.[1085]

H. Accounting Audits under the Financial Instruments and Exchange Act

814. Under the Financial Instruments and Exchange Act, an audit certification by certified public accountant or audit firm that has no special interest in the company will be required for the financial statements and consolidated financial statements, such as the balance sheet and profit and loss statement, of listed companies.[1086] If the audit certification contains any false statement on important matters or lacks a statement on important matters that should be stated or material facts that are necessary for avoiding misunderstanding, the certified public accountant or audit firm will be liable to compensate damages sustained by persons who acquired the securities of the company without knowing the existence of the false statement or lack of such statement.[1087] However, the certified public accountant or audit firm will not be liable if they did not provide the inappropriate audit certification intentionally or negligently.[1088] The certified public accountant or audit firm may also be liable for aiding and abetting the companies that submitted false disclosure documents.[1089]

815. The management members of a listed company will be required to evaluate its internal control system on finance and accounting and other information and submit an internal control report together with the annual securities report to the relevant authorities.[1090] Unlike the internal controls required by the Companies Act (see paragraph 693), the internal controls required under the Financial Instruments and Exchange Act are limited to financial reports. This is intended to ensure the appropriateness of corporate disclosures by requiring the management members of the companies to evaluate the internal controls of the company which they are required to establish. In addition, an audit certification of certified public accountant or audit firm will be required for the internal control reports.[1091]

1085. Article 429, para. 2, item 4, Companies Act.
1086. Article 193-2, para. 1, Financial Instruments and Exchange Act.
1087. Article 22; Art. 24-4, Financial Instruments and Exchange Act.
1088. Article 21, para. 2, item 2, Financial Instruments and Exchange Act.
1089. Article 197, para. 1, item 1; Art. 207, para. 1, item 1, Financial Instruments and Exchange Act.
1090. Article 24-4-4, para. 1, Financial Instruments and Exchange Act.
1091. Article 193-2, para. 2, Financial Instruments and Exchange Act.

§6. COMPANIES WITH NOMINATING COMMITTEE, ETC. (*SHIMEI IINKAITOU SETCHI KAISHA*) AND COMPANIES WITH AUDIT AND SUPERVISORY COMMITTEE (*KANSATOU IINKAI SETCHI KAISHA*)

I. Companies with Nominating Committee, Etc.

A. Overview

816. The corporate governance system of Companies with Committees, etc. (*Iinkaitou setchi kaisha*) was originally established in the amendment to the Commercial Code in 2002. Companies with Committees, etc., were renamed as 'Companies with Committees' (*Iinkai setchi kaisha*) in the 2005 amendment, and as 'Companies with Nominating Committee, etc.' (*Shimei iinkaitou setchi kaisha*) in the 2014 amendment to the Companies Act (this revision was made because the 2014 amendment separately introduced 'Companies with Audit and Supervisory Committee' (*Kansatou iinkai setchi kaisha*), another type of company with committees).

817. The characteristic of Companies with Nominating Committee, etc., is that they have three committees inside the board of directors, namely, a nominating committee, audit committee and compensation committee, and the management of the company will be delegated to executive officers and representative executive officers.[1092] Companies with Nominating Committee, etc., may not appoint company auditors.[1093] As a so-called monitoring model, the board of directors may, except for certain limited matters, delegate the decisions on the operations to executive officers and focus on its role to mainly oversee the executive officers. In each of the three committees, majority of the committee members must be outside directors to enhance the independence of the committees (see paragraph 658).[1094]

818. Companies may become Companies with Nominating Committee, etc., by prescribing to such effect in the articles of incorporation.[1095] Whether or not to adopt the Companies with Nominating Committee, etc., structure is left to the judgment of the company. They may also choose traditional management structures. As corporate governance systems, both Companies with Nominating Committee, etc., and Companies with Company Auditor(s) are reasonable structures, so the choice is left up to the autonomy of each company. However, few companies have chosen to become Companies with Nominating Committee, etc. (as of 31 March 2015, only fifty-nine listed companies).

1092. Article 2, item 12; Art. 402, para. 1; Art. 420, para. 1; Art. 418, Companies Act.
1093. Article 327, para. 4, Companies Act.
1094. Article 416, para. 4; Art. 400, para. 3, Companies Act.
1095. Article 326, para. 2, Companies Act.

B. Directors and Board of Directors

819. In Companies with Nominating Committee, etc., the directors are appointed at shareholders meetings; provided, however, that the candidates to be nominated in the proposal for the appointment of directors are determined by the nominating committee.[1096] There must be at least three directors, of which two or more must be outside directors because each of the committees must consist of a majority of outside directors.[1097]

820. The term of office of a director is until the conclusion of the annual shareholders meeting for the last business year within one year from the time of his or her election (see paragraph 668).[1098] This means that the directors of Companies with Nominating Committee, etc., must be reappointed by the shareholders each and every year. One of the reasons for such a short-term of office is that the board of directors of Companies with Nominating Committees, etc., is entitled to determine dividends of surplus without shareholder resolution (see paragraph 639).[1099]

821. As it is intended in Companies with Nominating Committee, etc., to delegate the operations to executive officers and split the role of supervision and operations, a director may, in principle, not execute the operations of the company in his or her capacity as a director.[1100] However, it is possible for directors to be appointed concurrently as executive officers.[1101] Therefore, a director may be involved in the execution of operations in his or her capacity as executive officer. In such case, it is likely that more operational information will be provided to the board of directors. On the other hand, there may be a concern that the role of directors in overseeing the executive officers may be weakened, but such role is expected to be performed by the committees comprised of a majority of outside directors.

822. Directors are prohibited from serving concurrently as managers or other employees of the company.[1102] Therefore, in Companies with Nominating Committee, etc., an employee may not serve concurrently as director. This is because it is not suitable for an employee who serves under the directions and orders of executive officers to act concurrently as a director whose main responsibility is to oversee the executive officers.

823. Companies with Nominating Committee, etc., must have a board of directors.[1103] The board of directors will decide the operations of the company, such as basic management policy, and oversee the performance of duties of the directors and

1096. Article 329, para. 1; Art. 404, para. 1, Companies Act.
1097. Article 400, para. 3, Companies Act.
1098. Article 332, para. 3, Companies Act.
1099. Article 459, Companies Act.
1100. Article 415, Companies Act.
1101. Article 402, para. 6, Companies Act.
1102. Article 331, para. 3, Companies Act.
1103. Article 327, para. 1, item 4, Companies Act.

executive officers.[1104] The board of directors must make decisions on the following:[1105]

(i) Basic management policy.
(ii) Matters prescribed by the applicable ordinance of the Ministry of Justice as those necessary for the performance of the duties of the audit committee (see paragraph 824).
(iii) In case where there are two or more executive officers, matters regarding the interrelationship between executive officers, including the division of duties between executive officers and hierarchy of commands of executive officers.
(iv) The directors to receive requests from executive officers to convene board meeting.
(v) Development of a mechanism necessary to ensure that the performance of duties by executive officers complies with laws and regulations and the articles of incorporation and other systems prescribed by the applicable ordinance of the Ministry of Justice as systems necessary to ensure the properness of operations of the company (see paragraph 825).

These matters may not be delegated to individual directors.[1106]

824. The following matters are prescribed by the applicable ordinance of the Ministry of Justice as those necessary for the performance of duties of the audit committee:[1107]

(i) Matters relating to the directors and employees who will assist the duties of audit committee.
(ii) Matters relating to the independence of the directors and employees in item (i) above from executive officers.
(iii) The framework for the executive officers and employees to report to the audit committee and other frameworks relating to the reporting to the audit committee.
(iv) Other frameworks to ensure that the audit by audit committee will be carried out effectively.

825. The following items are prescribed by the applicable ordinance of the Ministry of Justice as systems necessary to ensure the properness of operations of the company:[1108]

(i) Framework for preservation and management of information relating to the execution of duties by the executive officers.
(ii) Internal rules relating to the control of risk of losses and other frameworks.

1104. Article 416, para. 1, Companies Act.
1105. Article 416, para. 2, Companies Act.
1106. Article 416, para. 3, Companies Act.
1107. Article 112, para. 1, Ordinance for Enforcement of the Companies Act.
1108. Article 112, para. 2, Ordinance for Enforcement of the Companies Act.

(iii) Framework to ensure that the performance of executive officers will be carried out effectively.
(iv) Framework to ensure that the employees comply with laws and regulations and the articles of incorporation.
(v) Framework to ensure proper operations of the corporate group comprising such company, its parent company and its subsidiaries.

826. The board of directors of Companies with Nominating Committee, etc., may, by its resolution, delegate the decisions on the operations of the company to executive officers; provided, however, that such delegation to executive officers may not be permitted on certain matters, including the following:

(i) Decisions on approval of the transfer of shares with restrictions on transfer.
(ii) Prior decisions on matters concerning acquisition of the company's shares.
(iii) Convocation of shareholders meeting.
(iv) Decisions on the proposals to be submitted to the shareholders meeting.
(v) Decisions on the appointment or dismissal of committee members.
(vi) Appointment or dismissal of executive officers.
(vii) Appointment or dismissal of representative executive officers.
(viii) Decisions on partial exemption of liability of directors and executive officers.
(ix) Approval of financial statements.
(x) Decisions on the terms of merger agreements.[1109]

C. Powers of the Three Committees

827. The nominating committee determines the proposals regarding the election and dismissal of directors to be submitted to the shareholders meeting.[1110] In the past, there were quite a few cases where certain persons such as the representative director had in fact decided the directors to be nominated. It is expected in Companies with Nominating Committee, etc., in which the nominating committee is composed of a majority outside directors, that the directors will be nominated independently from the executive officers.

828. The audit committee audits the performance of duties by directors and executive officers and prepares the audit reports.[1111] Companies with Nominating Committee, etc., may not have company auditors.[1112] An audit committee member may not concurrently serve as executive officer or executive director of such company or its subsidiaries, or as accounting advisor, manager or other employees of its subsidiary.[1113] The board of directors must decide the matters prescribed in the

1109. Article 416, para. 4, Companies Act.
1110. Article 404, para. 1, Companies Act.
1111. Article 404, para. 2, Companies Act.
1112. Article 327, para. 4, Companies Act.
1113. Article 400, para. 4, Companies Act.

applicable ordinance of the Ministry of Justice as the matters necessary for the performance of duties of the audit committee (see paragraph 824).[1114] In addition, the board of directors is required to develop a mechanism to ensure that the performance of duties by the executive officers complies with laws and regulations and the articles of incorporation (see paragraph 825).[1115] The main responsibility of the audit committee is to oversee whether the internal control department of the company is properly established and operated.

829. Audit committee members appointed by the audit committee may at any time request reports on the performance of duties from other directors, executive officers and employees, or investigate the operations and financial status of the company.[1116] If it is necessary for the purpose of performing duties of the auditing committee, such audit committee members may request reports on the business from the company's subsidiary or investigate the operations and financial status of such subsidiary.[1117] If audit committee members find that executive officers or directors engage in or are likely to engage in misconduct, or that there are facts in violation of laws and regulations or the articles of incorporation or grossly improper facts, the audit committee members must report to the board of directors.[1118] In addition, in cases where an executive officer or director engages or is likely to engage in an act outside the scope of the purpose of the company or other acts in violation of laws and regulations or the articles of incorporation, if such act is likely to cause substantial detriment to the company, the audit committee members may demand that such executive officer or director cease such act.[1119]

830. The audit committee has the authority to determine the proposal on the election and dismissal of accounting auditors and the refusal to re-elect accounting auditors to be submitted to shareholders meeting.[1120]

831. The compensation committee determines the remunerations of individual directors and executive officers.[1121] The compensation committee must prescribe the policies on deciding the remunerations for individual directors and executive officers.[1122] The compensation committee must also determine the following: (i) in cases of remunerations in a fixed amount, the amount for each individual person, (ii) in cases of remunerations that are not fixed in amounts, the specific method for calculating that amount for each individual person and (iii) in cases of remunerations that are not monetary, the specific contents thereof for each individual person.[1123]

1114. Article 416, para. 1, item 1(b), Companies Act.
1115. Article 416, para. 1, item 1(e), Companies Act.
1116. Article 405, para. 1, Companies Act.
1117. Article 405, para. 2, Companies Act.
1118. Article 406, Companies Act.
1119. Article 407, para. 1, Companies Act.
1120. Article 404, para. 2, item 2, Companies Act.
1121. Article 404, para. 3, Companies Act.
1122. Article 409, para. 1, Companies Act.
1123. Article 409, para. 3, Companies Act.

832. Where an executive officer serves concurrently as employee, including manager, the compensation committee will also determine the contents of such employee's remuneration as employee.[1124]

D. Operation of the Three Committees

833. Companies with Nominating Committee, etc., must establish three committees: nominating committee, audit committee and compensation committee.[1125] The three committees may be convened by any director who is a committee member of such committee.[1126] In convening the committees, a notice must be dispatched to each committee member no later than one week in advance (or if a shorter period is prescribed by the board of directors, such shorter period of time).[1127] The convocation procedures will not be required if the consent of all committee members of such committee is obtained.[1128] If requested by the committee, directors and executive officers must attend the committee meeting and explain the matters requested by such committee.[1129]

834. Resolutions of committee meeting will be passed by a majority of the committee members present at the meeting where the majority of committee members entitled to participate in the vote are present.[1130] With regard to the quorum and requirements for resolution, a higher proportion may be prescribed by the board of directors. Committee members having special interest in the resolution may not participate in the vote.[1131] The minutes of committee meetings must be prepared and kept at the head office for ten years.[1132]

835. One or more committee members appointed by the committee must report the performance of duties of such committee to the board of directors without delay.[1133] If committee members make the following requests to the company with respect to the performance of their duties, the company may not refuse such request except in cases where it proves that the expenses or payables relating to such request are not necessary for the performance of duties of such committee members: (i) advancement of expenses, (ii) indemnification of expenses paid and interests thereon from and including the day of the payment or (iii) payment of payables incurred to the creditor.[1134]

1124. Article 404, second sentence of para. 3, Companies Act.
1125. Article 2, item 12, Companies Act.
1126. Article 410, Companies Act.
1127. Article 411, para. 1, Companies Act.
1128. Article 411, para. 2, Companies Act.
1129. Article 411, para. 3, Companies Act.
1130. Article 412, para. 1, Companies Act.
1131. Article 412, para. 2, Companies Act.
1132. Article 412, para. 3; Art. 413, para. 1, Companies Act.
1133. Article 417, para. 3, Companies Act.
1134. Article 404, para. 4, Companies Act.

*E. Executive Officers (*Shikkouyaku*) and Representative Executive Officers (*Daihyou Shikkouyaku*)*

836. Executive officers are elected by resolution of the board of directors.[1135] The term of office of an executive officer continues until the conclusion of the first board meeting called after the conclusion of the annual shareholders meeting for the last business year ending within one year from the time of their election.[1136] Executive officers may be dismissed at any time by the resolution of the board of directors.[1137] A dismissed executive officer may demand damages arising from such dismissal from the company, except in cases where there were justifiable grounds for such dismissal.[1138]

837. Disqualification grounds of executive officers are the same as those of directors (see paragraph 666).[1139] Non-Public Companies may also provide in the articles of incorporation that the executive officers must be the shareholders of the company.[1140]

838. In Companies with Nominating Committee, etc., executive officers make the decisions on the operations of the company delegated by the resolution of the board of directors and execute the operations of such company.[1141] Executive officers must report on the performance of their duties to the board of directors at least once every three months.[1142] If requested by the board of directors, executive officers must attend the board meeting and provide explanations on the matters requested by the board.[1143] Executive officers have the authority to convene board of directors meeting.[1144] In addition, if executive officers detect any fact likely to cause substantial detriment to the company, they must immediately report such fact to the audit committee members.[1145]

839. If more than one executive officer has been elected, one or more representative executive officers must be appointed by the resolution of the board of directors.[1146] If there is only one executive officer, such officer will be deemed to have been appointed as the representative executive officer.[1147] The representative executive officers may be removed at any time by the resolution of the board of directors.[1148] The name and address of representative executive officer must be registered

1135. Article 402, para. 2, Companies Act.
1136. Article 402, para. 7, Companies Act.
1137. Article 403, para. 1, Companies Act.
1138. Article 403, para. 2, Companies Act.
1139. Article 402, para. 4; Art. 331, para. 1, Companies Act.
1140. Article 402, para. 5, Companies Act.
1141. Article 418, Companies Act.
1142. Article 417, para. 4, Companies Act.
1143. Article 417, para. 5, Companies Act.
1144. Article 417, para. 2, Companies Act.
1145. Article 419, para. 1, Companies Act.
1146. Article 420, first sentence of para. 1, Companies Act.
1147. Article 420, second sentence of para. 1.
1148. Article 420, para. 2, Companies Act.

in commercial registration.[1149] As with representative directors, a similar provision is provided for representative executive officers on apparent representative executive officers (see paragraph 707).[1150] In addition, the provisions relating to representative directors apply *mutatis mutandis* to representative executive officers on certain matters, including the scope of authority to represent the company.[1151]

F. *Liability of Directors and Executive Officers*

840. The contractual relationship between the company and directors or executive officers is governed by the provisions on 'mandate' (*inin*) under the Civil Code.[1152] Therefore, directors and executive officers are subject to duty of due care to the company and will be liable for the damages if they failed to perform their duties.[1153] This liability may not be exempted without the consent of all shareholders; provided, however, that as with other stock companies, certain limited exemption is available for the directors and executive officers of Companies with Nominating Committee, etc., to the extent that the relevant director or executive officer is without knowledge and not grossly negligent in performing his or her duties (see paragraphs 735–736).[1154]

841. Similar rules apply to the liabilities relating to illegal dividends and conflict of interest transactions (see paragraphs 739–740). The shareholders may file derivative actions not only against directors but also against executive officers.[1155] In the event that the company files a lawsuit to pursue the liability of executive officers, the company will be represented by the audit committee members appointed by the audit committee.[1156]

842. Liabilities of directors and executive officers in Companies with Nominating Committees, etc., to third parties are essentially the same as with other stock companies (see paragraph 749). If they are with knowledge or grossly negligent in performing their duties, they will be liable to third parties for damages arising as a result thereof.[1157] In such case, the liabilities of directors and executive officers will be joint and several.[1158]

1149. Article 911, para. 2, item 22(c).
1150. Article 421, Companies Act.
1151. Article 420, para. 3, Companies Act.
1152. Article 330; Art. 402, para. 3, Companies Act.
1153. Article 644, Civil Code; Art. 423, para. 1, Companies Act.
1154. Articles 424–427, Companies Act.
1155. Article 847, para. 1, Companies Act.
1156. Article 408, para. 1, Companies Act.
1157. Article 429, Companies Act.
1158. Article 430, Companies Act.

II. Companies with Audit and Supervisory Committee

A. *Overview*

843. The 2014 amendment to the Companies Act introduced the Companies with Audit and Supervisory Committee. Companies with Nominating Committee, etc., introduced in the 2002 amendment, provided a system for the oversight of executive officers by the board of directors, centred around three committees, in each of which a majority of members are outside directors. This sought to realize the 'monitoring model' through the separation of the execution and supervision of management (see paragraph 817). However, only a few companies adopted the Companies with Nominating Committee, etc., structure. One reason that companies in practice showed reluctance to transition to that structure is because of the compulsory establishment of a nominating committee and a compensation committee. Therefore, the new system was designed to make nominating committees and compensation committees unnecessary while retaining the audit and supervisory role filled by a committee in which a majority of members are outside directors (the audit and supervisory committee).

844. Unlike Companies with Nominating Committee, etc., Companies with Audit and Supervisory Committee do not have executive officers or representative executive officers. Instead, a representative director represents the company, as in Companies with Company Auditor(s) and Companies with Board of Auditors. However, if a majority of the directors are outside directors or if so prescribed in the articles of incorporation, the powers of the board of directors may be largely delegated to the representative director or other directors. This allows for swift decision-making, as in Companies with Nominating Committee, etc. Companies with Audit and Supervisory Committee cannot have company auditors. The audit and supervisory committee possesses the same power as the audit committee members in a Company with Nominating Committee, etc. The election and dismissal of directors is decided at the shareholders meeting, but the audit and supervisory committee has the right to state their opinion at those meetings (the same rule applies when deciding remuneration). Because these points expand the committee's power beyond only auditing, the name 'audit and supervisory committee' was chosen. The audit and supervisory committee is given the same power on ensuring independence as in the case of company auditors. For these reasons, Companies with Audit and Supervisory Committee can be said to occupy a middle ground between Companies with Company Auditors/Board of Auditors and Companies with Nominating Committee, etc.

B. *Directors and Board of Directors*

845. Directors of Companies with Audit and Supervisory Committees are elected at the shareholders meeting.[1159] Directors who are also audit and supervisory

1159. Article 329, para. 1, Companies Act.

committee members must be elected separately from other directors.[1160] The term of office of directors who are not audit and supervisory committee members is one year (which can be shortened through the articles of incorporation or a resolution of the shareholders meeting), but the term of office of directors who are audit and supervisory committee members is two years.[1161] Although the term of office of the former can be shortened through the articles of incorporation or a resolution of the shareholders meeting, the term of office of the latter cannot. The dismissal of directors who are not audit and supervisory committee members can be accomplished through an ordinary resolution of the shareholders meeting, but the dismissal of directors who are audit and supervisory committee members requires a special resolution of the shareholders meeting.[1162] The remuneration, etc., of directors is determined by a resolution of the shareholders meeting if not provided in the articles of incorporation.[1163] However, the remuneration, etc., of directors who are audit and supervisory committee members must be prescribed separately from that of other directors.[1164] Directors who are audit and supervisory committee members may state their opinion on such remuneration, etc.[1165] These rules are to ensure the independence of directors who are audit and supervisory committee members.

846. Directors who are audit and supervisory committee members cannot simultaneously serve as executive directors, managers or other employees of the company or its subsidiaries.[1166] There must be three or more directors who are audit and supervisory committee members, and a majority of them must be outside directors.[1167]

847. Companies with Audit and Supervisory Committee must have a board of directors.[1168] They cannot have executive officers (*shikkouyaku*). As a result, the execution of the company's business is carried out by the board of directors and the representative director (executive directors, etc.). This is the same as in Companies with Company Auditor(s) and Companies with Board of Auditors. However, if a majority of the directors are outside directors or if so prescribed in the articles of incorporation, the matters to be decided by the board of directors may be largely delegated to individual directors through a resolution of the board of directors.[1169] The scope of matters that may be delegated to individual directors is effectively the same as that which can be delegated to executive officers in Companies with Nominating Committee, etc. This makes it possible to conduct business execution similar to that in Companies with Nominating Committee, etc., if this delegation system is adopted.

1160. Article 329, para. 2, Companies Act.
1161. Article 332, paras 1 and 3, Companies Act.
1162. Article 309, para. 2, item 7, Companies Act.
1163. Article 361, para. 1, Companies Act.
1164. Article 361, para. 2, Companies Act.
1165. Article 361, para. 5, Companies Act.
1166. Article 331, Companies Act.
1167. Article 331, para. 4, Companies Act.
1168. Article 327, para. 1, item 3, Companies Act.
1169. Article 399-13, paras 5 and 6, Companies Act.

C. Powers of Audit and Supervisory Committee

848. The audit and supervisory committee audits the directors' performance of their duties and prepares audit reports.[1170] Companies with Audit and Supervisory Committee must have accounting auditors.[1171] The audit and supervisory committee determines the contents of resolutions related to the election, dismissal, and non–re-election of accounting auditors that are submitted to the shareholders meeting.[1172]

849. The powers of audit and supervisory committees are the same as Companies with Nominating Committee, etc. Additionally, an audit and supervisory committee member elected by the committee may state the committee's opinion on the election of directors who are not audit and supervisory committee members and their remuneration, etc., at the shareholders meeting.[1173] Unlike nominating committees and compensation committees in Companies with Nominating Committee, etc., the audit and supervisory committee cannot determine election and dismissal proposals or remuneration; however, a similar effect is achieved in the form of the committee stating its opinion.

850. In Companies with Audit and Supervisory Committee, where directors who are not audit and supervisory committee members personally entered into a transaction with the company (see paragraph 731), they will not be presumed to have neglected their duties (see paragraph 738) if they had obtained approval for the transaction from the audit and supervisory committee.[1174] However, such special rule does not apply to directors who are audit and supervisory committee members.

851. It is not mandatory to have full-time committee members on the audit and supervisory committee (see paragraph 772 regarding the board of auditors). This is because, as is the case with audit committee members in Companies with Nominating Committee, etc., the auditing committee members can make use of the company's internal control system. For this reason, directors in Companies with Audit and Supervisory Committee must establish the internal control system, even if the company is not a Large Company.[1175]

D. Operation of Audit and Supervisory Committee

852. The audit and supervisory committee is formed of all directors elected at the shareholders meeting to serve as audit and supervisory committee members.[1176] Each audit and supervisory committee member has the right to convene a meeting

1170. Article 399-2, para. 3, item 1, Companies Act.
1171. Article 327, para. 5, Companies Act.
1172. Article 399-2, para. 3, item 2, Companies Act.
1173. Article 342-2, para. 4; Article 361, para. 6, Companies Act.
1174. Article 423, para. 4, Companies Act.
1175. Article 399-13, para. 1, item 1(c), Companies Act.
1176. Article 399-2, paras 1 and 2, Companies Act.

of the committee.[1177] Notice of the convocation of the committee must be given at least one week before the date of the meeting.[1178] In the case of the three committees of Companies with Nominating Committee, etc., that notification period can be shortened if the board of directors so provides, but shortening such period for the audit and supervisory committee requires a corresponding provision in the articles of incorporation.[1179]

853. Resolutions of the audit and supervisory committee require the attendance of a majority of the committee members entitled to vote in the resolution and the approval of a majority of those attending members to pass.[1180] The requirements for resolutions cannot be changed. Audit and supervisory committee members with special conflict of interest in the resolution cannot participate in the vote.[1181] Minutes of the meetings must be prepared,[1182] and any committee member who participated in the resolution but did not have their objection recorded in the relevant minutes will be presumed to have agreed to that resolution.[1183]

1177. Article 399-8, Companies Act.
1178. Article 399-9, para. 1, Companies Act.
1179. Article 411, para. 1 and others, Companies Act.
1180. Article 399-10, para. 1, Companies Act.
1181. Article 399-10, para. 2, Companies Act.
1182. Article 399-10, paras 3 and 4, Companies Act.
1183. Article 399-10, para. 5, Companies Act.

Chapter 5. Dissolution and Liquidation of Stock Companies

§1. DISSOLUTION

I. Grounds for Dissolution

854. Dissolution will cause the company to lose its status as juridical person. The grounds for dissolution are the following:[1184]

(i) The expiration of the duration of the company provided in the articles of incorporation.
(ii) The grounds for dissolution provided in the articles of incorporation.
(iii) Shareholder resolution.
(iv) Merger (limited to mergers where such stock company is liquidated as a result of the merger).
(v) Ruling to commence bankruptcy procedures.
(vi) Judgment that orders dissolution.

In addition, there is (vii) a deemed dissolution of dormant companies.[1185] Items (i) through (iv) are grounds for dissolution based on the will of shareholders and items (v) through (vii) are grounds for dissolution not based on the will of shareholders.

855. If a stock company is dissolved, the company must go into liquidation, except for cases of dissolution by merger or bankruptcy.[1186] Upon the completion of liquidation proceedings, the company ceases to exist. Dissolution of a company must be registered in the commercial registration.[1187]

II. Dissolution Order (*Kaisan Meirei*) and Dissolution Ruling (*Kaisan Hanketsu*)

856. One of the grounds for dissolution that are not based on the will of shareholders is a judgment by the court that orders dissolution. This type of dissolution can be split into dissolution orders and dissolution rulings.

857. Dissolution order is a court order for dissolution of the company in response to a petition by the Minister of Justice, shareholders, creditors or other interested parties in the following cases and to be granted if it court finds that the existence of the company is unallowable for securing public interests:[1188]

1184. Article 471, Companies Act.
1185. Article 472, Companies Act.
1186. Article 475, item 1, Companies Act.
1187. Article 926, Companies Act.
1188. Article 824, Companies Act.

(i) The company was incorporated for an illegal purpose.
(ii) The company fails to commence its business within one year from its incorporation or suspends its business continuously for one year or more, without justifiable grounds.
(iii) In cases where an executive director, executive officer or partner executing the business has committed an act that goes beyond, or abuses, the authority of the company prescribed by laws and regulations or the articles of incorporation or that violates criminal laws and regulations, if such person commits such act continuously or repeatedly despite receiving a written warning from the Minister of Justice.

858. Dissolution ruling is a court ruling to order dissolution in the cases listed below and if there are unavoidable circumstances based on an action filed by a shareholder who holds at least 10% (or a lesser proportion if so prescribed in the articles of incorporation) of the voting rights of all shareholders or a shareholder having at least 10% (or a lesser proportion if so prescribed in the articles of incorporation) of the total number of issued shares:[1189]

(i) Company faces extreme difficulty in executing business and suffers or is likely to suffer irreparable harm.
(ii) The management or disposition of property of the company assets is extremely unreasonable and puts the existence of the company at risk.

859. Whereas the dissolution order is intended to secure public interests, the dissolution ruling protects the interests of the shareholders. The dissolution ruling allows the filing of such action as the right of minority shareholders, especially in situations where a special resolution at the shareholders meeting necessary to approve dissolution was not passed and there is no other viable solution other than to dissolve the company to protect the legitimate interests of the shareholders.

III. Deemed Dissolution of Dormant Companies

860. The grounds for dissolution include a deemed dissolution of dormant companies because an inconsistency between the commercial registration and reality, which may arise if companies that are not engaged in any actual business activities for a prolonged period continue to exist legally (i.e., in the commercial registration), may adversely effect other companies to freely choose their trade names or harm the security of transactions. In a deemed dissolution, the Minister of Justice will give a public notice in the official gazette to the company which has not made any changes in the registration for twelve years that such company should submit a notice that it has not yet abolished its business to the registry which has jurisdiction over the area of the company's head office. If the company fails to submit such

1189. Article 833, Companies Act.

notice within two months from the date of the public notice, such company shall be deemed to have been dissolved upon the expiration of such two-month period.[1190]

861. In the Commercial Code, companies were deemed to be dissolved as dormant companies after five years since the last commercial registration. This five-year period was set taking into account that the term of office of a director is two years, which means that there will be a registration matter (e.g., appointment of directors) at least once every two years. Under the Companies Act, as the term of office of directors in certain companies may be extended to ten years by the articles of incorporation (see paragraph 669), no registration matter may arise in such companies for ten years. Therefore, the period for the deemed dissolution was set under the Companies Act to be after twelve years since the last commercial registration.

§2. Liquidation

I. Overview

862. Upon dissolution, a stock company will enter into liquidation proceedings, except in cases of mergers or bankruptcy.[1191] In liquidation proceedings, the residual assets of the company will be distributed to the shareholders in a fair manner after the legal relations involving the company are liquidated. The company continues to exist within the scope of the purpose of liquidation until the completion of the liquidation.[1192] In addition to ordinary liquidation (*tsujyou seisan*), special liquidation (*tokubetsu seisan*) will apply in certain cases, such as the existence of circumstances prejudicial to the implementation of ordinary liquidation.[1193]

II. Liquidators

863. If a company enters into liquidation proceedings, the directors lose their positions. However, in principle, the directors at the time of dissolution will perform the duties as liquidators.[1194] Other liquidators may also be appointed by the articles of incorporation or shareholders resolution.[1195] If there is no such liquidator appointed or the company was dissolved by a court ruling of invalidation of incorporation or share transfer (*kabushiki iten*), the court will appoint the liquidator in response to the petition by an interested party.[1196] If the company was dissolved by a dissolution order or dissolution ruling, the court will appoint the liquidator in

1190. Article 472, para. 1, Companies Act.
1191. Article 475, item 1, Companies Act.
1192. Article 476, Companies Act.
1193. Article 510, Companies Act.
1194. Article 478, para. 1, item 1, Companies Act.
1195. Article 478, para. 1, items 2 and 3, Companies Act.
1196. Article 478, paras 2 and 4, Companies Act.

response to the petition of an interested party or the Minister of Justice or ex officio.[1197]

864. Except in cases where the liquidator was appointed by the court, the liquidator may be dismissed by an ordinary resolution at the shareholders meeting.[1198] Certain minority shareholders may also file a petition to the court for dismissal of the liquidator.[1199]

865. The liquidators will perform the duties of conclusion of current business, collection of debts and performance of obligations, and the delivery of residual assets.[1200] A liquidated company must appoint one or more liquidators.[1201] While the liquidators may in general have the power to represent the company, the company may also appoint representative liquidators from among the liquidators in the articles of incorporation or through appointment by the liquidators from among themselves pursuant to the applicable provisions of the articles of incorporation or by a resolution at the shareholders meeting.[1202] If there are two or more liquidators, the business of the company must be determined by a majority of the liquidators unless otherwise provided in the articles of incorporation.[1203] It is also possible to establish a board of liquidators as prescribed by the articles of incorporation.[1204] In such case, the board of liquidators must appoint representative liquidators from among the liquidators and may remove such representative liquidators if necessary.[1205]

III. Ordinary Liquidation

866. Liquidators will administrate the liquidation to complete the affairs which were not completed at the time of dissolution. (e.g., purchase of goods to fulfil a sales contract, collection of debts, performance of obligations). With regard to performance of obligations, the liquidators will give a notice that the creditors should state their claims within a certain period (two months or more) and may perform its obligations to all creditors who stated their claims after this period has elapsed.[1206] After these obligations have been performed, the liquidators may distribute the residual assets of the company to the shareholders.[1207] The residual assets are, in principle, distributed in proportion to the number of shares held by each shareholder.

1197. Article 478, para. 3, Companies Act.
1198. Article 479, para. 1, Companies Act.
1199. Article 479, para. 2, Companies Act.
1200. Article 481, Companies Act.
1201. Article 477, para. 1, Companies Act.
1202. Article 483, para. 1; Art. 483, para. 3, Companies Act.
1203. Article 482, para. 2, Companies Act.
1204. Article 477, para. 2, Companies Act.
1205. Article 489, paras 3 and 4, Companies Act.
1206. Articles 499–501, Companies Act.
1207. Articles 504–506, Companies Act.

867. Under the Companies Act, it is possible to distribute residual assets in properties other than cash payments. In such case, the shareholders have the right to demand the distribution of cash payments.[1208] In such case, a cash payment equivalent to the value of the residual assets will be made to such shareholders. Here, the value of the residual assets will be the market price as calculated by the method prescribed in the applicable ordinance of the Ministry of Justice in cases where the assets have market value and, in other cases, the amount determined by the court in response to a petition by the company.[1209]

868. Once the administration of liquidation has concluded, the liquidators must prepare the settlement of accounts without delay.[1210] In a company with board of liquidators, the settlement of accounts requires the approval of the board of liquidators.[1211] The liquidators will be required to submit or provide the settlement of accounts to the shareholders meeting and obtain approval.[1212] The liquidators must register the completion of liquidation at the location of the head office within two weeks from the approval of the settlement of accounts by the shareholders meeting.[1213] The company ceases to exist upon the registration of the completion of liquidation.

IV. Special Liquidation

869. Special liquidation is a liquidation proceeding initiated upon a court order based on certain grounds. The grounds for commencement of the special liquidation proceedings are as given below:[1214]

(i) Existence of circumstances prejudicial to the implementation of liquidation.
(ii) Suspicion that the company is insolvent.

870. A petition for special liquidation may be filed by a liquidator, creditor, company auditor or shareholder.[1215] If it is suspected that the company is insolvent, the liquidator must file a petition for the commencement of special liquidation.[1216]

871. While the liquidators will also administrate the liquidation in a special liquidation, the liquidators will be subject to duty to perform the liquidation administration fairly and in good faith in relation to creditors, the company and shareholders.[1217]

1208. Article 505, para. 1, Companies Act.
1209. Article 505, para. 3, Companies Act.
1210. Article 507, para. 1, Companies Act.
1211. Article 507, para. 2, Companies Act.
1212. Article 507, para. 3, Companies Act.
1213. Article 929, item 1, Companies Act.
1214. Article 510, Companies Act.
1215. Article 511, para. 1, Companies Act.
1216. Article 511, para. 2, Companies Act.
1217. Article 523, Companies Act.

872. If an order to commence special liquidation is issued, the liquidation will be subject to the supervisions by the court.[1218] The court may order the company at any time to report the status of its administration of the liquidation and assets, or otherwise conduct investigations necessary for the supervision of liquidation.[1219] In addition, where necessary, the court may effect the disposition ordering investigations by investigators into matters such as: (i) circumstances that resulted in the commencement of special liquidation, (ii) the status of the business and assets of the company and (iii) whether or not there is a need for temporary restraining order, in each case in response to a petition from the liquidators, company auditors, creditors who have claims of at least 10% of the total amount of the claims of creditors that have stated their claims and other creditors known to the company or shareholders who have held shares or voting rights of at least 3% of all shareholders for a consecutive period of six months or more, or ex officio.[1220]

873. If it is necessary to implement the special liquidation, a creditors' meeting may be convened.[1221] Although the meeting will, in principle, be convened by the company, certain creditors may convene the meeting with the permission of the court.[1222] The creditors' meeting will be directed by the court.[1223] A resolution will be passed by the consent of a majority of the voting rights holders present at the meeting, and the consent of persons who hold the voting rights in excess of 50% of the total voting rights of those holders present at the meeting.[1224]

874. The company may offer an agreement (*kyoutei*) to the creditors' meeting.[1225] In the agreement, the terms and conditions must be provided regarding the changes of some or all of the rights of the creditors (e.g., debt reduction, extension of terms).[1226] The changes of rights under the agreement must be equal among the creditors.[1227] An agreement offered by the company may be approved or modified at the creditors' meeting. To approve an agreement, the consent of a majority of the voting rights holders present at the meeting, and the consent of those persons who hold two-thirds or more of the total voting rights of those holders present at the meeting will be required.[1228]

875. The court may, if it finds necessary, appoint one or more supervisors (*kantoku iin*), who will have the authority to supervise the company's operations and management of assets.[1229] In a special liquidation, the company must obtain the permission of court to carry out the following acts: disposal of an asset, taking out of

1218. Article 519, para. 1, Companies Act.
1219. Article 520, Companies Act.
1220. Article 522, Companies Act.
1221. Article 546, para. 1, Companies Act.
1222. Article 546, para. 2; Art. 547, Companies Act.
1223. Article 552, para. 1, Companies Act.
1224. Article 554, para. 1, Companies Act.
1225. Article 563, Companies Act.
1226. Article 564, Companies Act.
1227. Main text of Art. 565, Companies Act.
1228. Article 567, para. 1, Companies Act.
1229. Article 527; Art. 528, Companies Act.

a loan, filing of an action, settlement or entering into an arbitration agreement, waiver of rights and other acts designated by the court, provided, however, that the court may grant the authority to give consent to the supervisor in lieu of the permission of the court.[1230]

876. The court may appoint one or more investigators (*chousa iin*) in cases where it issues an investigation order.[1231]

877. The court will hand down a ruling on the conclusion of special liquidation when the special liquidation has been completed or where it is no longer necessary.[1232] If the special liquidation is completed, the company will cease to exist. On the other hand, if the special liquidation is no longer necessary, the company will either move to ordinary liquidation or will continue to exist. After the commencement of special liquidation, the court will make an ex officio ruling on the commencement of bankruptcy procedures in accordance with the Bankruptcy Act if: (i) there is no prospect of an agreement, (ii) there is no prospect that the agreement will be implemented or (iii) special liquidation is contrary to the general interests of the creditors.[1233] If an agreement is not adopted or a ruling to reject the agreement has become final and binding after the commencement of special liquidation, and the court finds facts which constitute a ground for the commencement of bankruptcy procedures, the court may make an ex officio ruling for the commencement of bankruptcy procedures in accordance with the Bankruptcy Act.[1234]

1230. Article 535, main text of para. 1; Art. 527, para. 1, Companies Act.
1231. Article 533, Companies Act.
1232. Article 573, Companies Act.
1233. Article 574, para. 1, Companies Act.
1234. Article 574, para. 2, Companies Act.

Chapter 6. Business Combination

878. If a company intends to develop new business or expand its existing business, the company may consider acquiring an existing business of another company as a more efficient means than to plan a capital expenditure of its own. An acquisition may be achieved through, among others, mergers (*gappei*), business transfers (*jigyou jouto*) and tender offer (*koukai kaitsuke*). In a merger, shareholders of the absorbed company typically become the shareholders of the surviving company, whereas in a business transfer in which the assets of the assignor will be transferred to the assignee, the shareholders of the assignor will not become the shareholders of the assignee. A tender offer (takeover bid (TOB)) is a means to acquire the shares of a reporting company of annual securities reports under the securities regulations. While mergers and business transfers will need to be agreed by the target company of the acquisition, a tender offer may be implemented without the target company's consent and is therefore sometimes used as a means to implement hostile takeover.

§1. Merger

I. Overview

879. In a merger of two or more companies, the absorbed company will be merged into the surviving company and will be dissolved by operation of law (or the companies will be consolidated into a new company incorporated by the merger), and as a result the shareholders of the absorbed company will typically become the shareholders of the surviving company (or the shareholders of the companies will become the shareholders of such new company).

880. There are absorption-type mergers and consolidation-type mergers. In an absorption-type merger, one of the companies will continue to exist and the other will be dissolved, while in a consolidation-type merger, all of the companies will be dissolved and a new company will be incorporated simultaneously. In Japan, the absorption-type merger is used in most cases because it is less burdensome in obtaining necessary governmental permits to continue the merging companies' businesses and the registration and license tax can also be saved.

881. Merger is a typical method of business combination. In addition to the purpose of expanding the size of the parties' businesses, the parties typically intend in a merger to reduce costs, avoid competition and redress weaknesses. A merger may also be used to restructure a financially distressed company.

882. Under the Companies Act, mergers are permitted between any types of companies.[1235] Therefore, stock companies may merge not only with other stock

1235. Article 748, Companies Act.

companies but also with membership companies (i.e., general partnership companies, limited partnership companies and limited liability companies). In a consolidation-type merger, either the stock company or membership company may become the new company incorporated by the merger. In an absorption-type merger, either the stock company or membership company may become the surviving company.

883. In a merger, the Act on Prohibition of Private Monopolization and Maintenance of Fair Trade (Anti-Monopoly Act) prohibits mergers where the effect of the merger may substantially restrain competition in a particular field of trade or where unfair trade practices have been employed in the course of the merger.[1236] In addition, the plan of merger by domestic companies must be notified to the Fair Trade Commission in advance.[1237] Further, mergers of banks or other companies engaged in certain specialized business require the approval of competent ministers (e.g., Article 30, paragraph 1, Banking Act).

II. Merger Procedures

A. *Execution of Merger Agreement*

884. Companies intending to merge must enter into a merger agreement.[1238]

885. The merger agreement must provide certain mandatory matters required by the Companies Act. Any lack of such matters may invalidate the merger. The merger agreement may also provide certain matters which do not contravene the nature of merger or laws and regulations. The following refers to mergers between stock companies.

886. The matters to be provided in a merger agreement differ for absorption-type mergers and consolidation-type mergers. The mandatory matters to be prescribed in the merger agreement of an absorption-type merger are as follows:[1239]

(i) The trade names and domiciles of the surviving company and absorbed company.
(ii) If the surviving company is to deliver to the shareholders of the absorbed company cash or other properties in lieu of its shares, certain matters concerning the cash or other property (matters are listed separately for shares, bonds, share options, bonds with share options, property other than shares, etc.).
(iii) In cases of item (ii) above, certain matters concerning allotment of cash or other properties to the shareholders of the absorbed company.

1236. Article 15, para. 1, Anti-Monopoly Act.
1237. Article 15, para. 2, Anti-Monopoly Act.
1238. Article 748, Companies Act.
1239. Article 749, para. 1, Companies Act.

(iv) If the absorbed company has issued share options, certain matters concerning the share options of the surviving company or cash which the surviving company will deliver in lieu of the share options to the holders of such share options.
(v) In cases of item (iv) above, certain matters concerning allotment of the share options of the surviving company or cash to the holders of the share options of the absorbed company.
(vi) The date on which the absorption-type merger becomes effective.

887. The matters to be prescribed in the merger agreement of a consolidation-type merger are as follows:[1240]

(i) The trade names and domiciles of the companies consolidated by the merger.
(ii) The purpose, trade name, location of the head office and total number of authorized shares of the new company to be incorporated by the merger.
(iii) In addition to item (ii) above, the matters to be provided in the articles of incorporation of the new company incorporated by the merger.
(iv) The names of directors at the time of incorporation of the new company incorporated by the merger.
(v) The names of the accounting advisors (if the new company incorporated by the merger is Company with Accounting Advisors), the names of the company auditors (if the new company incorporated by the merger is Company with Company Auditor(s)) and the names of the accounting auditors (if the new company incorporated by the merger is Company with Accounting Auditors), in each case at the time of incorporation.
(vi) The number of shares of the new company incorporated by the merger to be delivered to the shareholders of the companies consolidated by the merger or its calculation method, and matters concerning the amount of stated capital and capital reserves of the new company incorporated by the merger.
(vii) Certain matters concerning allotment of the shares of item (vi) above to the shareholders of the companies consolidated by the merger.
(viii) If the new company incorporated by the merger is to deliver bonds, etc., in lieu of its shares to the shareholders of the companies to be consolidated by the merger, certain matters concerning such bonds, etc. (matters are listed separately for bonds, share options and bonds with share options).
(ix) In cases of item (viii) above, certain matters concerning allotment of bonds, etc., to the shareholders of the companies to be consolidated by the merger.
(x) If the companies to be consolidated by the merger have issued share options, certain matters concerning the share options of the new company incorporated by the merger or cash to be delivered in lieu of the share options to the holders of such share options.
(xi) In cases of item (x) above, certain matters concerning allotment of the share options of the new company incorporated by the merger or cash.

1240. Article 753, Companies Act.

888. The surviving company of absorption-type merger must keep the merger agreement and other matters prescribed by the applicable ordinance of the Ministry of Justice at its head office for a period starting from two weeks before the shareholders meeting approving the merger agreement until six months after the effective date of the merger. The absorbed company is subject to the disclosure obligations until the effective date of the merger.[1241] These disclosure requirements are intended to assist the shareholders and company creditors to make appropriate decisions with regard to the merger.

B. Resolution at Shareholders Meeting

889. The absorbed company will be required to obtain approval of the absorption-type merger agreement by a special resolution at the shareholders meeting on or before the day immediately preceding the effective date of the merger; provided, however, that if all or part of the cash or other properties to be delivered to the shareholders of the absorbed company is certain equity interests of a membership company or those prescribed by the applicable ordinance of the Ministry of Justice, the consent of all shareholders must be obtained.[1242] In cases where the absorbed company is corporation with class shares, if all or part of the consideration is shares with restrictions on transfer of the surviving company, an extraordinary resolution of the class shareholders will be required.[1243] If the absorbed company is a membership company, the consent of all members of the membership company will be required.[1244]

890. In the surviving company, the merger agreement needs to be approved by a special resolution at the shareholders meeting on or before the day immediately preceding the effective date of the merger.[1245] The directors must give an explanation at the shareholders meeting in cases where: (i) the amount of liabilities of the absorbed company to be succeeded by the surviving company exceeds the amount of succeeded assets or (ii) the book value of cash or other payments to be delivered to the shareholders or members of the absorbed company exceeds the amount calculated by subtracting the succeeded amount of liabilities from the succeeded amount of assets.[1246] In cases where a membership company continues to exist, the consent of all members will be required.[1247]

891. Shareholders who provided notice to the merging company prior to the shareholders meeting that they dissent from the absorption-type merger, and

1241. Article 782, para. 1, Companies Act.
1242. Article 783, para. 1; Art. 309, para. 2, item 12; Art. 783, para. 2, Companies Act.
1243. Article 783, para. 3; Art. 324, para. 3, item 2, Companies Act.
1244. Article 793, Companies Act.
1245. Article 795, para. 1; Art. 309, para. 2, item 12, Companies Act.
1246. Article 795, para. 2, items 1 and 2, Companies Act.
1247. Article 802, para. 1, items 1 and 2, Companies Act.

dissented from such merger at the shareholders meeting may demand that the company purchase their shares at fair price.[1248] The shareholders who are unable to exercise voting rights at the shareholders meeting, such as those shareholders having shares with no voting rights, will also have the right to demand their shares be purchased.[1249] Share option holders will also have such right under certain limited circumstances.[1250]

C. *Summary Procedures (*Ryakushiki Tetsuzuki*)*

892. If the surviving company is a 'special controlling company' (*tokubetsu shihai kaisha*) of the absorbed company, the shareholders resolution of the absorbed company will not be required.[1251] Special controlling company means a company which holds at least 90% of all voting rights of another company.[1252] While the purpose of these summary procedures is to simplify the process under certain limited circumstances, it will not be available in the event that all or part of the value of merger to be delivered to the shareholders of the absorbed company is shares with restrictions on transfer and the absorbed company is a Public Company and not a corporation with class shares.[1253]

893. If the absorbed company is a special controlling company of the surviving company, no shareholder resolution of the surviving company will be required.[1254] However, if all or part of cash or other value to be delivered to the shareholders of the absorbed company is shares with restrictions on transfer and the surviving company is not a Public Company, the shareholder resolution of the surviving company may not be omitted.[1255]

894. The dissenting shareholders will have the right to demand the company to purchase their shares in the summary procedures.[1256] The shareholders subject to the summary procedures who are likely to suffer disadvantage may demand that the company refrain from the merger if there is violation of laws and regulations or the articles of incorporation or the price is grossly improper in light of the financial status of the companies.[1257]

1248. Article 785, para. 1; Art. 797, para. 1, Companies Act.
1249. Article 785, para. 2, item 1(b).
1250. Article 787, Companies Act.
1251. Article 784, main text of para. 1, Companies Act.
1252. Article 468, para. 1, Companies Act.
1253. Article 784, proviso to para. 1, Companies Act.
1254. Article 796, main text of para. 1, Companies Act.
1255. Article 796, proviso to para. 1, Companies Act.
1256. Article 785; Art. 797, Companies Act.
1257. Article 784, para. 2; Art. 796, para. 2, Companies Act.

*D. Simplified Merger (*Kanyi Tetsuzuki*)*

895. In cases where the size of the absorbed company is relatively small that the merger will be insignificant for the surviving company, it may not worth forcing the surviving company to hold a shareholders meeting. Therefore, where the amount of merger consideration is 20% or less of the total net assets of the surviving company, the approval at the shareholders meeting of the surviving company will not be required.[1258] However, such simplified merger is not available if: (i) the merger results in losses for the surviving company or (ii) in the event that the surviving company is not a Public Company and all or part of cash or other value to be delivered to the shareholders of the absorbed company are shares with restrictions on transfer of the surviving company.[1259]

896. In a simplified merger, notice must be given to the shareholders or a public notice must be posted.[1260] If the shareholders who dissent from the simplified merger reach a certain minimum number, the simplified merger will not be available.[1261] Such minimum number is the smallest of the following:

(i) the number obtained by multiplying (a) the total number of shares (designated shares) entitled to exercise voting rights at the shareholders meeting approving the merger by (b) 1/2 (or the minimum ratio provided in the articles of incorporation as the quorum to pass the resolution) and further (c) by 1/3 (in cases where there is a provision in the articles of incorporation that a certain ratio of voting rights held by shareholders of designated shares (designated shareholders) are required to pass the resolution, the ratio obtained by subtracting such minimum ratio from one) and then adding one;
(ii) in cases where there is a provision in the articles of incorporation that certain minimum number of shareholders is required to pass such resolution in the shareholders meeting, the 'number of designated shares held by designated shareholders who sent a notice of opposition' if the number obtained by subtracting the number of designated shareholders who sent a notice of opposition from the total number of designated shareholders is less than such minimum number;
(iii) in cases where there is a provision in the articles of incorporation a requirement to pass such resolution other than as provided in items (i) or (ii) above, if such resolution will not be passed when all of the shareholders who sent a notice of opposition oppose the resolution at the shareholders meeting, such number of designated shares held by the designated shareholders who sent a notice of opposition; and
(iv) certain number prescribed in the articles of incorporation.[1262]

1258. Article 796, main text of para. 3, Companies Act.
1259. Article 796, proviso to para. 3, Companies Act.
1260. Article 797, paras 3 and 4, Companies Act.
1261. Article 796, para. 4, Companies Act.
1262. Article 197, Ordinance for Enforcement of the Companies Act.

897. In a simplified merger, the dissenting shareholders may still exercise the appraisal right to demand the company to purchase his or her shares.[1263]

E. *Consideration for Merger*

898. Merger ratio is one of the most important terms of a merger provided in the merger agreement which indicates the ratio to exchange the shares of the absorbed company with the shares of the surviving company.[1264] The merger ratio takes into account the overall assessment of factors such as the company's profit and loss, assets, financial conditions, share price and future potential development.

899. In an absorption-type merger, the consideration to be paid to the shareholders of the absorbed company may be cash or other assets in lieu of the shares of the surviving company.[1265] The flexibility in merger consideration was realized in the Companies Act as it was strongly requested by the business community to allow reorganizations in a flexible manner.

900. In connection with the flexibility in merger considerations, reorganizations may be implemented as follows. A squeeze out merger may be implemented by delivering cash in lieu of the shares of the surviving company to the shareholders of the absorbed company. In a triangular merger, the shares of the parent company of the surviving company will be delivered to the shareholders of the absorbed company and therefore the shareholders of the absorbed company will become the shareholders of the parent company of the surviving company. For example, a foreign company may acquire a Japanese target company without any cash payment if such foreign company has its Japanese subsidiary enter into a merger with the Japanese target company and deliver the shares of the foreign (parent) company to the shareholders of such Japanese target company without making cash payment.

901. In the process of drafting the Companies Act, some concerns were expressed by the business community that allowing flexibility in merger consideration could result in an increase of hostile takeovers, which would damage the value of the company. Taking such concerns into account, the effective date of the part of the Companies Act relating to the flexibility of merger considerations was postponed for one year from the enactment of the Companies Act.[1266] This one year delay was intended to ensure an opportunity for the companies to introduce measures against takeovers by amending the articles of incorporation at the annual shareholders meeting. It should be noted, however, that a merger will not be achieved if the parties are in hostile relationship because in such case the parties will not agree on a merger agreement.

1263. Article 785; Art. 797, Companies Act.
1264. See Art. 749, para. 1, item 2; Art. 753, para. 1, item 6, Companies Act.
1265. Article 749, para. 1, item 2; Art. 751, para. 1, item 3, Companies Act.
1266. Article 4, Supplementary Provisions of the Amendment to the Companies Act.

F. Procedures for Creditor Protection

902. As a merger will have significant influence on the company, the Companies Act requires creditor protection procedure. Each company must make public notice in the official gazette to the company creditors, and must also send a notice to each known creditor, that if any creditor has an objection to the merger, it must state such objection within a certain period of not less than one month.[1267] However, the notice to known creditors need not be sent if, in addition to the public notice in the official gazette, the public notice is made in a daily newspaper which publishes news on current affairs or by an electronic public notice, as prescribed in the company's articles of incorporation as the method of public notice. If a creditor does not file objection within the set period, such creditor will be deemed to have approved the merger.[1268] In addition, with regard to the creditors who have stated objection, the company must make payment, provide reasonable security or entrust equivalent property to a trust company, unless there is no risk of harm to such creditor in the contemplated merger.[1269]

903. A resolution of the bondholders' meeting will be required for bondholders to file objection.

904. In cases where the company is in violation of creditor protection procedures, the company creditors may file an action seeking invalidation of the merger (see paragraph 908).

*G. Post-Merger Disclosure (*Jigokaiji*) and Registration (*Touki*)*

905. The surviving company must prepare without delay following the effective date of the merger, documents or electromagnetic records stating or recording the rights and obligations succeeded from the absorbed company by the absorption-type merger and other items prescribed in the applicable ordinance of the Ministry of Justice, and must keep them at the head office for six months.[1270] The Ministry of Justice ordinance prescribes the following items: (i) the effective date, (ii) the process of the procedures in the absorbed company for the share purchase demand (i.e., appraisal rights), the demand for purchase of share options and for creditors' objections, (iii) the process of the procedures in the surviving company for share purchase demand (i.e., appraisal rights) and the creditors' objections, (iv) items relating to the important rights and obligations succeeded by the surviving company, (v) items described or recorded in the disclosure documents or electromagnetic records kept by the absorbed company, (vi) the date of the changes to the registration and (vii) other important items regarding the absorption-type

1267. Article 789, para. 3; Art. 799, para. 3; Art. 810, para. 3, Companies Act.
1268. Article 789, para. 4; Art. 799, para. 4; Art. 810, para. 4, Companies Act.
1269. Article 789, para. 5; Art. 799, para. 5; Art. 810, para. 5, Companies Act.
1270. Article 801, paras 1 and 3, Companies Act.

merger.[1271] The shareholders and creditors of the surviving company may request to inspect or copy such documents or records at any time during the business hours of the company.[1272] Such post-merger disclosure is also required in the companies newly incorporated by consolidation-type merger.[1273]

906. After an absorption-type merger, the absorbed company must register dissolution and the surviving company must register the changes upon merger at the location of their respective head offices within two weeks after the merger.[1274] In cases of two or more companies forming a consolidation-type merger, dissolution of the dissolved companies and the incorporation of the new company must be registered.[1275]

III. Enjoinment and Invalidation of Merger

A. *Enjoinment of Merger*

907. When an absorption-type merger violates the applicable laws and regulations or the articles of incorporation, if the shareholders of the surviving company or the absorbed company are likely to suffer disadvantages, then the shareholders may demand to the company that the merger be ceased.[1276] Additionally, when a merger is conducted through summary procedures (see paragraph 892), if the consideration for that merger is extremely improper in light of the financial status of either the absorbed company or the surviving company or other circumstances, then the shareholders of the surviving company or the absorbed company may demand that the merger be ceased.[1277] While consideration for mergers is generally approved through a resolution of the shareholders meeting, mergers through summary procedures are not subject to the shareholder approval and therefore could be subject to enjoinment demands if the consideration is extremely improper.

B. *Invalidation of Merger*

908. While a defect in the procedures of merger may invalidate the merger, invalidation of merger may be raised only by the filing of an action because there is a need to protect the transactions involving the merged companies after the merger.[1278] The grounds for invalidation are not specified in the Companies Act and are interpreted to include cases such as when the merger agreement becomes invalid or is rescinded due to mistake, fraud or duress, the absence of resolution on the

1271. Article 200, Ordinance for Enforcement of the Companies Act.
1272. Article 801, para. 4, Companies Act.
1273. Article 815, Companies Act; Art. 211, Ordinance for Enforcement of the Companies Act.
1274. Article 921, Companies Act.
1275. Article 922, Companies Act.
1276. Article 784-2, item 1; Article 796-2, item 1, Companies Act.
1277. Article 784-2, item 2; Article 796-2, item 2, Companies Act.
1278. Article 828, para. 1, items 7 and 8, Companies Act.

merger or when the procedures for protection of creditors were not taken. A judicial precedent ruled that even if the merger ratio is unjust or unfair, it will not constitute a ground for invalidation.[1279]

909. Invalidation of a merger may be asserted by the company's shareholders, directors, executive officers, company auditors, liquidators, bankruptcy trustees, creditors who did not approve the merger or the Fair Trade Commission within six months after the merger. If a judgment on invalidation of merger becomes final and binding, changes to the surviving company, dissolution of the newly incorporated company and the recovery of the dissolved company will be registered ex officio.[1280] The finalized judgment on invalidation of merger will be effective against third parties but does not have retroactive effect.[1281]

§2. ASSIGNMENT OF BUSINESS

910. 'Assignment of business' (*jigyou jouto*) is defined as an assignment of assets organized for certain business purpose that function as one organic unit. This is different from disposal of important assets.[1282] As assignment of business has a significant impact on the company as one of the measures of business combination, the Companies Act requires a special resolution at the transferor's shareholders meeting upon an assignment of all or significant part of the business of the transferor to protect the interests of the shareholders.[1283] In addition, a special resolution of the transferee's shareholders meeting will be required if the transferee acquires the entire business of another company.[1284] The same restrictions also apply to entering into, changing or termination of a contract for the lease of the entire business, a contract for the entrustment of the management of the entire business and a contract for sharing with others all profits and losses of business and other equivalent contracts.[1285] As with mergers, shareholders who dissent from the assignment of business may demand that the company purchase their shares at fair price.[1286]

911. In cases where the company acquiring the business is a special controlling company of the transferor (see paragraph 892), the resolution at the transferor's shareholders meeting will not be required.[1287] In addition, upon the acquisition of another company's entire business, the resolution at the transferee's shareholders meeting will not be required if the total value of consideration does not exceed 20% of the net assets of the transferee.[1288] Unlike mergers, an assignment of business

1279. Judicial precedent of the Tokyo High Court, 31 Jan. 1990, *Shojihomu Documents* 77–193.
1280. Article 937, Companies Act.
1281. Article 838, Companies Act; Art. 839, Companies Act.
1282. Article 362, para. 4, item 1, Companies Act.
1283. Article 467, para. 1, items 1 and 2; Art. 309, para. 2, item 11, Companies Act.
1284. Article 467, para. 1, item 3; Art. 309, para. 2, item 11, Companies Act.
1285. Article 467, para. 1, item 4, Companies Act.
1286. Article 469, Companies Act.
1287. Article 468, para. 1, Companies Act.
1288. Article 468, para. 2, Companies Act.

will not result in the transfer of rights and obligations by operation of law and requires the consent of each creditor for any assumption of liabilities. As a result, no statutory creditor protection procedures are provided for assignment of business.

912. As is the case with mergers, the Anti-Monopoly Act prohibits assignment of business where the assignment of business may substantially restrain competition in a particular field of trade or where unfair trade practices have been employed in the course of an assignment of business.[1289] In this regard, the assignment of business of more than a certain size must be notified to the Fair Trade Commission in advance of the closing.[1290]

§3. Tender Offer

I. Overview

A. *Tender Offer Regulations*

913. Tender offer or TOB is an attempt to acquire the control of a target company through an offer to the shareholders to purchase shares, etc., outside of the stock exchange market upon certain disclosures, including the tender offer period, number of shares to be purchased and tender offer price.

914. Tender offer regulations were introduced in Japan by the amendment to the Securities Exchange Act (the current Financial Instruments and Exchange Act) in 1971. It was intended to enhance the disclosure requirements in the secondary market to protect the shareholders and other investors and achieve the overall purpose of the Securities Exchange Act. Although tender offers are frequently used in Europe and the United States as a means of corporate takeover, tender offers were rarely used in Japan until recent years because a corporate takeover was not widely accepted in the society at large or by the employees of target companies. However, in recent years, the number of tender offers have increased dramatically as corporate takeovers, including management buyout (MBO) transactions, have gradually gained recognition in Japan as a means of corporate strategy.

915. In tender offers, a public notice will be made to provide all shareholders an equal opportunity to sell their shares. In this regard, tender offers may be used by the issuing company as a means to purchase its own shares equally from the shareholders, subject to the financial restrictions under the Companies Act (see paragraph 389). Under the Financial Instruments and Exchange Act, tender offers by the issuing company and tender offers by parties other than the issuing company are distinguished as 'tender offer of listed share certificates by the issuing company' (Chapter II-2, section 2) and 'tender offer of shares, etc., by a person other than the issuing company' (Chapter II-2, section 1).

1289. Article 16, para. 1, item 1, Anti-Monopoly Act.
1290. Article 16, para. 2, Anti-Monopoly Act.

B. Tender Offer Requirements

916. Tender offer is defined as the purchase of share certificates or other securities (shares, etc.) of the target company implemented outside of the stock exchange market through an offer of purchase or a solicitation for offer of sale of shares, etc., by a public notice.[1291]

917. A tender offer will be required upon certain purchase of shares, etc., issued by a reporting company (*yuka shouken houkokusho teishutsu kaisha*).[1292] For example, a tender offer will be required if, as a result of the purchase, the shares, etc., to be owned by the purchaser amount to more than 5% of the voting rights of the company.[1293] However, the purchases from ten persons or fewer within sixty-one days are excluded from the tender offer requirements; provided, however, that the shareholding ratio of shares, etc., of the purchaser after the purchase is not in excess of one-third (see paragraph 918).[1294] The reporting companies under the Financial Instruments and Exchange Act are (i) companies which have submitted a securities registration statement, (ii) companies issuing securities listed on a stock exchange, (iii) companies issuing securities registered as OTC with the Association of Financial Instrument Business Operators and (iv) companies where the number of owners of securities issued by the company is 1000 or more.[1295]

918. The Tokyo Stock Exchange provides certain off-floor sales transaction services called Tokyo Stock Exchange Trading NeTwork System (ToSTNeT) to allow implementation of large transactions smoothly. In March 2005, Livedoor, a Japanese corporation, acquired more than one-third of the voting rights of Nippon Broadcasting System using ToSTNeT-1 without implementing a tender offer. There, an issue arose as to whether or not such purchase by Livedoor outside of the trading floor was a transaction within the securities market where the tender offer regulations would not apply. The Tokyo High Court ruled that Livedoor's purchase would not trigger the tender offer requirement because ToSTNeT-1 was considered as a securities exchange market (23 March 2005, *Shojihomu* 1728-41). However, even though ToSTNeT-1 was considered as a securities exchange market, it was argued that the tender offer regulations should apply to such purchase by Livedoor causing a change of control in the target company, taking into account the nature of ToSTNeT-1 as a negotiated transaction. Given the above, the Securities Exchange Act was amended in 2005 to require tender offers in such transactions to the extent that the percentage of ownership by the purchaser after the purchase exceeds one-third.[1296]

1291. Article 27-2, para. 6, Financial Instruments and Exchange Act.
1292. Article 27-2, para. 1, Financial Instruments and Exchange Act.
1293. Article 27-2, para. 1, item 1, Financial Instruments and Exchange Act.
1294. Article 7, para. 4, Order for Enforcement of the Financial Instruments and Exchange Act.
1295. Article 3-6, para. 4, Order for Enforcement of the Financial Instruments and Exchange Act; Art. 24, para. 1, Financial Instruments and Exchange Act.
1296. Article 27-2, para. 1, item 3, Financial Instruments and Exchange Act.

919. There was another issue relating to the tender offer requirements when an investment fund initially purchased shares not exceeding one-third of the voting rights of the target company from a small number of persons (ten or less) outside of the market and subsequently followed by a purchase on the market which would not trigger the tender offer requirements (see paragraph 917), resulting in the collective purchase of over 40% of the voting rights of the target company (acquisition of the shares of Hanshin Electric Railway Co., Ltd. by Murakami Fund). Under the tender offer regulations at the time, the tender offer requirements would be triggered only upon a purchase outside the market resulting in the shareholding ratio in excess of one-third (e.g., if a purchase is made outside of the market up to 32% of the voting rights and then 2% was to be purchased on the market, it was technically possible to acquire more than one-third of the voting tights without triggering the tender offer requirement). Given the above, the Securities Exchange Act was amended in 2006 to require tender offers in such combination of transactions on and outside of the market if the shareholding ratio after the purchase results in excess of one-third.[1297]

II. Disclosure Requirements in Tender Offers

920. In a tender offer, first, a public notice must be made in a daily newspaper which publishes news on current affairs, setting forth, among others, the purpose of tender offer, purchase price, 'number of shares, etc., to be purchased' (*kaitsuke yotei su*) and purchase period.[1298] On the date of the public notice, the tender offeror must submit a tender offer statement (*koukai kaitsuke todokedesho*) which provides the details of the tender offer, including the terms and conditions of purchase and purpose of the purchase, as well as certain attachments prescribed in the applicable cabinet office ordinance, to the local finance bureau.[1299] After the tender offer registration statement has been submitted, the tender offeror must immediately send a copy of the tender offer registration statement to the target company and the financial instruments exchange or the Association of Financial Instrument Business Operators, as may be applicable.[1300]

921. Before the amendment to the Securities and Exchange Act in 1990, the filing of a tender offer would in principle become effective after the elapse of a ten-day review period (waiting period) by the finance minister (prior filing requirement). A public notice would be made after the filing had become effective upon which solicitation of purchases would permitted. Under such prior filing requirement, however, there was a possibility of insider trading during the waiting period. As it was a unique requirement not customary outside Japan, the prior filing requirement was abolished by the amendment in 1990.

1297. Article 27-2, para. 1, item 4, Financial Instruments and Exchange Act.
1298. Article 27-3, para. 1, Financial Instruments and Exchange Act.
1299. Article 27-3, para. 2, Financial Instruments and Exchange Act.
1300. Article 27-3, para. 4, Financial Instruments and Exchange Act.

III. Tender Offer Regulations

922. Except for certain limited situations, the statutory tender offer period is twenty to sixty business days.[1301] In purchasing the shares from shareholders, a tender offer explanation statement (*koukai kaitsuke setsumeisho*), which provides information identical to the tender offer registration statement, must be delivered to the shareholders so that sufficient information will be provided to the shareholders directly for their decision on whether to accept the tender offer.[1302]

923. Tender offers are subject to the following requirements to ensure the equal treatment of the shareholders of the target company:

(i) The terms and conditions of the tender offer must be equal to all shareholders.[1303]
(ii) In cases where the shares tendered by the shareholders exceed the number of shares planned to be purchased in the tender offer, the tender offeror must purchase from each tendering shareholder on a pro-rata basis.[1304]
(iii) During the tender offer period, the tender offeror is prohibited from purchasing the securities subject to the tender offer by means other than the tender offer (prohibition of purchases outside the tender offer, Article 27-5, Financial Instruments and Exchange Act).

924. Prior to the amendment to the Securities and Exchange Act in 1990, certain administrative matters relating to tender offers were required to be performed by a securities firm acting as tender offer agent (*koukaikaitsuke dairinin*). It was explained at the time the tender offer rules were introduced in Japan that this requirement would further ensure the investor protections. However, the requirement of tender offer agent was abolished in the 1990 amendment because Japanese companies had gradually gained experience in using tender offers outside of Japan, and moreover, it was criticized that such requirement could effectively prevent hostile tender offers. However, the administrative matters relating to storage, return and payment of purchase price for the shares, etc., will need to be handled by a credible third-party institution such as securities firms (financial instruments business operator) or banks.[1305]

925. After the completion of the tender offer period, the tender offeror must send without delay a written notification of purchase (*kaitsuke tsuchi sho*) in the tender offer, setting forth the results of the tender offer to the tendering shareholders.[1306]

1301. Article 27-2, para. 2, Financial Instruments and Exchange Act; Art. 8, Order for Enforcement of the Financial Instruments and Exchange Act.
1302. Article 27-9, Financial Instruments and Exchange Act.
1303. Article 27-2, para. 3, Financial Instruments and Exchange Act.
1304. Article 27-13, para. 5, Financial Instruments and Exchange Act.
1305. Article 27-2, para. 4, Financial Instruments and Exchange Act.
1306. Article 8, para. 5, Order for Enforcement of the Financial Instruments and Exchange Act.

926. While the tender offerors are prohibited from purchasing the shares, etc., outside the tender offer (see paragraph 923 (iii)), those persons (other than the tender offeror) who already hold more than one-third of the voting rights of the target company used to be permitted to freely purchase more shares of the company (i.e., tender offer would be required if the shareholding was one-third or less). This discrepancy was pointed out to be unfair particularly in situations where the tender offeror was fighting to obtain control of the target company. In the amendment to the Securities and Exchange Act in 2006, a shareholder holding more than one-third of the voting rights of the target company would also be required to implement a tender offer during the tender offer period of another tender offeror if such shareholder purchases more than 5% of additional shares.[1307]

927. In addition, the tender offeror will be required to purchase proportionately if the shares tendered by the shareholders exceed the number of shares planned to be purchased in the tender offer (see paragraph 923 (ii)). In such case, the tendering shareholders may not be able to sell all of their shares (leftover shares). In cases where the shareholding ratio of the tender offeror after the completion of the tender offer is quite large, the remaining shareholders could be subject to the risk that the shares may be delisted. Taking into account such risk, the amendment to the Securities and Exchange Act in 2006 required the tender offerors to purchase all of the tendered shares in cases where the shareholding ratio after the completion of the tender offer is two-thirds or more (i.e., introduction of obligation to purchase all tendered shares).[1308] The amendment also included a mandatory requirement of the target company to provide a position statement (*iken hyoumei houkoku*) relating to the tender offer (and the right of the target company to inquire questions to the tender offeror) and certain deregulation with regard to the withdrawal or changes to the terms and conditions of the tender offer.

IV. Tender Offers by the Issuing Company

928. Companies may carry out a tender offer to purchase its own shares (see paragraph 391). In such case, tender offer regulations applicable to tender offerors other than the issuing company will in general apply *mutatis mutandis*; provided, however, that the filing of position statement by the target company will not be required because the issuing company itself is the tender offeror and the consideration will be limited to cash only (Article 27-4 of the Financial Instruments and Exchange Act will not apply *mutatis mutandis)*.[1309] However, in order to

1307. Article 27-2, para. 1, item 5, Financial Instruments and Exchange Act.
1308. Article 27-13, para. 4, Financial Instruments and Exchange Act; Art. 14-2-2, Order for Enforcement of the Financial Instruments and Exchange Act.
1309. Article 27-10, Financial Instruments and Exchange Act.

prevent insider tradings, if undisclosed material facts exist with regard to the issuing company, which intends to acquire its own shares through the tender offer, the issuing company must make a public announcement of such facts before submitting the tender offer statement.[1310]

1310. Article 27-22-3, Financial Instruments and Exchange Act.

Chapter 7. Regulations on Shareholding

929. In general, the purpose of equity investment will be either net investment using surplus funds or acquisition to enhance its influential power against, or to gain control of, another company. In a capitalist society, investors should be allowed to invest in shares freely at their own discretion as part of their private economic activities. It should be noted, however, that if the equity investment exceeds certain level, there is a possibility that other economic activities may be affected in various ways.

930. First, substantial adverse effects may be caused by a business combination resulting in monopolization of economic activities. In Japan, the adverse effects of monopolization of economic activities are mainly regulated by the Anti-Monopoly Act. Under the Anti-Monopoly Act, holding companies were previously prohibited to prevent the control of corporate groups by a small amount of capital but such prohibition was lifted by the amendment in 1997.

931. The cross-shareholding among companies is regulated in the Companies Act. Although cross-shareholding is not directly prohibited, certain rules have been established to regulate company controls by eliminating voting rights. Meanwhile, since large shareholding in a specific listed company will have significant influence on the investment decisions of other investors in the stock market, certain disclosure obligations are provided in the Financial Instruments and Exchange Act with regard to large shareholdings.

§1. Holding Companies (*Mochikabu Kaisha*)

I. Prior Prohibition on Holding Companies

932. In Japan, holding companies were previously prohibited, whether newly incorporated or converting into a holding company.[1311] Holding companies may be in the form of 'pure holding company', whose business purpose is solely to control other companies, or 'business holding company', which will operate its own business activities while controlling other companies. Article 9 of the former Anti-Monopoly Act was difficult to apply as such business holding companies could not be easily distinguished with other general business companies.

933. Holding company controls a company by holding the shares of such company and, by the same token, such controlled company would hold the shares of another company. A pyramid control relationship will be created through such share ownership mechanism. This will potentially allow enormous capital and manufacturing capability to be controlled exclusively by a relatively small capital in the holding company.

1311. Article 9, paras 1 and 2, former Anti-Monopoly Act.

934. Before the Second World War, the economic and political power possessed by the conglomerate organizations *(zaibatsu)* was enormous. After the war, the Allied Forces dismantled the conglomerates as they were deemed to be the economic pillars of the Japanese Imperial Army. One of the primary tools to dismantle conglomerates was to prohibit holding companies. In addition to the purpose of destroying the economic power of the conglomerates, it was also intended to democratize the economy by establishing market competition. The prohibition on holding companies was provided as a rule to protect the democratization of economy from private monopoly.

II. Deregulation of Holding Companies

935. The Anti-Monopoly Act banned holding companies whose principal business was to control the business activities of domestic companies through ownership of shares.[1312] However, as a result of the structural reforms of economy to ensure the international competitiveness of companies in Japan, such ban on holding companies was deregulated, to the extent not contravening the purpose of the Anti-Monopoly Act. Specifically, by the amendment in 1997, the ban on holding companies was lifted except for those that could cause excessive concentration of economic power.[1313]

936. 'Holding companies' are defined as companies whose ratio of the total acquisition value of the shares of subsidiaries to the total assets of the company exceeds 50%. Here, subsidiaries are those companies whose shareholding ratio held by the holding company directly or indirectly exceeds 50%.[1314]

937. 'Excessive concentration of economic power' means any of the following:

(i) where the scale of the holding company group's overall business is extremely large in a considerable number of fields of business (i.e., according to the relevant guideline, companies where the total assets of the holding company group is over JPY 15 trillion and where the holding company has companies having total assets of more than JPY 300 billion in approximately five or more key business fields);
(ii) where there is substantial influential power against other business operators arising from transactions pertaining to funds (i.e., according to the relevant guideline, in cases where the company holds a financial institution (*kinyu kaisha*) which has a total amount of assets of more than JPY 15 trillion and a company whose total amount of assets in a business field other than finance or business closely related to finance (debt guarantees, venture capital, leases, etc.) is more than JPY 300 billion); or

1312. Article 9, para. 3, Anti-Monopoly Act prior to amendment.
1313. Article 9, paras 1 and 2, Anti-Monopoly Act.
1314. Article 9, para. 4, Anti-Monopoly Act.

(iii) where the national economy is substantially affected and promotion of fair and free competition is hindered by the company holding a powerful position in a significant number of business fields which are closely connected to one another (i.e., according to the relevant guideline, cases where the holding company has a separate powerful company (a company whose market share is at least 10% or is in the top three ranking companies) in approximately five or more key business fields which are closely connected to one another (where the scale of the industry is particularly large, three or more companies depending on the degree of the company's power)).[1315]

938. To monitor whether or not there is excessive concentration of economic power, if the sum of the assets of the holding company and its subsidiaries is over JPY 300 billion, an annual report will be required on the business of the company after the end of each business year. Separately, a filing must be submitted upon establishment of a new holding company.[1316]

III. Lifting the Ban on Financial Holding Companies (*Kinyu Mochikabu Kaisha*)

939. As the ban on holding companies was lifted by the amendment to the Anti-Monopoly Act, holding companies were permitted to have subsidiaries engaged in financial services (financial holding companies). First, bank holding companies were permitted in the Banking Act.[1317] An authorization (*ninka*) to be granted by the FSA will be required to establish a bank holding company. Other than banks, bank holding companies may own a financial instruments business operator or insurance company as its subsidiary, subject to approval of the FSA. In addition, insurance holding companies were permitted in the Insurance Business Act.[1318] Insurance holding companies also require a license by the FSA. An insurance holding company may, upon obtaining a separate license by the FSA, own life insurance companies, non-life insurance companies, banks and financial instruments business operators as its subsidiaries.

IV. Share Exchange (*Kabushiki Koukan*) and Share Transfer (*Kabushiki Iten*)

940. Holding companies may be useful to operate a corporate group, not only in financial services but also in other businesses, efficiently. For this purpose, convenient tool to create a holding company was necessary to facilitate organizational changes. It was also important to allow companies other than holding companies to acquire other companies as wholly-owned subsidiaries. On such basis, share

1315. Article 9, para. 3, Anti-Monopoly Act.
1316. Article 9, para. 5, Anti-Monopoly Act.
1317. Article 52-17, Banking Act.
1318. Articles 271-8 et seq., Insurance Business Act.

exchange and share transfer were established in 1999 with certain measures to protect the interests of the shareholders of the parent company.

941. Share exchange is a method of business combination where a stock company will have all of its issued shares acquired by another stock company or LLC.[1319] A share transfer is also a method of business combination where one or more stock companies will have all of its issued shares acquired by a newly incorporated stock company.[1320]

942. In a share exchange, all shares held by the shareholders of company *a* will be transferred to company *b*, typically in exchange for the shares of company *b*. As a result, the shareholders of company *a* become the shareholders of company *b* and company *a* becomes a wholly-owned subsidiary of company *b*. Share exchange may be used in cases where company *b* already exists. In cases where company *b* is to be newly incorporated, a share transfer will be used. In a share transfer, the shares held by the shareholders of company *a* will be transferred to the newly incorporated company *b*, typically in exchange for the shares issued upon incorporation of company *b*. As a result, company *a* becomes a wholly-owned subsidiary of company *b*, and shareholders of company *a* will become the shareholders of company *b*.

943. Share exchange will have significant influence on the status of both the shareholders of the acquired company and the shareholders of the acquiring company. In this regard, a share exchange agreement must be executed by the parties setting forth certain statutory required items relating to the new shares to be issued by company *b* upon the share exchange.[1321] The share exchange agreement will be kept at the head office for disclosure prior to its completion.[1322] Shareholder approval must be obtained by each of company *a* and company *b* by a special resolution at the shareholders meeting.[1323] Shareholders who dissent from the share exchange, as well as holders of certain share options, may exercise the appraisal right to demand the company to purchase their shares or share options.[1324] In a share transfer, there will be significant impact on the status of the shareholders of the company which is to become the wholly owned subsidiary. Therefore, the same procedures as share exchange will be required to protect the rights of such shareholders.

944. In cases where the company which is to become a wholly-owned subsidiary in share exchange or share transfer has issued share options (see paragraph 461), the company to become the parent company may succeed to the obligations related to such share options.[1325] If after the share exchange the share options were to be exercised against the acquired company as originally contemplated, it would prevent the 100% ownership intended to be created by the parties. Therefore, the

1319. Article 2, item 31, Companies Act.
1320. Article 2, item 32, Companies Act.
1321. Article 768, Companies Act; Art. 767, Companies Act.
1322. Article 782; Art. 794, Companies Act.
1323. Article 783; Art. 795; Art. 308, para. 2, item 12, Companies Act.
1324. Article 785, para. 1, item 3; Art. 797, Companies Act.
1325. Article 769, para. 4, Companies Act.

parties may provide certain statutory required items in the share exchange agreement to cause the parent company to succeed to the obligations relating to the share options.

945. In cases where company *b* is significantly larger than company *a*, the impact of share exchange on the shareholders of company *b* may be minimal. In this regard, if the amount obtained by multiplying the shares to be delivered upon the share exchange by company *b* by the net asset value per share is not in excess of 20% of the net asset value of company *b*, company *b* may implement a simplified share exchange without obtaining the special resolution at its shareholders meeting.[1326]

946. After the completion of share exchange or share transfer, the shareholders who had owned the shares of company *a* may only be involved in the management of company *a* through the election of directors of company *b*. Therefore, the Companies Act allows the shareholders of the parent company to oversee the directors of the subsidiaries by certain disclosure available to the shareholders of the parent company. In other words, with the permission of the court, the shareholders of the parent company may request to inspect the minutes of the shareholders meetings, the minutes of the board meetings, the articles of incorporation, the shareholder registry, accounting books and other documents of the subsidiary, where it is necessary for the purpose of exercising their rights; provided, however, that the right to inspect the accounting books will be limited to shareholders who hold at least 3% of the total number of issued shares of the parent company.[1327]

947. In share exchange or share transfer, unlike merger, liabilities of company *a* will not be transferred to company *b*. In addition, no assets will flow out of the parent company to the extent that the consideration to be delivered to the shareholders of the acquired company will be the shares of the parent company. Therefore, in principle, there is no need to protect the creditors. However, the bonds with share options issued by company *a* may be succeeded by company *b*, in which case, the liabilities associated with the bonds will be transferred from company *a* to company *b*. In addition, in a share exchange, the consideration to be delivered to the shareholders of company *a* may be properties other than the shares of company *b*. In these cases, there is a need for creditor protection procedures.[1328]

V. Company Split (*Kaisha Bunkatsu*)

948. By the amendment to the Commercial Code in 2000, company split was introduced to facilitate reorganizations. Company splits consist of an incorporation-type split (*shinsetsu bunkatsu*), where certain business of the splitting company will

1326. Article 796, para. 3, Companies Act.
1327. Article 318, para. 5; Art. 371, para. 5; Art. 31, para. 3; Art. 125, para. 4; Art. 433, para. 3, Companies Act.
1328. Article 789, para. 1, item 3; Art. 799, para. 1, item 3, Companies Act.

be split to a newly incorporated company, and an absorption-type split (*kyushu bunkatsu*), where certain business will be succeeded by an existing company.[1329]

949. In a company split, there is spin-off (*butteki bunkatsu*), where the shares to be issued by the succeeding company as consideration in the company split will be allocated to the splitting company, and split-off (*jinteki bunkatsu*), where such shares will be allocated to the shareholders of the splitting company. In cases where company *a* which has division *c* and division *d* is to split division *c* to company *b* by company split, in a spin-off, the shares to be issued by company *b* will be allocated to company *a*. As such, a parent and subsidiary relationship between company *a* and company *b* will be established by the company split. In a split-off, the shares of company *b* will be allocated to the shareholders of company *a*. Therefore, for example, if company *a* is owned by a holding company (company *e*), a sister company relationship will be created between company *a* and company *b*, with company *e* as the parent company. In the Companies Act, if there is a split-off, the consideration will be initially delivered to company *a*, and then distributed to the shareholders of company *a* as dividends of surplus (dividends in kind, in cases of dividends other than cash payments). Therefore, a company split under the Companies Act means the abovementioned spin-off.

950. In a company split, certain rights and obligations in connection with the company's business will be transferred to the succeeding company or newly incorporated company. In exchange, the splitting company will receive shares or other consideration from the succeeding company or newly incorporated company. Therefore, there will be significant impact on the shareholders of the companies involved.

951. A company split plan (in cases of incorporation-type company split) or company split agreement (in cases of absorption-type split) must be prepared or executed.[1330] Such plan or agreement must be approved by a special resolution at the shareholders meeting.[1331] As in the case of a merger, simplified procedures and summary procedures are permitted.[1332] The dissenting shareholders may exercise the appraisal right to demand the company to purchase their shares.[1333] In addition, the creditors will be given an opportunity to state their objections after the company provides certain disclosures, including public notice. If a creditor stated objection, the company must take certain measures, such as to pay off its debts or provide reasonable security.[1334]

952. In an incorporation-type split, part of the rights and obligations related to the business of the splitting company may be transferred to the company established through the incorporation-type company split (the newly incorporated company). However, there were cases where splitting companies that had fallen into

1329. Article 2, item 30; Art. 2, item 29, Companies Act.
1330. Article 757; Art. 762, Companies Act.
1331. Article 783; Art. 795; Art. 309, para. 2, item 12, Companies Act.
1332. Article 784; Art. 796; Art. 805, Companies Act.
1333. Article 785; Art. 797; Art. 806, Companies Act.
1334. Article 789; Art. 799; Art. 810, Companies Act.

financial distress would leave the unprofitable business divisions or liabilities in the splitting company and transfer only the assets and liabilities of the profitable business divisions to the newly established company. The 2014 amendment aimed to protect creditors involved in such fraudulent company splits. Specifically, if a splitting company implements an absorption-type company split while knowing that it will harm the creditors who will not be transferred to the succeeding company (i.e., the remaining creditors), unless the succeeding company at the time that the absorption-type company split took effect did not know that the remaining creditors would be harmed, the remaining creditors may request performance on their claims from the succeeding company up to the amount equivalent to the succeeded property.[1335] If remaining creditors do not either demand performance or give notice of their intent to do so within two years from finding that the splitting company conducted an absorption-type company split with the knowledge that it would harm the remaining creditors, the succeeding company's liability to those creditors will extinguish.[1336] The succeeding company's liability will also extinguish when twenty years have passed from the effective date of the company split.

§2. Restrictions on Shareholding

I. Restrictions on Shareholding by Business Companies

A. *Excessive Concentration of Economic Power*

953. A company may not be established if it will cause an excessive concentration of economic power by ownership of shares of other companies.[1337]

954. In addition, an existing company may not have excessive concentration of economic power in Japan by acquiring or owning the shares of other domestic companies.[1338] Whether or not a company falls under such category will be determined on the basis of the corporate group (i.e., the company, its subsidiaries and other domestic companies) (a company and its subsidiaries and other companies in Japan whose business activities are controlled by the said company).[1339]

955. It is necessary to prevent not only holding companies but also business companies from gaining excessive concentration of economic power ('Opinions on companies with excessive concentration of economic power', Guidelines on the Interpretation and Operation of Article 9 of the Anti-Monopoly Act published by the Fair Trade Commission).

1335. Article 759, para. 4, Companies Act.
1336. Article 759, para. 6, Companies Act.
1337. Article 9, para. 1, Anti-Monopoly Act.
1338. Article 9, para. 2, Anti-Monopoly Act.
1339. Article 9, para. 3, Anti-Monopoly Act.

B. Lessening of Competition and Unfair Trade Practices

956. In cases where a company would substantially lessen competition in certain field of trade by acquiring or owning shares in another company, such acquisition or holding of shares will be prohibited. Acquisition or holding of shares through unfair trade practices will also be prohibited.[1340]

957. In addition, companies of a certain size will be required to submit periodic reports relating to its shareholding to the Fair Trade Commission to ensure the effectiveness of the regulations on corporate shareholding.[1341]

958. Any person or entity other than a company is also prohibited from acquiring or holding shares where there will be substantial lessening of competition in certain field of trade and where such acquisition or holding of shares will be implemented through unfair trade practices.[1342]

II. Restrictions on Shareholding by Banks and Insurance Companies

959. Banks and insurance companies may not acquire or own more than 5% of the voting rights of other companies (10% in the case of companies engaging in the insurance business).[1343] Such restrictions were especially needed to prevent excessive control by these financial institutions, taking into account the historical background in Japan of financial institutions controlling business companies through their financing capabilities.

960. Prior to the amendment in 1977, limitation on the percentage of shareholding was 10%. However, due to the increase in share ownership by financial institutions, there was an increased risk of control. Therefore, the percentage was reduced to 5%, except for insurance companies. With regard to insurance companies, the restrictions on shareholding were eased as there was less risk of controlling other companies due to their different role from banks in terms of loans and taking into account the importance of their asset management as institutional investors.

961. The separation policies relating to the business of financial institutions (see paragraph 532) have been eased. Namely, banks may acquire a majority of the issued shares of securities companies (financial instruments business operators), insurance companies and other companies upon obtaining permission from the

1340. Article 10, para. 1, Anti-Monopoly Act.
1341. Article 10, para. 2, Anti-Monopoly Act.
1342. Article 14, Anti-Monopoly Act.
1343. Article 11, para. 1, Anti-Monopoly Act.

FSA.[1344] In addition, insurance companies may own life insurance companies, non-life insurance companies, banks and securities companies as their subsidiaries.[1345]

§3. Cross-Shareholding (*Kabushiki Sougohoyu*) and Voting Rights

I. Overview

962. Cross-shareholding means that companies hold shares in each other. It has been criticized that such cross-shareholding harms the capital of the company. In other words, if company *a* and company *b* simultaneously increase their capital by subscribing for each other's shares, although the stated capital technically increases, the money paid by each company will be set-off, resulting in no increase of capital in substance. Moreover, the voting rights of such shares may be exercised in a collusive manner at the shareholders meeting of each company to unfairly maintain the positions of current management members. In addition, as such shares are rarely sold, the increase of such shares may cause reduction of floating stocks in the market and adversely effect the fairness of share prices.

II. Regulations on Cross-Shareholding

A. *Relationship between Parent Company and Subsidiaries*

963. Under the Companies Act, subsidiaries are prohibited from acquiring the shares of its parent company.[1346] However, certain exceptions are permitted as follows:

(i) if the subsidiary accepts an assignment of entire business of another company which owns the parent company's shares;
(ii) if the subsidiary succeeds to the parent company's shares as a result of merger;
(iii) if the subsidiary succeeds to the parent company's shares as a result of absorption-type company split;
(iv) if the subsidiary succeeds to the parent company's shares from another company as a result of an incorporation-type company split; and
(v) in other cases prescribed in the applicable ordinance of the Ministry of Justice.[1347]

In these cases, the acquired shares must be disposed of at an appropriate time.[1348]

1344. Article 16-2, para. 4, Banking Act.
1345. Article 106, para. 1, Insurance Business Act.
1346. Article 135, para. 1, Companies Act.
1347. Article 135, para. 2, Companies Act; Art. 23, Ordinance for Enforcement of the Companies Act.
1348. Article 135, para. 3, Companies Act.

964. Under the Companies Act, a 'subsidiary' is defined as any entity which is prescribed by the applicable ordinance of the Ministry of Justice as the juridical person, the management of which is controlled by a company, including a stock company a majority of all votes in which are owned by the company.[1349] On the other hand, a 'parent company' is defined as any entity which is prescribed by the applicable ordinance of the Ministry of Justice as a juridical person which controls the management of a stock company, including but not limited to a company which has a stock company as its subsidiary.[1350] Here, in addition to the numerical criteria of owning the majority of all votes, there is a substantive criteria concerning the control of companies. In the ordinance of the Ministry of Justice, such control is described as 'cases of control over the decisions on financial and business policies'.[1351]

965. The 'cases of control over the decisions on financial and business policies' are provided as follows:[1352]

(i) Cases where the percentage of the voting rights held on its own account (including its subsidiary companies, subsidiary legal persons and others) vis-à-vis the total number of voting rights of the other company is more than 50%.
(ii) Cases where the percentage of the number of voting rights held on its own account vis-à-vis the total number of voting rights of the other company is 40% or more and comes under one of the following: (a) the percentage of the total number of voting rights held on its own account, by persons who will exercise their voting rights in the same manner as the company by virtue of the close relationship with the company in terms of contribution, personnel affairs, funds, technology, transactions or other matters, and by persons who agreed to exercise their voting rights in the same manner as the company, is more than 50%, (b) the percentage of the number of its own officers, employees or others vis-à-vis the total number of members of the board of directors or an equivalent organ of the other company is more than 50%, (c) there is a contract pursuant to which the company has control over the decisions on important financial and business policies, (d) the percentage of the amount of loan that the company has provided vis-à-vis the total amount of financing of the other company is more than 50% or (e) there are other facts which suggest that the company has control over the decisions on financial and business policies of the other company.
(iii) Cases where the percentage of voting rights owned (including cases where the company does not own voting rights on its own account) vis-à-vis the total amount of voting rights of the other company is more than 50% and comes under one of the matters given in (b) through (d) of item (ii) above.

1349. Article 2, item 3, Companies Act.
1350. Article 2, item 4, Companies Act.
1351. Article 3, paras 1 and 2, Ordinance for Enforcement of the Companies Act.
1352. Article 3, para. 3, Ordinance for Enforcement of the Companies Act.

B. Relationship of Cross-Shareholding

966. Exercise of voting rights will be restricted on cross-shareholding. In cases where company *a* owns over 25% of the voting rights of all shareholders of company *b*, company *b* may acquire the shares of company *a* as it is not a subsidiary of company *a*. However, no voting rights may be exercised by company *b* with respect to such shares of company *a*.[1353] In addition, even if company *a* only holds 8% of the shares of company *b*, if company *c*, which is a subsidiary of company *a*, owns 20% of the shares of company *b*, company *b* may not exercise the voting rights on the shares of company *a*.

967. Such restrictions on cross-shareholding do not prohibit the acquisition of shares per se but intend to prevent the creation of control indirectly by restricting the exercise of voting rights. However, it is customary in Japan that many companies hold a small number of the shares of each other within a certain corporate group. As such, the restrictions have not achieved successful results.

§4. Disclosure Relating to Large Shareholdings

I. Overview

968. Recently, there has been an increase in the number of cases where a large volume of shares of stock companies is bought up for the purpose of management participation or selling off at higher prices. Such buy up of shares may lead to wild fluctuation in share prices, potentially causing unforeseen damages to retail investors. Therefore, the Financial Instruments and Exchange Act requires certain disclosure on the acquisition, ownership and sale of shares and other securities to ensure the fairness and transparency of the market. The disclosure requirements relating to large shareholdings that are customary in Europe and the United States were introduced in 1990 to boost the development of Japanese market as an international market.

II. Disclosure Requirements (5% Rule)

969. A holder of share certificates, convertible bond certificates and other securities (hereinafter collectively referred to as 'share certificates') of listed companies or OTC companies whose ownership percentage of share certificates is over 5% (large volume holders) must submit a large shareholding report (*tairyouhoyu houkokusho*) to the local finance bureau within five business days of becoming a large volume holder.[1354]

1353. Article 308, para. 1, Companies Act.
1354. Article 14-4, para. 2; Art. 27-23, para. 1, Financial Instruments and Exchange Act.

970. The large shareholding report will be required to describe the following information, which may allow other investors to judge the nature of shareholding and potential future activities of the large volume holder:[1355]

(i) Name of issuing company, location of head office, classification of listed companies and OTC companies.
(ii) In cases where the large volume holder is an individual, the name, address, date of birth, place of work, and in cases of a juridical person, the name, location of head office, date of incorporation, name of representative and primary business.
(iii) Purpose of shareholding.
(iv) Total number of shares held, shareholding ratio and breakdown by classes of share certificates and subscription warrants (certificates).
(v) Status of acquisition and disposition, transaction date, classes of shares, quantity and price per share over the last sixty days relating to the shares issued by the issuing company.
(vi) Important agreements, such as security agreement, relating to the shares.
(vii) Acquisition funds for share certificates held.

971. If a holder is in agreement with other holders (joint holders) to the joint acquisition of share certificates, the shareholding ratio will be calculated by combining the share certificates of such joint holders.[1356] In addition, if the shareholding ratio of large volume holders increases or decreases by 1% or more after the report has been submitted, such holders must submit an amendment report on the changes within five business days from such change.[1357] For the convenience of investors, the amendment report must provide, in principle, not only the changes but also all other information to be provided in the large shareholding report at the time of such amendment report.[1358] When submitting the amendment report, in cases where more than a half of the holder's ownership percentage of shares is reduced within sixty days, as a result of which a decrease of more than 5% in ownership percentage occurs, the amendment report must also disclose counterparties to the transfer and the transfer price.[1359] Practically, this disclosure requirement should have a restraining effect on the so-called 'assumption at high prices' (*takane katagawari*).

972. Furthermore, when the large volume holder submits a large shareholding report or amendment report to the local finance bureau, a copy of such large shareholding report or amendment report must be delivered, without delay, to the issuing

1355. Article 2, Cabinet Office Ordinance on the Disclosure of the Status of Large Volume Shareholding.
1356. Article 27-23, paras 3 and 4, Financial Instruments and Exchange Act.
1357. Article 27-25, para. 1, Financial Instruments and Exchange Act.
1358. Article 8, same Cabinet Office Ordinance.
1359. Article 14-8, Ordinance on the Financial Instruments and Exchange Act.

company and listed financial instruments exchange or association of financial instruments business operators.[1360] These reports must be kept at the local finance bureau, and a copy must be kept at the listed financial instruments exchange or association of financial instruments exchange operators, available for public inspection for five years.[1361]

973. In cases where the large shareholding report or amendment report has not been submitted or a false entry has been made in such reports, up to five years of imprisonment with work or a fine of up to JPY 5 million may be imposed (in cases of a juridical person, a fine of up to JPY 500 million).[1362] In addition, in cases where a false report has been delivered, up to one year of imprisonment with work or a fine of up to JPY 1 million may be imposed.[1363]

§5. Demand for Shares, Etc., Cash-Out (*Kabushikitou Uriwatashi Seikyu*) by Special Controlling Shareholders

974. There are cases where an acquirer obtains, through a tender offer or other such means, a controlling interest in the target company and then squeezes out the remaining minority shareholders to make that target company a wholly-owned subsidiary.

975. One of the methods to squeeze out such minority shareholders is to use 'shares subject to wholly call' (see paragraph 353). The shares subject to wholly call was originally intended to enable corporate rehabilitation of distressed companies smoothly but the insolvency criteria was removed during the legislative process. It was then used in practice as a means of squeezing out remaining minority shareholders after a large-scale share acquisition. Specifically, the acquirer will squeeze out the remaining shareholders and make the target company a wholly-owned subsidiary as follows:

(i) the acquirer obtains a controlling interest that would be sufficient to pass special resolutions at the shareholders meeting through a tender offer;
(ii) the acquirer passes a special resolution at the shareholders meeting to make all shares issued by the target company subject to wholly call;
(iii) the target company acquires all shares subject to wholly call;
(iv) in exchange for the shares subject to wholly call, the target company allocates to the shareholders another class shares in a proportion such that all shareholders other than the acquirer (i.e., minority shareholders) will be allocated only with fractions of less than one full share; and
(v) (instead of delivering such fractions of shares) the minority shareholders will receive cash equivalent to the value of the fractions of such shares.

1360. Article 27-27, Financial Instruments and Exchange Act.
1361. Article 27-28, Financial Instruments Exchange Act.
1362. Article 197-2, item 6; Art. 207, para. 1, item 2, Financial Instruments Exchange Act.
1363. Article 200, item 11, Financial Instruments Exchange Act.

976. In the 2014 amendment, a new method to facilitate the squeeze out of minority shareholders was introduced. In this new method, special controlling shareholders (*tokubetsu shihai kabunushi*) can demand that the minority shareholders cash-out their shares without holding a shareholders meeting. A 'special controlling shareholder' means a person who directly or indirectly holds 90% or more of the voting rights of a company (a percentage greater than this can be prescribed in the articles of incorporation).[1364] Eliminating minority shareholders (making the target company a wholly-owned subsidiary) by payment of cash consideration for shares, including this demand for shares, etc., cash-out, is in general called a 'cash-out' transaction.

1364. Article 179, para. 1, Companies Act.

Chapter 8. Taxation on Stock Companies

§1. CORPORATION TAX (*HOUJIN ZEI*)

977. Corporation tax will be imposed on the income of stock companies.[1365] Taxable income is, first, the income for each business year. In other words, tax will be levied on the balance of gross revenue and deductible expenses of each business year.[1366] As the tax rate of corporation tax applies proportionately, the tax rate is 30% for all stock companies; provided, however, that from the perspective of protecting small and medium-sized businesses (i.e., enterprises with stated capital of JPY 100 million or less), a reduced tax rate of 22% is applicable to the part of annual income of such enterprises up to JPY 8 million.[1367]

978. The amendment in 2002 introduced consolidated taxation. In a consolidated taxation, the parent company will declare and pay corporation tax in one tax return form (consolidated tax return) by listing the total amount of income of the entire group (consolidated income) – the parent company and its subsidiaries fully controlled by the parent company.[1368] Here, 'fully controlled' means directly or indirectly holding all of the issued shares or equity interests (excluding treasury shares).[1369] In principle, each company will not need to make a separate tax return or payment.[1370] The corporation tax rate on the consolidated income is ordinarily 30%, if the amount of stated capital or contributions is in excess of JPY 100 million, and if the amount is JPY 100 million or less, it will be 22% with regard to the part of the consolidated income up to JPY 8 million and 30% for the part of the consolidated income in excess of JPY 8 million.[1371]

979. As a supplement to the tax on income of each business year, there is a tax to be imposed on liquidation income. In cases where a stock company is dissolved or enters into liquidation proceedings, tax will be levied on the balance of residual assets of the company and the aggregate of capital and accumulated profits (*rieki tsumitatekin*) at the time of dissolution.[1372] A tax rate of 27.1% applies to the liquidation income of stock companies.[1373]

980. The Corporation Tax Act also provides special treatment for family companies where the total number of shares held by one group of associated persons is at least 50% of the total number of issued shares of the company. In such family companies, profits are often not distributed to the shareholders or distributed only in a significantly small amount of dividend. Hence, if undistributed earnings

1365. Article 4, para. 1, Corporation Tax Act.
1366. Article 22, para. 1, Corporation Tax Act.
1367. Article 66, paras 1 and 2, Corporation Tax Act.
1368. See Art. 81-22, Corporation Tax Act.
1369. Article 4-2, Corporation Tax Act.
1370. Article 81-28, Corporation Tax Act.
1371. Article 81-12, Corporation Tax Act.
1372. Article 93, para. 1, Corporation Tax Act.
1373. Article 99, para. 1, Corporation Tax Act.

exceeds certain amount, a special tax rate will be added to the ordinary tax rate on certain undistributed taxable earnings (*kazei ryuho kingaku*) (i.e., undistributed amount for current term minus certain deductions).[1374]

981. Stock companies must pay corporate enterprise tax (*houjin jigyou zei*) for the income of each business year, as well as the liquidation income, to the relevant prefectural government. The standard rate of corporate enterprise tax for other ordinary corporations is 9.6% (provided, however, that a tax rate of 5% will apply to the part of income up to JPY 4 million and a rate of 7.3% will apply to the amount in excess of JPY 4 million and up to JPY 8 million).[1375] The tax reform of 2003 introduced a business tax (*jigyou zei*), which combines income taxation and pro forma standard taxation (*gaikei hyoujun kazei*), the application of which is limited to corporations where the stated capital, etc., is over JPY 100 million. In such corporations, tax will be levied on the aggregate of the amount of prorated added value, prorated stated capital and prorated income.[1376] In addition, corporations must pay municipal tax.[1377]

982. In Japan, there has been a trend of so-called 'incorporation movement' (*houjin nari*), where sole proprietorships convert into a corporate enterprise. In such cases, the salaries of president (business owner) and family employees may be deductible expenses for the purpose of calculating corporate income tax and corporate enterprise tax. In addition, employment income exemptions (*kyuyo shotoku koujo*) are permitted in the calculation of income tax of such individuals. The conversion will be implemented typically if the tax burden will be lowered by operating the business as a corporate enterprise rather than sole proprietorship.

§2. Double Taxation Issue on Corporation Tax and Income Tax

983. Dividends distributed by a stock company to individual shareholders are subject to income tax. However, corporation tax has already been levied on the income of the company. This gives rise to the issue of double taxation.

984. While interest payments will also cause company funds to flow out, the amount of interest payments are deductible expenses which will not be subject to corporation tax. On the other hand, distribution of profits are not deductible expenses and will be taxed at both the company level and shareholder level. To handle this double taxation issue, first, dividend tax deductions on the dividends received by individual shareholders were introduced. In the tax reform of 1950 based on the recommendations by the Shoup Mission, the 35% corporation tax at the time was considered as a prepayment of income tax by shareholders, and, at the

1374. Article 67, Corporation Tax Act.
1375. Article 72-22, para. 1, Local Tax Act.
1376. Article 72-2, para. 12, Local Tax Act.
1377. Articles 294 et seq., Local Tax Act.

shareholder level, the received dividends were added to the total income of the individual for purposes of calculating income tax but the amount equivalent to 25% of the received dividends were deducted from the income tax. Thereafter, such deductions were gradually lowered and, at present, it has been fixed at 10% of the amount of received dividends.[1378]

985. In the tax reform of 1961, further to the foregoing adjustment at the shareholder level, a new adjustment was also introduced by way of reduced tax rate on paid dividends at the company level. There, different tax rates would apply where the paid dividends will be subject to a tax rate 10% lower than that of the retained profits. This was also aimed to boost share issuance and enhance the companies' equity capital. However, the reduced tax rate on paid dividends were abolished in 1991 by the tax reform of 1988 as no improvement was found in the equity capital ratio in stock companies, and moreover there was a need to simplify the tax system. As such, the adjustment of double taxation was once again made by the adjustment at the shareholder level.

986. In cases where the shareholder is a juridical person, it would be necessary to avoid an overlap in the imposition of corporation taxes on its received dividends. In principle, an amount equivalent to 50% of the received dividends will be excluded from the gross revenue to calculate the shareholder's corporation tax.[1379]

§3. Taxation on Interest Income and Dividend Income

987. Under the Income Tax Act, companies must, in principle, withhold income tax upon the payment of interests and dividends, and pay such withheld amount to the tax authorities by the tenth day of the following month.[1380] Presupposing a consolidated income, interest payments will be withheld at a tax rate of 15%.[1381] Currently, a special measure of uniform separate withholding tax (*gensen bunri kazei*) applies, where the income tax on interest income is concluded by such withholding of 15% tax.[1382] However, there used to be a tax-free small-sum savings system (so-called tax-free small deposits system) to encourage national savings, where the interest income of bonds, etc., along with interests on savings and dividends of joint trusts, were not taxable up to a principal amount of JPY 3 million. However, by the amendment in 1987, it was reorganized into a limited tax exemption applicable only to persons at the age of at least 65 and disabled persons. Later, in 1996, such elderly persons also lost eligibility.[1383]

1378. Article 92, Income Tax Act; provided, that if the amount of the total taxable gross income is over JPY 10 million, the deduction will be 5% with regard to the excess part.
1379. Article 23, para. 1, Corporation Tax Act.
1380. Article 181, para. 1, Income Tax Act.
1381. Article 182, item 1, Income Tax Act; moreover, an additional residence tax of 5% will also be imposed.
1382. Article 3, Special Measures Act.
1383. Article 9-2, Income Tax Act; Art. 3-4, Special Measures Act.

988. With regard to dividend income, first, it will be withheld at a 20% tax rate.[1384] In the tax reform of 2003, a reduced tax rate of 10% (income tax of 7%, residence tax 3%) was applied to the dividends of listed shares for five years from April 2003 to the end of March 2008. This was a special measure to promote equity investment by individual investors. From April 2003, the consolidated taxation of dividends and other income was permanently replaced where no tax return will be required if the dividends were subject to the withholding.[1385]

989. If a listed company acquires its own shares as treasury shares through a tender offer, no deemed dividend tax will be imposed on the amount of money delivered to the shareholders who accepted the tender offer that are in excess of the amount of State capital, etc., of such listed company corresponding to the shares accepted in the tender offer.[1386]

§4. Taxation on Capital Gains

990. Since 1953, capital gains on sales of securities were, in principle, not taxable. This was aimed to encourage equity investment and transfer of shares and develop a healthy stock market. However, in 1987, the tax exemption on small-sum savings was revised to be taxable. In 1990, tax exemption on capital gains were also abolished, taking into account that the exemption mainly benefited only high-income earners.

991. Previously, upon transfer of listed shares through a securities company (financial instruments business operator), to the extent that separate withholding tax was selected, it was sufficient for the seller to simply make a tax payment of 1% of the transfer price (i.e., the income was deemed to be 5% of the transfer price – temporarily 5.25%– subject to a withholding tax rate of 20%). However, such separate withholding tax was abolished in 2002, and was unified with separate self-assessment taxation (*shinkoku bunri kazei*). In such case, individual investors must, in principle, pay taxes of 20% (15% income tax, 5% residence tax) for the capital gains on securities (i.e., income after deducting the brokerage commission, etc.) each year.[1387] In cases where listed shares are sold at loss, it may be offset with the capital gains in the following three years (i.e., deductible from the capital gains through the tax return).[1388] By the tax reform of 2003, a special measure was newly established, making the tax rate for capital gains 10% (7% income tax, 3% residence tax) in cases of selling listed shares over the five-year period from January 2003.[1389] This amendment was also intended to encourage individual investors to actively participate in the market.

1384. Article 182, item 2, Income Tax Act.
1385. Article 8-5, Special Measures Act.
1386. Article 9-6, Special Measures Act.
1387. Article 37-10, para. 1, Special Measures Act.
1388. Article 37-12-2, Special Measures Act.
1389. Article 37-11, para. 2, Special Measures Act.

992. A simplified tax payment method known as specified accounts (*tokutei kouza*), where securities companies stand in for part of the tax payment procedures, commenced in January 2003 accompanying the abolition of separate withholding tax on capital gains. Under this payment method, tax payment may be made either by securities companies withholding the income tax on capital gains or by the investors filing a tax return using the annual transaction report issued by the securities company.

993. In the tax reform of 1953, the securities transaction tax was introduced as an alternative to the tax exemption on capital gains. The securities transaction tax was imposed based on the sale and purchase price of securities regardless of gains or losses on the investment. However, it was abolished on 1 April 1999 to revitalize the long-term stagnation of the stock market.

994. In response to the introduction of share exchange (*kabushiki koukan*) and share transfer (*kabushiki iten*) in the amendment to the Commercial Code (see paragraph 940), a special measure of tax exemption was provided to individual shareholders of the specified subsidiary. Namely, if individual shareholders of specified subsidiaries (i.e., companies which will become the wholly-owned subsidiary as a result of the share exchange or share transfer) were allotted shares of the specified parent company in share exchange or share transfer, the shares of the specified subsidiary were deemed not to have been transferred at that point.[1390]

995. Separately, there was an issue as to whether the economic benefits obtained by the exercise of stock options by directors or employees should be categorized as employment income, miscellaneous income (consideration for services) or temporary income (consideration not for services). The National Tax Agency had viewed such economic benefits as employment income since 1998. On 25 January 2005, the Supreme Court ruled that such economic benefits are categorized as employment income.

1390. Article 37-14, Special Measures Act.

Part II. Other Forms of Joint Ventures

996. Sole proprietorship is the simplest form to run a business. However, despite its merit to take all profits generated from the business, the financial capacity and labour force will be limited. In addition, all losses will need to be borne individually. Therefore, a joint venture is often formed to cover these disadvantages.

997. In Japan, the Companies Act anticipates a typical form of joint venture in membership companies (*mochibun kaisha*), in addition to the stock companies discussed in Part I above. There are also silent partnerships (*tokumei kumiai*) under the Commercial Code and partnerships (*kumiai*) under the Civil Code as forms of joint ventures which are not corporate organizations. Mutual companies (*sougo kaisha*) and cooperatives (*kyoudo kumiai*) also exist for the purpose of mutual aid.

Chapter 1. Membership Companies (*Mochibun Kaisha*)

998. Under the Companies Act, 'companies' are defined to include stock companies, general partnership companies (*goumei kaisha*), limited partnership companies (*goushi kaisha*) and limited liability companies (*goudo kaisha*).[1391] General partnership companies, limited partnership companies and limited liability companies are collectively referred to as 'membership companies', the details which are provided in Part III of the Companies Act.

999. In membership companies, the rules governing the relationship among members, as well as the relationship between members and the company (i.e., internal relations), may, in principle, be determined flexibly by the articles of incorporation. In this regard, similar features are found in partnerships under the Civil Code. In addition, there are no rules on the establishment of corporate governance mechanism as required in stock companies.

1000. Membership companies focus on the individuality of members. Therefore, such companies are sometimes referred to as personal companies (*jinteki kaisha*). In a stock company, assets of the company are more important than the individuality of members. Therefore, stock companies are sometimes referred to as property companies (*butteki kaisha*).

1001. A general partnership company is a company where all members are subject to unlimited liability. It is a form of business which is best suited to very small businesses such as family-run business. A limited partnership company is a company with both unlimited liability members and limited liability members. The addition of limited liability members makes it possible to run businesses that are larger than a general partnership company. An LLC is a company where all members assume limited liability. LLC was newly established by the Companies Act. It is possible to give higher dividends – regardless of the percentage of contribution – to the members who possess exceptional skills, and is generally a form suited for venture companies. Since LLCs also take the form of enterprise having certain flexibility of a partnership pursuant to its articles of incorporation, they are categorized as one of the membership companies that are governed by the same rules as those of general partnership companies and LLCs.

1002. A membership company may become a different type of membership company by an amendment to the articles of incorporation. For example, a general partnership company may convert into a limited partnership company by adding limited liability members. If all unlimited liability members were to become limited liability members, it will convert into a LLC. A limited partnership company may also become a general partnership company or LLC by changing the scope of liability of its members. Withdrawal of unlimited liability members may cause the company to become a LLC (if the limited liability members withdraw, then it becomes

1391. Article 2, item 1, Companies Act.

a general partnership company). A LLC may also become a general partnership company or limited partnership company. In membership companies, the unanimous consent of all members will be required to change the articles of incorporation.[1392] Changing the type of company from one membership company to another is not legally characterized as an entity conversion.

1003. The Companies Act allows entity conversion between a membership company and a stock company (mergers, etc., are also allowed). In principle, such entity conversion requires the consent of all members or shareholders, as the case may be.[1393] Issuance of bonds by membership companies is also permitted. Therefore, the Companies Act is organized to provide Bonds (Part IV) and Entity Conversion, Mergers, Company Splits, Share Exchanges and Share Transfers (Part V) after Part II: Stock Companies and Part III: Membership Companies.

§1. General Partnership Companies (*Goumei Kaisha*)

1004. The name 'general partnership company' derives from the French *société en nom collectif* (i.e., a company where the names of all members will be listed in its trade name). However, unlike a French general partnership company, only the words 'general partnership company (*goumei kaisha*)'– and not the names of its members – will be required in the trade name of a general partnership company in Japan.[1394]

1005. Members (*shain*) of a general partnership company will be subject to unlimited liability for the liabilities of general partnership company.[1395] In other words, the members will be jointly and severally liable directly towards the company creditors without limitation. Therefore, in cases where the debts are not fully paid by the company assets, each member will be required to pay the company debts with their personal assets.

1006. To incorporate a general partnership company, those persons who intend to become members must prepare the articles of incorporation and register the incorporation in commercial registration.[1396] The matters required to be provided in the articles of incorporation are as follows:[1397]

(i) Purposes of the company.
(ii) Trade name.
(iii) Location of head office.
(iv) Names and addresses of members.

1392. Article 637, Companies Act.
1393. Article 781, para. 1; Art. 776, para. 1, Companies Act.
1394. Article 6, para. 2, Companies Act.
1395. Article 576, para. 2, Companies Act.
1396. Article 912, Companies Act.
1397. Article 576, para. 1, Companies Act.

(v) Classification as to whether the members are unlimited partners or limited partners (in a general partnership company, only unlimited liability partners are permitted).
(vi) Subject-matter of, and the value and standard of evaluation of, the member.

As the names and addresses of the members will be provided in the articles of incorporation, the members will be fixed upon the preparation of the articles of incorporation (see paragraphs 228 and 235, Stock companies). Juridical persons may also become members.

1007. Contributions of the members may be made by money or contribution in kind, as well as by providing credits or services.[1398]

1008. Incorporation of general partnership companies may be subject to an action seeking invalidation (*mukou*).[1399] It may also be subject to an action seeking rescission (*torikeshi*).[1400] One unique feature of general partnership company is that if incompetence (*ishi munouryoku*) or mistake (*sakugo*) of a member is found in the acts of incorporation, not only is the member not permitted to participate, but also the incorporation of the company itself may become invalid. This is because the individual characteristics of members are important in general partnership company. It is possible, however, to continue the company with remaining members after the withdrawal of such member.

1009. The membership of general partnership company takes the form of equity interest (*mochibun*). Unless otherwise provided in the articles of incorporation, transfer of equity interest requires approval of all members.[1401] Amendment to the articles to incorporation must be made to add members as such new members will need to be listed in the articles of incorporation. Such amendment will require consent of all members.[1402]

1010. Unless otherwise provided in the articles of incorporation, a member may withdraw from the company at the end of each business year by giving a notice six months in advance.[1403] In addition, a member will withdraw from the company upon the following grounds: (i) the occurrence of an event provided in the articles of incorporation, (ii) the consent of all members, (iii) death, (iv) merger (limited to cases where the member which is a juridical person is liquidated as a result of the merger), (v) a ruling to commence bankruptcy procedures, (vi) dissolution, (vii) being subject to a decision on the commencement of guardianship and (viii) removal.[1404] Death is one of the grounds for withdrawal (item (iii) above) in which case the equity interest is not passed on but the heir will receive a refund of

1398. See Art. 576, para. 1, item 6, Companies Act.
1399. Article 828, para. 1, item 1, Companies Act.
1400. Article 832, Companies Act.
1401. Article 585, paras 1 and 4, Companies Act.
1402. Article 576, para. 1, items 4–6, Companies Act.
1403. Article 606, paras 1 and 2, Companies Act.
1404. Article 607, para. 1, Companies Act.

the equity interest. A removal of member (item (viii) above) will be permitted upon certain grounds, including failure to perform the obligation of contribution or engagement in misconduct.[1405] The withdrawing member will receive a refund of the equity interest.[1406]

1011. Unless otherwise provided in the articles of incorporation, all members will execute the business of general partnership company as the organ of company.[1407] As a result, the organ of company will be established by preparation of the articles of incorporation, together with determining the members (see paragraphs 230 and 239). The business of general partnership company will, in principle, be determined by a majority of the members.[1408] In addition, each of the members will have the right to represent the company; provided, however, that one or more members may be appointed from among the members who execute the business to represent the company pursuant to the articles of incorporation or through appointment by the members themselves in accordance with the articles of incorporation.[1409]

1012. The members executing business will be subject to the duty care of a prudent manager and the duty of loyalty.[1410] Where a member has failed to perform his or her duties, such member will be liable for losses arising as a result thereof.[1411] If a member was with knowledge or grossly negligent in performing its duties, such member will be liable to compensate loss arising in a third party as a result.[1412]

1013. Unlike stock companies, there are no strict restrictions on dividends with regard to the distribution of profits in a general partnership company (see paragraph 635). Therefore, it is not illegal to distribute the company assets to the members even if no profits exist in the company.

1014. General partnership companies will be dissolved upon the occurrence of certain statutory grounds for dissolution.[1413] The grounds for dissolution are as follows: (i) expiration of the duration provided in the articles of incorporation, (ii) occurrence of the grounds for dissolution provided in the articles of incorporation, (iii) consent of all members, (iv) absence of all members, (v) merger (in cases where the company will be liquidated as a result of the merger), (vi) ruling for commencement of bankruptcy procedures and (vii) judgment ordering dissolution.

1015. Under the Companies Act, single-member companies are permitted as the number of members being reduced to one has been removed from the grounds for dissolution.

1405. Article 859, Companies Act.
1406. Article 611, Companies Act.
1407. Article 590, para. 1, Companies Act.
1408. Article 590, para. 2, Companies Act.
1409. Article 599, para. 3, Companies Act.
1410. Article 593, paras 1 and 2, Companies Act.
1411. Article 596, Companies Act.
1412. Article 597, Companies Act.
1413. Article 641, Companies Act.

§2. Limited Partnership Companies (*Goushi Kaisha*)

1016. The origin of limited partnership company is found from the 'commenda' agreements used in the commercial cities of the Mediterranean coast in the Middle Ages. Namely, there was a contract pursuant to which investors provided funds to entrepreneurs engaged in maritime trades who agreed to distribute the profits from their maritime trades to such investors. Such contracts were later divided into those where both the investor and entrepreneur made external appearance as joint entrepreneurs and those where only the entrepreneur appeared externally and the investor remained behind the scenes. The former turned into limited partnership company and the latter turned out to be silent partnership (*tokumei kumiai*) (see paragraph 1033 below). This section describes the rules of membership companies applicable to limited partnership companies that are different from general partnership companies.

1017. A limited partnership company is composed of unlimited liability members and limited liability members. Whether or not the liability of partners is limited or unlimited must be specified in the articles of incorporation and commercial registration.[1414] Unlimited liability members are subject to direct liability for the liabilities of the company to company creditors in the same manner as the members of a general partnership company. In contrast, limited liability members are also subject to directly liability to the company creditors but only to the extent of the value of their contribution.[1415] Limited partnership companies must use 'limited partnership company *(goushi kaisha)*' in their trade name.[1416]

1018. Contributions to be made by the limited liability members will be limited to money or other assets.[1417] In contrast, contributions to be made by unlimited liability partners may also be services or credits.

1019. Limited liability members who do not execute operations of the company may transfer all or part of their equity interest to a third party, if they obtain approval of all members who execute the business operations.[1418]

§3. Limited Liability Companies (*Goudo Kaisha*)

1020. LLC was newly introduced by the Companies Act. As there must be at least one unlimited liability member in general partnership companies and limited partnership companies, there was a need to form a company where all members are

1414. Article 576, para. 1, item 5; Art. 913, para. 1, item 6, Companies Act.
1415. Article 580, para. 2, Companies Act.
1416. Article 6, para. 2, Companies Act.
1417. Article 576, para. 1, item 6, Companies Act.
1418. Article 585, para. 2, Companies Act.

subject to limited liability while the internal relations in the company could be regulated in the same manner as those of partnerships under the Civil Code. LLC was modelled on overseas LLCs.

1021. With regard to the naming of *g d kai sha* (LLC), it has been explained that no favourable candidate was presented in the course of deliberations of the legislation and, taking into consideration that the same regulations as those for general partnership companies *(g mei kai sha)* and limited partnership companies *(g shi kai sha)* will apply, it was decided that the name should likewise consist of four characters and start with '*g*' and end with '*kaisha*' (company).

1022. LLCs and stock companies have in common that the liability of members or shareholders is limited. Therefore, the same procedures for creditor protection are established for LLCs as with stock companies. LLCs must prepare balance sheet and profit and loss statement.[1419] Creditors of the company may request to inspect or copy these documents.[1420] In addition, a full payment requirement was adopted with regard to the contributions of the members so that the assets of the company will be reserved properly. Rules similar to stock companies will also apply with regard to the distribution of profits in that distribution of dividends will not be permitted if no profits are reserved by the company.[1421]

1023. In stock companies, a shareholders meeting and directors must be established as organs of the company (see paragraph 547) and, in general, the principle of shareholder equality is applied to the rights of shareholders (see paragraph 311). In contrast, in LLCs, the structuring of organs and rights of members will be determined mostly by the articles of incorporation.

1024. As far as the limited liability of members or partners is concerned, limited liability partnerships (LLPs) (*yugen sekinin jigyou kumiai*) under the Limited Liability Partnership Act (Japanese version of LLPs) also permits the limited liability of partners while applying the partnership rules to the internal relations. In this respect, there are similarities between LLC and LLP. However, whereas the LLC has a legal personality, the LLP does not. In addition, not all of the members are required to be responsible for the execution of operations in LLC, whereas in an LLP, all partners must be involved in the execution of operations in some form. In addition, whereas limited liability companies are allowed to have just one member, an LLP cannot exist with one partner.

1025. LLCs are subject to corporation tax. Whether or not the number of LLCs will increase in the future, as has been the case with LLCs in the United States, will depend very much on whether pass-through taxes will be allowed in the Japanese tax system.

1419. Article 617; Art. 618, Companies Act.
1420. Article 625, Companies Act.
1421. Article 628, Companies Act.

Chapter 2. Partnerships (*Kumiai*) under the Civil Code

1026. A partnership under the Civil Code will be established by a partnership agreement. The partnership agreement is an agreement where at least two persons make contributions and agree to run joint business.[1422] Unlike companies, partnerships engage in business activities but they are not juridical persons.

1027. Contributions to partnerships may be made in money or by services.[1423] In addition, it has been construed that contributions may be made by any form of property with value, such as contribution of credits.

1028. In principle, each partner has the authority to manage the business of partnership. The management of partnership business will be determined by a majority of the partners.[1424] However, matters in ordinary course of business (*joumu*) may be performed individually by each partner without such majority resolution.[1425] One or more operating officers (*gyoumu shikkousha*) may be delegated to manage the partnership business.[1426] In principle, the operating officers must indicate the names of all partners in entering into an external transaction. However, due to the complexity caused by such requirement, a judicial precedent permitted that an act performed in the name of a representative of the partnership will be binding against all partners.[1427]

1029. Assets of the partnership will be jointly owned by all partners.[1428] The partners may not request division of the assets during the duration of the partnership.[1429] In addition, distribution of profit or loss will be based on the value of contribution made by each individual partner unless otherwise provided in the partnership agreement.[1430]

1030. Creditors of the partnership have the right to claim against the partnership assets. At the same time, the creditors may request payment from individual partners in accordance with the proportion of the loss-sharing of each partner at the time the claim arose. If the creditor does not know the proportion of the loss-sharing of the partners, such creditor may exercise his or her rights against each partner in equal proportions.[1431]

1031. Partnerships under the Civil Code will be dissolved upon termination of the partnership agreement. Causes for dissolution of a partnership are as follows:

1422. Article 667, para. 1, Civil Code.
1423. Article 667, para. 2, Civil Code.
1424. Article 670, para. 1, Civil Code.
1425. Article 670, para. 3, Civil Code.
1426. Article 670, para. 2, Civil Code.
1427. 31 Jul. 1961, Supreme Court Collection of Court Decisions on Civil Actions 15-1982.
1428. Article 668, Civil Code.
1429. Article 676, para. 2, Civil Code.
1430. Article 674, Civil Code.
1431. Article 675, Civil Code.

(i) successful completion of the business which was the partnership's object or by the impossibility of such successful completion and (ii) request for dissolution by a partner based on unavoidable grounds.[1432]

1032. If the partnership is dissolved, liquidation procedure will be carried out by the appointed liquidators. In principle, all partners become liquidators.[1433] However, one or more partners may be appointed as liquidators pursuant to the agreement or by a majority of all partners.[1434]

1432. Article 682; Art. 683, Civil Code.
1433. Article 685, para. 1, Civil Code.
1434. Article 685, paras 1 and 2, Civil Code.

Chapter 3. Silent Partnerships (*Tokumei Kumiai*)

1033. Silent partnership involves one or more silent partners (*tokumei kumiaiin*) providing funds to the proprietor (*eigyousha*), without having its name appear externally, to receive the distribution of profits to be generated from the business.[1435] Silent partnerships are joint business where the business activities of the proprietor will be carried out using the funds of the silent partners.

1034. As is the case with partnerships under the Civil Code, silent partnerships will be formed by an agreement. However, contribution by a silent partner will not form the assets of silent partnership. Namely, contribution by the silent partner will become the assets of the proprietor.[1436] Silent partnerships are similar to limited partnership companies, to the extent that a joint business will be formed by an investor and business operator. However, the significant difference is that whereas limited partnership company is a juridical person jointly owned by the parties, silent partnership is an individual enterprise run by the proprietor.

1035. Contributions by silent partners are limited to money and other properties and may not be made in the form of labour or credits.[1437] If profits are generated by the business, the silent partner will receive the distribution of profits from the proprietor in accordance with the terms of the silent partnership agreement. Unless otherwise provided in the agreement, the profits will be distributed in proportion to the contributions of each silent partner.[1438]

1036. The business of silent partnership will be operated by the proprietor and the silent partner will not participate in the operations.[1439] Therefore, the silent partner does not have any legal relationship externally with third parties with regard to the business. However, if the silent partner permits its name or trade name to be used as the trade name of the proprietor, the silent partner will be subject to the liability jointly and severally with the proprietor.[1440]

1037. Silent partnership is a contractual relationship formed on the basis of the credit of the proprietor. Therefore, the proprietor may not assign its contractual status (*keiyaku jou no chii*) to another person without the consent of silent partner. On the other hand, unless the silent partner obtains consent from the proprietor, it may not assign its contractual status to another person.

1038. The parties to the silent partnership may give notice to counterparties six months in advance of its intention to terminate the silent partnership agreement at

1435. Article 535, Commercial Code.
1436. Article 536, para. 1, Commercial Code.
1437. Article 536, para. 2, Commercial Code.
1438. Article 674, para. 1, Civil Code.
1439. Article 536, para. 3, Commercial Code.
1440. Article 537, Commercial Code.

the end of the business year.[1441] In addition, the statutory grounds for termination of the agreement are as follows: (i) confirmation of the success or impossibility of success in the intended business under the silent partnership agreement, (ii) death or commencement of guardianship of the proprietor and (iii) bankruptcy of the proprietor or silent partner.[1442]

1039. Upon termination of the silent partnership, the proprietor must refund to the silent partner the amount of contribution made by such silent partner.[1443]

1441. Article 540, Commercial Code.
1442. Article 541, Commercial Code.
1443. main text of Art. 542, Commercial Code.

Chapter 4. Mutual Companies (*Sougo Kaisha*)

1040. Insurance business must be engaged in the form of stock company or mutual company.[1444] In Japan, a large number of life insurance businesses were run in the form of mutual company (in 1991, sixteen out of the twenty-six domestic life insurance companies were mutual companies, including all of the top ten companies). In contrast, most non-life insurance businesses take the form of stock company. Until the Second World War, life insurance businesses also took the form of stock companies, but under the influence of the post-war occupational policy to dissolve the conglomerates (*zaibatsu*) and democratize companies, there was a shift from stock companies to mutual companies. However, recently, insurance companies in the form of mutual company have changed into the form of stock company (in 2012, there are five mutual companies in Japan) (see paragraph 1049).

1041. Mutual companies are mainly regulated by the Insurance Business Act, which requires a governmental license to engage in the life insurance business.[1445] Although the name 'company' is used in mutual companies, it is not a company under the Companies Act.

1042. A mutual company is a juridical person.[1446] Scholarly views construe mutual companies as 'incorporated associations' (*shadan houjin*) having the purpose to engage mutually in the insurance of its members. Unlike stock companies, mutual companies do not aim to gain profits (see paragraphs 114 and 115).

1043. In mutual companies, subscribers of insurance become members of the company. Therefore, the insurance premiums paid by the subscribers correspond to contributions into the mutual company. The members are subject to limited liability to the extent of their insurance premiums with regard to the liabilities of the company.[1447]

1044. In mutual companies, there is a general meeting of members, which corresponds to the shareholders meeting of a stock company. Whereas one voting right is granted to one share at the shareholders meeting, one voting right is allocated to each member of the general meeting of members.[1448] Under the Insurance Business Act, many of the provisions concerning the shareholders meeting of a stock company are applied *mutatis mutandis* to the general meeting of members.[1449]

1045. In mutual companies, a general meeting of representative members (*shain soudai kai*) may be established to replace the general meeting of members.[1450] The reason is that the number of members of a mutual company can be extremely large

1444. Article 5-2, Insurance Business Act.
1445. Article 3, Insurance Business Act.
1446. Article 18, Insurance Business Act.
1447. Article 31, Insurance Business Act.
1448. Article 37, Insurance Business Act.
1449. Article 41, Insurance Business Act.
1450. Article 42, para. 1, Insurance Business Act.

and it would be practically difficult to hold a meeting if all members were allowed to attend the general meeting of members. In cases where a general meeting of representative members is established, only the representative members may attend and participate in the general meeting of representative members. As such, unlike the stock company, where the right to attend shareholders meeting is permitted to all shareholders, in a mutual company, only a limited number of members will be permitted to participate in the decision-making organ of the company. Moreover, in reality, the representative members of mutual companies are selected by the company from among the members, which has led to the criticism that the general meeting of representative members has no substance.

1046. In mutual companies, directors will be appointed as the organ to execute operations and company auditors will be appointed as the organ to audit the operations. The provisions of stock companies are applied *mutatis mutandis* to directors and company auditors of mutual companies.[1451]

1047. In mutual companies, financing for the insurance business will be made by the payment of insurance premiums by the members. There is no equivalent to the capital of a stock company. However, in mutual companies, a fund (*kikin*) may be obtained in the form of borrowing to finance the funds necessary to commence the insurance business.[1452] Unlike stock company, the fund is not an equity contribution by the members and is a loan from company creditors, which must eventually be repaid. The repayment of such fund will be subordinated to the claims of other creditors in the order of distribution of assets upon liquidation.[1453]

1048. Mutual companies will be dissolved by the following causes for dissolution:[1454] (i) merger, (ii) bankruptcy, (iii) court-ordered dissolution, (iv) rescission of license, (v) resolution provided in Article 62, paragraph 2 of the Insurance Business Act at the general meeting of members (general meeting of representative members) and (vi) comprehensive transfer (*houkatsu iten*) of all insurance agreements. In cases where the mutual company is dissolved by a reason other than items (i) or (ii) above, liquidation procedures will commence. In such case, other than the special provisions for the liquidation of mutual companies in the Insurance Business Act, the provisions of the Companies Act apply *mutatis mutandis*; provided, however, that in light of the unique characteristics of the Insurance Business Act, where the courts would be involved under the Companies Act in matters such as appointment or dismissal of liquidator and the supervision of the liquidation administration, it would in many cases be the authority of the FSA under the Insurance Business Act.[1455]

1451. Article 53-15, Art. 53-20, Insurance Business Act.
1452. Article 6, Insurance Business Act.
1453. Article 181, Insurance Business Act.
1454. Article 152, para. 2 and para. 3, Insurance Business Act.
1455. Articles 180–182; Arts 183–184; Arts 174–176; Art. 178; Art. 179, Insurance Business Act.

1049. In the past, the Insurance Business Act permitted a stock company to convert into mutual company but a mutual company was not permitted to convert into stock company.[1456] However, as it was necessary to reinforce the financing capabilities of insurance companies and process capital alliance with companies in other industries, and moreover, to make a strategic move to break into other industries such as banking, mutual companies were permitted to convert into stock company under the new Insurance Business Act enacted in 1995 (see paragraph 1040).[1457]

1050. Moreover, under the former Insurance Business Act, life insurance business and non-life insurance business could not be run together by a single company.[1458] While such prohibition still exists under the new Insurance Business Act, the regulations on running both businesses have been eased and it is now possible to enter into the other business through a subsidiary.[1459]

1456. Article 19, former Insurance Business Act.
1457. Article 85, Insurance Business Act.
1458. Article 5; Art. 7, former Insurance Business Act.
1459. Article 3, item 3; Art. 106, Insurance Business Act.

Chapter 5. Cooperatives (*Kyoudo Kumiai*)

1051. Cooperatives are established with a purpose of mutual cooperation by persons in weak economic position. In Japan, there is Japanese Consumers Cooperative Union (*shouhi seikatsu kyoudo kumiai*), which is a cooperative for consumers, as well as *shinkin* banks, credit cooperatives and *shouko chukin* banks, which are cooperatives for small and medium-sized enterprises. In addition, there are The Norinchukin Bank, agricultural cooperatives and fisheries cooperative associations, each of which are for agriculture, forestry and fishery operators.

1052. The organization and business of the cooperatives are provided in each special act on cooperatives. In general, the eligibility to join a cooperative will be restricted by the business purpose of each cooperative. A general meeting will be held as the decision-making body of the cooperative. In addition, a director (*riji*) will be appointed to execute the operations, which will be audited by an inspector (*kanji*). Certain procedures, such as approval of the cooperative, will be required upon transfer of the interests held by the members.

1053. Unlike companies under the Companies Act, the cooperative is not intended to generate profit. This is similar in some ways to mutual company (see paragraph 1042). In addition, unlike partnerships under the Civil Code, cooperatives are granted with independent legal personality (see paragraph 1026).

Index

The numbers here refers to paragraph numbers.

Index

Index

Index

Index

Index

www.ingramcontent.com/pod-product-compliance
Lightning Source LLC
Chambersburg PA
CBHW071604040526
44394CB00004B/735
9789041168542